Journey through the Manual of *A Course in Miracles*

Manual for Teachers

Clarification of Terms

Journey through the Manual
of
A Course in Miracles

Manual for Teachers

Clarification of Terms

KENNETH WAPNICK, Ph.D.

Foundation for A Course in Miracles®

Foundation for A Course in Miracles®
375 N Stephanie St, Suite 2311
Henderson, NV 89014
www.facim.org

Copyright 2007 by the
Foundation for A Course in Miracles®

All rights reserved under International and Pan-American Copyright Conventions. No part of this book may be reproduced or transmitted in any form or by any means, electronic or mechanical, including photocopying, recording, or by any information storage and retrieval system, without permission in writing from the publisher.

2nd edition
Second printing, 2019

Portions of *A Course in Miracles* copyright 1992,
Psychotherapy: Purpose, Process and Practice copyright 1976, 1992
The Song of Prayer copyright 1978, 1992,
The Gifts of God copyright 1982,
by the Foundation for Inner Peace
used by permission.

ISBN 978-1-59142-919-7

CONTENTS

Preface vii
Acknowledgments vii

MANUAL FOR TEACHERS

GENERAL INTRODUCTION 3

Introduction 5
1. Who Are God's Teachers? 11
Introduction to Sections 2 and 3 15
2. Who Are Their Pupils? 19
3. What Are the Levels of Teaching? 23
4. What Are the Characteristics of God's Teachers? 29
5. How Is Healing Accomplished? 53
6. Is Healing Certain? 63
7. Should Healing Be Repeated? 67
8. How Can Perception of Order of Difficulties Be Avoided? 71
9. Are Changes Required in the Life Situation of God's Teachers? 75
10. How Is Judgment Relinquished? 79
11. How Is Peace Possible in This World? 83
12. How Many Teachers of God Are Needed to Save the World? 87
13. What Is the Real Meaning of Sacrifice? 93
14. How Will the World End? 99
15. Is Each One to Be Judged in the End? 105
16. How Should the Teacher of God Spend His Day? 109
17. How Do God's Teachers Deal with Magic Thoughts? 117
18. How Is Correction Made? 125
19. What Is Justice? 131
20. What Is the Peace of God? 137
21. What Is the Role of Words in Healing? 143
22. How Are Healing and Atonement Related? 149
23. Does Jesus Have a Special Place in Healing? 155
24. Is Reincarnation So? 161
25. Are "Psychic" Powers Desirable? 167
26. Can God Be Reached Directly? 173
27. What Is Death? 179
28. What Is the Resurrection? 185
29. As for the Rest 191

CLARIFICATION OF TERMS

General Introduction 199

Introduction 201
1. Mind – Spirit 207
2. The Ego – The Miracle 211
3. Forgiveness – The Face of Christ 217
4. True Perception – Knowledge 221
5. Jesus – Christ 227
6. The Holy Spirit 233
Epilogue 239

Complete Index of References to *A Course in Miracles* 243

Foundation for A Course in Miracles®

Preface

This is the second presentation to be published on the three books of *A Course in Miracles*. The first, the eight-volume *Journey through the Workbook of A Course in Miracles*, was published in 2005. My third presentation, *Journey through the Text of A Course in Miracles,* is forthcoming. My commentary on "What It Says," the third part of the Course's preface, was released in 2006.

This whole project began, innocently enough, with a recorded series of classes on the workbook that I gave in the 1990s at our Center in Roscoe, New York. We then decided to transcribe these talks and expand them into the aforementioned line-by-line commentary.* It was after this decision was made that it seemed logical to continue this procedure for the text and manual. Finally, for the sake of completion, we included the third part of the preface, scribed by Helen Schucman in 1976, which nicely serves as an introductory overview to the teachings of *A Course in Miracles*.

The current book on the manual for teachers and clarification of terms was prepared in a fashion similar to the other two. My series of lectures, held at the Foundation's Center in Temecula, California, in 2003, was transcribed and then edited to enhance readability. Unlike the book on the workbook lessons, however, very little material has been added, as befitting the briefer manual.

The last of the three scribed books, the manual for teachers, summarizes some of the more important themes and principles of the text, focusing on the meaning of being a teacher of God. It is organized in question and answer form, and is a most useful adjunct to the other two books. It is the smallest of the three and the most simply written, and thus is perhaps the most accessible of the Course books for students to read and study. For that reason in fact, many students prefer to begin their study of *A Course in Miracles* with the teacher's manual. Though dwarfed in size and scope by the text and workbook, the manual nonetheless remains an essential part of the Course's curriculum, mandatory for all serious students.

Acknowledgments

I am grateful to a long list of people whose help has made this book possible. I should especially like to express my gratitude to the members of the Foundation staff who worked so tirelessly to bring this book to fruition: Jennye Cooke, Jackie Futterman, Loral Reeves, Elizabeth Schmit, and Virginia Tucker. I would gratefully like to single out Rosemarie LoSasso, our Director of Publications, for her remarkable editing skills and consistent fidelity to the work of the Foundation. And to my wife Gloria, my love-filled gratitude for her keen editorial assistance that has made this book what it is.

---

* For a more detailed account of that book's preparation, please see the Preface to *Journey through the Workbook of A Course in Miracles*.

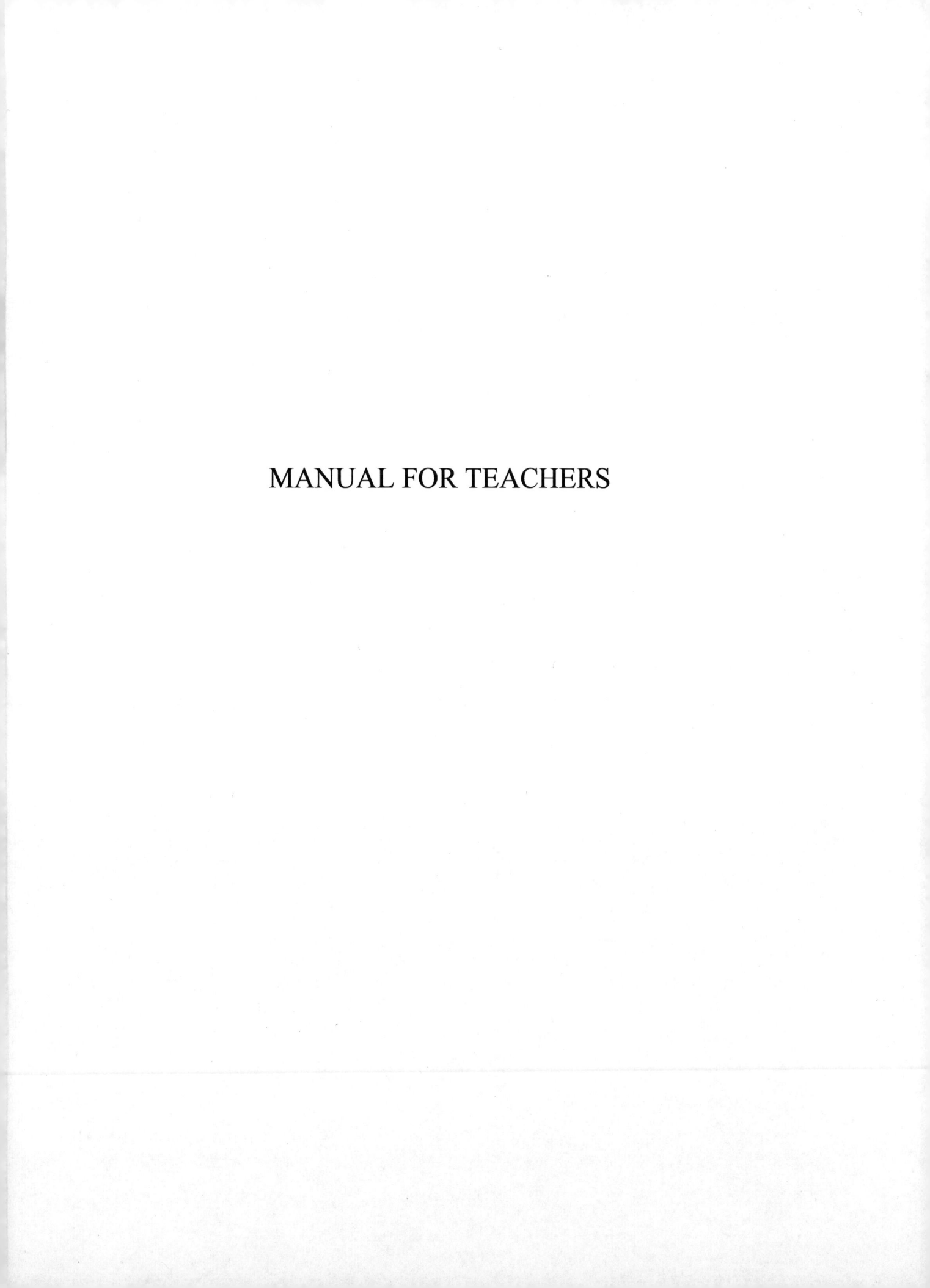

MANUAL FOR TEACHERS

GENERAL INTRODUCTION

My presentation on the text* followed a musical format, taking not only Jesus as my inspiration, obviously, but Beethoven as well. Our journey was like a symphony within a symphony, each lecture built around the various themes of the text's thirty-one chapters, which reflected the symphonic nature of the text itself. Although the form is slightly different, I have done the same thing in these lectures on the manual for teachers, using music as the inspiration for their structure, and, again, Beethoven as the model, specifically the third movement of Beethoven's Ninth Symphony. This adagio movement comes between the towering first two movements and the awesome fourth and final movement —superlatives can never do this music justice. The third movement is built around two themes, and variations on one of them. It begins with a celestial adagio—*adagio* being the Italian word for "very slow," the basic tempo of the piece. This is followed by the second theme, marked *andante*, which means "walking," a leisurely, slow—but not too slow—tempo. That theme does not share the otherworldly nature of the opening adagio, but rather plumbs the depths of human feeling. Both are stunningly beautiful. Then Beethoven devotes the rest of the movement to variations of the first theme, interspersed with a single restatement of the second.

As I thought about the structure for these classes, this movement came to mind because the manual itself is organized around two themes and variations of these two themes, specifically the first. This first one—mentioned in its full form in the manual's opening question, "Who Are God's Teachers?"—is the theme of *separate versus shared interests*. In that first question, Jesus states that the qualifications for a teacher of God "consist solely in this; somehow, somewhere he has made a deliberate choice in which he did not see his interests as apart from someone else's" (M-1.I.2). This theme is stated virtually in that same form in many other places, and also in several variations, one example being that *giving and receiving are the same*. Moreover, *shared interests* is at the core of *A Course in Miracles*' concept of forgiveness, and is also the basis of the important topic that Jesus discusses at great length in the text: the distinction between *form* and *content*. The content of this theme makes healing possible, and we will also recognize it in the equation Jesus makes at the beginning of the manual between teaching and learning, and in the major variation of the giving up of judgment.

This idea of shared interests—not seeing someone else's interests as apart from one's own—is at the heart of the message of *A Course in Miracles*. It is the first great theme in the manual, unifying all the seemingly disparate questions posed. It emphasizes that we are all the same, which reflects the much larger theme that is not as clearly articulated in the manual as it is in the text and the workbook: the oneness of God's Son, and his perfect unity with his Creator and Source. As we are told in the text, however, "the concept of a Oneness joined as One" is totally meaningless to us here (T-25.I.7:1). There is no way that we, in our separated state, can understand what it means. Yet we can understand and be taught the reflection of this Oneness, its principal form being the ability to see someone else's interests as not separate from our own.

The second theme is equally important. In fact, it would not be possible to learn that our interests are shared without it. Yet it does not undergo the extensive variations of the first. It simply is what it is. We are speaking of the importance of *asking the Holy Spirit for help*—the key to practicing *A Course in Miracles*. By asking help of our inner Teacher, we become aware of our wrong-minded thought system and the hateful, cruel, and separating ways in which we manifest it. In what the Course refers to as our right mind, the Holy Spirit gently corrects our misperceptions.

My line-by-line presentation of the manual is thus organized around these two themes. There are subsidiary ones as well, just as in Beethoven's great movement there is other material holding the theme and its variations together. In one sense, the purpose of this book is to demonstrate the masterful way in which Jesus weaves together his basic message, with the musical form of themes and variations guiding us on our journey. We have, again, seen this within the larger symphonic structure of the text.

---

* #CD-61, V-12.

We begin the journey with the title, *manual for teachers*, discussing this on two levels: *form* and *content*. The *form* is what the words actually refer to, and the *content* is what the book is really about—its underlying meaning. This is somewhat akin to Freud's famous distinction between a dream's *manifest* and *latent* content. *A Course in Miracles* is organized in a curricular format: textbook, workbook for students, and manual for teachers—similar to what one might find in a high school or college class, at least in the years when I went to school. Thus, there would be a textbook for students to read and study, which presented the basic material from which the instructor taught; a workbook or companion to the text, which helped students integrate the more theoretical material of the text; and, finally, a book the students never saw, as it was meant only for the teacher—a manual that organized the material to be presented to the students throughout the semester.

In *A Course in Miracles*, however, specifically in the opening pages of the manual, Jesus emphasizes that the line of demarcation between teachers and pupils is spurious, because there is no difference between the two groups. This is a variation of our first theme: we have no separate interests because we are the same. The perception of differences is part of the ego's strategy to have us believe that separation is real, and thus differences are real and important, for they are the means of distinguishing our identities and holding ourselves apart from each other. Again, teachers and pupils are the same, not in *form*, certainly, but in sharing one *content*. They share the same need, purpose, and interest: to awaken from the ego's dream of separation and specialness, and thus awaken to the truth that they are God's *one* Son, totally at one with their Creator and Source:

> God shares His Fatherhood with you who are His Son, for He makes no distinctions in what is Himself and what is still Himself. What He creates is not apart from Him, and nowhere does the Father end, the Son begin as something separate from Him (W-pI.132.12:3-4).

This is our "Oneness joined as One," the Oneness of Christ joined at one with the Oneness of God.

Thus, on the one hand, the manual has its place in the curriculum by virtue of its role in explaining how we should teach this course, which means how we should *learn* it. Manuals are typically set up as "how-to" books, instructing their readers how to successfully complete a task—teach a class, repair a car, or operate a computer. The purpose of this manual is to have us learn how to become a teacher of God. In one way or another, each section is about learning how to accomplish this. Once again, at the heart of this process of becoming teachers of God is learning to see another's interests as one with our own. Stated differently, we learn the importance of giving up judgment—the core of forgiveness.

There is one final point before we embark on our journey through the manual, and one that hopefully will help students avoid a common ego trap. Recall that one of the important variations of our theme of shared interests is *form and content. Form* divides and separates, as, for example, we see in bodies, which clearly demarcate where one self ends and another begins. That is why Jesus states in the text, "Nothing so blinding as perception of form" (T-22.III.6:7). Form blinds us to the truth that we are one. Again, we do not have to understand the true *content* of Oneness—the "Oneness joined as One"—but we can understand the reflection of that Oneness: we are the same because we are on the same journey. We share the same thought system of the ego: hate, cruelty, guilt, suffering, pain, specialness, and death; we share the same correction in our right minds: forgiveness, healing, and peace; and we share the same capacity of the mind to choose between the ego's wrong-minded and the Holy Spirit's right-minded thought system. In other words, we have the same split mind and need: to awaken from this dream of death to the eternal life we never lost. Form confuses us about this awakening because it keeps us in the dream of separation. Therefore, when Jesus speaks of teachers and teaching, he does not speak of form—one body teaching another, whether the subject is arithmetic, history, science, or *A Course in Miracles*. In the Introduction to the manual, he specifically discusses that teaching means demonstration, and in a wonderful passage in the text he says:

> Teach not that I died in vain. Teach rather that I did not die by demonstrating that I live in you (T-11.VI.7:3-4).

Thus, the teaching Jesus speaks of is not that of talking to a group, for example, but the teaching that comes through demonstration. We will see what this means as we set out on our journey through the manual for teachers of God.

INTRODUCTION

Jesus begins by setting forth the purpose of his manual for teachers, implicit in which is its place in the overall curriculum of *A Course in Miracles*. Even though one can certainly start one's work with the Course by reading the manual, it is clearly implied that students reading it are already somewhat familiar with the text and workbook. Again, that does not mean that one must first read the text and do the workbook lessons; however, students should be aware that some of the concepts in the manual would be difficult to understand without the theoretical basis provided by the text. We will see an example of this in the second section when we discuss the topic of *time*.

(1:1-2) The role of teaching and learning is actually reversed in the thinking of the world. The reversal is characteristic.

The world has things backward because it operates on the premise that one's own interests are separate from everyone else's. This results in judging the world on the basis of whether or not it serves our interests. For example, we do not care about others unless this caring serves our interests in some way. This is the reversal Jesus speaks of here, and what he attempts to undo through his course. He therefore asks us to learn to make judgments based on *content*, not *form*, which means asking ourselves which teacher we are listening to: the ego or the Holy Spirit. He asks us as well to see everything in this world as an opportunity to learn the lesson of shared interests, and, above all, to be motivated to learn that lesson. This means that we begin to recognize how very painful it is to live a life thinking only of ourselves, or our family, nationality, country, race, or religion—all at the expense of others outside our group. Only when we experience the pain and discomfort that comes from such misperceptions will we be motivated to learn the lessons Jesus would have us learn: we share the one interest of awakening from the dream of separation.

(1:3) It seems as if the teacher and the learner are separated, the teacher giving something to the learner rather than to himself.

Giving and receiving are seen as separate activities in the world: When I give something to you, you receive it and I now no longer have it. This is the underpinning of the common experience of teachers, therapists, or others in helping roles—formal or informal—feeling fatigued after an activity of helping. They believe they are drained because *they* are the ones who have been giving and giving—their energy, time, love, and wisdom—which means they lack the energy another has received, who is the beneficiary of their largesse, kindness, generosity, and love, while they are left feeling wasted and empty.

This is not genuine giving, and certainly is not love. When we proceed from our right minds, on the other hand, we do nothing: The love of Jesus works through us and gives us the same love that is extended through us. Thus there is no loss, for no one loses and all parties gain, as Jesus teaches in the text (T-25.VII,VIII). Yet, again, this is not how the world sees giving and receiving, which always entails a sense of loss—an example of the "reversal" Jesus speaks of in this passage from the text:

> All choices in the world depend on this; you choose between your brother and yourself, and you will gain as much as he will lose, and what you lose is what is given him. How utterly opposed to the truth is this, when all the lesson's purpose is to teach that what your brother loses *you* have lost, and what he gains is what is given *you* (T-31.IV.8:4-5).

(1:4) Further, the act of teaching is regarded as a special activity, in which one engages only a relatively small proportion of one's time.

We generally equate teaching with form. We may say that by profession we are teachers who teach certain subjects in which we have expertise, which might include *A Course in Miracles*. This is based on having something our pupils lack, and we are going to supply them with it. While this analysis is correct on the level of form, we need to remember that this is a course in *content*, which is the meaning of this statement from the text: "This is a course in cause and not effect" (T-21.VII.7:8). *Effect* is the form or behavior, having to do only with bodies and the world, whereas *cause* is in the mind and reflects either the ego's content—guilt, separation, fear, and hate—or the Holy Spirit's—forgiveness, peace, and healing. The Course, therefore, emphasizes only content, and so teaching according to the manual has nothing to do with behavior or form.

(1:5) The course, on the other hand, emphasizes that to teach *is* to learn, so that teacher and learner are the same.

My true interest as a teacher on the level of form is the same as your interest as a student on the level of form: to learn that the Holy Spirit's thought system is true and the ego's is false; the former brings peace, happiness, and joy, and the latter conflict and pain. Therefore, we are the same in content—what I teach, I learn; what you learn, you teach. To state it once again, teachers and learners alike share the thought systems of the ego and the Holy Spirit, and the power to choose between them.

(1:6) It also emphasizes that teaching is a constant process; it goes on every moment of the day, and continues into sleeping thoughts as well.

We are taught in *A Course in Miracles* that there is no difference between being awake or asleep in the body, since these states pertain only to the mind that decides for the ego—choosing to remain asleep—or the Holy Spirit—choosing to awaken. This decision occurs whether we are physically awake or asleep, for the mind is always active, and so teaching is ongoing because we are always teaching the mind's *content*, not the body's *form*. The next paragraph—and indeed the rest of this section—elaborates on this important point.

(2:1-2) To teach is to demonstrate. There are only two thought systems, and you demonstrate that you believe one or the other is true all the time.

Again, Jesus is not speaking of form. It is not my demonstration of expertise in a particular subject matter that is important, but the demonstration that either the ego's or Holy Spirit's thought system is true. I teach the ego's separation by my special relationship with you, while I teach the Holy Spirit's Atonement by transcending specialness, choosing to see our interests as shared. I thus accept that there are no differences between us in *content*, although there may be major differences in *form*—e.g., gender, age, cultural upbringing, or religious persuasion. These differences, although significant in the world, have no relevance to our salvation; thus they are superficial.

(2:3) From your demonstration others learn, and so do you.

Your "learning" reinforces the decision you made for the thought systems of separation or Atonement. Thus, for example, your special relationship with me—regardless of its form—reflects that you believe that separation is real and your needs have to be fulfilled at my expense. If I am coming from that same point of view, my interaction will tell you that you made the right choice. Since egos *are* attack and I have identified with my ego, I will attack you. Thus do I give the ego's gift by reinforcing its message that you are an innocent victim, and you, of course, reciprocate. And so we continue our dance of death: my decision for the ego reinforces your own, which strengthens my decision that in turn strengthens yours—and both of us lose.

However, when I am in my right mind and not defensive—i.e., I do not judge or attack you—and I perceive our shared interests, my right-mindedness calls you to choose peace as I have. The peace you experience coming through me is now yours, if you so choose. Yet, if you are in your right mind and I am not, and I attack you as the object of my specialness, your defenseless non-judgment teaches me, even though I may be in the role of teacher. As an illustration, let us say that as your teacher I humiliate you, and you do not take it personally. Your not becoming upset demonstrates that my attack had no effect, and thus you remind me that I have another choice.

(2:4-5) The question is not whether you will teach, for in that there is no choice. The purpose of the course might be said to provide you with a means of choosing what you want to teach on the basis of what you want to learn.

Jesus reiterates that teaching occurs all the time —from the ego or the Holy Spirit—and my behavior reflects the mind's choice. *A Course in Miracles* helps me understand that if I feel unfairly treated and my anger and judgments are justified, it is only because I want to learn that separation is real and salvation's principle is *one or the other*. Therefore, if I am to survive and be happy, I must see someone else as the sinful victimizer—my salvation and happiness come at another's expense. Since that is what I want to learn, that is what I will teach. If, however, I want to learn that in the end Jesus is right and I am wrong—no thought of attack or judgment is ever justified—I will see daily happenings only as opportunities for me to make another choice.

(2:6) You cannot give to someone else, but only to yourself, and this you learn through teaching.

I may not be aware that I have chosen my ego, but seeing how defensive, cruel, or selfish I am toward you helps me understand that I have chosen against the Holy Spirit. As Jesus says in the text, the world is "the outside picture of an inward condition" (T-21.in.1:5). Because I am not aware of my mind—the "inward condition"—I do not know I decided for my ego; I do not even know I have a mind that can make such a decision. However, I can learn of my mind by letting Jesus instruct me to pay attention to my relationships. This will help me realize that what I see in you is a projection of what I do not want to acknowledge in myself.

(2:7) Teaching is but a call to witnesses to attest to what you believe.

I want you to prove I am right. If I choose my ego, I want you to join me on its dance floor of specialness and death. I need you to feel unfairly treated by me so I can be justified in feeling unfairly treated by you. I want you to witness to the fact that by choosing the ego I have chosen the truth. If, however, I choose the Holy Spirit, the witnesses to that choice will be my new perception that sees everyone as either calling for love or expressing it, a perception that is independent of what is done. No matter how egregious the sin or heinous the crime, I will yet see it as a call for love, which makes real the love in our minds. Moreover, if you call for love, you must know it is there even if you have buried it, the happy fact I happily remind you of by witnessing to its presence in me.

(2:8-11) It is a method of conversion. This is not done by words alone. Any situation must be to you a chance to teach others what you are, and what they are to you. No more than that, but also never less.

I convert my mind's mistaken decision for the ego to the Holy Spirit, Who is the Correction. Thus, when I see the ego in action I am reminded of the opportunity for conversion, because Jesus teaches me that when I am upset or disquieted physically and/or emotionally, it comes from the mind's decision, which I can reverse. Every situation now becomes an opportunity for me to choose again, converting the ego's anger and despair to the Holy Spirit's peace and joy. My words are the external effects of this decision, reflecting my choice for the Holy Spirit.

(3:1) The curriculum you set up is therefore determined exclusively by what you think you are, and what you believe the relationship of others is to you.

As we see here and throughout *A Course in Miracles*, Jesus repeats his themes over and over, in different ways. He varies the symbols—the words—but the content remains the same. He wants us to understand how the manual fits into the larger curriculum of his course. Everything comes down to what I believe I am: a child of the ego or a child of God. What I believe I make real for myself, and attempt to support through my perceptions of the world.

(3:2) In the formal teaching situation, these questions may be totally unrelated to what you think you are teaching.

If you are teaching arithmetic, for example, more than likely you are unaware that you are also teaching the identity you have made real for yourself. What matters is the *way* you teach arithmetic. When we think back over our early lives, we most likely do not remember *what* our teachers taught us, but do remember *how* they interacted with us, whether they were kind or mean, understanding or humiliating. This content is what taught us and has lasted over the years.

(3:3) Yet it is impossible not to use the content of any situation on behalf of what you really teach, and therefore really learn.

The word *content* here refers to the *form* of teaching. In that sense we use our teaching of arithmetic or *A Course in Miracles* as the framework in which we teach the Holy Spirit's Love. My interests as a teacher are not different or separate from yours as a pupil, for we are united in that one Love.

(3:4-7) To this the verbal content of your teaching is quite irrelevant. It may coincide with it, or

it may not. It is the teaching underlying what you say that teaches you. Teaching but reinforces what you believe about yourself.

What underlies the verbal content of our teaching is what truly teaches us. If I teach from Jesus, I will teach forgiveness, regardless of the form; i.e., teaching that our interests are the same for we are not truly different. If I teach from my ego, however, I will teach guilt, punishment, and separate interests. When my students do poorly, therefore, I will make them feel bad about themselves, a projection of my own poor self-image. This is reinforced by my negative judgments of my students—not that they made a mistake, but that they *are* a mistake. The proper role of teachers is thus not really correcting mistakes of *form*, but of *content*.

(3:8-10) Its fundamental purpose is to diminish self-doubt. This does not mean that the self you are trying to protect is real. But it does mean that the self you think is real is what you teach.

We diminish self-doubt by seeking proof we are right—either as an ego or a Son of God. This begins with the mind's decision, to which the external is irrelevant. By calling this book *manual for teachers*, Jesus attempts to help us understand that we teach what we learn, and we learn what we teach. It comes down to the same decision: to which teacher do I want to listen? who do I want to be?

(4:1-3) This is inevitable. There is no escape from it. How could it be otherwise?

It is inevitable that I will teach the self I think I am because *ideas leave not their source*. A most important principle in the text and workbook, it is not mentioned in the manual at all. Yet it is the foundation of the concept that we but teach and learn who we are. Everything we do reflects the choice for the ego or the Holy Spirit. It cannot be otherwise because there is nothing outside us; everything comes from the mind and can never leave its source.

(4:4-7) Everyone who follows the world's curriculum, and everyone here does follow it until he changes his mind, teaches solely to convince himself that he is what he is not. Herein is the purpose of the world. What else, then, would its curriculum be? Into this hopeless and closed learning situation, which teaches nothing but despair and death, God sends His teachers.

In the world's curriculum, I teach myself that I am the ego's son and not God's because I am separate from others, as are my interests. Thus my salvation, peace, and joy come at other people's expense. The world's purpose is to convince us we are what we are not, and therefore it has inevitably become a place of despair and death, not happiness and joy. The world, never having left its source in the ego's wrong-minded thinking, teaches we are separate. Moreover, separation is good, as are individuality, uniqueness, separate interests, and having our special needs met. How could such thinking *not* lead to despair and death, for it reinforces the idea we left our home, our Source, our Self? We find happiness and joy only when we begin the process of leaving the world and awakening to the Heaven where true peace abides.

(4:8) And as they teach His lessons of joy and hope, their learning finally becomes complete.

The lessons of joy and hope are the simple lessons that teach we were wrong and the Holy Spirit right. Realizing this is the only joy the world holds, our learning makes us happy and hopeful. Yet we all try to defend—ultimately to our death—the idea that we are right: separation is real and salvation comes at the expense of others. We thus erect huge systems of hate, cruelty, and specialness to keep the ego's thought system alive in our minds. It is indeed a welcomed relief to lay down the awesome burden of guilt, and with a happy and grateful sigh exclaim: "Thank you, Jesus. I was wrong and you were right." This is the only lesson we wish to learn, and therefore the only lesson we will teach.

(5:1) Except for God's teachers there would be little hope of salvation, for the world of sin would seem forever real.

The world of sin seems forever real in the mind, which is why it seems forever real in the body. We seem to live in a world of good and evil from which there is no escape, except to be shown that the world comes from a decision in the mind. Yet we first must realize we have a mind before we can change it. We learn this as we teach others, who act as a screen onto which we project our "secret sins and hidden hates" (T-31.VIII.9:2). Thus we become each other's savior, without which opportunity we would have no way of moving from the outside to the inside—the world's picture being a projection of the mind's condition. To borrow Freud's wonderful phrase, the world of our special relationships becomes the *royal road* that leads us back to the mind that chose them, wherein lies our hope.

(5:2-5) The self-deceiving must deceive, for they must teach deception. And what else is hell? This is a manual for the teachers of God. They are not perfect, or they would not be here.

When we choose the ego, we deceive ourselves about our identity. Therefore everything we say and do reflects that deception, as we attempt to deceive the world so as to reinforce our mistaken choices. This place of self-deception is hell, in which we believe we are what we are not. Indeed, no one here is perfect, not even teachers of God, as we are told here. In the text, Jesus speaks of the shadows of guilt, reminding us that these deceptions are opportunities for us to move beyond them. Thus we need not be upset by the ego, for its defenses are the means of escaping from it:

> Trust not your good intentions. They are not enough. But trust implicitly your willingness, whatever else may enter. Concentrate only on this, and be not disturbed that shadows surround it. That is why you came. If you could come without them you would not need the holy instant (T-18.IV.2:1-6).

(5:6-7) Yet it is their mission to become perfect here, and so they teach perfection over and over, in many, many ways, until they have learned it. And then they are seen no more, although their thoughts remain a source of strength and truth forever.

This is what Jesus means when he says, "To teach is to demonstrate." I teach perfection by increasingly identifying with the perfection of forgiveness, which reflects the perfection of the Holy Spirit's correction that in turn reflects Heaven. Teachers of God "are no longer visible" when the ego thought system is gone from their minds, a reference to the Teachers of teachers, addressed later in the manual (M-26.2:2).

(5:8-12) Who are they? How are they chosen? What do they do? How can they work out their own salvation and the salvation of the world? This manual attempts to answer these questions.

This ends Jesus' introduction to the manual, and he has already alluded to some of its most important themes, helping us understand what it means to be a teacher of God and how to go about becoming one. The question "How can they work out their own salvation and the salvation of the world?" forms an important subtheme, a variation of the theme of shared interests. My salvation is the world's because the world is my mind's projection —there is no world out there, as we learn in the workbook (W-pI.132.6:2), and the mind of God's Son is one. To say "the world is saved" is to say that the mind that thought it up is saved from its belief in guilt. Again, Jesus will elaborate on this as we continue our journey through the manual.

1. WHO ARE GOD'S TEACHERS?

In this first section Jesus explains, in answer to the title question, that a teacher of God is someone who has chosen the Holy Spirit as his Teacher, and has thus made the right-minded choice. There are, in fact, but two choices: to be a teacher of the ego or a teacher of God. Needless to say, to be a teacher of God does not mean we "teach God"; rather, we teach the subject matter of God, or the forgiveness that reflects His Love in the world.

(1:1-2) A teacher of God is anyone who chooses to be one. His qualifications consist solely in this; somehow, somewhere he has made a deliberate choice in which he did not see his interests as apart from someone else's.

This is our first great theme, the foundation of this book. My right-minded choice establishes me as a teacher of God; it is my response to realizing that my tolerance for suffering has been eclipsed—I can no longer stand the pain of judging and finding fault with everyone. Thus I plead: "There must be another way, another teacher, another way of perceiving." To perceive that my brother is myself is this other way: our interests are the same, for we share the same need to awaken from this moribund dream of darkness and despair.

(1:3) Once he has done that, his road is established and his direction is sure.

The recognition that our interests are the same sets us on the journey, a symbol Jesus uses throughout *A Course in Miracles*. To shift symbols, we can say that this is what sets our feet on the right ladder. The ego's ladder goes nowhere, as it is the ladder of separation and separate interests. Seeing that another's interests are not apart from ours, even for a moment, finds us on the right ladder with the right Teacher. Our journey has begun.

(1:4-5) A light has entered the darkness. It may be a single light, but that is enough.

I may have had only an instant of recognition, but in that instant I acknowledged, whether I was aware of it or not, that I have a right mind that contains the correction for the separation. Now at last there is genuine hope, an ending to my nightmarish existence.

(1:6-8) He has entered an agreement with God even if he does not yet believe in Him. He has become a bringer of salvation. He has become a teacher of God.

Jesus is not talking about the *form* of belief, but its *content*. A teacher of God brings salvation to the world by accepting it for himself, as Jesus says in the lesson "I am among the ministers of God" (W-pI.154). God's ministers are His messengers, but the messages they deliver to the world they must first accept for themselves. To restate this happy fact, a teacher of God is anyone who sets his foot on the right ladder, which begins with the recognition that our interests are not separate from another's.

(2:1-2) They come from all over the world. They come from all religions and from no religion.

We again find the theme of form and content, a variation of the theme of shared interests. Form is not important, for location and religious belief are irrelevant to true spirituality.

(2:3-5) They are the ones who have answered. The Call is universal. It goes on all the time everywhere.

Call is capitalized because it refers to the Holy Spirit. This is an intimation of our second theme—the importance of asking the Holy Spirit's help. His Call is universal and continuous, because we all have a right mind, no matter where we are, whom we are with, or whether we are awake or asleep. This is the Call we took with us into the dream—the memory of Who we are as God's Son, reflecting the Atonement that says the separation never happened.

(2:6) It calls for teachers to speak for It and redeem the world.

Jesus' point has nothing to do with specifics, for he refers to the presence of the Atonement that calls to us: "Choose love instead of fear."

(2:7) Many hear It, but few will answer.

This echoes the line in the text, "All are called but few choose to listen" (T-3.IV.7:12), which corrects the biblical "Many are called but few are chosen" (Matthew 20:16b, 22:14). *All*, not *many*, are called; few, however, choose to answer. Here Jesus tells us that all are called because the Call is universal. Many hear It, but few—one could even say very few—will actually answer. Some people know there is another way and another teacher, but still they stubbornly choose to hold onto their grievances and judgments—their good-versus-evil mentality—and to the idea that some have to suffer for what *they* have done. This is believed even though they know there is another way and have studied *A Course in Miracles* for years. Again, many hear the Call, but still choose not to answer It.

(2:8-9) Yet it is all a matter of time. Everyone will answer in the end, but the end can be a long, long way off.

In the next section we will speak more about time, but suffice it for now to say that here Jesus teaches that within the illusion of time, the end can indeed be a long way off. Nonetheless, everyone will eventually answer because in our minds is the truth that the separation never happened, which means the world of time never happened. We all will answer that Call because It is within us, and there is no one to whom this does not apply. Remember that everyone shares the same split mind: the 100 percent thought system of the wrong mind—hate, cruelty, suffering, and guilt—the 100 percent thought system of the right mind—forgiveness, peace, joy, and healing—and the power to choose between them.

(2:10-12) It is because of this that the plan of the teachers was established. Their function is to save time. Each one begins as a single light, but with the Call at its center it is a light that cannot be limited.

We will discuss what Jesus means by *plan* in the next section. The point here is that the light cannot be limited because the mind of the Sonship is one. Not only are we one as Christ in Heaven, but as a split mind as well. The separation that seemed to fragment the Sonship into billions and billions of pieces is part of the illusion, and so we remain one Son in separation, as we are one Son in Heaven. Therefore, we all share the same Call to return.

(2:13-14) And each one saves a thousand years of time as the world judges it. To the Call Itself time has no meaning.

Time has no meaning because in the right mind there is only the reflection of eternity. In the wrong mind, however, our belief in sin, guilt, and fear leads to the perception of linear time, a topic we will consider in more detail later. Jesus develops this notion in Chapter 1 of the text, where he talks about the miracle minimizing the need for time (T-1.II.6).

(3:1) There is a course for every teacher of God.

Not for some, but for *every* teacher of God—all will awaken one day from the dream. The most evil of evildoers will awaken from the dream because the Holy Spirit is in them. Origen, the prominent third-century Christian teacher likewise taught that in the end even Satan would learn his lessons, for no creation of God could fail to return to Him. If any were exempt from the unity of God's Son, the Sonship would not be unified, which would mean God's Son were but a parody or travesty of God's one creation (T-24.VII.1:11; 10:9).

(3:2-5) The form of the course varies greatly. So do the particular teaching aids involved. But the content of the course never changes. Its central theme is always, "God's Son is guiltless, and in his innocence is his salvation."

While the "particular teaching aids" in various spiritualities differ, the meaning or content of their message never varies. The reality of God's Love is the content behind every spiritual path, whether it is spiritual in form or not. Our all-important theme of shared interests reflects that Oneness and Wholeness. If our interests are shared we are not separate, and thus there is no sin—nothing happened in the seeming separation. Therefore, we are *all* guiltless—not just some, not just the good people. No one is deserving of our judgment, condemnation, hatred, or need to punish. No one! If we believe someone is so deserving, it is only because we secretly believe we are.

(3:6) It can be taught by actions or thoughts; in words or soundlessly; in any language or in no language; in any place or time or manner.

In other words, the form does not matter. You can lecture a group about *A Course in Miracles* by reading from the phone book, and if you read with love and peace, that is what people will receive, and they will understand the Course. They may not understand what you are doing, but they will feel something different because of who you are. On the other hand, if you explain the Course's metaphysics perfectly, the sequence of the ego thought system and its undoing by the Holy Spirit's forgiveness, but you do not come from love—that is, you believe you have something others lack—people will hear only separation, believing *A Course in Miracles* is about specialness and not its undoing. Thus the *form* does not matter, only the *content*, which always comes back to this simple question: to which teacher do I choose to listen?

(3:7-10) It does not matter who the teacher was before he heard the Call. He has become a savior by his answering. He has seen someone else as himself. He has therefore found his own salvation and the salvation of the world.

The salvation of the world is one with the teacher's, because salvation reflects Heaven's Oneness. Because our interests are the same, we are not separate from each other. To save myself is thus to save the world, which is only a projection of my thought. To heal my brother heals myself; to heal myself heals my brother: when we are healed, we are not healed alone (W-pI.137).

(3:11) In his rebirth is the world reborn.

Rebirth occurs when we reject the ego and declare we are a Son of God. We are born again—not in the fundamentalist sense—and therefore the world is reborn as well, being nothing but the mind's projection of separation and guilt.

(4:1-2) This is a manual for a special curriculum, intended for teachers of a special form of the universal course. There are many thousands of other forms, all with the same outcome.

This is the answer for students who seek to make *A Course in Miracles* special, falling into the trap of spiritual specialness. The Course is certainly unique, for its specifics differ from other paths; yet being only one form among many thousands it is not better or worse than any other.

(4:3-5) They merely save time. Yet it is time alone that winds on wearily, and the world is very tired now. It is old and worn and without hope.

The idea of saving time refers to not having to remain asleep a moment longer, suffering from nightmares of fear and death. The world is "old and worn and without hope" because *we* are—tired and worn because of our continual and futile attempts to make the world work for us. The body and world can never bring us lasting happiness or peace, and so there is no hope here. *A Course in Miracles* offers hope *because* it offers no hope in the world, thus allowing room for us to go within to choose our only Hope. Musicologist H.C. Robbins Landon wrote of Mozart (*Mozart's Last Years*; Thames and Hudson, New York, 1999) in words that, when paraphrased, express well the hope *A Course in Miracles* brings:

> *A Course in Miracles* is as good an excuse for mankind's existence as we shall ever encounter and is perhaps, after all, *a still, small hope* for our ultimate survival (p. 10).

As Jesus states in the Course:

> Learn now, without despair, there is no hope of answer in the world.... Seek not another signpost in the world that seems to point to still another road. No longer look for hope where there is none.... No pathway in the world can lead to Him, nor any worldly goal be one with His [the Holy Spirit]. What road in all the world will lead within, when every road was made to separate the journey from the purpose it must have unless it be but futile wandering? All roads that lead away from what you are will lead you to confusion and despair (T-31.IV.4:3,5-6; 9:3-5).

Once we recognize there is no hope in the world, we can move from the *form* of our lives to the *content* of our thinking; hopeful because the Call of hope lies in each of us—*we can yet make another choice*. Therefore, attempts to make something work that was made never to work is indeed frustrating and enervating. The good news, though, is:

(4:6-7) There was never a question of outcome, for what can change the Will of God? But time, with its illusions of change and death, wears out the world and all things in it.

Wearing out the world was the ego's idea all along. Yet, never knowing why it was being worn out, we kept trying to save it, and always failing in the end.

(4:8-10) Yet time has an ending, and it is this that the teachers of God are appointed to bring

about. For time is in their hands. Such was their choice, and it is given them.

Choice is a seminal theme running through all three books of *A Course in Miracles*, and the text ends with "Choose Once Again" (T-31.VIII). The purpose of the manual is to help us learn that becoming a teacher of God means changing our minds and our perceptions. We learn to say "no" to the ego's thought system of separation, and "yes" to the Holy Spirit's thought system of shared interests.

This, the essence of forgiveness, is what will eventually bring about the end of time—our hearing the Call and accepting the Atonement:

> How lovely is the world whose purpose is forgiveness of God's Son! How free from fear, how filled with blessing and with happiness! And what a joyous thing it is to dwell a little while in such a happy place! Nor can it be forgot, in such a world, it *is* a little while till timelessness comes quietly to take the place of time (T-29.VI.6).

INTRODUCTION TO SECTIONS 2 AND 3

Before I continue my commentary on the manual, I would like to briefly address two important topics: *A Course in Miracles*' distinctive use of language and its theory of time, as the next two sections are heavily based on these dimensions of the Course. I have discussed these topics at length many times before,* so I will go through them relatively quickly here.

The Language of *A Course in Miracles*

Jesus tells us in the Introduction to the clarification of terms that "this course remains within the ego framework, where it is needed" (C-in.3:1). He is talking about the Course on the external level of form, having to do with the body and words. Later in the manual Jesus explains that "words are but symbols of symbols. They are thus twice removed from reality" (M-21.1:9-10). Made to keep us separate from God, words remain within the ego's framework, and yet, as with everything else the ego made, they can serve a different purpose; not only reinforcing separation, but reflecting the thought system that ends separation. Therefore, since we are creatures of the ego's world of duality and experience ourselves in the body, Jesus speaks to us on the level we can understand.

In my introduction, I quoted the phrase from the beginning of Chapter 25 that the concept of "a Oneness joined as One" is totally meaningless to us, for it is the language of non-duality: there is the Oneness of God and nothing else. This is not understandable because, again, our experience is that we live in a world of separation and separate interests. Therefore, the language of *A Course in Miracles* has to be pitched at a level we can accept without fear of disappearing into the abyss of nonexistence. However, even though the words themselves may not be true, they *reflect* the truth in terms of their purpose of leading us to it.

The Course also tells us that the ego speaks first and is wrong (T-5.VI.3:5; 4:2); consequently, Jesus' answer falls within the framework of the ego's first statement so we can understand it. Whatever the ego says—wrong without exception—is always some expression of the belief that the separation happened: duality is reality and non-duality an illusion. The ego thus proclaims that our physical/psychological selves embody the ego's fact of existence. Therefore, Jesus' answer must come in the context of this concept we have about ourselves and reality—shadowy fragments of the ego's myth of separation: we sinned against God, Who in His retaliative rage sends the Holy Spirit into our minds to fulfill His plan to save us through atonement. This plan means vengeance and sacrifice, as explained in "The Laws of Chaos" (T-23.II)—guilt demands punishment, which our sin deserves.

Jesus therefore uses the language and contours of the ego's myth, but instead of a tale of horror, he offers a tale of hope—the same myth but with a different purpose. In Jesus' version, God also has an answer to the separation, but it is loving rather than punitive. Yes, God "sends" the Holy Spirit, but to lovingly remind, not punish. He is now the memory in our dream of Who we really are as children of a loving Father. Again, Jesus uses the dualistic language of the world, but with a different content. God's plan is simply God: His Love, Oneness, and Will. It is thus not a plan as the world conceives it, yet Jesus uses the term as the correction for the ego's plan of punishment and sacrifice.

As will be obvious when I discuss time, God cannot send teachers or assign people roles, because there are no people. Nothing real can be separate. Therefore, to correct the belief that God sends people to punish us or even to give us what we need, Jesus talks about God "sending" people, but only to reflect His one Will. They are "sent" to remind us we can choose again. In fact, as we will see in section 4, Jesus says that "God gives special gifts to His teachers," but then explains that he does not mean what the words literally say (M-4.1:4-7).

In light of all this, students of *A Course in Miracles* need to move beyond the literal meaning of the words—beyond their *form* to the underlying *content*, which expresses God's Love in a way we

---

* See, for example, my *The Message of A Course in Miracles: Volume Two – Few Choose to Listen*, Chapters 2-3; *A Vast Illusion*; "Duality as Metaphor in *A Course in Miracles*"; "From Time to Timelessness"; and "The Time Machine."

can understand and accept. This Love—perfect and non-specific Oneness—is not understandable here. To reiterate, God does not send us people, nor does He appoint special people to carry out His "plan" of teachers—we are *all* teachers. The Course's words often suggest that He does, but only so we could understand its message of forgiveness and shared interest. Thus Jesus uses the language of duality to reflect non-dualistic love. In that same passage in Chapter 25 where Jesus speaks of "a Oneness joined as One," he says that the message of that Oneness must come to us in a form we can accept in the condition in which we think we are in; that is, in the dualistic condition of being separate from God:

> It is apparent that a mind so split could never be the Teacher of a Oneness which unites all things within Itself. And so What is within this mind, and does unite all things together, must be its Teacher. Yet must It use the language that this mind can understand, in the condition in which it thinks it is. And It must use all learning to transfer illusions to the truth, taking all false ideas of what you are, and leading you beyond them to the truth that *is* beyond them (T-25.I.7:2-5).

I end this brief discussion of the Course's language with the reminder that, even though throughout the manual Jesus uses terms such as *God's plan*—which occur frequently in the workbook as well—he employs them simply as metaphorical or symbolic expressions that reflect the non-dualistic reality that lies beyond all dualism and form, to the truth of which we are happily led by the Course's right-minded, albeit illusory words.

Time in *A Course in Miracles*

Sections 2 and 3 are the only places in the manual where Jesus truly discusses time, although there are a few isolated statements elsewhere that bear on it. The Course's understanding of time appears throughout its three books, but never in a coherent statement. There are passages in the text, workbook, and this one in the manual, which, when taken together, however, do form a coherent presentation. Yet as Jesus makes clear to us, there is no way we can understand the nature of time, by which he means its unreality:

> There is no need to further clarify what no one in the world can understand. When revelation of your oneness comes, it will be known and fully understood. Now we have work to do, for those in time can speak of things beyond, and listen to words which explain what is to come is past already. Yet what meaning can the words convey to those who count the hours still, and rise and work and go to sleep by them? (W-pI.169.10)

Nonetheless, some summary statement of the Course's view of time will be helpful before looking at these next two sections.

Reality is eternity, in which there can be no time. When the ego thought system began to develop—which in truth, never happened at all—it formed around the unholy trinity of sin, guilt, and fear. Our separating from God was deemed a *sin*, for which we felt overwhelmed by a *guilt* that reinforced our belief in separation, which in turn led to our *fear* of the punishment the ego told us was inevitable. Thus our sin against God was reciprocated, for He would steal back the life we believe we stole from Him. Needless to say, all this occurred only in minds made mad by guilt (T-13.in.2:2).

This thought system gets projected from the mind, as a means, the ego assures us, of saving us from God's retaliative wrath. Once projected, the thoughts of *sin, guilt,* and *fear* give rise to linear time: *past, present,* and *future*: I sinned in the past, experience guilt in the present, and fear the inevitable future. The thought of separation from God now takes the form of a body separate from other bodies in a world of time and space. The same moment this thought system was projected, the one Son of God, who imagined he was separate from his Source, split into billions and billions of fragments. These represent the quasi-infinite ways the original thought of separation found expression, similar to the shattering of a huge pane of glass. Though in different shapes and sizes, each little piece remains glass. So are we different bodily shapes and sizes, but remain embodiments of the one thought of separation.

Another way of understanding this process is to think of the ego's thought system as an unrolling carpet of time (T-13.I.3). On it are found the many ways in which we, as seemingly separate Sons in relationship with other seemingly separate Sons, have acted out the ego's time-less trinity of sin, guilt, and fear in our special relationships. Remember that time is illusory, and that we have all identified with the wrong-minded ego that contains the world of time and space. That is why none of this is truly understandable to us. Having identified with the ego, the mind has programmed the brain not to understand time's unreality—specifically, that everything is happening at once, has already happened, and in reality never happened at all. Our brains have an intellect in order to think, but only as they have been designed to think in terms of separation and linearity. Most especially, our brains have been made to make sense of the morass of misery that is the world, therein to find some hope. They were never programmed to move beyond themselves to the mind that programmed them. That is why thinking about this will never be fruitful.

At the same time the carpet unrolled, it also rolled back. This process occurs through our forgiveness of wrong-minded thoughts and behaviors. Thus in that one instant, the ego arose, with all its permutations and combinations of guilt, specialness, cruelty, fear, and death. Yet, in that same instant, the correction arose as well. For each thought or expression in form of the ego thought system of separation, there is a corresponding correction—the Holy Spirit. Each thought of the ego was answered by the correction: separation by Atonement, guilt by forgiveness, the special relationship by the holy relationship.

In the manual, God's or the Holy Spirit's "plan" of Atonement consists of rolling back the carpet. The plan is illusory because it undoes the ego's plan, which is also illusory—an illusory thought of the correction undoes the illusory thought of the mistake. Thus, when the carpet of time rolls back, it is as if it never happened—because it never did! Again, none of this is understandable, and is not meant to be, which is why no systematic presentation exists in the Course. In the workbook, as we have just seen, Jesus reiterates our inability to understand this. He continues by encouraging us to return to what we can understand, which is learning to forgive—our part in the "plan":

> Suffice it, then, that you have work to do to play your part. The ending must remain obscure to you until your part is done (W-pI.169. 11:1-2).

In the context of our discussion of the manual, our part in the plan of forgiveness is learning to see shared instead of separate interests.

When we finally experience guiltlessness—the mind's experience in which there is no separation or specialness—this all becomes clear; not through the intellect, but through the experience that infuses the intellect. Fortunately, progress in *A Course in Miracles* is not contingent on our understanding. That is why Jesus says:

> You are still convinced that your understanding is a powerful contribution to the truth, and makes it what it is (T-18.IV.7:5).

We are asked only to understand that choosing selfish interests makes us unhappy, and choosing shared interests brings us joy. That alone is what we can understand, and thus learn and teach.

2. WHO ARE THEIR PUPILS?

We need to keep in mind that teachers and pupils are one and the same in *content*, not *form*. Therefore, even though our experience is of the body by necessity, the process of recognizing our shared interests occurs in the mind.

(1:1-4) Certain pupils have been assigned to each of God's teachers, and they will begin to look for him as soon as he has answered the Call. They were chosen for him because the form of the universal curriculum that he will teach is best for them in view of their level of understanding. His pupils have been waiting for him, for his coming is certain. Again, it is only a matter of time.

The "assignment" relates to the correction of the relationship that happened with the original fragmentation. To return to the analogy I used in my discussion of time, when the pane of glass shattered into fragments, some fell close together. These adjacent fragments can be understood as what later manifested as our meaningful relationships: the families we are born into and those we establish in adulthood; our colleagues, friends, and enemies—our special love and hate partners. These, then, are the "assigned" relationships, which we have already made real. Their *forms* do not matter—only the ego's *content* of guilt.

Therefore, to speak of the relationship as an assignment acknowledges it has already happened, and we can now choose to review it, as the workbook says:

> For we but see the journey from the point at which it ended, looking back on it, imagining we make it once again; reviewing mentally what has gone by (W-pI.158.4:5).

I can thus choose to re-experience my relationship with you; i.e., look at it with Jesus instead of the ego. The relationship that was made to reinforce guilt now becomes the means of undoing it. I could also choose to re-enact the relationship and strengthen the guilt even more, which means that you and I will wait until one of us decides to choose again. This is Jesus' point here—we wrote the ego's script of guilt and established the curriculum of special relationships that span the carpet of time, and we also chose to correct our mistake and choose the holy relationships of forgiveness instead. In reality, the rolling out of the carpet spans one unholy, unreal instant in which we chose the ego as our teacher, while the carpet's rolling back spans one holy, unreal instant with the Holy Spirit teaching us. This fundamental unreality of the carpet is what makes the phenomenon of time so difficult to understand.

(1:5) Once he has chosen to fulfill his role, they are ready to fulfill theirs.

Note the emphasis on *choice*. Once God's teachers have chosen to fulfill their role, which means they no longer see another's interests as separate from their own—even for an instant—they lay aside their grievances. That holy instant is all it takes for teachers to invite their pupils to fulfill their roles and choose to be in their presence. The pupils thus choose a life in which the teachers become a part because they offered them another opportunity to choose again. Whether the pupils make that choice is up to them, yet they are now in their teachers' lives because they want to see that their right-minded choice is available to them as well.

(1:6-7) Time waits on his choice, but not on whom he will serve. When he is ready to learn, the opportunities to teach will be provided for him.

Again, the provision is not made by the Holy Spirit, but by my accepting life as the script I wrote, which I can now walk through with a Teacher Who will help me forgive and find peace, rather than making myself and others miserable. Importantly, the *I* is not the physical self I think I am, but the mind's decision maker.

(2:1) In order to understand the teaching-learning plan of salvation, it is necessary to grasp the concept of time that the course sets forth.

Here Jesus is saying that we need to understand time, even though he tells us elsewhere, as I explained above, that this is impossible. Yet it is important to recognize the metaphysical foundation for his teachings. The manual is the least metaphysical of the Course's three books, for there is little in it about the nature of the illusory universe, unlike what is found in the text and workbook. However, there are intimations that what underlies this belief in shared interests is our perfect oneness as God's perfect creation, perfectly at one with our Creator.

In order to appreciate the importance of looking at everyone differently and asking Jesus' help to do so, it is necessary that we accept that everything has already happened and will continue to happen in our deluded minds as long as we choose to remain asleep. Jesus is helping us understand there is a method in the world's madness, even though it makes no sense. Though the world is indeed a terrible, pain-filled place "where starved and thirsty creatures come to die" (W-pII.13.5:1), meaning can yet be found here, allowing our experience to change as we choose to learn that our interests are not apart from anyone else's.

(2:2-8) Atonement corrects illusions, not truth. Therefore, it corrects what never was. Further, the plan for this correction was established and completed simultaneously, for the Will of God is entirely apart from time. So is all reality, being of Him. The instant the idea of separation entered the mind of God's Son, in that same instant was God's Answer given. In time this happened very long ago. In reality it never happened at all.

The Atonement corrects what never was because it itself is an illusion. The carpet of time reversing itself is as illusory as the carpet of time spinning out, but we need the correction as long as we believe in the reality of the ego problem. We have already seen that in the original instant all the mistakes were made as split-off parts of the original one; and in that same instant all the answers were given as fragmentary reflections of the original answer. Indeed, everything that ever happened occurred then, as we read from "The Little Hindrance":

> The tiny tick of time in which the first mistake was made, and all of them within that one mistake, held also the Correction for that one, and all of them that came within the first. And in that tiny instant time was gone, for that was all it ever was. What God gave answer to is answered and is gone (T-26.V.3:5-7).

Again, there is no way of understanding this, because if it never happened at all, we are not even here to ponder it. Since we experience ourselves as being here, therefore, statements such as the above make no real sense to us. Yet it is important to understand that we are talking about an illusion correcting an illusion, leaving only the reality of God. But it is the correction of that illusion that makes our lives meaningful and will have us end the world that is weary, worn, and without hope. The hope does not come from within the world, but from the shift in our minds.

(3:1-5) The world of time is the world of illusion. What happened long ago seems to be happening now. Choices made long since appear to be open; yet to be made. What has been learned and understood and long ago passed by is looked upon as a new thought, a fresh idea, a different approach. Because your will is free you can accept what has already happened at any time you choose, and only then will you realize that it was always there.

Stating this once again, the original error and its subsequent forms have already happened; the undoing of the error has happened as well—the carpet of time spun out and rolled back in that single illusory instant. We think we are walking on it, as if for the first time. However, we are simply reviewing in our minds what has past (W-pI.158.3-4). In other words, everything in the world is a form of *déjà-vu*.

I will not elaborate any further. Suffice it to say, what is necessary is understanding we are not choosing the script, relationships, or circumstances in our lives. We choose the teacher with whom we will join to re-experience these relationships and circumstances. Thus it is not the form that is important—what my body does with another body or within itself—but the way in which I look at my body and its relationship to other bodies. This is a course in *cause*—the mind—not in *effect*—the body. Jesus continues with what we truly choose:

(3:6-8) As the course emphasizes, you are not free to choose the curriculum, or even the form in which you will learn it. You are free, however, to decide when you want to learn it. And as you accept it, it is already learned.

The reference here is to the text's Introduction where Jesus makes the same point:

> This is a course in miracles. It is a required course. Only the time you take it is voluntary. Free will does not mean that you can establish the curriculum. It means only that you can elect what you want to take at a given time (T-in.1:1-5; italics omitted).

College students have nothing to say about the courses listed in the school catalog, but they are free to pick which courses they will take when—at least with regard to electives. Our situation is similar. Our decision maker has already established the curriculum of our lives, but our choice now lies with which teacher we choose to re-experience this script: the ego or the Holy Spirit. Therefore, when we accept the curriculum, "it is already learned"—we simply accept the learning that is there.

Once again, it comes down to the manual's central theme: Do I choose to see my relationship with you as expressing the separate interests the ego tells me is the truth, or do I choose to see the reflection of shared interests the Holy Spirit knows as the truth? To see this as the only issue simplifies our extremely complicated lives, personally and collectively: Do I see my interests as separate from this doctor, lawyer, family member, friend, or colleague; from my president or prime minister? Do I see myself with conflicting interests, or interests shared in common? And, given that I have already chosen to do both in that original instant, my choice comes within the context of a movie I have already made. Yet I am now free to re-experience the drama through the eyes of the ego or the Holy Spirit. That alone is my choice.

(4:1) Time really, then, goes backward to an instant so ancient that it is beyond all memory, and past even the possibility of remembering.

We are not asked to return to the ontological moment when we believed as one Son in the separation from God. That memory is so buried it is almost impossible to access it. Yet we are not asked to do so because we are reliving it right now, in the present choice to see our relationship with others as justifying separation.

(4:2) Yet because it is an instant that is relived again and again and still again, it seems to be now.

I believe I am a body localized in a particular time and space, and that is how I experience the original error. Again, I do not have to decide for or against God, but simply to decide for or against you in what I believe to be my present. This means I can choose to see us as sharing the same split mind, or as separate in the sense that our interests conflict.

(4:3) And thus it is that pupil and teacher seem to come together in the present, finding each other as if they had not met before.

But we have already "met." Our entire lives here, again, are literally one *déjà vu*—we have already seen this, done that. When we become sick and tired of the specialness we constantly live through, day in and day out, we will let it go simply by choosing not to see our interests as special—apart from another's.

(4:4-8) The pupil comes at the right time to the right place. This is inevitable, because he made the right choice in that ancient instant which he now relives. So has the teacher, too, made an inevitable choice out of an ancient past. God's Will in everything but seems to take time in the working out. What could delay the power of eternity?

These ideas are so essential, we see how frequently Jesus repeats them. Not only did the ego thought system happen long ago, its undoing through the Holy Spirit happened long ago as well, and we simply revisit them now. The ending is inevitable, as is said twice in the text: "The outcome is as certain as God" (T-2.III.3:10; T-4.II.5:8). The only question is *when* we will choose to make certain our experience that the outcome has already happened. How long will we attempt to walk this long and wearying path, when in an instant we could leave it and go home?

(5:1-3) When pupil and teacher come together, a teaching-learning situation begins. For the teacher is not really the one who does the teaching. God's Teacher speaks to any two who join together for learning purposes.

Here we see the confluence of our journey's two great themes: In order to see shared interests and realize we are one in purpose, we need a Teacher Who will so instruct us and give meaning to every circumstance in our lives. In the text, this meaning is reflected in "the holy encounter" (T-8.III.4:1), wherein every relationship has the potential for holiness because it can serve the Holy Spirit's holy purpose of providing an opportunity to choose again—to see separate interests as wrong and hurtful, and shared interests as helpful.

(5:4) The relationship is holy because of that purpose, and God has promised to send His Spirit into any holy relationship.

The important theme of *purpose* returns. I do not have to change the relationship, simply the purpose my specialness has given it. Changing the form is irrelevant, for it is the mind's shift in purpose that makes the relationship holy.

"God has promised to send His Spirit into any holy relationship": Remember, the Holy Spirit is there already as the memory we took with us into the dream when we fell asleep. That is why God does not "send" the Holy Spirit. We are simply reminded of His Presence.

(5:5) In the teaching-learning situation, each one learns that giving and receiving are the same.

I have briefly discussed the equality of giving and receiving, and we will continually return to this subsidiary theme. Giving and receiving are the same because teacher and pupil are the same—one in content and purpose. When I give guilt by attacking you, I reinforce it in myself, thereby receiving it. When I let forgiveness extend through me to you, I reinforce it in myself, thereby receiving it—giving and receiving are the same and there is no loss.

(5:6) The demarcations they have drawn between their roles, their minds, their bodies, their needs, their interests, and all the differences they thought separated them from one another, fade and grow dim and disappear.

Separate interests are born of the belief that I want to be separate and my ego to be right. My being in a body and seeing yours as different from mine reinforces this. When I choose a different Teacher and different lesson, however, recognizing our interests are the same, everything of the ego begins to disappear. Our bodies do not literally disappear, but the ego's interpretation of the body "flickers and fades and finally is gone" (*The Gifts of God*, p. 64). I will no longer see you and me as separate, but look beyond our superficial differences to the same content: we share the same ego, Holy Spirit, and capacity to choose between the two.

(5:7) Those who would learn the same course share one interest and one goal.

Our wonderful theme returns. You do not have to share that interest in order for this to work; it is enough that I do. You may have died already, or no longer be physically present to me, but you remain in my mind. The interest we share is there, and when this mind is healed of its belief in separate interests, it becomes one with the Sonship. Remember that since this is a dream, there is literally no one out there to be forgiven. Seeing our shared interests corrects my first having seen them as separate. As I learn, step by step, that our interests are the same and we are one, I grow in understanding that we are literally cut from the same cloth—fragments of the same pane of glass; and, ultimately, we are one in Christ. Yet I begin my learning where I think I am—in a body separate from yours.

(5:8-9) And thus he who was the learner becomes a teacher of God himself, for he has made the one decision that gave his teacher to him. He has seen in another person the same interests as his own.

You can see the centrality of this theme to the manual, for it returns repeatedly. Here it is stated in its original form; however, as I mentioned in the Introduction, we will also see it in many variations before our journey is complete.

3. WHAT ARE THE LEVELS OF TEACHING?

In this section, Jesus talks about three forms or levels of relationships: superficial, intense and circumscribed by time, and lifelong. Despite the obvious differences in form, all relationships are the same. The section is, in fact, a commentary on the first principle of miracles: there is no order of difficulty among them (T-1.I.1). This means there is no hierarchy of illusions and no levels of teaching. This first principle concludes with: "All expressions of love are maximal" (T-1.I.1:4), and we will see the word *maximal* used again in this section. Thus it does not matter whether one is involved in superficial encounters or lifelong relationships. The potential for total healing is always present, because whatever the level, it is possible to see another's interests as shared. Approaching relationships this way brings unity to our days, and indeed can unify our lives. It does not matter whether we do something significant or insignificant; whether we are with important or unimportant people, with those who mean a great deal to us or with strangers. Everything is the same because the Holy Spirit and ego are always with us. Therefore the opportunity is continually present to project separation and guilt or extend sharing and forgiveness—the theme of this section.

(1:1-2) The teachers of God have no set teaching level. Each teaching-learning situation involves a different relationship at the beginning, although the ultimate goal is always the same; to make of the relationship a holy relationship, in which both can look upon the Son of God as sinless.

Teaching-learning situations are different in form but the same in content, for we share the goal of making each relationship holy. On a deeper level, we share the same content because we are part of the same sinless Sonship that has never left its Source, and therefore we all need to awaken from the nightmare dream of sin. The differences in the form of our relationships, if taken seriously, serve merely to reinforce our belief in separation.

(1:3) There is no one from whom a teacher of God cannot learn, so there is no one whom he cannot teach.

It is not that you teach me something on the level of form (history, cooking, etc.). I first teach separation by projecting guilt and seeing you as the object of my special love or hate. My awareness of the pain this causes motivates me to ask for help and make another choice. Thus we can learn from anyone, because anyone can be the object of our projected guilt, the precursor to our teaching and learning forgiveness.

(1:4-8) However, from a practical point of view he cannot meet everyone, nor can everyone find him. Therefore, the plan includes very specific contacts to be made for each teacher of God. There are no accidents in salvation. Those who are to meet will meet, because together they have the potential for a holy relationship. They are ready for each other.

In a world of six and a half billion people, we are not going to meet everyone. The "plan" thus includes specific contacts as representative of the relationships we have already experienced, leaving no room for accidents because everything has already happened. We choose to be with a certain person, either from the point of view of the ego—to fulfill its purpose of separation—or the Holy Spirit—to fulfill His purpose of salvation. And, of course, we can always change our minds. We can be in a relationship for what could have been the purpose of healing, and then become fearful and attack, or vice versa—yet the potential for forgiveness is always there. Now the first level:

(2:1-4) The simplest level of teaching appears to be quite superficial. It consists of what seem to be very casual encounters; a "chance" meeting of two apparent strangers in an elevator, a child who is not looking where he is going running into an adult "by chance," two students "happening" to walk home together. These are not chance encounters. Each of them has the potential for becoming a teaching-learning situation.

It cannot be said often enough that the Holy Spirit does not orchestrate these meetings. The decision-making mind sets them up for one of two purposes, and we are free to choose either at any moment; moreover, we have seen how we can go back and forth between the ego and the Holy Spirit. It should be emphasized that none of this discussion should be taken to mean that we "attract" people or situations into our lives. Our decision maker—outside time and space—chooses when and with whom we will have our experiences, and what they will be.

(2:5-8) Perhaps the seeming strangers in the elevator will smile to one another; perhaps the adult will not scold the child for bumping into him; perhaps the students will become friends. Even at the level of the most casual encounter, it is possible for two people to lose sight of separate interests, if only for a moment. That moment will be enough. Salvation has come.

Every situation is an opportunity, so we should not minimize any encounter: the one who checks us out at the supermarket; the salesperson at a clothing store; someone we do not really meet, but our cars "meet" on the highway; those in our work and personal lives; the ones we "meet" on television and in the news. All these are opportunities for us first to project the ego, and then ask for help to look at the relationship differently. Remember, "all expressions of love are maximal"; there is no hierarchy of love or expressions of love, for love is total.

(3:1-3) It is difficult to understand that levels of teaching the universal course is a concept as meaningless in reality as is time. The illusion of one permits the illusion of the other. In time, the teacher of God seems to begin to change his mind about the world with a single decision, and then learns more and more about the new direction as he teaches it.

Time and levels of teaching are meaningless concepts in reality, because time and space are the same illusion of separation, taking different forms (T-26.VIII.1:3). Our experience is that we make a decision and then nourish, reinforce, and attack it, and then return to it. Yet all this acts out something that has already happened—in the mind. However, nothing can happen in the world for the body does not do anything, as the Course teaches again and again. Thus, as we have seen, we merely revisit what has already happened: the ego script of separation and specialness, or the Holy Spirit's correction script of shared interests and forgiveness.

(3:4) We have covered the illusion of time already, but the illusion of levels of teaching seems to be something different.

We really think there is a difference between our important and unimportant relationships, a concept the ego loves, for it reinforces the notion of a hierarchy of illusions—its first law of chaos (T-23.II.2-3). A hierarchy implies separation, or ordering, but in Heaven there is only *one* order: God. In discussing the trinity, for example, Jesus explains that God is the First, and there is no second or third:

> The first in time means nothing, but the First in eternity is God the Father, Who is both First and One. Beyond the First there is no other, for there is no order, no second or third, and nothing but the First (T-14.IV.1:7-8).

Since God is One, how can there be anything else? The ego, therefore, loves anything that proves the existence of a hierarchy; judging, for example —some people are better or worse than others, some relationships are more important than others. In the context of our daily experience, Jesus helps us understand that the content is always the same, regardless of the form.

(3:5-7) Perhaps the best way to demonstrate that these levels cannot exist is simply to say that any level of the teaching-learning situation is part of God's plan for Atonement, and His plan can have no levels, being a reflection of His Will. Salvation is always ready and always there. God's teachers work at different levels, but the result is always the same.

There is only one content: either the ego's separate interests, or the Holy Spirit's shared interests that reflect the one level of God's Will. There is nothing else. Having this as our foundation unifies our day and gives it meaning.

(4:1) Each teaching-learning situation is maximal in the sense that each person involved will learn the most that he can from the other person at that time.

The word *maximal* is important because it returns us to the first principle of miracles: "All expressions of love are maximal" (T-1.I.1:4). Each teaching-learning situation is maximal, whether it is a five-second superficial encounter or an ongoing relationship—the ego is always there, as is the Holy

Spirit. Recall that the mind is outside time and space, where there is no large or small. The ego's thought system never diminishes, being 100 percent sin, guilt, and fear. The Holy Spirit's right-minded correction is also unchanging, being 100 percent forgiveness, peace, and love's reflection. What changes is the decision maker's choice, and both the ego and Holy Spirit disappear when we accept the Atonement, which gently fades away when its purpose is fulfilled. What then remains is the Oneness of God's Son.

At any given moment, therefore, the entirety of the ego's thought system can be activated, as can the entirety of the Holy Spirit's—whether on the freeway, supermarket checkout counter, or with a person with whom you live or work. The lack of difference is what is important. Never forget this is not a course in behavior—the *form*—but in changing one's mind—the *content*. Teaching occurs through demonstration, and we always demonstrate one thought system or the other; behavior, being the effect, is secondary.

(4:2-3) In this sense, and in this sense only, we can speak of levels of teaching. Using the term in this way, the second level of teaching is a more sustained relationship, in which, for a time, two people enter into a fairly intense teaching-learning situation and then appear to separate.

We have seen that the first level of teaching includes superficial, seemingly chance meetings, and the second level the more sustained, intense relationships. This second level therefore includes those who are married for a short period of time, have an intense though short-lived love affair, or are our closest friends in school whom, after graduation, we never see again; people with whom we work closely, and when one or both parties leaves, we lose all contact; or a doctor/therapist-patient relationship. Indeed, all intense relationships provide us with excellent opportunities to project the ego onto another. Yet this also means we have the opportunity to look at our projections with Jesus, seeing that what we judge against another is a projection of what we have judged against ourselves.

(4:4-7) As with the first level, these meetings are not accidental, nor is what appears to be the end of the relationship a real end. Again, each has learned the most he can at the time. Yet all who meet will someday meet again, for it is the destiny of all relationships to become holy. God is not mistaken in His Son.

The meaning of the last sentence, "God is not mistaken in His Son," is that we remain as He created us—one. Therefore every relationship on the carpet of time in which we have made separation real to prove that God is mistaken in His Son, will be healed. We do not have to undo each and every relationship, however. We are taught that when we forgive one person, behind him stand thousands more, and behind each one of those stand another thousand (T-27.V.10:4). This is the meaning of "all who meet will someday meet again"—we meet in each other. Incidentally, this is another of many places where Jesus implies a belief in reincarnation, a topic he addresses later in the manual. Yet whether or not you believe in reincarnation, within the illusion of time it would appear as if this is not the only time we have come. Passages such as these strongly suggest that we "come" many times.

Whatever has not been healed in my relationship with you will be healed again. Perhaps not on the bodily level, but on some level in the mind every relationship will be healed—God is not mistaken in His Son. We are not separate, and when we have finally accepted the Atonement all special relationships will be undone in the same holy instant because they were held together by our belief in separate interests, a belief that ultimately stems from the belief that God and His Son are separate. God, however, wills His Oneness, and wills His Son be forever a part of Him. This means we cannot be individuals, with separating interests apart from His Will. And now the third level:

(5:1) The third level of teaching occurs in relationships which, once they are formed, are lifelong.

These relationships include, for example, friends from school who remain part of our lives; people we meet, with whom we remain friends; those we marry, and stay married to. While nuclear families are not specifically mentioned here, they certainly belong in this category. Regardless of what happens to a family—people die, move away, or have nothing more to do with each other—they continue to exist in the mind. We take our parents, siblings, and

3. What Are the Levels of Teaching?

children with us, whether they are physically present or not.

(5:2-3) These are teaching-learning situations in which each person is given a chosen learning partner who presents him with unlimited opportunities for learning. These relationships are generally few, because their existence implies that those involved have reached a stage simultaneously in which the teaching-learning balance is actually perfect.

What keeps people together is that they can learn from each other. Yet they can choose not to learn, as we will see in the next few sentences, and can choose to separate instead. In this regard, it is vitally important to understand that nothing in this section, or anywhere in *A Course in Miracles* should be taken to mean that it is sinful to separate from a friend or spouse, since Jesus says nothing about form. If you are in a relationship that is problematic and you can no longer tolerate it, Jesus would not say you should remain there, as long as you know that whatever issues remain unhealed in you will surface again, either with this person or another who represents the same dynamic. The idea is not to feel guilty because you leave a situation—whether at work or a relationship that is abusive, hurtful, or simply difficult. Realize, again, that whatever is unhealed will come up again; and when you are ready to deal with it, you will. Since time is not real, whenever you experience Jesus pressuring you, know that he is not the source of the pressure, *you* are. Yet in time, everyone will learn to forgive and be healed.

(5:4-5) This does not mean that they necessarily recognize this; in fact, they generally do not. They may even be quite hostile to each other for some time and perhaps for life.

Couples often do not recognize they are ideally suited, in the sense that they offer each other wonderful opportunities to forgive and be healed. Many of us know marriages that last forty, fifty, or sixty years, in which judgment and hatred are constant and there is no apparent love present. Yet there is something that keeps the couple together, which means there is, at least on some level, a right-minded view that says their interests are not separate, even though that may not be expressed at all. Thus one often finds in this kind of relationship a deep-seated loyalty that in the end transcends the daily bickering and bitterness. Their loyalty extends not only to their spouse, but to themselves, for on some level it is recognized that salvation—learning the lesson of shared interests—is best served by preserving the *form* of marriage, which reflects the *content* of joining of minds. This exemplifies the principle that nothing is accidental. Our lives are scripts in which we chose to separate and attack, yet the same scripts contain the potential for healing. Both the ego and Holy Spirit help us review mentally what has already occurred in the script we wrote in the beginning. Thus can conflicting interests dissolve into the single interest of awakening from the dream of separation.

(5:6) Yet should they decide to learn it, the perfect lesson is before them and can be learned.

The perfect lesson is that *God's Son is sinless*, reflected in learning that his interests are not separate from another's. The lesson is there because the Holy Spirit's thought of Atonement is in the shared right mind. Since somewhere in our scripts we have chosen to accept it, it is accepted. *When* we choose to re-experience this acceptance is our only choice. We cannot choose not to accept it, because we have already done so—an essential point of these early sections.

(5:7-8) And if they decide to learn that lesson, they become the saviors of the teachers who falter and may even seem to fail. No teacher of God can fail to find the Help he needs.

Here again is our second theme: asking the Holy Spirit's or Jesus' help. When I learn the lesson of seeing my interests as not separate from another's, no matter whom I am with, I will demonstrate that lesson by my very presence, for I have become the teacher and savior of others. Again, in the illusion this may seem to take a long time, and may seem to be almost impossible. In reality, however, salvation has already happened because all have returned to the home they never left. All have accepted the Atonement for themselves because the separation never occurred. It is therefore only a question of how long we choose to remain asleep in our misery. Our function as teachers of God is to learn that lesson, and to let our new teacher live his lesson of forgiveness through us. To repeat this wonderful quote:

Teach not that I died in vain. Teach rather that I did not die by demonstrating that I live in you (T-11.VI.7:3-4).

The demonstration that Jesus' presence is alive and well in us reflects the principle that we are one, and that the ego has no power over God's Son; separation has no power over our shared interests.

4. WHAT ARE THE CHARACTERISTICS OF GOD'S TEACHERS?

This section is the longest in the manual and contains much rich material. It helps students get a better understanding not only of what it means to be a teacher of God, but a teacher of God who has matured spiritually. In the manual generally, and specifically in this section, Jesus delineates three levels of God's teachers. Recall that everyone can choose to be a teacher of either the ego or God. Choosing to see another's interests as not separate from your own means that you have chosen to be one of *God's teachers*. This reflects our common need to awaken from the ego's dream and return home. Using the image of the ladder, which I alluded to earlier, seeing another's interest as your own places you on the bottom rung of the right ladder. The ego's ladder of separate interests, bearing the emblem "seek and do not find," goes nowhere. The Holy Spirit's ladder, on the other hand, leads us home.

The three levels of God's teachers discussed in the manual correspond to three levels of the ladder. The bottom rungs represent the beginning of the journey and learning that our interests are not separate from another's—manifested in our everyday lives by letting go of judgments and grievances, not attacking others by making them scapegoats for our guilt, and not perceiving ourselves as victims of the world. However, when Jesus discusses the ten characteristics of a teacher of God, he speaks of the characteristics of *advanced teachers*—those who have grown up spiritually and are now on the upper rungs of the ladder. The actual process of getting from the bottom to the top is discussed below under "The Development of Trust," which Jesus describes as a six-stage process.

The journey begins when you first make the decision not to judge another. This does not require that you withdraw judgments from everyone, but just a simple withholding of judgment from someone who may have bumped into you or cut you off on the freeway. This is all it takes to get you onto the bottom rung of Jesus' ladder. The rest of the journey consists of generalizing this holy instant to all relationships and situations.

The top rung, the final stage in this process, is the real world, though it is not mentioned as such here. Just beyond the real world the ladder disappears and you are home. When you reach the very top, the ladder fades and you become a *Teacher of teachers*, a term used specifically later in the manual (M-26.2:2). This level includes people like Jesus, or any others who can be considered enlightened, who need not be physically present in the world. They are at the ladder's top rung, after which God takes the last step, reaching down to lift us unto Himself. This is not a concept covered here in the manual, but is often described in the text (e.g., T-7.I.6-7; T-11.VIII.15).

We begin with two introductory paragraphs as we embark on our study of the ten characteristics of an advanced teacher of God.

(1:1-2) The surface traits of God's teachers are not at all alike. They do not look alike to the body's eyes, they come from vastly different backgrounds, their experiences of the world vary greatly, and their superficial "personalities" are quite distinct.

This relates to *form*, wherein everyone looks different, speaks differently, and has different messages. "Personalities" is placed in quotes because they are illusory. We all seem to have them, just as we all seem to have physical characteristics that distinguish us from each other; but both our physical and psychological selves are superficial and mean nothing. It is the underlying *content* alone that is important, and this is a variation of our first theme that we share the same interests because we share the same mind.

(1:3-4) Nor, at the beginning stages of their functioning as teachers of God, have they yet acquired the deeper characteristics that will establish them as what they are. God gives special gifts to His teachers, because they have a special role in His plan for Atonement.

On the lower rungs of the ladder, when we first see someone else's interests as our own, we have not yet acquired the deeper characteristics—the ten described in this section—that will establish us as advanced teachers of God.

We are already familiar with the principle that God does not "give" anything, as we will see reflected in sentence 6. He does not give special gifts, even though our experience seems to suggest He does. In reality, the gifts are our own, since it is our script of separation. The talents and abilities we developed over the course of our holographic journey through time and space we would have used first for ego purposes: advancing our specialness by getting others to worship at our personal altars and shrines. Eventually, when we realize our interests are not apart from another's, we make a shift: the abilities that were separating now serve the holy purpose of Atonement. Realizing our interests are the same, the need to dominate, control, seduce, or harm is gone.

(1:5) Their specialness is, of course, only temporary; set in time as a means of leading out of time.

Each of these characteristics, although positive, are nonetheless illusory because they do not exist in Heaven. In fact, at the end of this section we will be told what characteristics of God's Son do exist there; but we will also be told that these are beyond the curriculum of *A Course in Miracles*.

(1:6) These special gifts, born in the holy relationship…

This is the key—these gifts are not given by God, but are within us. When we choose the holiness of the Holy Spirit's purpose instead of the ego's *un*holiness, the latter is out of the way, leaving only the Atonement Thought that the separation never happened. The reflection of Heaven's truth—kindness and gentleness—then shines through us. This reflection, then, becomes our traits, but not because God has granted them to us. These "special gifts"—the ten characteristics—are an inherent part of our right minds, born in the holy relationship because its forgiveness undoes the barriers to our awareness of them.

(1:6) These special gifts, born in the holy relationship toward which the teaching-learning situation is geared…

This statement expresses the purpose of *A Course in Miracles*, as well as any relationship initially made by the ego to separate. Choosing the Holy Spirit as our Teacher shifts the purpose, undoing the separation through forgiveness. Indeed, all teaching-learning situations are geared toward this shift.

(1:6-7) … become characteristic of all teachers of God who have advanced in their own learning. In this respect they are all alike.

It is not some, the best, or the enlightened ones; it is *all* teachers of God because the Atonement Thought is in *everyone*. If there is no separation, there is only the Love of God, and so *all* teachers share these characteristics. The content of love, however, will be expressed differently because people need to be taught in ways they can accept without fear, as this wonderful passage from the text explains:

> The value of the Atonement does not lie in the manner in which it is expressed. In fact, if it is used truly, it will inevitably be expressed in whatever way is most helpful to the receiver. This means that a miracle, to attain its full efficacy, must be expressed in a language that the recipient can understand without fear. This does not necessarily mean that this is the highest level of communication of which he is capable. It does mean, however, that it is the highest level of communication of which he is capable *now*. The whole aim of the miracle is to raise the level of communication, not to lower it by increasing fear (T-2.IV.5).

The value of the Atonement, therefore, has nothing to do with behavior. When people are right-minded, for example, their words come through in whatever form is most helpful, contingent upon the need of others, just as *A Course in Miracles* came in a form we can understand and accept, written in a language and idiom with which we are familiar. And so, when we make the choice to see our interests as shared instead of separate, Jesus' love flows through us and whatever we say or do is helpful. Incidentally, our behavior may be totally different from what we say or do to someone else, or to the same person on a different day—it is only the *content* that determines the importance of our words or deeds.

(2:1) All differences among the Sons of God are temporary.

If the differences are temporary, they must be illusory since truth is eternal. They are thus superficial because they are based on form—traits of the physical body and its personality. What is constant is God's non-specific and abstract Love, present in our minds through the Holy Spirit and His Atonement principle. Though the expressions in form are legion, the content of Atonement remains one, reflecting the eternal One.

(2:2) Nevertheless, in time it can be said that the advanced teachers of God have the following characteristics:

Within time there are certainly differences among us, and referring to himself in this regard, Jesus says that he is no different from any of us in eternity, although in the illusion he is clearly wiser:

> There is nothing about me that you cannot attain. I have nothing that does not come from God. The difference between us now is that I have nothing else. This leaves me in a state which is only potential in you.
>
> "No man cometh unto the Father but by me" does not mean that I am in any way separate or different from you except in time, and time does not really exist (T-1.II.3:10-13; 4:1).

Using the analogy of the ladder we can say that Jesus is higher than we; in fact, he is not on the ladder at all. Advanced teachers therefore are on the higher rungs, having the ten characteristics we now examine.

I. Trust

The first characteristic is trust and, as will become evident, the other nine are based on this. Trust is probably the most important expression thus far on our journey of the second theme in our *opus* of themes and variations—asking for and trusting the Holy Spirit's help. This means withdrawing trust in the ego and placing it in Him, allowing us literally to look at the world differently. Even though our eyes may see the same world we saw before, our interpretation of what we see will be quite different. Specifically, we would not be affected by anything external, for we would have learned that God's peace and Love remain forever unchanged within our minds, and nothing in this world has the power to take them away, *unless we give it that power*. Only we can remove peace from our experience; not people, objects, or circumstances. Thus everything rests on trust, and in particular, the teacher in whom we place it.

(1:1-3) This is the foundation on which their ability to fulfill their function rests. Perception is the result of learning. In fact, perception *is* learning, because cause and effect are never separated.

This is a variation of our theme of shared interests. Everything is one, which means everything is the same—cause and effect are not separated. A crucial principle—stated directly fourteen times in the text and workbook—is that *ideas leave not their source*. Worded differently, this principle states that *effects leave not their cause*. When applied to the world, this means that the world has not left its cause (source) in the mind, which means there is no world outside our minds.

Perception therefore follows directly from our decision to learn from the ego or the Holy Spirit. The one we choose will be the eyes through which we perceive the world; not what our physical eyes see—perceptual facts such as color, shapes, or behavior—but *the way in which we see*—our interpretation of these facts. By choosing the ego we see through the judgmental eyes of separation and separate interests; by choosing the Holy Spirit we see through vision's eyes of joining and shared interests:

> Vision or judgment is your choice, but never both of these (T-20.V.4:7).

That is why perception is not only the result of learning, but *is* learning—there is no difference between inner and outer. This is one of the main points of the early workbook lessons: the world is the projection of the thoughts in the mind; i.e., the inner teacher with whom we choose to identify.

(1:4-7) The teachers of God have trust in the world, because they have learned it is not governed by the laws the world made up. It is governed by a power that is *in* them but not *of* them. It is this power that keeps all things safe. It is through this power that the teachers of God look on a forgiven world.

This passage can easily be taken out of context to mean that the Holy Spirit is going to make everything right in this world—He will bring peace to the Middle East, prevent wars in Africa, and end world poverty. Yet this is the exact opposite of Jesus' teaching. The world does not change; it is what it is and has never left its source in the mind. As an illusion, the world cannot change into something other than itself. What does change, however, is the mind's choice of teacher in whom it puts its trust. Once we have faith in what Jesus tells us—the world is a projection of our thought—and shift from thoughts of separation and guilt to forgiveness and shared interests, we look on everything differently. Our eyes report the same sensory data, but our response is based on the realization that everyone either expresses love or calls for it. No other perception is possible once we have chosen to see through Christ's vision.

Everyone wants to be loved, and the natural response to a call for love or its expression is love. The forms of that expression differ widely, but their content remains the same. Thus, choosing the Holy Spirit's peace allows you to walk the world in a state of peace, despite what goes on around you. In the midst of cruelty, murder, and exploding bombs, you are peaceful. Cause and effect are not separate: identify with the thought of peace and love—the *cause*—and the *effect* must be peace and love. In your right mind there is nothing else.

This, of course, does not mean you do not respond behaviorally to situations; but if you do, it is through the vision that sees everyone's interests as the same. Thus, even though behaviorally you might be taking sides—and there is nothing in *A Course in Miracles* that says not to do that—in your heart of hearts you know everyone is your brother or sister: victims and victimizers, oppressed and oppressors. All call for the same love; otherwise they would not be here. This is the power Jesus speaks of, which brings peace regardless of the events in your personal world or the world at large. It does not oppose or triumph, for its love can only embrace the perfect oneness that is itself, reflected in the world of separation by Christ's vision that embraces all people as one in purpose.

(2:1) When this power has once been experienced, it is impossible to trust one's own petty strength again.

A major theme in *A Course in Miracles* is the contrast between our weakness and the strength of Christ in us. It does not appear often in the manual, but it is prevalent in the text, especially at its conclusion, "Choose Once Again" (T-31.VIII.2:3-7). Thus, as Jesus says here, when we experience this peace—"which passes all understanding" (Philippians 4:7)—we will never again place trust in the ego's little strength.

(2:2-3) Who would attempt to fly with the tiny wings of a sparrow when the mighty power of an eagle has been given him? And who would place his faith in the shabby offerings of the ego when the gifts of God are laid before him?

Jesus teaches us to contrast the gifts of the ego—guilt and anxiety—with the gifts of God—love and peace—and see the causal connection between our choice of teachers and how we feel. In choosing the ego's separate interests, we experience depression, discomfort, and disease. In choosing the Holy Spirit's shared interests, we experience happiness and joy. This is why our second theme of asking the Holy Spirit for help is so crucial. We need an inner Teacher to help us see this contrast clearly and make the correct choice.

(2:4) What is it that induces them to make the shift?

What follows in the "Development of Trust" is the answer to this question, which reflects what we have just seen as the contrast between choosing the ego and the Holy Spirit. The choice for separate interests leads to opposition and war in the world, and pain and unhappiness in our personal lives; while the choice for shared interests leads to real and lasting peace—personally and collectively. The right choice occurs as we develop our trust in the Holy Spirit's thought system, a process to which we now turn.

A. Development of Trust

We begin by summarizing the six stages in the development of trust, followed by a line-by-line commentary. This section traces the process of moving from the bottom rungs of the ladder—a beginning teacher—to the top rungs—an advanced teacher. A word of caution: It is a mistake to take these six stages literally and attempt to determine which stage you are at, or anyone else is at for that matter. Falling into that trap reflects the competitive endeavor in which the gods of specialness revel. These stages are intended to describe only the general process of releasing the ego, and are not meant to be taken as literal, sequential, or linear stages. They merely express the general process of letting go of the ego and its thought system of sacrifice and specialness.

The first three stages are experienced as somewhat painful, in that they deal with relinquishment. The first stage is *a period of undoing*, which pertains to our experience of external changes in our world. Here, we still do not know there is an internal state—the mind—and so we are very much affected by external events such as losing one's job or pension, relocating due to a company decision, a loved one's death, one's body becoming ill, war breaking out, or the stock market plummeting. Our immediate response, of course, is to experience these situations as bad and painful, and it is that perception that needs to be undone.

The second stage—*a period of sorting out*—occurs as we begin to understand that everything has the capacity for being helpful if we look at it properly. This stage involves sorting out the valuable from the valueless, the helpful from the unhelpful. We learn that the valueless is anything that keeps us rooted in the dream, and the valuable is what helps end our identification with the dream; in particular, end our identification with the figure in the dream we call ourselves. We begin to accept that letting go of the ego's specialness is helpful, and holding onto it is harmful.

The third stage is *a period of relinquishment*. This is the actual process of letting go of what is not helpful, and because of our need for specialness is usually experienced as painful and difficult.

Once we relinquish what is not helpful, we enter the fourth stage; a state of reasonable peace, *a period of settling down*. This involves the realization that we feel better when we let go of the ego, which means letting go of our victimization history and attitude of finding fault with everyone and everything. The temptation at this stage is to rest on one's laurels, thinking that the journey is done and we have attained the goal of *A Course in Miracles*.

We begin to realize, however, that we are not finished, for we are nowhere near the top of the ladder. Yet we are not at the bottom either, because it has dawned on us that we never really knew the difference between what is valuable and valueless. Learning this is the burden of *a period of unsettling*, the fifth stage. It had never occurred to us how much we cherished this self-identity, thinking that *we* forgive, *we* ask the Holy Spirit for help, *we* are this body, and *we* are the ones through whom the love of Jesus acts. Suddenly we begin to realize that *A Course in Miracles* is not about bolstering our sense of self, or becoming a happier person. We recognize instead that this is a course about realizing we are not actually a self at all, and that the person we thought we were is inherently valueless. We learn that what is truly valuable is continuing the process that helps us let go of our individual egos, which means we let go of *all* judgment.

When we finally release our identification with the ego, we are at the top of the ladder—the attainment of the real world and the final stage: *a period of achievement*. At this point the remaining nine characteristics of God's teachers become our own, and trust is certain.

Now to the commentary:

(3:1-3) First, they must go through what might be called "a period of undoing." This need not be painful, but it usually is so experienced. It seems as if things are being taken away, and it is rarely understood initially that their lack of value is merely being recognized.

Jesus is referring to the teachers of God who are on the right ladder, which means they are with the right teacher, following the right principle of shared interests.

In the text, Jesus explains that the Holy Spirit does not take away our special relationships, but transforms them by shifting their purpose (e.g., T-15.V.5; T-17.IV.2:3; T-18.II.6). Things of the world always change: bodies, circumstances, the weather, financial markets, governments, etc. The ego frequently interprets these changes as deprivation, the justified punishment for our sins. Whether we are conscious or not, these perceptions are in our minds, and it is these that need to be undone. Our task, however, is simply to look differently at the world and recognize its inherent lack of value.

(3:4) How can lack of value be perceived unless the perceiver is in a position where he must see things in a different light?

We are asked to see through Jesus' eyes instead of the ego's. He leads us to the mind, where we look differently on who we are. The ego has us look outside and make what we see real and important. To the ego, therefore, some things are judged as valuable and others valueless; happiness arising only when we take what is valuable and hold on to it. Jesus helps us look outside, too, but only as means of directing our attention within.

(3:5-7) He is not yet at a point at which he can make the shift entirely internally. And so the plan will sometimes call for changes in what seem to be external circumstances. These changes are always helpful.

Jesus says "what seem to be external circumstances" because, in truth, there are no external circumstances. In fact, there is no external anything because "There is no world! This is the central thought the course attempts to teach" (W-pI.132. 6:2-3). Therefore, it is only my perceptions of the world that have to change. These changes are helpful in that they bring to the surface what I previously did not know was going on in my mind. Again, this is not God's doing, nor is the Holy Spirit playing chess with my life by setting up situations that would be difficult, challenging, or painful. *I* am the one who write my script, since I am the one who believes in illusion. All the Holy Spirit "does" is be the loving Presence of Atonement in my mind, through which I look differently at my life. If my perception is that things are being taken from me, I can use that as an opportunity to re-examine my mind's decision for the ego, the cause of my experiencing deprivation and sacrifice. Knowing I have a mind, I have a basis for learning that the world is "an outside picture of an inward condition" (T-21.in.1:5). The external change has enabled me to get in touch with the internal condition—my mind's choice to believe in the ego.

(3:8) When the teacher of God has learned that much, he goes on to the second stage.

Recall that these are not precisely sequential stages. Proceeding from one stage to the next is not like walking through a room, closing the door behind you, and finding yourself in a new space. Jesus is describing the process of letting go of the ego—of our looking at the ego thought system and saying: "I do not want this any more." Toward that end, we are beginning to understand that an external change is helpful—whether it is deemed positive or negative—because of the opportunity it provides us to project from the mind, recognize the projection, and thus see what we were previously unaware of. Asking Jesus for help, therefore, should not be for the purpose of fixing the external situation, but only to help us look at it differently.

(4:1-3) Next, the teacher of God must go through "a period of sorting out." This is always somewhat difficult because, having learned that the changes in his life are always helpful, he must now decide all things on the basis of whether they increase the helpfulness or hamper it. He will find that many, if not most of the things he valued before will merely hinder his ability to transfer what he has learned to new situations as they arise.

This concept of *transfer of training* is a key theme in the early workbook lessons, and the process unfolds as follows: I first apply what I learned to a difficult situation and notice that some change has occurred. I begin to understand that what happened turned out to be a real blessing. While I may not have seen it that way at first, on reflection I see the blessing because it enabled me to look at something in myself that I had not previously known was there. This does not mean thanking the Holy Spirit for the *form* of the situation, but rather being grateful for the opportunity of bringing the *form* to the mind's *content*, and choosing differently.

I now want to transfer what I learn to *every* situation—"all things"—that adversely affects my peace: what excites and exhilarates me, or depresses and disquiets me. Neither is the peace of God. My goal is to realize that this process of generalization includes everything: the "good" and the "bad"; when I get what I want and when I do not. I also learn that what is not helpful is the ego's interpretation of a situation or relationship, while Jesus' interpretation most definitely is. I recognize now that I can choose between the two—the valueless and the valuable, as we read:

(4:4) Because he has valued what is really valueless ...

This is a reference to workbook Lesson 133—"I will not value what is valueless"—in which Jesus teaches that one of the most important criteria for deciding value or valuelessness is whether it is eternal. Anything that does not last is valueless, while anything that does, or is a reflection of what lasts, is valuable. This eliminates everything in the world, because nothing here lasts—pleasure is fleeting, and the surcease of pain is temporary because it always returns in one form or another. Yet, we continually strive after the world's gifts. What alone lasts here, and is therefore valuable, is forgiveness, which reflects eternal love and leads to it—the basis for Jesus asking us to be dedicated to the eternal (T-19.I.16:1). In the second stage, therefore, we begin the process of sorting out the valuable from the valueless, recognizing that every situation in our lives is relevant for this process.

(4:4) Because he has valued what is really valueless, he will not generalize the lesson for fear of loss and sacrifice.

What we fear most is that we will lose our self, that this "six-stage" process of forgiveness requires the sacrifice of our identity. It is imperative to understand that this loss of self occurs only at the top of the ladder, when we have already decided to relinquish the ego. What we "lose" as we make our way are guilt, fear, anger, depression, and pain. At the very end the entire self dissolves, because the guilt that held it in place is gone.

The ego is so afraid of our ascending the ladder that it continually attempts to keep us at the bottom rungs, or, even better, on *its* ladder, which is why we so easily fall back into holding grievances and bearing grudges, indulging in special love and hate, coveting our fears and concerns, and cherishing our guilt. The ego warns us that if we keep to this path and climb the ladder with Jesus, we will end up nowhere, disappearing into oblivion. The ego's real fear, of course, is that *it* will disappear, for when we hold Jesus' hand we end up Everywhere, joyfully echoing the lovely line from the workbook:

> Let me not forget myself is nothing, but my Self is all (W-pII.358:1:7).

(4:5-7) It takes great learning to understand that all things, events, encounters and circumstances are helpful. It is only to the extent to which they are helpful that any degree of reality should be accorded them in this world of illusion. The word "value" can apply to nothing else.

Often in the text Jesus talks about a "little willingness," but here he says that "great learning" is required to become an advanced teacher and to understand that "all things, events, encounters, and circumstances" have the potential to help us on our journey. In fact, they have value *only* to the extent that they advance us in this process of leaving behind our belief in separate interests, and in identifying more and more with the principle of shared interests. This theme is vital, and our little willingness to recognize its truth commences the journey, allowing us to begin the process of generalizing our learning to all situations and relationships as we progress. Yet we are still only in the second stage, which means that we are not yet able to correctly evaluate *all* situations in terms of their potential to help or hinder our progress up the ladder, or even keep us off it. What becomes evident, however, is that it is not the world that is important, but the way we look at it.

(5:1-2) The third stage through which the teacher of God must go can be called "a period of relinquishment." If this is interpreted as giving up the desirable, it will engender enormous conflict.

This is a critical point. In Chapter 2 of the text, Jesus speaks of our discomfort when what we do conflicts with what we want (T-2.VI.5-6). In other words, we will do what we think is spiritually correct —to forgive—but we really do not want to. We will do the right thing, whatever "right" is, because we think that is Jesus' will, when we are really opposed to doing so. We will follow the workbook because, after all, it is an integral part of *A Course in Miracles* and we want to prove to ourselves and others we are good students, yet we really do not want to give up the ego. Instead, we wish to have the ego's cake of separation and enjoy it, which means we want to be spiritual, but without giving up our special and individual selves—we want Jesus on our terms, not his. We certainly understand on one level the inherent valuelessness of our specialness, and want what is truly valuable; yet our heart's desire is to have *both*. Since this is not possible, conflict reigns supreme.

Our journey consists of the day-in and day-out practice of asking Jesus to help us look at the ego, in all situations. Specifically, this means looking at how it wants us to feel unfairly treated, justify defensiveness, attack, see separate interests, and keep us from realizing we are part of one family. The family may be insane, to be sure, but it nevertheless is a unity, and each member is as important as every other. If we do not see it that way, we but bring guilt and conflict into our spiritual path. We will have made this course difficult and accuse it of failing us, when in truth we have not done what it said. Thus Jesus said to Helen when she complained about his course not working:

You complain that this course is not sufficiently specific for you to understand it *and use it*. Yet it has been *very* specific, and *you have not done what it specifically advocates*. This is not a course in the *play* of ideas, but in their *practical application*. Nothing could be more specific than to be told, very clearly, that if you ask you *will* receive (*Absence from Felicity*, p. 297).

(5:3) Few teachers of God escape this distress entirely.

Based on the words Jesus uses—*somewhat difficult, painful, distress*—we know this is not an easy path. Looking at one's ego is painful. It need not be, but our tenacious hold on it, resisting its release, makes it difficult, painful, and distressing. And in these first three stages Jesus lets us know that he knows this will be difficult. Yet he urges us to continue with him through the darkness, because his path will take us to the light.

(5:4-5) There is, however, no point in sorting out the valuable from the valueless unless the next obvious step is taken. Therefore, the period of overlap is apt to be one in which the teacher of God feels called upon to sacrifice his own best interests on behalf of truth.

In this period of overlap—indicating that these are not discrete stages—we tend to believe Jesus is asking us to give up what we need, what we want, and who we are. Needless to say, this is a complete reversal of his message to us, yet since we believe he is asking us to sacrifice our best interests on behalf of truth, we are willing to do so. We might then devote our lives to helping people, studying this course, giving up our jobs, etc.—all because we think this is what Jesus wants us to do. The truth, however, is that Jesus does not want us to do or sacrifice anything. He does not care about what we *do*, only what we *think*. We need always to remember that this is a course in cause, not effect (T-21.VII.7:8), and so he teaches that whatever we do behaviorally should come from love instead of guilt. He cares only for what is in our minds because, seeing through Christ's vision, he sees nothing else. How can Jesus see a world that does not exist? He does "see" the thoughts that made the world, and it is these he asks us to change, with his help. He cannot change our minds for us, yet he patiently waits our making the right choice, and his patience is infinite (T-5.VI.11:6-7).

(5:6) He has not realized as yet how wholly impossible such a demand would be.

Sacrifice is totally unknown in Heaven (T-3.I.4:1), for it is a notion known only to the ego's god and its version of truth. It makes loss real, for it declares there is a real problem of sin that has to be atoned for. The truth, however, is that there is no problem to be atoned for since nothing happened—"not one note in Heaven's song was missed" (T-26.V.5:4). Nothing changed—God remains God; Oneness remains One. Though we may think the ego has the power to render perfect thought imperfect, the meaning of the Atonement is that it does not. God and His Son are one, and neither has been sacrificed for the Other:

> Merely a tiny instant has elapsed between eternity and timelessness. So brief the interval there was no lapse in continuity, nor break in thoughts which are forever unified as one. Nothing has ever happened to disturb the peace of God the Father and the Son (W-pII.234.1:2-4).

Since we demanded sacrifice of no one, it is impossible it be demanded of us.

(5:7) He can learn this only as he actually does give up the valueless.

As you continue your practice, you come to recognize that what you see yourself as giving up is really nothing, for nothing here has any value. As Jesus says in describing the real world, you will wake up one morning and realize "in glad astonishment, that for all this you gave up *nothing!*" (T-16.VI.11:4). At the top of the ladder we indeed realize this, and so there was no loss. To achieve this state, Jesus asks us to look at what we value in the world, questioning whether this is what we truly want. We are the ones to remove the ego's gifts of sacrifice because we put them in our hands in the first place. Jesus asks that we see these gifts for what they are: the ego's shabby offerings that will never bring us peace.

(5:8) Through this [giving up of the valueless], he learns that where he anticipated grief, he finds a happy lightheartedness instead; where

he thought something was asked of him, he finds a gift bestowed on him.

This is the segue into the fourth stage. We are learning that we are not asked to give up anything of value—only what is hurting us. The situation is analogous to a parent taking scissors from a small child (T-4.II.5:2), who, attracted to its glitter and movement, cries because it wants its "toy" and feels that sacrifice of its happiness is being demanded. It is only when the child is older that it realizes it was asked to give up what was hurting it. Similarly, we are all Jesus' spoiled baby brothers and sisters, demanding what we want when we want it. We therefore experience him as taking our happiness from us. Yet in truth he takes nothing from us, but patiently waits our realizing for ourselves that what we desire is not helpful. When we are able—voluntarily!—to let go of what was hurting us—our guilt and projections—we have reached the fourth stage:

(6:1-4) Now comes "a period of settling down." This is a quiet time, in which the teacher of God rests a while in reasonable peace. Now he consolidates his learning. Now he begins to see the transfer value of what he has learned.

Notice the qualifying adjective, *reasonable*. At the end—the final stage—Jesus talks about real peace. At this stage, however, it is only *reasonable*. Yet that does not mean our peace is inauthentic; it is just not what we thought it was. Formerly, there was a period of *sturm und drang*, turmoil and struggle. Now all is quiet because we realize we are holding onto nothing. There is still a sense of self—an "I"—but we have learned the value of letting go of guilt, judgment, and specialness. We realize how much better we feel when we forgive, and understand we will feel even better when we forgive not only selected individuals, but *everyone*. Further, we no longer see people having power to entrap, imprison, or victimize us, for no one has the power to bring us pain or take away our peace. We therefore can go anywhere with anyone and be at peace. While we are not at the point of realizing we are one, we are far enough along now to realize we all have the same wrong mind, right mind, and decision maker, recognizing "the transfer value" of our learning. Though our belief in self remains, we are gratefully no longer the unknowing child who began the journey.

(6:5-8) Its potential is literally staggering, and the teacher of God is now at the point in his progress at which he sees in it his whole way out. "Give up what you do not want, and keep what you do." How simple is the obvious! And how easy to do!

We do not want our grievances and judgments, and we do want forgiveness. This is non-conflicting once we recognize that holding onto grievances is painful. Yet as long as we define ourselves by specialness, we will believe we are asked to sacrifice our self.

(6:9-10) The teacher of God needs this period of respite. He has not yet come as far as he thinks.

This is one of the factors that distinguishes *A Course in Miracles* from many spiritual paths. This is not about living more happily within the dream, but about awakening from the dream entirely; not about resting comfortably in the middle of the ladder, but about getting to the top and then beyond.

(6:11-13) Yet when he is ready to go on, he goes with mighty companions beside him. Now he rests a while, and gathers them before going on. He will not go on from here alone.

The mighty companions Jesus speaks of are symbols or thoughts. In the text, he discusses the importance of taking his hand on the journey and walking with him (e.g., T-8.V). He is thus a mighty companion, as are all thoughts and memories of our positive experiences when we released the ego. They are like money in the bank that we never withdraw; always there when we need it. When we are therefore tempted to hold onto a grievance or judgment, certain we are right, we need to think back to those "mighty companions"—the memories of how good it felt when we let go of attack thoughts. That is the point of this passage.

(7:1-2) The next stage is indeed "a period of unsettling." Now must the teacher of God understand that he did not really know what was valuable and what was valueless.

You are no longer on the bottom rung of the ladder, but well along the way. Yet at this stage in the journey to Heaven, all hell breaks loose. This is what Christian mystics refer to as the "dark night of the soul," which, in the Course process, occurs when you suddenly realize what Jesus is talking about. The "you" he addresses is not the "you" you see every morning in your bathroom mirror, the one who reads and practices his words, or the self you thought was forgiving and peaceful. The object of Jesus' teaching is thus not a specific individual, but the decision-making part of the mind that chose wrongly, and now can choose the Holy Spirit.

Teachers of God who learned the value of forgiveness now recognize that Jesus meant something much deeper than they originally thought. The process does not end with simply forgiving another. What awakens us from the dream and returns us home is the realization that the reason there is nothing to forgive because nothing was ever done to us, is that there is no "us." That is the final step in our learning. We integrate our understanding of the difference between the valuable and the valueless with the realization that our self is inherently valueless. Even when it is peaceful, forgiving, kind, and gentle, it is still "self," and therefore without true value.

This essential stage in the journey accounts in large measure for the extreme difficulty students have with this course. We have intimations that selflessness is its goal, even though we may still have a long way to go. It is therefore important that we be repeatedly reminded that we do not lose our self as we journey on, but simply feel more happy and peaceful, less anxious, angry, and afraid. At some point, however, we come to realize that the process of differentiating the valuable from the valueless leads to this stage of acknowledging there is no "we."

(7:3-6) All that he really learned so far was that he did not want the valueless, and that he did want the valuable. Yet his own sorting out was meaningless in teaching him the difference. The idea of sacrifice, so central to his own thought system, had made it impossible for him to judge. He thought he learned willingness, but now he sees he does not know what the willingness is for.

This is about returning to the original choice point in our minds and saying to the Holy Spirit: "You were right and I was wrong. I chose a teacher that made real the separation from my Creator and Source, and thus made real my individual and special self. I was wrong." Our practice of forgiveness, realizing we share the same interest and goal, has brought us to the point where we begin to look at the first—and only—mistake, and realize that in the end there is no "I." Thus we learn that willingness is not limited to giving up grievances and specialness, but extends to letting go of what we believed to be our self:

> What you think you are is a belief to be undone (W-pI.91.6:7).

In that sense, I and the Course are one; I and the Course's source are one. Yet, my ego is still tempted to see my journeying with Jesus as sacrifice—I am going to lose my identity.

(7:7) And now he must attain a state that may remain impossible to reach for a long, long time.

Be cautious of those who tell you this course is easy and they are in the real world. While Jesus does say forgiveness takes only an instant, he also says it can take "a long, long time." It does not have to—remember, time is an illusion—but our resistance to losing this self keeps us from moving along too quickly.

(7:8) He must learn to lay all judgment aside, and ask only what he really wants in every circumstance.

Our most important judgment comes in laying aside the belief we exist. We all truly want to return home, yet this is impossible to do on the shoulders of our individuality. While this separated self will take us far along the journey, it will not allow us to pass through Heaven's gates. Accordingly, at some point we must realize this very self is the hindrance. Thus while it is essential to shift from a wrong-minded to a right-minded self, the ultimate goal—what alone brings true happiness—is to remember we are a non-physical, non-special Self.

(7:9) Were not each step in this direction so heavily reinforced, it would be hard indeed!

Each time we step up the ladder we feel better—the positive reinforcement that helps us continue—for we identify less with the ego's goal of specialness and more with Jesus' goal of unity.

(8:1-3) And finally, there is "a period of achievement." It is here that learning is consolidated. Now what was seen as merely shadows before

become solid gains, to be counted on in all "emergencies" as well as tranquil times.

We have reached the top of the ladder, having learned the lessons that not only do we all share the same interests, but we all share the same Self. In *The Song of Prayer*, Jesus says that the ladder of prayer ends when we realize, not just that we and our brothers walk together, but that *we and our brothers are one* (S-1.V.3:12). This final step consolidates our learning and the ultimate resolution of the theme of shared interests—the interest each of us shares in remembering:

> I am one Self, united with my Creator, at one with every aspect of creation, and limitless in power and in peace (W-pI.95.11:2; italics omitted).

Because differences are no longer perceived among the Sonship, we are outside the ego's dream of separation and in the real world. From there, all worldly things are seen as the same—good and bad, special love and special hate, success and failure—for they share the single purpose of reinforcing belief in the self and glorifying its reality. And thus all situations are related to in the same way, for the inherent powerlessness of illusions to affect anything is recognized.

(8:4) Indeed, the tranquility is their result; the outcome of honest learning, consistency of thought and full transfer.

Learning we share the same Self is what Jesus means by "honest learning," which is the process of bringing this realization to fruition. All thought becomes consistent, for everything within the Holy Spirit's thought system of Atonement is accepted as one. If the separation never happened, we are the same in our need to remember our oneness as Christ. This is the "full transfer" wherein we have learned that no perception of differences is ever justified. The happy result of perfect peace allows us to be seen in the world as a body, while at the same time knowing we are not here—how Jesus was when his body appeared, although his self remained outside the dream.

(8:5) This is the stage of real peace, for here is Heaven's state fully reflected.

This stage of real peace contrasts with the *reasonable* peace of stage four (paragraph 6). It is not contingent on anything other than itself. The separated self—the home and source of conflict—is now gone, for we have become the full reflection of Heaven's Oneness and Love. We are still aware of the dream, but our identity is no longer with the physical, psychological self the world sees, for we are one Self.

(8:6-10) From here, the way to Heaven is open and easy. In fact, it is here. Who would "go" anywhere, if peace of mind is already complete? And who would seek to change tranquility for something more desirable? What could be more desirable than this?

When we reach the top, the ladder disappears and we are home. Part of God's Oneness, we had said in our delusional state that His peace and Love were not enough—we wanted something more than everything, to be more than everywhere, to be a self greater than the Self of Christ. Thus we return to the beginning when we made such insane declarations, looking at what we chose and realizing our mistake. The decision for individuality was the mistake's origin, and the separated self traveled rapidly down the ladder into a world of specialness. It was this same self, however, that chose the correction, enabling it to climb the ladder and disappear into the Heart it never left. Jesus thus asks us to consider why we would ever want anything but to be with our Creator and Source, part of Its living and loving Oneness.

We continue with the next nine characteristics of God's teachers, having discussed the process of climbing from the ladder's bottom rungs to the top, becoming advanced teachers of God as we make our way. As we go through these nine, all in one sense contained in *trust*, we shall re-present our two themes—shared interests and choosing the Holy Spirit—as well as some variations. We shall also see, interestingly, that these positive traits really consist of undoing the ego's negative ones. Thus, *trust* undoes trust in the ego; *honesty*, the dishonesty of conflict; *tolerance*, judgment; *gentleness*, harmfulness; *joy*, fear, pain, and attack; *defenselessness*, defensiveness; *generosity*, selfishness; *patience*, impatience; *faithfulness*, faith in the ego; and *open-mindedness*, the close-mindedness of judgment.

II. Honesty

Interestingly, Jesus' description of honesty does not center on behavior—verbal or physical—but on thought. Thus *honesty* is defined as "consistency" —what you say reflects what you think or believe. Achieving this consistency results in the end of the conflict typical of the third stage of the development of trust, where you do or say what you do not really want to. Honesty, therefore, means proceeding from a thought of love where everything you do or say is loving. In form, for example, it might be what the world calls a "white lie," where the purpose is not to deceive or hurt but to be helpful and kind. In this sense it is a variation of our theme of shared interests, based on the oneness that unites the individual fragments of the Sonship through bodily actions that emanate from loving minds.

(1:1-3) All other traits of God's teachers rest on trust. Once that has been achieved, the others cannot fail to follow. Only the trusting can afford honesty, for only they can see its value.

As he discusses each of the nine remaining characteristics, Jesus continually refers back to the previous ones, teaching us their inherent unity—they are not separate traits at all, but different aspects of one. Therefore, when you put your trust in Jesus as your teacher, you cannot but be honest, kind, gentle, patient, open-minded, etc.

(1:4-9) Honesty does not apply only to what you say. The term actually means consistency. There is nothing you say that contradicts what you think or do; no thought opposes any other thought; no act belies your word; and no word lacks agreement with another. Such are the truly honest. At no level are they in conflict with themselves. Therefore it is impossible for them to be in conflict with anyone or anything.

Everything is of one piece. About sixteen hundred years ago St. Augustine said: "Love and do what you will." When love is in your heart, everything you do will reflect it—the honesty and consistency Jesus speaks of here. He is saying that we should not judge according to the *form*—i.e., behavior—which is the way the world looks at everything. Rather, he tells us to look to the *content* —i.e., thought or motivation—for if the content is loving and right-minded, whatever is said or done will be helpful. Thus, the teacher you have chosen represents the Oneness of Heaven, and his love is automatically reflected in your perception by seeing the oneness of God's Son in everyone. As you will no longer see separate interests, there can be no conflict with anyone, regardless of behavior. This greatly simplifies our lives, making peace of mind inevitable:

(2:1-2) The peace of mind which the advanced teachers of God experience is largely due to their perfect honesty. It is only the wish to deceive that makes for war.

Without conflict, peace is all there is. As Jesus explains, war is rooted in the wish to deceive. Governments lie because individuals lie. Indeed, the very foundation of individuality is a lie; and therefore everything that flows from separation is untrue —*ideas leave not their source*. As you release identification with your special self, you reach the point where you no longer seek to justify the ego's thought system of separation and specialness.

(2:3) No one at one with himself can even conceive of conflict.

Whenever we are in conflict with anyone or anything, including our sick or failing body, it is because we are not at one with ourselves. Choosing the ego as our teacher means we cannot be unified within. Since the world is the projection of the original conflict with God, born of the mind's choice to believe the ego, we inevitably believe everyone is in conflict with us. When we change that wish and choose to identify with the Holy Spirit, we share the oneness of His vision in which conflict ends and peace is unmistakable, since the guilt is gone that demands God be at war with us. Our vision, therefore, embraces all people as one, for nothing remains in the mind to reinforce external conflict. This makes life uninteresting as the world sees it, which finds excitement in differences—*vive la différence*, as the French say. This works if we want to be differentiated from our Source and His creation, but it will not bring us happiness or peace, for the desire to be separated breeds thoughts of conflict that can only lead to war, anxiety, and dis-ease.

(2:4) Conflict is the inevitable result of self-deception, and self-deception is dishonesty.

Jesus does not speak of dishonesty with words, but of dishonesty within ourselves. We are self-deceiving when we choose the ego, which results in deception in everything we say or do. It is therefore not the words we want to change to become more honest, but our identification with the dishonest ego to the identification with the honest self of the right mind.

(2:5-6) There is no challenge to a teacher of God. Challenge implies doubt, and the trust on which God's teachers rest secure makes doubt impossible.

Bravery or courage means surmounting obstacles, meeting challenges, and defeating enemies. Whether you climb Mount Everest, beat up evil people around the world, or achieve a difficult goal, there is always a challenge to meet and overcome. Society calls such people heroes, which indeed they are—*heroes of the dream*, wherein bodies conquer other bodies, glorifying themselves and exulting in their triumphs. Yet, in truth, meeting a challenge comes from projecting self-doubt. Instead of looking at uncertainty within, we confront it outside, magically hoping that by conquering the projection we can undo it in ourselves. Fanatics—in religion, politics, or *A Course in Miracles*—do nothing more than defend against self-doubt. When we are certain of who we are, there is nothing but calm certainty; no need to prove anything or convince anyone. We merely choose peace, and quietly let it extend through us. Thus, advanced teachers of God are not courageous or brave; they simply *are*—consistently honest within themselves.

(2:7-12) Therefore they can only succeed. In this, as in all things, they are honest. They can only succeed, because they never do their will alone. They choose for all mankind; for all the world and all things in it; for the unchanging and unchangeable beyond appearances; and for the Son of God and his Creator. How could they not succeed? They choose in perfect honesty, sure of their choice as of themselves.

Note again the word *all*. Jesus uses it once in sentence 8, and three times in sentence 10. You do not choose for yourself alone—the selfish interest of the ego—because you are part of the *all*. Accordingly, if you choose guilt and conflict, you reinforce the ego self in others. On the other hand, when you choose the end of conflict by asking the Holy Spirit for help, you choose for everyone, reinforcing the mind's power of decision. Remember, this choice for the Holy Spirit must embrace *all* people because you have chosen against the ego's separation. Accepting the Holy Spirit's memory of the unchanging and unchangeable Christ, you remember your one Self.

III. Tolerance

Tolerance is giving up judgment. It does not refer to a holier-than-thou, condescending attitude that "tolerates" bad behavior of individuals or groups. Jesus speaks instead of tolerance in its highest sense of not judging *anyone*.

(1:1-2) God's teachers do not judge. To judge is to be dishonest, for to judge is to assume a position you do not have.

Remember that these ten characteristics describe advanced teachers. When Jesus says "God's teachers do not judge," he is speaking of those already high on the ladder. If I engage in judging, it means *I* know what is best; for example, *I* know who is to be saved, for *I* can distinguish between good and evil. I thus assume a role I do not have, which is a shadowy fragment of what we did at the beginning when we usurped God's role of creator and became self-creators. This is why it is essential that we prefer to be happy and not right (T-29.VII.1:9); happily telling Jesus we are glad we are wrong. The fact is that we cannot judge, as important a theme in the manual as it is in the text and workbook. It is easily recognized as a variation of our theme of seeing shared interests. If you judge, you but see others as separate from you. The only judgment that is justified is the Holy Spirit's: *everyone* calls for love or expresses it.

(1:3-5) Judgment without self-deception is impossible. Judgment implies that you have been deceived in your brothers. How, then, could you not have been deceived in yourself?

Being "deceived in your brothers" means that someone has disappointed you, such as saying something unacceptable. We are not aware, however, that we want to be deceived because that proves *they* are sinful, while we retain our innocence. Yet if I am deceived in others, how could I not be deceived in myself?

(1:6-11) Judgment implies a lack of trust, and trust remains the bedrock of the teacher of God's whole thought system. Let this be lost, and all his learning goes. Without judgment are all things equally acceptable, for who could judge otherwise? Without judgment are all men brothers, for who is there who stands apart? Judgment destroys honesty and shatters trust. No teacher of God can judge and hope to learn.

Judgment is inherent in our thought system and very existence, because the ego was born of its judgment of God. Thus if we are serious about becoming an advanced teacher, it is necessary to know how we are continually tempted to judge, find fault, and criticize—thus re-reading the above paragraph would be helpful. When we judge we put our trust in the ego; otherwise we could not make the judgments that destroy honesty and shatter trust, saying we are different from others, with separate and conflicting interests. *Our* interest lies in proving the world wrong! Judgment, therefore, is one of the key elements in the ego thought system, and, consequently, forgiving ourselves for *not* giving up judgment is an essential part of becoming an advanced and non-judgmental teacher of God.

IV. Gentleness

Gentleness is giving up harmfulness—the desire to hurt others. As we have seen, and will see again, right-minded traits are merely the undoing of wrong-minded ones.

(1:1-2) Harm is impossible for God's teachers. They can neither harm nor be harmed.

Harm is impossible because only a body can be harmed. This does not give you license to hurt other members of the Sonship, however, for although the body is illusory, it does not mean you can harm with impunity, as Jesus now explains:

(1:3-4) Harm is the outcome of judgment. It is the dishonest act that follows a dishonest thought.

You would not seek to hurt others if you had not first harbored hurtful thoughts in your mind that you sought to get rid of through projection. Judgment, of course, is just another form of inflicting harm.

(1:5) It is a verdict of guilt upon a brother, and therefore on oneself.

This is a variation of the theme of shared interests. Since we are one, if we see another as guilty we see ourselves the same way, as is the case with innocence. Our inherent sameness goes against the ego's principle of *one or the other*, which establishes our guiltlessness by another's guilt, and vice versa. Since the ego has us believe it is better to be guiltless so that God will not punish us, it is in our interest to prove others guilty. As it is in their interest to do the same with us, it must be we are different, seen from our differing points of view. This underscores the importance of shared interests, born of our natural oneness. If we insist that another is the guilty, evil one, we but make ourselves the home of the same guilt and evil.

(1:6-7) It is the end of peace and the denial of learning. It demonstrates the absence of God's curriculum, and its replacement by insanity.

Recall this early statement: "To teach is to demonstrate" (M-in.2:1). If you seek to harm, you demonstrate the insanity of the ego thought system that says attack will bring you what you want.

(1:8) No teacher of God but must learn,—and fairly early in his training,—that harmfulness completely obliterates his function from his awareness.

Our function is forgiveness—seeing no one's interests as apart from our own. Fear of this function is why we seek to harm, judge, and see ourselves unfairly treated. It is certainly true that people here are treated unfairly, and often cruelly. Yet, even those inflicting suffering believe they have been unfairly treated themselves, which justifies their cruelty toward others. Such attack is the history of the world, because attack is the ego's game. In fact it is the very reason for being in a physical universe, which came into existence to defend the belief we treated God cruelly. Our selfish need to be special is preserved by hiding the mind's guilt in the body. That is why Jesus asks us to look at what we are doing and see that harming another harms ourselves. Imagine if heads of state looked at issues from that perspective! War would disappear. Seeking to harm groups different from one's own, regardless of any attempts at justification, harms oneself, one's country, race, or religion—one cannot be harmed without harming everyone. The principle of *shared interests* remains vital to our salvation.

(1:9-10) It will make him confused, fearful, angry and suspicious. It will make the Holy Spirit's lessons impossible to learn.

We return to our second theme: choosing the Holy Spirit as our Teacher. Implicit in this choice is that if we do not want to learn His lessons, we need only attack, judge, and perceive separate interests. These ensure we will not learn from the Holy Spirit and climb the ladder home, thus forever remaining separate and alone.

(1:11-12) Nor can God's Teacher be heard at all, except by those who realize that harm can actually achieve nothing. No gain can come of it.

Later in the manual, Jesus tells us that it is so difficult to hear God's Teacher that very few hear Him at all (M-12.3:3), and in the text that we cannot hear the Holy Spirit's Voice as long as we identify with specialness:

> What answer that the Holy Spirit gives can reach you, when it is your specialness to which you listen, and which asks and answers? Its tiny answer, soundless in the melody that pours from God to you eternally in loving praise of what you are, is all you listen to. And that vast song of honor and of love for what you are seems silent and unheard before its "mightiness." You strain your ears to hear its soundless voice, and yet the Call of God Himself is soundless to you (T-24.II.4:3-6).

In this world, those who do not identify with specialness are very, very few indeed; which means very, very few actually hear God's Voice. This is because the Holy Spirit speaks only of unity and shared interests, and would never encourage anything that would hurt God's Son. If you believe, therefore, that the Holy Spirit tells you to do something harmful, you can rest assured the voice is not His. It could only be the ego's voice, whose purpose is to keep us rooted in individuality and then blame everyone else for it.

(2:1-4) Therefore, God's teachers are wholly gentle. They need the strength of gentleness, for it is in this that the function of salvation becomes easy. To those who would do harm, it is impossible. To those to whom harm has no meaning, it is merely natural.

God's advanced teachers are not partially gentle, they are *wholly* and *always* gentle because there is no thought of conflict or guilt that would cause them to harm anyone. Knowing the oneness of God's Son, they know that to harm another is to harm oneself. An advanced teacher of God no longer listens to the ego's lies and so can only be gentle and kind.

(2:5-6) What choice but this has meaning to the sane? Who chooses hell when he perceives a way to Heaven?

Who would fly with the tiny wings of a sparrow when he could fly with the mighty wings of an eagle? Who, knowing the love of Heaven, would ever choose the hatred of hell?

> Those with the strength of God in their awareness could never think of battle. What could they gain but loss of their perfection? For everything fought for on the battleground is of the body; something it seems to offer or to own. No one who knows that he has everything could seek for limitation, nor could he value the body's offerings.... And what is there that offers less, yet could be wanted more? Who with the Love of God upholding him could find the choice of miracles or murder hard to make? (T-23.IV.9:1-4,7-8)

Jesus continually encourages us to contrast the ego's teachings with his own. Seeing the contrast motivates us to shift teachers and learn the forgiveness that helps us ascend the ladder and return home.

(2:7) And who would choose the weakness that must come from harm in place of the unfailing, all-encompassing and limitless strength of gentleness?

To the world, amassing armies and stockpiles of weapons is a sign of strength. Yet all they do is conceal underlying weakness and vulnerability. Christ's strength is not external and cannot be found in dominating or destroying others, for its gentleness comes from our oneness with each other. Since the only way to harm another is to project guilt, if there is no guilt—having trusted the right Teacher—there is nothing to project and therefore there can be no attack. Gentleness alone remains, which is why it is natural and need only be accepted, not striven for.

(2:8-10) The might of God's teachers lies in their gentleness, for they have understood their evil thoughts came neither from God's Son nor his Creator. Thus did they join their thoughts with Him Who is their Source. And so their will, which always was His Own, is free to be itself.

Evil thoughts came from the illusory and shabby substitute for the Self of God, of which joining with others gently reminds us. We do not join by actively doing anything, but by accepting our common Source. This is achieved by taking Jesus' hand, allowing him to lead us gently and patiently on the journey. Only then can we begin to see our unified purpose, reflecting our one Self. Happily, our giving up guilt and judgment frees us to return to our Source.

V. Joy

Joy comes from forgiveness, although it is not specifically mentioned here. We think of joy coming from getting what we want, which means it is dependent on something external. The world's only joy, however, comes in knowing we are forgiven, which occurs when we place our trust in the right Teacher.

(1:1-2) Joy is the inevitable result of gentleness. Gentleness means that fear is now impossible, and what could come to interfere with joy?

Joy is our natural state, as are honesty and gentleness. It is attained once we put ourselves in the natural state of right-mindedness with our natural Teacher. Once the ego's obstacles are gone, we feel the joy that is our "sacred right" (T-30.V.9:10).

(1:3) The open hands of gentleness are always filled.

Our hands are closed to keep out the truth, which is why Jesus asks us, in "The Gifts of God," to open them to him:

> How can you be delivered from all gifts the world has offered you? How can you change these little, cruel offerings for those that Heaven gives and God would have you keep? Open your hands, and give all things to me that you have held against your holiness and kept as slander on the Son of God.... Give me these worthless things the instant that you see them through my eyes and understand their cost (*The Gifts of God*, p. 118).

This characteristic foreshadows the last one—open-mindedness.

(1:4-8) The gentle have no pain. They cannot suffer. Why would they not be joyous? They are sure they are beloved and must be safe. Joy goes with gentleness as surely as grief attends attack.

The body suffers when guilt expresses itself in pain, but with guilt gone, we no longer identify with the body and so *we*—the decision-making mind—do not experience pain. We may be aware our bodies are suffering, but the mind's love and peace are unaffected. Therefore, if there is no guilt, whatever happens to the body has nothing to do with us, for the peace of God is there, as is the kind gentleness that embraces all people as one—the right mind has not changed just because the body has.

(1:9-10) God's teachers trust in Him. And they are sure His Teacher goes before them, making sure no harm can come to them.

Our second theme returns. The Holy Spirit's shield does not prevent people from hurting the body, or microorganisms from making us sick, but it does keep the light of Christ in the mind because there is nothing else. The Holy Spirit thus does nothing but reinforce the idea we are safe because of Who we are. Hence, if we do not experience safety in the world, it is because we do not experience safety in the mind—our guilt demands punishment. This guilt is projected onto the world we made, in which we feel vulnerable and unsafe. It could not be otherwise—bodies *are* vulnerable because they come from a vulnerable thought. The solution is thus to change the thought and its author; our experience changes accordingly.

(1:11) They hold His gifts and follow in His way, because God's Voice directs them in all things.

The Holy Spirit does not direct *some* things, but *all* things. Importantly once again, this does not mean that the Holy Spirit tells you what to do, since

4. What Are the Characteristics of God's Teachers?

He does not care about what does not exist. Remember, this course has nothing to do with behavior. The reason He is there for all things is that all things come from thought, and His is the one Thought that brings the others together to undo them. Thus, when you shift your thought from the ego to the Holy Spirit you are safe. That is the source of all happiness, peace, and joy.

(1:12-15) Joy is their song of thanks. And Christ looks down on them in thanks as well. His need of them is just as great as theirs of Him. How joyous it is to share the purpose of salvation!

The purpose of salvation is to undo guilt. Since the mind of God's Son is one, if guilt is undone in anyone it is undone in everyone—such is the joy of salvation and the cause of our gratitude.

VI. Defenselessness

Defenselessness undoes defensiveness, and arises from recognizing you need no defense because you cannot be harmed. With guilt undone there is no demand that you be punished, and so harm is impossible. Although the body may be harmed, as you journey on you come to realize you are not your body. Therefore you no longer use it as proof that you are right and God is wrong, which is the ego's ultimate use for the body: "If pain is real, there is no God" (W-pI.190.3:4). If, therefore, you want to prove there is no God—in fact, that *you* are God—then make physical or emotional pain. Nonetheless, Jesus' lesson is that, regardless of the body's state, peace awaits the mind's decision.

(1:1-2) God's teachers have learned how to be simple. They have no dreams that need defense against the truth.

Not having dreams in need of defense simplifies your life. To live in fear, requiring barricades and defenses, is complicated since you must then be vigilant for who is going to get you next. Sometimes people will indeed attack your body, but if you perceive them so, it is because you want the attack in order to demonstrate your innocence and their guilt. While you are not necessarily responsible for what they do—i.e., you do not always cause others to hurt you—you are responsible for your interpretation of their behavior and reactions to it. In other words, if you are the innocent victim of another's sin, the Sonship is not one and God is wrong: His Son is *not* as He created him.

(1:3-5) They do not try to make themselves. Their joy comes from their understanding Who created them. And does what God created need defense?

Teachers of God "do not try to make themselves," in that they do not support the original ego thought of self-creation. Recall the Course's distinction between *make* and *create*—the ego makes and spirit creates—and how the Holy Spirit teaches us to distinguish between the illusory self we made and the glorious Self that God created—a variation of our second theme. Therefore, when you seek to protect yourself from a hostile and threatening world in which you are highly vulnerable, you affirm that God did not create you, for His creation—spirit—needs no defense. Yet do not take this to mean that you should ignore your body or deny its needs. Jesus asks only that you be aware that focusing on the body represents the mind's decision to focus on the ego. Gentleness Itself will then lead you to see the body's role in the ego's defensive system, for It would not deprive you of pleasure or bring you pain, nor take away your self. Its Voice teaches only that you are not what you seem to be, Its Love asking that you choose again.

(1:6) No one can become an advanced teacher of God until he fully understands that defenses are but foolish guardians of mad illusions.

We desperately try to defend against something that does not exist. The ego tells us God is hell-bent on destroying us for our sin, and we urgently need to protect ourselves. We project the mind's fear, so it now looks as if the world is out to destroy us. Therefore, what we attempt to protect ourselves *from* is the projection of our need to protect ourselves from the presence of God's wrath in the mind. Yet the truth is that there is no vengeful God. Like Don Quixote, we tilt at windmills, having made a world as a defense against an enemy that does not exist. This is not sinful or evil, but it does reflect the silliness of believing in an insane thought system.

(1:7-8) The more grotesque the dream, the fiercer and more powerful its defenses seem to

be. Yet when the teacher of God finally agrees to look past them, he finds that nothing was there.

The more grotesque the mind's dream of guilt, hate, and terror, the more powerful our defenses need to be to protect us. This is why the world becomes increasingly complicated, and why hate and cruelty are expressed now on a scale never before seen—in our civilization at least. We strive to protect a self that does not exist, as we strive mightily to keep its unreality from awareness. Each of us, however, will finally decide to look within, past defenses, and see that nothing was there; no sin requiring protection: God's Son—His Effect—never left the Cause that is his Source:

(1:9) Slowly at first he lets himself be undeceived.

This is a slow, gentle, and kind process of healing. We first allowed the ego to deceive us—better, we wanted the ego to deceive us—so now we must negate that choice and be *un*deceived. The right mind thus undoes the wrong mind that spoke first, as we deny our denial of truth. God is the only positive, for He is the only truth.

(1:10-15) But he learns faster as his trust increases. It is not danger that comes when defenses are laid down. It is safety. It is peace. It is joy. And it is God.

The ego fears our one day awakening to realize its world was made up, and since there was no sin, there was no need to defend it through fear of punishment. Psychologists tell us that giving up defenses leads to psychosis. Within the thought system of the world this is indeed true, but the world is psychotic. Why, then, ask the one thing in all the universe that does not know what reality, sanity, or health are to teach you about them (T-20.III.7-8), when the ego merely encourages defenses against nonexistent problems? These defenses, moreover, make no sense, since they reinforce the very fear they were made to protect us from (T-17.IV.7).

VII. Generosity

The essence of generosity is that giving and receiving are the same, which corrects the ego's dictum that they are different. To the ego, the giver loses and the receiver gains; for one to win, another must lose. This flows from the ego's fundamental principle of *one or the other*. In the true sense of generosity, however, you give from the abundance of God's Love coming through you, and therefore there is no loss of any kind—God's one Son can give only to himself.

(1:1-3) The term generosity has special meaning to the teacher of God. It is not the usual meaning of the word; in fact, it is a meaning that must be learned and learned very carefully. Like all the other attributes of God's teachers this one rests ultimately on trust, for without trust no one can be generous in the true sense.

We again see that everything relates to trust in the Holy Spirit to lead us from self to Self, a concept detailed in the next paragraph. From this trust we become honest, gentle, non-judgmental, and generous, so there is no need for the defense of withholding love.

(1:4-6) To the world, generosity means "giving away" in the sense of "giving up." To the teachers of God, it means giving away in order to keep. This has been emphasized throughout the text and the workbook, but it is perhaps more alien to the thinking of the world than many other ideas in our curriculum.

When you gives others what they lack, they now have it and you do not. This is not giving, but sacrifice. As a teacher of God, however, you give love so you will retain awareness that you *are* love. You forgive by letting go of grievances because this reinforces sin's absence in you; you relinquish judgment because there is nothing in you to be judged. This notion of "giving away in order to keep" is a key idea in the text, where near the beginning of Chapter 5 Jesus explains that ideas are strengthened when one gives them away (T-5.I.1-2). When we listen to the ego, on the other hand, we believe that when we give, we lose, whether it is our time, money, or ourselves, yet the truth remains that we only gain when we give with Jesus. Needless to say, we are speaking of *content*, not *form*, and so these comments should not be misconstrued to mean, for example, that Jesus is asking us to give away our money. The point is that we give away our ego desires by bringing them to him, leaving his love to guide our behavior.

(1:7-8) Its greater strangeness lies merely in the obviousness of its reversal of the world's thinking. In the clearest way possible, and at the simplest of levels, the word means the exact opposite to the teachers of God and to the world.

As stated earlier, the characteristics of God's advanced teachers entail undoing the ego's characteristics—correcting selfishness in this instance.

(2:1-2) The teacher of God is generous out of Self interest. This does not refer, however, to the self of which the world speaks.

This Self is not the separate interest of the ego self, but the Self interest that embraces God's Son as one, reflected by sharing *one* interest—a restatement of our first theme.

(2:3-6) The teacher of God does not want anything he cannot give away, because he realizes it would be valueless to him by definition. What would he want it *for*? He could only lose because of it. He could not gain.

As a teacher of God, we would not want anything that cannot be extended through us—thought, not materiality—for then we would lose Jesus' purpose of teaching us the value of shared interest. We want the Love and peace of God, and to be genuine, they must extend through us to embrace the entire Sonship. As Jesus says at the end of the text:

> Yet this a vision is which you must share with everyone you see, for otherwise you will behold it not (T-31.VIII.8:5).

We lose the vision if we do not let it extend to everyone we meet; not some, but *all*. This universality characterizes true giving and generosity. If love is of God, it must freely flow to bless the Sonship, without exception. Thus, a helpful guideline is that we should strive to have no thoughts or judgments we would not extend to everyone.

(2:7) Therefore he does not seek what only he could keep, because that is a guarantee of loss.

At the beginning, we believed we could keep what we stole from God, for it now belonged to us. In effect, this was the beginning of the end, and everything went quickly downhill from that point, as is seen by the nature of the world. People continue to steal, but camouflage their sin so it appears to be something wonderful in the name of democracy, freedom, benevolent dictatorships, or some other "ism." They believe they can take what another has, and that makes it theirs. The world acts this way because individuals do, because we originally stole love together.

(2:8-12) He does not want to suffer. Why should he ensure himself pain? But he does want to keep for himself all things that are of God, and therefore for His Son. These are the things that belong to him. These he can give away in true generosity, protecting them forever for himself.

We are one, and therefore if we truly want the Love of God we must want it for *all* people. Anything less causes us to suffer, which motivates us to ask Jesus for help in learning how to remember we are part of God's one Son.

VIII. Patience

Simply stated, patience undoes the ego's impatient use of time.

(1:1) Those who are certain of the outcome can afford to wait, and wait without anxiety.

Advanced teachers can wait without anxiety because nothing here can upset them. Living in the world, it is important that one is careful and considerate by doing things on time and doing them well. Yet these teachers are not slaves to any of the world's problems that impatiently demand a certain outcome at a certain time.

(1:2-5) Patience is natural to the teacher of God. All he sees is certain outcome, at a time perhaps unknown to him as yet, but not in doubt. The time will be as right as is the answer. And this is true for everything that happens now or in the future.

Patience is natural to the advanced teacher of God because, as explained earlier, linear time is a projection of sin, guilt, and fear. Consequently, without this unholy trinity, God's teachers will not perceive time as a potential victimizer. What happens in the world will not really affect them because the mind of these teachers remains at peace, even though they look and behave like normal bodies living in time.

(1:6-8) The past as well held no mistakes; nothing that did not serve to benefit the world, as

well as him to whom it seemed to happen. Perhaps it was not understood at the time. Even so, the teacher of God is willing to reconsider all his past decisions, if they are causing pain to anyone.**

The mistakes include the entire carpet of time, all of which can now serve the Holy Spirit's purpose of undoing our decision for the ego. We no longer beat ourselves up because of past mistakes, but instead see them as opportunities for forgiveness.

The past is over, but if you are aware you made mistakes and these still cause pain, returning to the place of love in your mind leads you to do whatever would alleviate the suffering. To simply dismiss it as an illusion—"it never happened anyway"—is the ego's rationalization to disguise the underlying hate and the mind's wish to let itself off the hook by not dealing with the guilt. Therefore, if you recognize the hurtfulness of your past behavior and it is still possible to undo it, you would do so because the love in the mind naturally extends to itself.

(1:9-10) Patience is natural to those who trust. Sure of the ultimate interpretation of all things in time, no outcome already seen or yet to come can cause them fear.

Patience emanates from trust. There is a certainty about the outcome of *all*—not *some*—things, for God's children are guiltless. The world is thus seen as a classroom that helps others attain the realization they are forgiven. This includes our learning it is the mind's *content* that is important, not the external *form*. Impatience, however, is always based on form—something has to be done at a certain time—which is why our world is governed by time, a cruel master indeed. Yet it is possible to be free of its dictates by being free of the wrong teacher. This leaves us at peace with whatever happens, allowing us to be kind, gentle, and loving to everyone in the world, for we know we are one.

IX. Faithfulness

Faithfulness, the ninth characteristic, is really generalization—correcting the ego's belief that although there may indeed be a Holy Spirit, He only works sometimes; and while He is very good at some problems, it is best not to bother Him with others. Generalization, the full transfer of learning, undoes this ego belief as we learn to put our faith and trust in the Holy Spirit *all* the time, because we realize there is nothing and no one else.

(1:1-4) The extent of the teacher of God's faithfulness is the measure of his advancement in the curriculum. Does he still select some aspects of his life to bring to his learning, while keeping others apart? If so, his advancement is limited, and his trust not yet firmly established. Faithfulness is the teacher of God's trust in the Word of God to set all things right; not some, but all.

Jesus is describing the process of generalization, a hallmark of those advancing up the ladder. Generalizing what we have learned, we see only shared interests and are at peace regardless of the external situation. This is the vision of Christ that sees all people as one, their egos notwithstanding. If we blame our loss of peace on outer circumstances we are being dishonest, because the cause of our distress is our choice for a dishonest teacher that teaches a dishonest thought. If we do not let love embrace everyone, it is not because of anything external, but because of the fear of losing our specialness and accepting the universality of God's Love.

Incidentally, the term *Word of God* in *A Course in Miracles* almost always refers to some aspect of the Atonement: the Holy Spirit's Thought of correction that the separation never happened.

(1:5-6) Generally, his faithfulness begins by resting on just some problems, remaining carefully limited for a time. To give up all problems to one Answer is to reverse the thinking of the world entirely.

Remember the first principle of miracles: there is no order of difficulty among them (T-1.I.1:1). All problems are solved in the same way because the miracle corrects them as one by undoing the single problem that underlies them all—the belief in separation—regardless of their different forms of expression:

> Miracles demonstrate that learning has occurred under the right guidance.... Its generalization is demonstrated as you use it in more and more situations. You will recognize that you have learned there is no order of difficulty in miracles when you apply them to all situations. There is no situation to which miracles do not apply, and by applying them to all situations you will gain the real world (T-12.VII.1:1-

4).

(1:7-10) And that alone is faithfulness. Nothing but that really deserves the name. Yet each degree, however small, is worth achieving. Readiness, as the text notes [T-2.V.4; VII.7], is not mastery.

You can begin the journey without yet being ready to complete it, proceeding by taking small steps. Each degree, however small, is well worth the effort, for salvation has been born the instant you do not judge anyone, for anything. Remember, *all expressions of love are maximal*. Thus it does not matter whether the miracle is large or small—problems of separate interests are ultimately the same.

In what follows, Jesus summarizes his previous discussion of the ten characteristics:

(2) True faithfulness, however, does not deviate. Being consistent, it is wholly honest. Being unswerving, it is full of trust. Being based on fearlessness, it is gentle. Being certain, it is joyous. And being confident, it is tolerant. Faithfulness, then, combines in itself the other attributes of God's teachers. It implies acceptance of the Word of God and His definition of His Son. It is to Them that faithfulness in the true sense is always directed. Toward Them it looks, seeking until it finds. Defenselessness attends it naturally, and joy is its condition. And having found, it rests in quiet certainty on that alone to which all faithfulness is due.

Jesus continues to emphasize that this is all one piece, as he shows us different facets of the jewel of the Holy Spirit's Atonement. As you begin to see these principles work in all circumstances, you have become faithful, for you put your faith in the Holy Spirit, letting Him be your only Teacher and Guide, rather than faithlessly trusting in the ego's nothingness. Relying on the Holy Spirit is our second theme, and in learning how to accept His Love and wisdom we find the other characteristics within ourselves.

X. Open-Mindedness

Open-mindedness, the tenth and final characteristic of God's advanced teachers, is a return to the third characteristic—tolerance—with Jesus exploring its meaning in greater depth.

(1:1) The centrality of open-mindedness, perhaps the last of the attributes the teacher of God acquires, is easily understood when its relation to forgiveness is recognized.

Open-mindedness corrects the ego's close-mindedness. When we chose the ego the right mind closed, and for all intents and purposes the Holy Spirit's Voice was drowned out. The ego closes the mind, however, not only against the Holy Spirit, but on itself by making up a world and body. This establishes the Son as mindless, and sees to it that he never returns to the mind that has now been closed to awareness. We begin opening the mind by acknowledging we have one, which enables us to see the body and world as the mind's projections. Once we are back within, we can choose again and open the mind to the Holy Spirit, reversing the ego's defense of close-mindedness. Now we see shared instead of separate interests, and let go of judgment through forgiveness, as the following passages explain:

(1:2-5) Open-mindedness comes with lack of judgment. As judgment shuts the mind against God's Teacher, so open-mindedness invites Him to come in. As condemnation judges the Son of God as evil, so open-mindedness permits him to be judged by the Voice for God on His behalf. As the projection of guilt upon him would send him to hell, so open-mindedness lets Christ's image be extended to him.

When we judge others, it is not only that we see guilt in them but also in ourselves—as the workbook says, we believe we are "the home of evil, darkness and sin" (W-pI.93.1:1). Yet because we do not want to see it in our minds, we project it so we now believe it exists outside us. The way we let Christ's image—the vision of Christ—be extended is by letting these barriers of judgment go. His image is always present in the mind, despite our closing it off, and our minds open when we release the judgments against ourselves, allowing us to release the judgment against others. At the same time, releasing our judgments of others releases our judgment of ourselves. Healing occurs from either direction, for the inner and outer are one—*ideas leave not their source.*

(1:6) Only the open-minded can be at peace, for they alone see reason for it.

The ego does not want to see peace for it thrives on conflict, having been born out of conflict. Thus without conflict there is no ego and no individual self.

(2:1-8) How do the open-minded forgive? They have let go all things that would prevent forgiveness. They have in truth abandoned the world, and let it be restored to them in newness and in joy so glorious they could never have conceived of such a change. Nothing is now as it was formerly. Nothing but sparkles now which seemed so dull and lifeless before. And above all are all things welcoming, for threat is gone. No clouds remain to hide the face of Christ. Now is the goal achieved.

These clouds are the beliefs in separate interests. In a sense, the rest of the discussion on this attribute is a variation of our first theme—not seeing separate but only shared interests.

The goal of complete forgiveness is achieved by seeing no exceptions in our worldly experience. Nothing and no one in this world has power to take the peace of God from us, because His peace is within each of us. This means not only that nothing in the world has power, but that there is nothing in the world. It therefore does not matter whether we speak of slingshots or atomic bombs. It is we alone who have the power—through the decision maker—to see or not. Everything changes, not because the world does, but because the world of the mind changes.

(2:9-13) Forgiveness is the final goal of the curriculum. It paves the way for what goes far beyond all learning. The curriculum makes no effort to exceed its legitimate goal. Forgiveness is its single aim, at which all learning ultimately converges. It is indeed enough.

Forgiveness leads us to the journey's end. What lies beyond is past the scope of *A Course in Miracles* and, therefore, not our concern. At the beginning of the text Jesus says that his course does not aim at teaching the meaning of love, for that is beyond what can be taught. However, it does aim at removing the blocks to the awareness of love's presence (T-in.1:6-7). Once we are aware of love, the carpet of time disappears and we are in the real world, leaving only the Love of God in our minds to lift us back unto Itself.

Remember that Jesus uses many symbols to describe the journey. Sometimes his words about the real world can be confusing, not being quite as absolute as I just presented it. The concepts of the *real world*, *Teachers of teachers*, and *God's last step* are different ways of referring to the culmination of a process we can in no way understand in our separated state. In a sense, these are Jesus' little white lies to us. He is not being dishonest but loving, since this is the only way he could speak to us of something we know nothing about, which is why he leaves it to the following summary to tell us:

(3:1-5) You may have noticed that the list of attributes of God's teachers does not include things that are the Son of God's inheritance. Terms like love, sinlessness, perfection, knowledge and eternal truth do not appear in this context. They would be most inappropriate here. What God has given is so far beyond our curriculum that learning but disappears in its presence. Yet while its presence is obscured, the focus properly belongs on the curriculum.

The curriculum of *A Course in Miracles* undoes the ego's blocks through forgiveness—our learning to demonstrate the truth of the right-minded thought system and the falsity of the wrong-minded one. This is the justification for the Course, including this manual. Recall that one of the latter's principal purposes is teaching that our function is to demonstrate what we learn from the Holy Spirit. The world beyond this curriculum—"love, sinlessness, perfection, knowledge and eternal truth"—is of no concern and, until we undo the ego, there is no way we could even understand it. That is why Jesus says it would be inappropriate to discuss it here.

(3:6-7) It is the function of God's teachers to bring true learning to the world. Properly speaking it is unlearning that they bring, for that is "true learning" in the world.

Jesus resumes speaking of our function as God's advanced teachers. We learn of the Holy Spirit by first recognizing what we learned from the ego. Only then can we say we no longer want the separated self. This is the decision to unlearn its thought system and see shared instead of separate interests.

4. What Are the Characteristics of God's Teachers?

(3:8-9) It is given to the teachers of God to bring the glad tidings of complete forgiveness to the world. Blessed indeed are they, for they are the bringers of salvation.

This idea of "bringing salvation" occurs throughout *A Course in Miracles*. The way God's teachers bring salvation to the world is by accepting salvation for themselves. This acceptance of the Atonement occurs when they release their guilt and shift their trust from the ego to the Holy Spirit. Love automatically flows through their minds and since the mind is one, the world is one with them, as is the Sonship. Thus the mind of God's Son is healed when a single mind is healed. Salvation, therefore, is not brought to the world; the mind *is* the world that is the projection of God's separated Son. When his mind is healed and he has accepted his salvation, the world is saved as well.

5. HOW IS HEALING ACCOMPLISHED?

Beginning with this section and continuing on through the next three, we find an important variation of the theme of shared versus separate interests. The variation focuses on the relationship between mind and body; specifically, the mind's decisions causing the body's experience, thereby shifting attention from the body to the mind. This all-important variation of our theme centers on sickness and healing.

This shift in awareness to the mind is a key theme in *A Course in Miracles* itself—the Holy Spirit's answer to the ego's strategy of moving our identity to the body, making us mindless. Being unaware we have a mind means we cannot change it and reverse the mind's original decision for the ego. In choosing against the Holy Spirit's Atonement, therefore, we ensured that we would never restore to our minds the awareness of Who we are as Christ.

To solidify this decision for mindlessness, thereby protecting itself, the ego made up an horrific tale of sin, guilt, and fear that we see reflected in this first section on healing. It tells of our egregious sin against God, which drives His hate-filled desire to annihilate us as punishment. Rather than deal with the mind's "fact," the ego counsels us to make a world and house our selves in the body, at the same time causing a veil of amnesia to fall across the mind so we have no awareness of the source of the world and body. Once we believe we are here, our bodily identity becomes the inevitable focus of our attention. Moreover, we now believe that sin and guilt are real, yet no longer reside in us but in the bodies around us. Everyone and everything in the world, then, become responsible for how terrible we feel. The Course equates this belief in sin and guilt with sickness, which is why we believe our interests are separate from everyone else's: we believe people are out to hurt us and, in view of this, our happiness can be attained only at their expense—*one or the other.*

This is the foundation on which our discussion of the next four sections will be based. In light of our first theme, sickness is understood as the belief that leads to the perception of separate interests. Healing, thus, undoes this belief, as we learn to recognize that interests are shared and, in fact, are one.

(1:1-2) Healing involves an understanding of what the illusion of sickness is for. Healing is impossible without this.

Purpose is another of our important themes. Understanding the ego's purpose for the physical world helps us undo belief in its reality. Similarly, we will not be able to undo the problems we experience here without first understanding the mind's purpose for them. The focus of Jesus' teaching, therefore, is on our shifting identification from the body to the mind. In Lesson 136 in the workbook, "Sickness is a defense against the truth," he explains the purposive nature of sickness and how it comes from the mind's decision. This same idea is reflected here.

I. The Perceived Purpose of Sickness

(1:1-2) Healing is accomplished the instant the sufferer no longer sees any value in pain. Who would choose suffering unless he thought it brought him something, and something of value to him?

The reason we choose to be in pain—indeed, the reason we choose to be in a body at all—is to avoid the annihilation the ego tells us is certain to occur if we remain within our minds. The ego, of course, never lets us recognize the paradox in its counsel: while it tells us we can escape the mind's annihilation by going into a body, yet the body into which we escape suffers and dies. Unfortunately, since we no longer know we have a mind, we are unable to question the ego's deception. Healing is therefore accomplished once we understand the ego's strategy and the value it places on sickness (all physical and psychological distress): perpetuating its thought of separation by keeping us as mindless bodies.

(1:3-6) He must think it is a small price to pay for something of greater worth. For sickness is an election; a decision. It is the choice of weakness, in the mistaken conviction that it is strength. When this occurs, real strength is seen as threat and health as danger.

5. How Is Healing Accomplished?

We choose sickness out of weakness because we fear the mind's healing. Sickness only seems to be in the body, for it is really a projection of a thought of weakness in the mind. Thus the body can never be healed because the body is not sick. The body's inherent nothingness and the mind's power to heal is the source of the ego's fear.

(1:7-9) Sickness is a method, conceived in madness, for placing God's Son on his Father's throne. God is seen as outside, fierce and powerful, eager to keep all power for Himself. Only by His death can He be conquered by His Son.

For the first time in the manual we are confronted with the real problem of our perceived relationship with God, the underpinning of all that Jesus teaches. In the statement "only by His death can He be conquered by His Son" we see the principle of *one or the other*—God or the ego—the source of the ego's belief in separate interests. Separation and oneness are mutually exclusive states and cannot coexist, and so if God exists, I as a separate and special self cannot. Similarly, if I exist, it means God has been sacrificed—*one or the other*. But the ego's story does not end here, for God somehow rises from the grave, "fierce and powerful, eager to keep all power for Himself." In other words, the ego's God will not share life with us, since He does not believe in sharing—it is either His way or no way. As this is unacceptable to the ego, we respond that we will have it *our* way. Sharing is now perceived as the enemy, because we do not want to share our separated life with God's Oneness. Because He will not share with us, we believe we are justified in destroying Him and placing ourselves on His throne. But keep in mind that this is all made up—the ego's nightmarish lie that engendered such terror that had we remained one instant longer in the mind, God would have destroyed us. This, then, is our motivation to leave the mind's battleground and seek refuge in the body, presumably safe from God's wrath. Sickness serves this purpose well, as our symptoms focus attention on the problematically ill body and away from the mind.

(2:1-2) And what, in this insane conviction, does healing stand for? It symbolizes the defeat of God's Son and the triumph of his Father over him.

Healing returns us to the mind, the only place where sickness can be undone. Yet, looking at this thought recalls the original defiance of God, labeled by the ego as *sin deserving punishment, even unto death*. This is why, in the ego's myth, healing symbolizes defeat at God's Hands, for it would return us to the battleground of the mind and certain death.

(2:3) It represents the ultimate defiance in a direct form which the Son of God is forced to recognize.

We realize we can no longer hide, despite our desperate attempts to conceal the terrifying experience of sin and guilt, convinced we would be punished for our sin, cast into oblivion and annihilated. Thus God would have taken back from us the life we stole from Him. In order to avoid dealing with this impossible situation, the ego hides our sin through projection, which results in our seeing it in other people's bodies. Healing, therefore, means returning to this thought of sin in our minds, which so terrifies us. We shall return to this dynamic in section 17.

(2:4) It [healing] stands for all that he would hide from himself to protect his "life."

"Life" is in quotes because the self is not really part of life, which is only the oneness of God's Son with his Source. We seek to protect our special existence by identifying with the ego and choosing never to correct the mind's original choice—becoming mindless ensures we can never change it. Should we choose to return to the decision-making part of the mind, however, we will certainly change it, thereby losing our "life"—the individual self—and disappearing into the Heart of God. To the ego this is annihilation, and sickness is one way it protects its existence.

(2:5-8) If he is healed, he is responsible for his thoughts. And if he is responsible for his thoughts, he will be killed to prove to him how weak and pitiful he is. But if he chooses death himself, his weakness is his strength. Now has he given himself what God would give to him, and thus entirely usurped the throne of his Creator.

The problem is that we do not want to be responsible for our thoughts, for then we would have to accept our perceived part in the separation. We fear that God will destroy us for what we believe to be the most horrendous sin imaginable, but if we punish ourselves, His punishment will be mitigated—thus the ego reasons in its insanity. Jesus makes this same point in the text (T-5.V.5:4-8). Thus by causing our sickness, up to and including death, we in effect say to God: "Yes, I did this terrible thing to You, but *I* will punish myself." We thus make God irrelevant—in love and in hate: we do not need His Love because we find our own in specialness, and we do not need His hate because we punish ourselves. This, then, is the essence of sickness: Sickness does not simply prove we are bodies and not minds—innocent victims of forces beyond our control—but further demonstrates our usurping of God's role. Having initially given Him a punitive function, we now take it back: we first usurp God's role on the throne of Love, and then His place on the throne of hate.

Healing, however, explodes the ego's myth—not only its nightmare of our sin and God's wrath, but also our individual existence, which is why we fear the healing of separation. Jesus tells us the only way we can be healed is to bring the problem from the body to the mind, recognizing that God is not our enemy. We thus recognize the illusion of *one or the other*, and that happiness and joy ultimately come from remembering we are part of God, sharing the same Will, Self, and Love. Indeed, we *are* that Will, Self, and Love. This truth is reflected in our practice of seeing shared interests in all relationships: no one is out to get us, just as God is not. It was only our projected guilt that made a world in which it appeared as if people were the enemy, justifying our desire to destroy them.

The necessity of shifting our focus from the body to the mind varies the theme of shifting from separate to shared interests. Bodies do not share the same interests because they were made *not* to share them, their purpose being to exist in a perpetual state of lack. This means that we need people to complete us, and since the need is reciprocal, we are here to feed off each other. The body, both physically and emotionally, was thus made to prove that separate interests is the truth and the only way we can be saved from healing. It is when we finally shift attention to the mind that we understand that the ego's religion of separate interests is not founded in reality; in truth we are one—as mind and as Mind.

II. The Shift in Perception

(1:1) Healing must occur in exact proportion to which the valuelessness of sickness is recognized.

We need to realize that sickness is purposeful, and when we no longer desire the purpose, the sickness will disappear. Remember that sickness has nothing to do with the external, and so has nothing to do with the body or physical symptoms. It is the belief that separate interests is salvation, beginning with our relationship with God. Healing, on the other hand, is the recognition that shared interests will save us—the meaning of forgiveness.

(1:2) One need but say, "There is no gain at all to me in this" and he is healed.

As sickness is the mind's distorted purpose, this discussion of sickness and healing will make sense only when you shift your perspective from the body and go above the world's battleground (T-23.IV). There, with Jesus in your mind, you look at the body differently and understand the purpose that sickness served. And you are healed.

(1:3-4) But to say this, one first must recognize certain facts. First, it is obvious that decisions are of the mind, not of the body.

We now read some clear statements about the cause-effect relationship between the mind and body; in particular, that the mind alone is the cause of our body's experience.

(1:5) If sickness is but a faulty problem-solving approach, it is a decision.

Sickness is a faulty problem-solving approach that is the ego's attempt to solve the problem of guilt, which in itself is a faulty problem-solving approach designed to solve the problem of the mind's having chosen separation. Sickness is especially faulty because it does not work. As the ego's solution to the problem of guilt, it does not bring us peace or safety, but merely reinforces anxiety and terror, which is why, to quote Thoreau: "The mass of men lead lives of quiet desperation." We are terrified of the guilt the ego told us is the mind's reality. Consequently, we desperately seek hope and comfort in the world, yet it always fails us. Healing occurs when we find our true hope and comfort—in the right mind.

(1:6-7) And if it [sickness] is a decision, it is the mind and not the body that makes it. The resistance to recognizing this is enormous, because the existence of the world as you perceive it depends on the body being the decision maker.

Jesus' point cannot be stressed enough. The reason sincere students of *A Course in Miracles* have trouble accepting sickness as the mind's decision is their resistance to understanding that *everything* is in the mind—nothing is in the body because there is nothing here.

Note that this is the only place in *A Course in Miracles* where the term *decision maker* actually appears, and the emphasis here differs slightly from how we typically use it. The ego has us believe that the body is the decision maker, and things happen because of what one body does to another. We believe that physical existence depends on the union of a sperm and an egg, and our birth has nothing to do with us. Thus the ego tells us that we are the *effect* of that union, not the *cause*. Accordingly, the world we perceive depends on the body being the decision maker or *cause,* and each of us as an individual self is the *effect*.

(1:8-10) Terms like "instincts," "reflexes" and the like represent attempts to endow the body with non-mental motivators. Actually, such terms merely state or describe the problem. They do not answer it.

We believe that people act in certain ways because of the body's reflexes: the famous knee-jerk reflex, for instance, which we account for by saying it was a reflex action of the body when the knee is tapped. In truth, however, that is not at all why the knee jerked. The leg goes up because the mind made the body so that it *would* act that way, for the purpose of providing still one more witness that what causes bodies to react is the body itself—ours or another's—and not the mind's decision. Consequently, words like *instincts* and *reflexes*—non-mental motivators; i.e., not of the mind—are used to explain why we act the way we do. Yet they merely describe what goes on and provide no true explanation of the physical event.

(2:1) The acceptance of sickness as a decision of the mind, for a purpose for which it would use the body, is the basis of healing.

Understanding that it is the mind that makes the decision, not the body, is the basis for healing. We become ill not because we caught a bacteria or virus, but because the mind decided to be sick, using the body to express its decision and conceal it. The sickness is our belief in separate interests, which says: "Look what people have done to me. Look what they are doing now. Look what I can expect from them and the world in the future." We conclude, therefore, that we have to take care of ourselves, with no awareness that we made the world to abuse, humiliate, reject, and betray us.

(2:2-6) And this is so for healing in all forms. A patient decides that this is so, and he recovers. If he decides against recovery, he will not be healed. Who is the physician? Only the mind of the patient himself.

This is another important passage. It is the decision-making part of our minds to which we appeal and to which we pray, because it is the mind that made the sickness by deciding for the ego and its belief in separate interests. Consequently, it is this same mind that needs to change itself by choosing to join with the Holy Spirit and learn that shared interests is the way home. Thus the healer is the mind—not God, the Holy Spirit, or Jesus. By joining with the Holy Spirit our minds are healed, for the power is within us to choose sickness or healing.

(2:7) The outcome is what he decides that it is.

Nothing outside has any effect on us. That is why it is crucial to be aware of the Course's non-dualistic metaphysics—there is nothing outside, for everything is a projection of what is within. If *ideas leave not their source*, what we believe is external to us has never left its source in the mind. Therefore, how can the *nothing* that is out there affect us? Stated another way, this is our dream, and as its dreamers if we feel ill, it is only because we chose illness; if we feel unfairly treated, it is only because we chose to feel that way. Believing otherwise is the sickness—the belief in the principle of *one or the other*, victim and victimizer. That is why Jesus makes the following statement in the text:

> Deceive yourself no longer that you are helpless in the face of what is done to you. Acknowledge but that you have been mistaken, and all effects of your mistakes will disappear.

It is impossible the Son of God be merely driven by events outside of him. It is impossible that happenings that come to him were not his choice (T-21.II.2:6–3:2).

(2:8) Special agents seem to be ministering to him, yet they but give form to his own choice.

The term *special agents* refers to what we think of as medicine, or what elsewhere is meant by *magic* (see, for example, T-2.IV.4; T-2.V.2; M-16.8-9). Thus, for example, I have a headache and take an aspirin (the special agent), and the pain is gone. I naturally believe the aspirin was responsible, when in truth the healing cause was the power of my mind that originally decided for guilt. However, my fear of accepting this power is enormous because I believe that the mind is the locus of my sin, the thought that God will stalk me until He inflicts the punishment I deserve. I therefore do not want to allow into awareness my mind's power to choose sin, and so I mindlessly believe that what made me ill was tension caused by the world or my body, and what made me feel better was this special agent or pill.

This does not mean that we should not take medicine, however. As long as we think we are a body, it is important to do whatever will make it feel better, at the same time remembering that true healing has nothing to do with external agents. What makes us sick is the mind's decision to be with the ego, and what heals is the decision to be with the Holy Spirit. It is that simple. Yet our resistance to true healing, again, is very great, because the ego tells us if we return to the mind we will misuse it again and thus be punished. We thus fear its power to hurt ourselves, others, and God. Rather than deal with the resultant guilt and fear, it is safer to believe that sickness and healing have nothing to do with the mind. Our focus, then, remains on the mindless body, as a source of sickness and means of healing.

(2:9-11) He chooses them [the special agents] **in order to bring tangible form to his desires. And it is this they do, and nothing else. They are not actually needed at all.**

My mind makes the decision to attack myself by giving me a headache; my mind makes a decision to let go of the headache. That is all. Yet rather than look at the mind's power to make me sick or well, I project it. The aspirin seems to work because it gives tangible form to my mind's decision. The same is true of surgery and diets because they express in bodily form the mind's decision to be well.

Even if we accept this concept intellectually, it is nonetheless alien to our experience. If we do not eat for several hours, for example, our bodies feel weak, which we explain by the lack of food. Thus we eat and feel strong again. The real reason the body became weak, however, is not that it went without food. What does food have to do with a thing that is lifeless and does not exist? Being hungry simply proves our vulnerability, which serves the ego's purpose of having us believe there are things in the world that make us strong. The result is that our focus stays rooted in the body, diverted from the mind. This is why bodies were made to need oxygen, water, and food, not to mention companionship, comfort, and love. Without these things, the ego tells us, we would not be able to survive. Jesus is therefore telling us that everything the ego has us believe is not true, and therefore its magic is not needed.

(2:12-13) The patient could merely rise up without their aid and say, "I have no use for this." There is no form of sickness that would not be cured at once.

As long as you continue to identify with the body, though, by all means take care of it: breathe, drink, eat, and see "magicians" whose special agents will help you with your physical or psychological pain. Plying your body with metaphysical axioms will not help, for what truly heals is the step-by-step process of realizing that your interests are not separate from another's. This realization helps break the bodily identification and gently moves you to the mind. Jesus tells us the use of magic is not sinful (T-2.IV.4-5), but we need to be aware that in using it we but treat an illusion.

(3:1-5) What is the single requisite for this shift in perception? It is simply this; the recognition that sickness is of the mind, and has nothing to do with the body. What does this recognition "cost"? It costs the whole world you see, for the world will never again appear to rule the mind. For with this recognition is responsibility placed where it belongs; not with the world, but on him who looks on the world and sees it as it is not.

Jesus repeats that sickness and healing are of the mind. *Cost* is in quotes because in reality there is no loss. We view the world as if it were real and had power over us instead of seeing it as a projection of an illusory and insane thought. The ego tells us that if we shift from body to mind, not only will we lose the world we see, we will lose the self we believe we are. Recall "The Fear of Redemption," where Jesus says that if we allowed ourselves to experience God's Love, the world we know would disappear and we would leap into Heaven (T-13.III.2:6; 4:3). That is our terror, for we do not fear crucifixion, which the ego craves, but redemption (1:10-11), both of which are in the mind. In the Course, *crucifixion* refers not only to the biblical tale, but symbolizes the ego's thought system of sin, guilt, and the belief we deserve punishment and death. We welcome crucifixion because it protects us from identifying with love, which means the end of the ego. Therefore, as long as we identify with the ego's thought system of individuality we will fear love. We will fear as well the true healing that would return love to our awareness.

(3:6-9) He looks on what he chooses to see. No more and no less. The world does nothing to him. He only thought it did.

We currently look on the world as if it does something to us. In particular, we believe the world gives us life and death, pleasure and pain, health and sickness, happiness and sadness. Despite this convincing belief that the world and its bodies affect us, they are nothing but the ingenious strategy of the ego—the part of our minds that wants to be on its own—to preserve itself by seeing to it that we never undo its source and sustenance: the mind's power to choose. As has been stated, it is the mistaken choice for the ego that is the sickness, and the corrected choice for the Holy Spirit that heals. To ensure that this corrected choice is never made, the ego conjures up a world and body, with the multitudinous problems we face here—physical, psychological, social, economic, political, etc. All these problems emanate from the same thought: I want to escape from the mind so I can protect my ego. Moreover, it is not only that the world does nothing to us, but we do nothing to the world, as Jesus now explains:

(3:10-11) Nor does he do anything to the world, because he was mistaken about what it is. Herein is the release from guilt and sickness both, for they are one.

The world does not victimize us, but neither are we its victimizer. Nothing has happened. The ego's unholy trinity of sin, guilt, and fear is an illusion, being simply the ego's nightmarish fairy tale to convince us to leave the mind. We never sinned against God because we never separated from Him. Thus there can be no guilt, without which there can be no fear. And without fear there is no need for a defense, such as the world or body, and thus no further need for sickness, which is here equated with guilt. More accurately, sickness is the *decision* for guilt, since guilt itself is unreal. Sickness therefore has nothing to do with physical or psychological symptoms.

(3:12) Yet to accept this release, the insignificance of the body must be an acceptable idea.

It is difficult to accept the body's insignificance because we think our bodies are special. Even as devoted students of *A Course in Miracles* we think our bodies are special—after all, Jesus is talking to us, or so we think. It is usually a long time in students' work with the Course before they recognize that Jesus is not talking to them as individuals, but is addressing them as decision-making minds. This is the clear implication of his discussion here—in fact, of his entire course: Jesus is speaking to the decision-making part of the mind, the source of the problem *and* the solution.

(4:1-2) With this idea is pain forever gone. But with this idea goes also all confusion about creation.

The body is insignificant because the body is merely an *effect*, not the *cause*. Jesus again moves from individual to ontological experience. The problem is that at the beginning we told God we no longer needed Him: we are now first cause and sit on the throne of creation. The ego's image of God then becomes the effect—a god who is punitive and vengeful, believing in separation, sin, sacrifice, and specialness.

(4:3-5) Does not this follow of necessity? Place cause and effect in their true sequence in one respect, and the learning will generalize and transform the world. The transfer value of one true idea has no end or limit.

We return to the important theme of generalization. We practice with our special relationships, in which we attribute the cause of our unhappiness to others. The Holy Spirit teaches we have merely mistaken cause for effect, and so we now withdraw this cause from the body—ours or another's—and restore it to its rightful place in the mind. We recognize that the mind is the *cause* and the body the *effect*, and the mind's decision to be an ego is the cause of the mind's guilt, which in turn is the cause of the world. With this understanding we recognize that the cause of everything in the world is an illusion, because there is no separation, sin, or guilt. Even believing we have a choice between the ego and the Holy Spirit is an illusion: a part of God—an extension of His living and loving Oneness—cannot choose, for there is nothing to choose between, and indeed, no chooser. Consequently, separation is not really a choice at all. Thus if the ego thought system is illusory, the cause of everything in this world must be unreal, which means the world itself is unreal:

> Yet if you are as God created you, you cannot think apart from Him, nor make what does not share His timelessness and Love. Are these inherent in the world you see? Does it create like Him? Unless it does, it is not real, and cannot be at all. If you are real the world you see is false, for God's creation is unlike the world in every way (W-pI.132.11:1-5).

Once this is recognized, we become aware of true cause and effect: God is first *Cause* and we, His Son, are the *Effect*. Since cause and effect are never separated, they remain forever united—*ideas leave not their source*; *effects leave not their cause*. Thus we have never left our Father's house and the separation never happened. This memory will dawn on our minds to the extent to which we can see that others are not the cause of our distress, for we are one.

(4:6) The final outcome of this lesson is the remembrance of God.

As we set aside the ego's cause-effect relationship and expose it for the lie it is, what remains is what it covered—the true Cause-Effect relationship: our relationship with God.

(4:7-8) What do guilt and sickness, pain, disaster and all suffering mean now? Having no purpose, they are gone.

Their purpose was to conceal from us Who we are—the Effect of First Cause. Once we truly desire the memory of our Self, it dawns on our minds. No longer needed to defend against the truth, guilt, sickness, and suffering are gone.

(4:9-11) And with them also go all the effects they seemed to cause. Cause and effect but replicate creation. Seen in their proper perspective, without distortion and without fear, they re-establish Heaven.

Heaven, of course, is re-established in our awareness, not in reality. By exposing the causal connection between the mind's decision for guilt and sickness, we put cause and effect in their proper sequence and undo what never was. This ultimately means we have not separated from God, nor usurped His place on creation's throne. A bad dream was all it was, with no effect upon reality.

III. The Function of the Teacher of God

The significance for others of changing our minds relates to the fact that the healed mind affects only the mind, because nothing else exists. This section therefore provides still another variation of the theme of body and mind: healing has nothing to do with the body, being the change of mind from guilt to forgiveness.

(1:1-3) If the patient must change his mind in order to be healed, what does the teacher of God do? Can he change the patient's mind for him? Certainly not.

Jesus is speaking of advanced teachers of God, as we saw in "The Characteristics of God's Teachers," addressing the function of those whose minds have been healed because they made the right choice. These advanced teachers do not attempt to brainwash (or "mindwash") another person, seeking to impose their will. Thus Jesus describes the Holy Spirit:

> The Voice of the Holy Spirit does not command, because It is incapable of arrogance. It does not demand, because It does not seek control. It does not overcome, because It does not attack. It merely reminds (T-5.II.7:1-4).

It is essential for teachers of God to understand —the Course's central idea—that they need to respect the mind's power to choose the ego or the Holy Spirit; otherwise they render powerless the only means that can help them, thereby making themselves helpless. The importance of respecting people's right to make the wrong choice is that only they have the power to make the right one. If you remove their power by denying the mind's ability to choose wrongly, you also make it impossible for them to choose correctly.

(1:4-7) For those already willing to change their minds he has no function except to rejoice with them, for they have become teachers of God with him. He has, however, a more specific function for those who do not understand what healing is. These patients do not realize they have chosen sickness. On the contrary, they believe that sickness has chosen them.

The world reflects the belief that things befall us without our bidding. We believe, for example, that sickness has chosen us; and we can freely substitute other words for sickness, such as *life*, for we also believe it has chosen us.

(1:8) Nor are they open-minded on this point.

Even dedicated students of *A Course in Miracles* may not be open-minded on its teaching on mind and body because it has not yet become part of their experience, even though they may intellectually accept the Course's truth. The problem is that the students still believe they are bodies—learning *about* spirituality and the mind—which means they are on the bottom rungs of the ladder. However, what helps their progress is the daily practice of not seeing people as enemies and saviors, with self-interests separate from their own.

(1:9-13) The body tells them what to do and they obey. They have no idea how insane this concept is. If they even suspected it, they would be healed. Yet they suspect nothing. To them the separation is quite real.

Jesus tells us in the text that to learn his course it is necessary to question every value that we hold (T-24.in.2); the same idea expressed here. This does not mean we have to change our values, but that we at least begin the process of questioning their validity. Our most fundamental value is individual existence, and Jesus asks that we question the belief in our physical reality; not that we let go of belief in the body, or pretend we do not have one. A major purpose of *A Course in Miracles* is to help us look open-mindedly at the belief that we are bodies living in a material world.

(2:1-3) To them God's teachers come, to represent another choice which they had forgotten. The simple presence of a teacher of God is a reminder. His thoughts ask for the right to question what the patient has accepted as true.

What patients have accepted as true is the reality of the body's identity. Moreover, they believe that the body is sick, and therefore in need of healing. The presence of a teacher of God—one who has accepted that healing is of the mind because sickness is of the mind—represents the choice the patient has forgotten. God's teachers remind patients, not in words, but by their very presence, that the choice they have made reflects the choice patients can make. This is *all* teachers of God do, for their ability to remind the Sonship of the truth is the essence of healing.

(2:4) As God's messengers, His teachers are the symbols of salvation.

We become symbols of salvation for others, as Jesus symbolizes one who accepted the Atonement and understands the dream-nature of the world. Thus are we asked in the clarification of terms to be what Jesus has been for us—an example of the right-minded Son whose mind has changed:

> Jesus became what all of you must be. He led the way for you to follow him (C-5.3:1-2).

(2:5-6) They ask the patient for forgiveness for God's Son in his own Name. They stand for the Alternative.

Here we see the return of our second theme: the Holy Spirit's role in our Atonement path. He is our Teacher, and we have now come to represent the mind's choice for Him. This is also a variation of the first theme of our oneness—what I have done, you can do; indeed, what I have done, you have already done. This reflects Jesus' words that we were with him when he arose (C-6.5:5)—his awakening is our own because we are one. We may choose to remain asleep, but a part of us has awakened because Jesus has. This makes no sense from our perspective on the world's battleground, because bodies *are* different and separate. We may believe that Jesus is awakened, but we are still here. Yet this is only because we *think* we are. Contrasting ourselves with Jesus, however, is just another attempt to prove the reality of the separation.

(2:7-9) With God's Word in their minds they come in benediction, not to heal the sick but to remind them of the remedy God has already given them. It is not their hands that heal. It is not their voice that speaks the Word of God.

Recall that the *Word of God* means some aspect of the Atonement principle. Having previously taught that healing is of the mind, Jesus tells us here *not* to heal the sick, meaning not to do anything external for the sake of healing symptoms. This is because healing has already occurred in the mind, a point that recurs in the sections to follow. Our function as teachers of God, like the Holy Spirit, is to remind others by our mere presence. Therefore we are not to heal the symptoms of those who are sick, which would merely reinforce the perception we are separate from them, but "to remind them of the remedy God has already given them." This alone is healing. Since sickness is guilt, which comes from the decision to believe in separate interests, healing recognizes its illusory nature. The text tells us "minds are joined; bodies are not" (T-18.VI.3:1)—for bodies were made to embody the mind's belief in separation. Thus we share the same interests because we share the same Self, and it makes no sense to do anything that belies this truth by reinforcing further separation.

In *The Song of Prayer*, Jesus speaks of "healing-to-separate" (S-3.III), wherein in effect we say to another: "You are sick and I am the healer who will fix you; I have something you lack, and I will give it to you." This message denigrates the mind's power to choose illness—the worst thing to do for anyone. Jesus never does, which is why he does not fix us in the world. To repeat, we are to remind others only that our power to choose Atonement is within them as well. When our minds are healed, we symbolize for others the peace and love they, too, can experience—we are not separate, and so the decision we made, they too can make.

Clearly, however, we act to help alleviate distress in others, but our bodily activities do not heal any more than an aspirin removes a headache. It is only love's presence that heals, for others experience our love because we have chosen its Voice instead of the voice of hate and guilt, the Voice of healing instead of the voice of sickness. In other words, it is not words or actions that heal, but the loving presence of peace that calls to others to choose again. This, then, is a variation of the theme that our interests are not separate because *we* are not separate.

(2:10) They merely give what has been given them.

This reflects the theme that giving and receiving are the same, which we saw previously under "Generosity" in section 4, and will see again. It varies the theme of shared interests, because you and I are one.

(2:11-12) Very gently they call to their brothers to turn away from death: "Behold, you Son of God, what life can offer you. Would you choose sickness in place of this?"

You do nothing else to heal, for it is your presence that asks others to question whether they would choose sickness instead of the peace they experience in you. You do not have to fix anyone, merely accept the Atonement for yourself. Once you accept this healing, you know that mind is everything and the body nothing, and sickness but the mind's mistaken decision while healing is its loving correction.

(3:1) Not once do the advanced teachers of God consider the forms of sickness in which their brother believes.

The theme of form and content returns. Forms separate because they come from the content of separation. Changing that thought restores to our awareness the fact we are already unified. Once again, we do nothing but remove this faulty thought from our minds through the Holy Spirit's help.

(3:2) To do this is to forget that all of them have the same purpose, and therefore are not really different.

All sickness is the same regardless of its form. That is why there is no hierarchy of illusions nor order of difficulty in miracles or healing. A major form of sickness such as cancer or AIDS, and a minor form such as a sprained ankle or slight cold are the same because their purpose is the same. Sickness comes from the decision to be a mindless body so that something else, not we, can be held responsible for our pain and misery—a germ, the weather, or another person. Thus the importance of learning to focus on purpose.

(3:3-4) They seek for God's Voice in this brother who would so deceive himself as to believe God's Son can suffer. And they remind him that he did not make himself and must remain as God created him.

You do not remind others they are as God created them by your words, but by your having identified with God's Son as He created him—perfect and whole—knowing that the only reality is oneness. In other words, you teach simply by being who you are. Helpful words will come through you, as will helpful actions. Remember that healing has nothing to do with form; only with the content of love, which reminds others that we are *all* children of love, not of guilt, hate, or sickness.

(3:5-6) They recognize illusions can have no effect. The truth in their minds reaches out to the truth in the minds of their brothers, so that illusions are not reinforced.

Illusions have no effect because their cause is unreal. This is the cause-effect connection we discussed in the previous subsection. Note that Jesus says nothing about bodies, for his message in *A Course in Miracles* is for us always to shift focus from body to mind. The healing I have accepted extends throughout the Sonship because it is one mind. As the workbook says: "When I am healed, I am not healed alone" (W-pI.137). Similarly, when I choose guilt I do not choose only for myself, because the Sonship is one and if in my mind I am guilty, I must believe that everyone else is guilty as well.

(3:7) They are thus brought to truth; truth is not brought to them.

This is the theme of bringing illusions to the truth, not truth to the illusion. The illusions of our separate identities as bodies have to be brought to the truth of the mind's oneness—God's one Son. It cannot be stated too often that we do not bring Atonement to others—thus bringing truth to illusion—but only remind them of its truth by the love and peace in our minds. This allows them to accept the same correction for themselves, when they are ready.

(3:8-9) So are they dispelled, not by the will of another, but by the union of the one Will with itself. And this is the function of God's teachers; to see no will as separate from their own, nor theirs as separate from God's.

Illusions are dispelled, but not by the will of another. I cannot teach you something that is not already in you; I cannot heal you unless the healing is there. I can only remind you of what you already know—that your mind is healed. This is what Jesus does in *A Course in Miracles*. He does not really teach us anything—we just think he does. He but reminds us we made the wrong choice and can now make the correct one. Indeed, that is what Plato taught twenty-five hundred years ago—that education is a remembrance, reminding students of what is already within them. Advanced teachers of God live out this truth for the Sonship.

We thus see a restatement of the theme of oneness. Not being separate from each other, we are not separate from God. Reality is oneness—of creation within itself and with its one Creator: "a Oneness joined as One" (T-25.I.7:1). We are asked only to live this oneness daily, by making the choice against separate interests. Thus do we teach, for our lives demonstrate that our choice for truth is the same for all, without exception.

6. IS HEALING CERTAIN?

This section expresses the theme of oneness and shared interests; namely, giver and receiver are no longer perceived as separate or different, but as one and the same, as are what is given and received. All is one, whether we listen to the ego or the Holy Spirit: if we believe separation and guilt are real, that is what we see in everyone; similarly, if we believe in forgiveness and love, that is what we see. Thus what we believe is what we give *and* receive.

We saw in the previous section that healing occurs when teachers of God accept healing for themselves, resulting in the patient being healed as well. The question specifically addressed here is: Is this really true?

(1:1-4) Healing is always certain. It is impossible to let illusions be brought to truth and keep the illusions. Truth demonstrates illusions have no value. The teacher of God has seen the correction of his errors in the mind of the patient, recognizing it for what it is.

You cannot bring darkness to the light without there being light, which dissolves the darkness into nothingness. Teachers of God see the correction of their errors in the mind of the patient, because they see it in themselves. This parallels the discussion in *Psychotherapy* that the therapist's mind is healed when he gives up judgment, which also heals the patient:

> The therapist sees in the patient all that he has not forgiven in himself, and is thus given another chance to look at it, open it to re-evaluation and forgive it. When this occurs, he sees his sins as gone into a past that is no longer here (P-2.VI.6:3-4).

> It is in the instant that the therapist forgets to judge the patient that healing occurs (P-3.II.6:1).

Thus healed, the therapist becomes an advanced teacher of God who symbolizes the decision the patient himself can make. Healing is therefore certain, because one mind's healing is every mind's healing. This is unlike the state of the world, where there is always a winner and loser—one who gives, one who receives—whose interests are clearly perceived as separate. However, shared interests is the only sane perception you can have within the right mind, which recognizes the oneness of God's Son within the dream—the same ego, Holy Spirit, and decision maker—and outside the dream—as Christ in Heaven. Because the truth of the Atonement has been accepted, healing cannot *not* be.

(1:5-6) Having accepted the Atonement for himself, he has also accepted it for the patient. Yet what if the patient uses sickness as a way of life, believing healing is the way to death?

Because healing returns us to the mind, wherein are found both problem and solution, the ego perceives it as death. By bringing the problem to the solution, the problem is undone. However, we experience healing as a threat because our existence is part of the problem of separation, which is the foundation of our life. Being healed, therefore, means the end of our individuality and specialness. Why, then, should we accept the healing that is offered? Instead, we erect barriers such as sickness to protect us. Yet despite the ego's best efforts, healing is inevitable when the Atonement has been accepted by another, since minds are joined.

(1:7-9) When this is so, a sudden healing might precipitate intense depression, and a sense of loss so deep that the patient might even try to destroy himself. Having nothing to live for, he may ask for death. Healing must wait, for his protection.

Again, Jesus speaks of healing on different levels. On the one hand healing has already occurred, so he refers to a person's fear of accepting what is there — the Atonement was accepted at the beginning because the separation never was. In the Western world, Jesus has come to symbolize one who accepted this Atonement—for all of us. Nonetheless, we chose not to accept it, and proceeded to make a world and body, sickness and death, as defenses that prevent us from accepting what another part of our minds already chose. Again, none of this is understandable unless you leave the dream with Jesus and look back on it. *A Course in Miracles*, therefore, can never be understood through the brain, which was programmed to think only in terms of time and space, while the Course comes from the atemporal and non-spatial mind. It speaks to us as decision makers who are beyond the world, yet have chosen to believe in it. Healing, however, is certain because, as Jesus says in the text, what can be more certain than a Son of God? (T-20.IV.8:12)

(2:1) Healing will always stand aside when it would be seen as threat.

It is not so much that healing stands aside—being in the mind through the Atonement, healing is always there. It is we who stand aside by distancing ourselves from healing, out of fear of losing our individual identity.

(2:2-4) The instant it is welcome it is there. Where healing has been given it will be received. And what is time before the gifts of God?

It makes no difference whether healing seems to take a day, month, year, century, millennium, or a million years, since God's Son is outside time and space. Thus the decision for sickness is timeless, as is healing.

(2:5-7) We have referred many times in the text to the storehouse of treasures laid up equally for the giver and the receiver of God's gifts. Not one is lost, for they can but increase. No teacher of God should feel disappointed if he has offered healing and it does not appear to have been received.

Healing *has* been received because it is already in the mind. It has just not yet been accepted. Yet the treasure or gift is there. As I mentioned earlier, education is a remembering, as is the Atonement. We remember our Identity as Christ we had chosen to forget, and forget the ego we had chosen to remember.

(2:8-9) It is not up to him to judge when his gift should be accepted. Let him be certain it has been received, and trust that it will be accepted when it is recognized as a blessing and not a curse.

Advanced teachers are certain within themselves that the problem has been healed, which means they feel no pressure to alleviate the pain of those who suffer. Such pressure to change others says they lack the power to make a decision; their right to be afraid is not respected. In wanting to remove that fear, as we discussed before, you denigrate the power of the person's mind to choose—fear or love, sickness or healing. When you feel pressured to have people believe what you believe, to be healed the way you want them to be healed, or to decide as you think they should, it is only because you doubt the truth of your Self. This means *you* are now sick, for you want the other person to accept healing only to demonstrate what you have doubted: the reality of the Atonement principle.

When *your* mind has been healed, you are certain of the Atonement and its healing. Thus you stand with Jesus outside time, where, again, it has no meaning. He expresses this perspective in "For They Have Come":

> What is a hundred or a thousand years to Them [God and Christ], or tens of thousands? When They come, time's purpose is fulfilled. What never was passes to nothingness when They have come (T-26.IX.4:1-3).

The term *patience* as it is commonly understood is virtually meaningless here. Jesus teaches that true patience comes from knowing there is nothing to wait for, because love's outcome is certain. And so there could never be a sense of urgency, which reflects the real meaning of the eighth characteristic of God's teachers.

Jesus therefore appeals to us not to forget what we know when we choose healing. In other words, we may choose healing and then become afraid, which causes us to fall back into uncertainty and, for example, find ourselves demanding witnesses and evidence that this course really works. Yet once we look for proof we will never find it, because we are searching for proof of the ego, reinforcing our own uncertainty. When we know from within that the oneness of love is all and the separation never happened, nothing outside will disturb us, even a loved one's "wrong choice." We understand that while it may be the wrong choice on one level, it is the only choice that person can make, and perhaps is prelude to a correct choice at some future point. We should take care not to stand in the way of other people's Atonement paths, nor the power of their minds to choose, because that power is the only thing in the universe that can help them. We therefore need to respect people's right to choose, even if that choice is a disaster. Remember, we want to heal the *content*, not the *form*, and what heals the content of separation, guilt, and fear is forgiveness, exemplified by our gentleness, patience, and peace.

(3:1-3) It is not the function of God's teachers to evaluate the outcome of their gifts. It is merely their function to give them. Once they have done that they have also given the outcome, for that is part of the gift.

We cannot be reminded too often that giving and receiving are the same. The outcome is part of the gift since cause and effect are not separated; so too with offer and acceptance. If I have offered you a gift, you must have accepted it because we are one. If I give you a gift and then worry if you have received it, I am saying we are separate, which means I believe in sickness—*my own*. Thus I am where the ego wants me—focusing on *form* instead of *content*. The content of healing is in the mind, and when I am right-minded I know that the Sonship is healed because the mind of God's Son is one.

(3:4-5) No one can give if he is concerned with the result of giving. That is a limitation on the giving itself, and neither the giver nor the receiver would have the gift.

True giving is based on oneness, the criterion for love. By contrast, false giving—giving-to-destroy—is concerned with the outcome of giving: will the recipient accept the gift or reject it? Thus we perceive and reinforce the separation the other person has chosen, for our minds have shifted from shared to separate interests, which, again, means we have chosen sickness and are now the ones who must ask for help and healing.

(3:6-8) Trust is an essential part of giving; in fact, it is the part that makes sharing possible, the part that guarantees the giver will not lose, but only gain. Who gives a gift and then remains with it, to be sure it is used as the giver deems appropriate? Such is not giving but imprisoning.

The word *trust* appears frequently now. Recall that it is the first and foremost characteristic of God's teachers. The statement "Trust is an essential part of giving" means trusting that what the Holy Spirit teaches about Atonement is true—the separation never happened, and so we are not separate from God or from each other. This is the basis of our shared interests. It also means not trusting what our eyes tell us, which only breeds further separation.

When I give the gift of healing I know it is received, for how could there be loss? By contrast, giving a gift and wanting to remain with it is giving-to-destroy—the ego's special love, which is really the imprisoning hate born of separate interests.

(4:1-2) It is the relinquishing of all concern about the gift that makes it truly given. And it is trust that makes true giving possible.

As I have said in different ways, these ideas make sense only when you are outside the dream, since only there can you realize you give but to yourself. "All that I give is given to myself," as Lesson 126 says, because in truth there is no one there to give. It is the choice to let go of guilt that allows love to extend through the mind of the Sonship. This is why giving and receiving are the same.

(4:3-4) Healing is the change of mind that the Holy Spirit in the patient's mind is seeking for him. And it is the Holy Spirit in the mind of the giver Who gives the gift to him.

The Holy Spirit is the Course's symbol to express the commonality that joins us as one. He is the Thought that unifies, the Link to God that reminds us that the separation never happened, which means you and I are not separate.

(4:5-9) How can it be lost? How can it be ineffectual? How can it be wasted? God's treasure house can never be empty. And if one gift is missing, it would not be full.

If one part of the Sonship is excluded from the rest, the Sonship ceases to be what it is. What makes the Sonship of Christ reality is its perfect wholeness. It is not the sum of integrated parts, but a wholeness in which there are no parts. Therefore, if you withhold your gift from a single person, you deny creation's unity and affirm the ego's belief in separation and fragmentation. This, once again, demonstrates your sickness.

(4:10-12) Yet is its fullness guaranteed by God. What concern, then, can a teacher of God have about what becomes of his gifts? Given by God to God, who in this holy exchange can receive less than everything?

These are mere words if you understand them with your brain, from a position on the battleground of separation. From outside the world, however, you

6. Is Healing Certain?

suddenly realize the meaning of "given by God to God"—we are all God because we are part of the one Source. We are not the Creator, but we are part of God's Self, and there can be no separation in Heaven. Understanding this oneness heals, and reflecting this understanding symbolizes healing for others. I need only accept the Thought of Atonement within my mind, which automatically extends throughout the Sonship. Healing then becomes a certainty, for what can be more certain than God?

7. SHOULD HEALING BE REPEATED?

The topic of healing's certainty, discussed in the preceding section, is continued here. If you believe healing is certain, you obviously do not have to repeat it.

(1:1-4) This question really answers itself. Healing cannot be repeated. If the patient is healed, what remains to heal him from? And if the healing is certain, as we have already said it is, what is there to repeat?

Healing is certain, as is Atonement, because God is certain. The inherent logic of the above series of statements is understandable only from beyond the world's experience, beyond the temporal and spatial limitations the body seems to impose on us. In truth, of course, it is the mind that imposes these limitations.

(1:5) For a teacher of God to remain concerned about the result of healing is to limit the healing.

The fact that Jesus said the very same thing in the previous section lets you know its importance. Repeating his argument, he expands on it:

(1:6-9) It is now the teacher of God himself whose mind needs to be healed. And it is this he must facilitate. He is now the patient, and he must so regard himself. He has made a mistake, and must be willing to change his mind about it.

If I believe you have a problem, *I* am the one who is sick. How could the perfect Son of God have a problem? I have let myself be drawn into the dream of separation and form, in which sickness comes from the body rather than the mind's decision. This decision, however, had no effect on reality because the separation never happened and "not one note in Heaven's song was missed" (T-26.V.5:4)—the principle of the Atonement. If I think there is a problem in the world or body, the problem is mine because I am looking through the ego's eyes that see separate interests. Since the truth is otherwise, if I see you as the problem I have become the patient, regardless of your condition. Perceiving separation anywhere reveals it is I who made a mistake. Therefore, proceeding from our first theme, if I perceive another with a problem I do not have, I affirm our separation. *That* is the sickness, for I have made the dream of separation real, thereby making God *un*real. If so, I obviously made His Son unreal as well. Shifting to a right-minded perspective undoes the error and restores God and His Son to Their rightful and unified place in Heaven.

(1:10) He lacked the trust that makes for giving truly, and so he has not received the benefit of his gift.

The word *trust* appears again, referring to our trusting the ego's separation instead of the Holy Spirit's Atonement.

(2:1-3) Whenever a teacher of God has tried to be a channel for healing he has succeeded. Should he be tempted to doubt this, he should not repeat his previous effort. That was already maximal, because the Holy Spirit so accepted it and so used it.

Do not continue attempts to heal others, sending them white light or healing thoughts. Send these but to yourself, because you are the one in need of healing, whose mind has plunged into the darkness of separation, guilt, and hate. The light, coming from your corrected choice, is needed for you. Remember, if you see darkness outside yourself, making it real by reacting to it as if it were real, it is only because you have projected your own perceived darkness. It is this projection that must be healed.

Jesus uses *maximal* again, which we have already noted is part of the first principle of miracles: "All expressions of love are maximal" (T-1.I.1:4). It is an all-or-nothing concept—if I choose love, I will see it in everything, *without exception*. Healing is the choice for the Atonement's all-inclusive love, for sickness is the choice for separation.

(2:4-5) Now the teacher of God has only one course to follow. He must use his reason to tell himself that he has given the problem to One Who cannot fail, and must recognize that his own uncertainty is not love but fear, and therefore hate.

In these sentences we see our second theme of asking for the Holy Spirit's help. Once I realize I am the one who is sick, I go to the Symbol of health and healing in my mind, which means the place of sanity wherein I choose against sickness and insanity. Moreover, since the ego thought system is of one piece, choosing against love and for fear means choosing hate. That is what makes this section so difficult, for Jesus is saying that when, out of a belief in separation we try to help people, we are really expressing hatred. Seeing others as separate, they become symbols of our separation, and of the guilt we hate above all else.

The ego compounds the terrible situation it caused by telling us if we are not happy, someone must have taken happiness from us. That is how we justify our hatred of others, as the fourth and fifth laws of chaos explain (T-23.II.9-13). Whenever we make separation real, we make the ego and its thought system of specialness real and, in the process, buy into its package of hate. However, we cannot buy part of the ego's package, having a little bit of hell in Heaven, as we will see again later. *A Course in Miracles* is an all-or-nothing system: all hell or all Heaven; all fear or all love. If we identify with the ego, therefore, we accept the entirety of its thought system: sin, guilt, fear, hate, judgment, pain, and death. If we choose the Holy Spirit, however, we choose His system: love, peace, forgiveness, healing, and joy.

(2:6-8) His position has thus become untenable, for he is offering hate to one to whom he offered love. This is impossible. Having offered love, only love can be received.

This means I have offered you not love but *special love*, which is based on separation. In *The Song of Prayer* we read about *healing-to-separate*, which we could also call *healing-to-destroy*, based on the idea that we are giving people what they lack (S-3.III). Yet how could they lack something when they are perfect, and how could we be separate and different when we are one? If we give them something we believe they lack but we have, we have again made separation real—the ego's "false empathy" (T-16.I) in which we see the Sonship as separated from ourselves: some people deserve empathy, love, and concern, while others do not. In true empathy, on the other hand, we allow God's Love to extend through us, embracing everyone as one. Love must be total if it is love. To repeat, "All expressions of love are maximal" (T-1.I.1:4), for love comes from oneness, and embraces oneness as one. Everything else is hate, for its source is the ego's thought system of hate.

(3:1-4) It is in this that the teacher of God must trust. This is what is really meant by the statement that the one responsibility of the miracle worker is to accept the Atonement for himself. The teacher of God is a miracle worker because he gives the gifts he has received. Yet he must first accept them.

As a teacher of God, I trust that when love is offered it is received, because giving and receiving are the same. Therefore, if I want to be truly helpful and an instrument of love, I must accept the help of the Love within me. It cannot be said too often that we are not separate, and so I cannot offer you what I do not have, and you cannot receive what I do not have. Love is all there is, as is the oneness of God's Son. This means that I need to be healed only of the belief in separation, trusting that love's oneness will work through me, guiding my words and deeds in whatever way will be the most helpful. I therefore have no investment in the outcome, which I know to be certain. This gift of trust is given by love to love, by God to God. My body might still act as if we are separate, but my healed mind knows we are one and loves accordingly.

(3:5-8) He need do no more, nor is there more that he could do. By accepting healing he can give it. If he doubts this, let him remember Who gave the gift and Who received it. Thus is his doubt corrected.

All we need do—and there is nothing more we can do—is accept the Atonement. Jesus here juxtaposes trust and doubt. Doubt says I am not sure healing is certain, which is another way of saying I am not sure Atonement is true and the ego an illusion. Above all, I am not sure *I* am an illusion. Trust says I believe that everything I have ever said or thought is false, because there is a Voice of truth in my mind from which I tried to separate. Trust in the Holy Spirit, then, is the correction for doubt—our second theme of asking Him for help.

(3:9-11) He thought the gifts of God could be withdrawn. That was a mistake, but hardly one to stay with. And so the teacher of God can only recognize it for what it is, and let it be corrected for him.

Guilt causes us to remain with the mistake, because it takes the *tiny, mad idea* seriously; and when we remembered not to laugh (T-27.VIII.6:2), the ego called it sin. Guilt, then, is indelibly stamped on our minds, which means we deserve to be punished. This in turn sets into motion the ego's insane defensive system of leaving the mind and making up a world and body. Thus we need to acknowledge our mistake: the separation was not a sin, but a mistaken choice that had no effect on reality; whatever effect it had on an illusion remains an illusion.

(4:1-3) One of the most difficult temptations to recognize is that to doubt a healing because of the appearance of continuing symptoms is a mistake in the form of lack of trust. As such it is an attack. Usually it seems to be just the opposite.

It is an attack on your Self as Christ, which is at one with my Self as Christ. By seeing you as prey to the body, I attack you because I take from you the mind's power to choose. On the surface, my continued concern appears to be kind, loving, and compassionate. Yet it is hateful because I reinforce the ego's separated and mindless reality. Therefore, the help I give is nothing but my attempt to erase self-doubt, which can hardly be called loving for it is another example of the ego's selfishness: I help you because I want to avoid the pain of looking at my guilt. As a result, no one is healed, which is why medicine will never truly heal disease—it looks in the wrong place. Disease is not of the body and does not come from microorganisms or a faulty organ, but from the mind's decision for guilt.

(4:4-7) It does appear unreasonable at first to be told that continued concern is attack. It has all the appearances of love. Yet love without trust is impossible, and doubt and trust cannot coexist. And hate must be the opposite of love, regardless of the form it takes.

Remember we are speaking of trust in the Holy Spirit, which means trust in the Atonement principle that says we are not separate. If I am concerned about you, I obviously see you as a body that is separated from me and from God—there is an *I* who am concerned about *you*. This does not reflect the Atonement's affirmation of unity, which means there could be no love present. Without love there must be hate, as expressed in this statement from the text: "What is not love is murder" (T-23.IV.1:10). It is a question of *one or the other*. If it is not the Holy Spirit's Love, it must be the ego's sin, guilt, fear, and hate. As we know, the ego's love is special love, which rests on separation and differences, whereas the Holy Spirit's Love rests on the gentle foundation of our inherent unity as God's one Son.

(4:8-9) Doubt not the gift and it is impossible to doubt its result. This is the certainty that gives God's teachers the power to be miracle workers, for they have put their trust in Him.

Again, our second theme. We put our trust in God, His Voice, and the Word It speaks. Whenever I find myself concerned, worried, and anxious about another—a loved one or any person in the world—I need to stop and realize this is not what it appears to be. If I truly want to be of help to this person whom I profess to love, I must first choose love within myself, shifting my focus from the outside—this body seemingly separate from me—to the person inside that I have made separate from God. That *inside*—the mind—is where healing must be. You are being most helpful, then, by watching your concern for another, and realizing this concern is not what it seems.

(5:1-2) The real basis for doubt about the outcome of any problem that has been given to God's Teacher for resolution is always self-doubt. And that necessarily implies that trust has been placed in an illusory self, for only such a self can be doubted.

I doubt who I am because I have dismissed the idea that I am the Self that God created one with Him. However, once we awaken from the dream and become aware of our Self as Christ, there is only oneness. Doubt—self-reflection—implies duality, and there can be no reflection of the non-dualistic Christ. As Jesus teaches near the end of the text, there is a concept of the self, but the true Self has none (T-31.V).

(5:3-8) This illusion can take many forms. Perhaps there is a fear of weakness and vulnerability. Perhaps there is a fear of failure and shame associated with a sense of inadequacy. Perhaps there is a guilty embarrassment stemming from false humility. The form of the mistake is not important. What is important is only the recognition of a mistake as a mistake.

7. Should Healing Be Repeated?

A mistake, not a sin—yet we must perceive it as a mistake: we chose the wrong teacher and identified with the wrong thought system. The problem, therefore, has nothing to do with the external, but only the decision maker's mistaken choice.

(6:1) The mistake is always some form of concern with the self to the exclusion of the patient.

This is a partial statement of our first theme—separate interests. I do not really care if you get well or not, but only that I not feel a sense of loss or failure. Your health will meet my needs of self-aggrandizement, and that is my only concern.

(6:2-4) It is a failure to recognize him as part of the Self, and thus represents a confusion in identity. Conflict about what you are has entered your mind, and you have become deceived about yourself. And you are deceived about yourself because you have denied the Source of your creation.

This is a variation of our second theme, and the interconnection of our two themes becomes more and more apparent as we continue the journey through the manual. I doubt my Source because I pushed Him away, making me my own creator. This established the perception that everything relates to preserving my selfish and self-centered interests, to the exclusion of everyone else. Moreover, I am confused about your identity because I am confused about mine—*projection makes perception* (T-21.in.1:1).

(6:5) If you are offering only healing, you cannot doubt.

This is so because true healing comes from love, which is oneness and certainty.

(6:6-9) If you really want the problem solved, you cannot doubt. If you are certain what the problem is, you cannot doubt. Doubt is the result of conflicting wishes. Be sure of what you want, and doubt becomes impossible.

And what is it we want?—Jesus asks us this over and over. Do we want independence, autonomy, freedom, specialness, individuality? If we answer "yes" to any or all of those—they are obviously the same—we have chosen the ego, making a conflicted self that is a defense against our unified Self. From that point, everything we do focuses on maintaining that identity. We make up a world and feel certain we understand what goes on in it, which ensures that we do not experience the self-doubt we feel as an ego. This is inevitable, because in making that self and world we have defended against the certainty of Who we are.

A primary source of our certainty is feeling there is a world that needs us—there are people who need our help; problems that need our solutions. Indeed, we think *we* know the problem and the solution. This arrogance is in fact a reaction against the underlying self-doubt and terror that we know nothing, and that our puny existence, which we attempt to make into something important, will be snuffed out in a moment. Self-doubt can only lead to this end, and recognizing this is an essential step toward one day replacing doubt with certainty, our self with our Self.

8. HOW CAN PERCEPTION OF ORDER OF DIFFICULTIES BE AVOIDED?

This section continues the discussion of looking past form—specifically, how we can move beyond the perception of symptoms to the commonality that underlies all our problems. In formulating his answer, Jesus returns to the theme of mind and body, asking us to focus not on the body's form but on the contents of the mind. There are two: the ego's separation, guilt, hate, and sickness; and the Holy Spirit's Atonement or forgiveness. Jesus begins with the perceptual world, describing it as "contrast." For example, as we look around a room we discern different shapes: chairs, tables, pictures on the wall, etc. We denote these differences because of contrast. If everything were the same—color, shape, and size—discernment would be impossible. In this world of separation and judgment, however, we see the projection of the original separation—the Son's judgment and perception of differences. Jesus proceeds to explain that all this comes from the mind, and not the body or world.

(1:1) The belief in order of difficulties is the basis for the world's perception.

We began with the original order, which was God and His Son. However, the Son did not like being second and so killed his Father, replacing Him on the throne of creation. From there arose the ego thought system, which culminated in a world that manifested this new order.

(1:2-7) It rests on differences; on uneven background and shifting foreground, on unequal heights and diverse sizes, on varying degrees of darkness and light, and thousands of contrasts in which each thing seen competes with every other in order to be recognized. A larger object overshadows a smaller one. A brighter thing draws the attention from another with less intensity of appeal. And a more threatening idea, or one conceived of as more desirable by the world's standards, completely upsets the mental balance. What the body's eyes behold is only conflict. Look not to them for peace and understanding.

Jesus describes our perceptual world, which we all take for granted. Indeed, what could exist here without such perceptions? The ego made the body and perceptual world so we would exist *by* perceiving such a world. We do not realize, however, that perception comes from the mind's decision. Since everything emanates from the original thought of conflict between God and the ego, everything in the world must conflict with everything else—*projection makes perception*: the perceptual world reflects the mind's world. Needless to say, this conflict exists in the ego's mind only; the true God knows nothing about it.

(2:1-3) Illusions are always illusions of differences. How could it be otherwise? By definition, an illusion is an attempt to make something real that is regarded as of major importance, but is recognized as being untrue.

"Illusions are always illusions of differences" because they come from the original difference between God and His Son. Yet deep within the mind we know we are not who we think we are, and we desperately try to prove the ego is right and God is wrong, as we now see:

(2:4-5) The mind therefore seeks to make it true out of its intensity of desire to have it for itself. Illusions are travesties of creation; attempts to bring truth to lies.

Recall that collectively we made a self that is a travesty of creation, what elsewhere Jesus refers to as a "parody" (T-24.VII.1:11), which we then sought to make real. The ego's way of accomplishing its goal was to brand separation as sinful, convincing us it actually happened. This led us to believe that God is separate from us and is the enemy. Again, projecting this conflict gave rise to a world of separation and differences, of victims and victimizers.

(2:6) Finding truth unacceptable, the mind revolts against truth and gives itself an illusion of victory.

The world represents this seeming victory—the defeat of God and establishment of a palpable world that is Heaven's opposite. Our brains tell us how real this perceptual world is, and so we tell God: "You lose. I told You I could do it and I did. I made up a world better than Yours, in which my specialness has the home You denied me in Heaven. Moreover,

I am not even responsible for this world; others are." This is the illusion of victory.

(2:7-8) Finding health a burden, it retreats into feverish dreams. And in these dreams the mind is separate, different from other minds, with different interests of its own, and able to gratify its needs at the expense of others.

In sentence 7, "health" refers to Atonement and oneness. Our defense of differences and separate interests is what needs correction and undoing. The paragraph's final phrases describe our special relationships, wherein we have different minds with competing interests, and have to gratify our needs at the expense of others. Thus the special relationship bargain that accentuates our differences: "I do not care about you, but only about your meeting my needs."

(3:1) Where do all these differences come from?

The focus shifts to the origin of these differences: in the mind, where they remain—*ideas leave not their source*:

(3:2-6) Certainly they seem to be in the world outside. Yet it is surely the mind that judges what the eyes behold. It is the mind that interprets the eyes' messages and gives them "meaning." And this meaning does not exist in the world outside at all. What is seen as "reality" is simply what the mind prefers.

Jesus is teaching that perception is interpretation. The issue is not what our eyes literally see, but how the mind interprets what they see. These interpretations come from either the ego—separation and attack are rampant, and guilt justified—or the Holy Spirit—the vision of underlying unity behind the superficial differences. This unity draws us together, and we are taught to see everyone as the same: either expressing love or calling for it. Thus, we learn that our right-minded world is about love; not hate, guilt, or fear.

(3:7) Its hierarchy of values is projected outward, and it sends the body's eyes to find it.

The hierarchy of values is that there is good and bad, victims and victimizers, innocent and sinful—and we know which is which. This is our perception, but deep within the mind we believe we are the sinners and God is innocent. We flip this around so that we become innocent of God's wrathful vengeance, and then through projection we retain our innocence while everyone else becomes victimizing sinners. Recall the ego's hungry dogs of fear, sent to pounce upon any shred of guilt they find, dragging it back mercilessly to its master (T-19.IV-A.12). We all are the ego's slaves, for the body's eyes are programmed to find separation, sin, guilt, and sickness.

(3:8-11) The body's eyes will never see except through differences. Yet it is not the messages they bring on which perception rests. Only the mind evaluates their messages, and so only the mind is responsible for seeing. It alone decides whether what is seen is real or illusory, desirable or undesirable, pleasurable or painful.

As we are taught throughout *A Course in Miracles*, eyes do not see, ears do not hear, brains do not think—they simply act as the mind directs (e.g., T-22.III.5-6; T-28.VI.2). Our senses come from the ego's thought of differences, which sends its messages into the world that are then perceived as if they were truly there. Understanding this dynamic helps us shift our focus from the body to the mind.

(4:1-5) It is in the sorting out and categorizing activities of the mind that errors in perception enter. And it is here correction must be made. The mind classifies what the body's eyes bring to it according to its preconceived values, judging where each sense datum fits best. What basis could be faultier than this? Unrecognized by itself, it has itself asked to be given what will fit into these categories.

Once again, it is not the world or body that is sick, but the mind—of which we are unaware—that believes in separation and differences. It is the great dictator of everything we see, which is some expression of sin and guilt—in others, not ourselves. Even if we accept some guilt, we still attribute it to someone or something else: our genes, parents, environment, even God. This, then, is the function the ego's perception serves: to see the separation and sin it is told to see, with our feeling no responsibility for its presence.

(4:6) And having done so, it concludes that the categories must be true.

We are always so sure we are right, though we continually add two and two and get five. We cannot *not* be wrong, because the mind has programmed the body, perceptual organs, and brain to get the incorrect answer. Yet the truth is that there is no separation, division, fragmentation, specialness, or sickness—we remain the unity that God created. Thus what we see is unreal, and we see it because we want to prove that the unreal is true. The source of the error never lies with the world perception sees, but with the mind that has chosen to see it.

(4:7-8) On this the judgment of all differences rests, because it is on this that judgments of the world depend. Can this confused and senseless "reasoning" be depended on for anything?

Our world rests on the belief that our categories of judgment are real, for our lives depend on what we perceive. We actually believe that what we see is there *because* we see it, and we do not realize that we see it because the mind has demanded we see separation as real and meaningful. Moreover, the separation we see is that others are guilty sinners and we the innocent ones who are sinned against. Thus, they will be punished and we saved. Everything here is based upon that judgment, but only because we put it here. In truth, there is nothing here but delusions and hallucinations.

(5:1-6) There can be no order of difficulty in healing merely because all sickness is illusion. Is it harder to dispel the belief of the insane in a larger hallucination as opposed to a smaller one? Will he agree more quickly to the unreality of a louder voice he hears than to that of a softer one? Will he dismiss more easily a whispered demand to kill than a shout? And do the number of pitchforks the devils he sees carrying affect their credibility in his perception? His mind has categorized them all as real, and so they are all real to him.

Underlying Jesus' words is the principle that an illusion is an illusion is an illusion—a large one is the same as a small one; one times zero is the same as a thousand times zero. The mind has judged the separation to be real, and has made up a body and world in which we all witness to this seeming fact by our belief in a hierarchy of perceptions.

(5:7-9) When he realizes they are all illusions they will disappear. And so it is with healing. The properties of illusions which seem to make them different are really irrelevant, for their properties are as illusory as they are.

To reiterate this important point, this will make no sense without an experience of the unreality of the world and your self. Without such awareness of what it means to be outside the dream, you will merely mouth inspiring words, yet all the while believing that bodies and the differences among them are real. You will watch the news and be troubled by what you hear, or become upset over a doctor's report, still believing in orders of difficulty in separation and perception. These mistakes cannot be corrected unless they are first acknowledged as illusions.

In this final paragraph, Jesus speaks of advanced teachers, and what it means to have a healed mind:

(6:1-3) The body's eyes will continue to see differences. But the mind that has let itself be healed will no longer acknowledge them. There will be those who seem to be "sicker" than others, and the body's eyes will report their changed appearances as before.

Jesus is not telling us to deny what our eyes see—separate bodies, each different from the other. Keep in mind that perception is not a fact but an interpretation. The world teaches that what eyes see are facts; however, we are asked to focus on the way we look at what our eyes see. Thus there will always be people who seem to be sicker than others, or more evil, cruel, kind, merciful, and spiritually advanced than others. The ego loves such comparisons, which is why we have orders of good and evil, innocence and sin, love and hate.

(6:4) But the healed mind will put them all in one category; they are unreal.

The eyes see differences: major and minor symptoms, major and minor problems. Yet the healed mind does not recognize them as such, knowing an illusion is an illusion. Big and little symptoms are part of an illusory body. Accepting this fact is the only way you can be healed, and thus be an instrument of healing for others by reminding them of what you have remembered—*in your mind.*

(6:5-9) This is the gift of its Teacher; the understanding that only two categories are meaningful

in sorting out the messages the mind receives from what appears to be the outside world. And of these two, but one is real. Just as reality is wholly real, apart from size and shape and time and place—for differences cannot exist within it—so too are illusions without distinctions. The one answer to sickness of any kind of healing. The one answer to all illusions is truth.

These are the two categories: *oneness*, reflected in the world of bodies by shared interests and goals; and *separation*, seen in the world as conflicting interests and goals. The Holy Spirit's reflection of love's reality is that *all* win or *all* lose. The ego's version is *one or the other*—you win, I lose; I win, you lose. The Holy Spirit's vision heals your mind and helps you recognize there is no order of difficulty in miracles. Indeed, this principle was Jesus' opening words to Helen when he began dictating—"The first thing to remember about miracles is that there is no order of difficulty among them"—and the ensuing course was a variation of that opening theme.

Thus you need to be aware of how you try to deny that truth. The first law of chaos (T-23.II.2:3) says the exact opposite, declaring there *is* a hierarchy of illusions, which means there is an order of difficulty in problems, symptoms, and sickness. At that point everyone becomes insane—the people who suffer and those who want to help them—because they see differences. If as a healer you think you are different from the ones you are healing—they are sick and you are not—you are just as sick. Remind yourself that it cannot be that only some are healed and not all; some are insane, and not all. That is why the word *all* is so important. To repeat:

(6:8-9) The one answer to sickness of any kind is healing. The one answer to all illusions is truth.

We suffer from the same illusion—our separate bodies are real—and share this common denominator of insanity. Consequently, we share the same need for the Answer, the Word of God that says the separation never happened. This means we are not separate from each other, and so on a daily basis we need to be aware of the temptation to fall into the trap of believing in separate problems and separate interests. This calls to mind, then, the need for the one answer to all problems: acceptance of God's healing Word of Atonement.

9. ARE CHANGES REQUIRED IN THE LIFE SITUATION OF GOD'S TEACHERS?

Though the shortest one in the manual, this section is significant as it addresses a question that is an important issue for students of *A Course in Miracles* who may feel that since the Course is so holy—and therefore they are so holy because they study it—they should not be involved in mundane matters such as marriage, families, jobs, earning money, carrying insurance, and so on. These students have been tempted, and many have unfortunately acted on the temptation, to leave their families, jobs, and insurance coverage, waiting for the Holy Spirit to provide for their needs. Jesus anticipated this mistake and seeks to correct it here.

(1:1-2) Changes are required in the *minds* of God's teachers. This may or may not involve changes in the external situation.

Changes are not required in anything external or physical, only in the mind. It must be so because the mind is the only thing there is—the source of the problem and its solution.

(1:3) Remember that no one is where he is by accident, and chance plays no part in God's plan.

This returns us to our earlier discussion of time. Jesus does not mean that God ordains specific events or that the Holy Spirit moves us around the board of life like chess pieces. We, not Them, wrote the script that occurred in the original instant, and so nothing could happen accidentally *now*, because it already happened *then*. Consequently, any circumstance, at any time, is the perfect instant for us to learn forgiveness—"God's plan." Projecting our guilt onto others provides the perfect opportunity to choose the Holy Spirit's script that shifts the mind's perceptions.

(1:4-5) It is most unlikely that changes in attitudes would not be the first step in the newly made teacher of God's training. There is, however, no set pattern, since training is always highly individualized.

This same thought is repeated almost word for word near the end of the manual: "the curriculum is highly individualized" (M-29.2:6). Since the training is "highly individualized," we can in no way know what anyone else should or should not do. There is no right or wrong approach in this sense—no right or wrong way of staying in or leaving a relationship or job, or even having one. The "right" way is acting without guilt, and the "wrong" way with guilt. These are the only meaningful criteria.

Jesus reinforces here what he has already taught: the need to shift our focus from the external—the world and body—to the thought system we have chosen in our minds. The decision for the ego is the problem, and changing thought systems is the answer. Thus we should not attempt to change the external in the magical hope of solving the problem—minds are not changed by changing behavior. Changing our minds may or may not change behavior, but if we are in our right minds what we do will not matter because it will always be loving, helpful, and kind.

(1:6) There are those who are called upon to change their life situation almost immediately, but these are generally special cases.

It is always intriguing to see—as we regularly saw in the early years of the Course—how many "special cases" there are. Students have been, and unfortunately continue to be tempted to think they are special cases, with the emphasis on the word *special*. I assure you, Jesus does not care where or if you work, where you live, or with whom. He cares only about your welcoming him back into your mind. How could he care about your behavior when he knows there is none? Recall this important line: "This is a course in cause and not effect" (T-21.VII.7:8). The *effect* is the external, having to do with the body, and the *cause* is the mind. Therefore, this is a course in changing the cause—from guilt to forgiveness.

(1:7-9) By far the majority are given a slowly evolving training program, in which as many previous mistakes as possible are corrected. Relationships in particular must be properly perceived, and all dark cornerstones of unforgiveness removed. Otherwise the old thought system still has a basis for return.

Note the words *slowly evolving*—as in being gentle, patient, kind, and merciful. This means there is no hurry to accomplish anything. Since we have already been healed—indeed, we have never *not* been healed—what is the rush? If, however, we feel a sense of urgency, it is only because we have made time real, thus making its source of sin, guilt, and fear real as well. The need for this slow evolution is our fear of love, which leads to our resistance against moving too quickly.

If we do not undo the guilt, it remains to return again and again in the form of attack, like a recurring nightmare. Guilt is undone by first recognizing how we have projected it onto everyone and everything. That is why the focus of *A Course in Miracles'* curriculum is on shifting relationships from special to holy—from the purpose of reinforcing guilt to undoing it; shifting from perceptions of separate to shared interests as we grow to realize we are *all* reflections of the Oneness of Heaven.

(2:1-2) As the teacher of God advances in his training, he learns one lesson with increasing thoroughness. He does not make his own decisions; he asks his Teacher for His answer, and it is this he follows as his guide for action.

Most readers are familiar with the "Rules for Decision" section in the text (T-30.I) and recall that Jesus stresses there, as he does here, the importance of asking the Holy Spirit for help—our second theme—and that we have only two choices available to us: the ego and the Holy Spirit. True help, of course, comes from the Holy Spirit, and Jesus tells us what this means in the next sentence:

(2:3) This becomes easier and easier, as the teacher of God learns to give up his own judgment.

The process of increasingly turning to the Holy Spirit becomes easier to the extent we can gladly say and mean: "Thank God I am wrong and You are right." The problem is that we are certain we understand what is wrong with the world, a friend, or our bodies, expressing absolute confidence in our judgments. Yet we are always wrong because we look in the wrong place, thinking problems are external and therefore in need of our doing something about them. Yet we do everything but go to the mind, where things have to be done differently: choosing again.

(2:4) The giving up of judgment, the obvious prerequisite for hearing God's Voice, is usually a fairly slow process, not because it is difficult, but because it is apt to be perceived as personally insulting.

It is personally insulting to be told we are wrong and do not understand anything. Moreover, not only do we not understand anything, we are incapable of understanding anything, as the next section explains.

In this part of the manual, judgment is treated as the major component of the ego thought system. The original judgment was against God for not giving the Son the specialness he demanded. Therefore, he made the judgment he would be happier on his own—and the ego was off and running. This is the source of our tendency to think we know better. We always think we understand how people should be— how they should behave, react, and think. However, the only meaningful judgment we can make is that we are wrong, but that there is Someone within us Who is right. As long as we stubbornly and arrogantly insist otherwise, we will never hear His Voice, for judgment drowns Him out, clearly saying that you and I are separate, expressing the special relationship in which you are either wonderful or hateful, my ally or my enemy. Therefore Jesus teaches that giving up judgment enables us to perceive everyone as sharing the same interests—our certain way home.

(2:5-6) The world's training is directed toward achieving a goal in direct opposition to that of our curriculum. The world trains for reliance on one's judgment as the criterion for maturity and strength.

We live in a society that values being an individual and self-assertive, making something of oneself. We may not all agree on the same criteria, but we would agree that we need to achieve our goals. Since we cannot do this without evaluating ourselves relative to some preconceived value, the process always involves judgment.

(2:7) Our curriculum trains for the relinquishment of judgment as the necessary condition of salvation.

Judgment in the world's terms involves judging a situation, and then resolving it. Thus we judge a relationship and act accordingly, with the goal uppermost in our minds of having our needs met. This type of judgment rests on the ego's bread-and-butter principle of *one or the other*, which invariably means that someone loses as another gains; someone is wrong and another is right. And we do everything possible to prove that we are the ones who are right. We know this makes the world go round because our original thought as one Son was that if I am right, God has to be wrong; both of us cannot be right. God "says": "You are my one Son, totally at One with Me." Our judgment counters: "That is unacceptable. I no longer want to be one with you. Therefore, separating from You is the right thing to do." Thus our original mistake was telling God: "You are wrong and I am right, and I will prove it." This conflict is the source of the thought system and world that followed, and is the core of everyone's authority problem. Remember the terrible twos: "No, I won't do it! I know what is best for myself, Mommy and Daddy—you don't!" We have never really abandoned that position, for we believe we know better than the authority, or anyone else for that matter, and behind every authority and relationship stands God.

Finally, our stubborn insistence we are right has never made us happy, but it has made us miserable by giving us the body and world, in which suffering is universal. That is why Jesus asks in the text: "Do you prefer that you be right or happy?" (T-29.VII.1:9). Our unhappiness has come because we judged we were right and God was wrong. A wonderful line in the text—one our egos hate—follows a description of the ego thought system: "And God thinks otherwise" (T-23.I.2:7). That is why we hate Him and try to block His Love. He thinks otherwise about this "wondrous" world we miscreated and the "wondrous" self we think we are. Of course, He does not really think at all because He does not see the world or its bodies, though the universe stands as testament to the fact that our judgments are correct. That is why the Course's curriculum places so much emphasis on our need to give them up.

10. HOW IS JUDGMENT RELINQUISHED?

In this section, Jesus tells us how to relinquish judgment, but he also helps us realize how silly it is, let alone insane, to believe we are capable of judging anything.

(1:1-2) Judgment, like other devices by which the world of illusions is maintained, is totally misunderstood by the world. It is actually confused with wisdom, and substitutes for truth.

We normally think wisdom has to do with people who can distinguish right from wrong, good from evil, what is helpful from what is not. This wisdom is based on the world and externals, with it sometimes being said that wisdom is acquired from long years of experience. But experience of what? A body learning how to get along with other bodies, which really means mastering the game of specialness that selfishly ensures that one's needs are met —always at another's expense. The people who are expert at this principle of *one or the other* we consider to be wise. They indeed may be wise in the ways of the world, but who would want the wisdom of an insane asylum, especially having seen it for what it is?

(1:3-6) As the world uses the term, an individual is capable of "good" and "bad" judgment, and his education aims at strengthening the former and minimizing the latter. There is, however, considerable confusion about what these categories mean. What is "good" judgment to one is "bad" judgment to another. Further, even the same person classifies the same action as showing "good" judgment at one time and "bad" judgment at another time.

All these judgments are relative, not absolute. The Greek sophists confronting Socrates declared that truth is relative, whereas he, and later his student Plato, taught the absolute and unchanging nature of truth. The first law of chaos reflects the sophist argument by stating there is a hierarchy of illusions (T-23.II.2)—some are more true than others. Jesus' point in these passages is that things are relative to us here. For example, what is good for one generation is bad for the next; what benefits one group is ruinous for another; adherents of one religion think another's is blasphemous—we do not agree on very much; and then there are days when we think something is acceptable, and when our needs change this judgment is reversed.

(1:7) Nor can any consistent criteria for determining what these categories are be really taught.

Consistent criteria are impossible if all is relative, for conclusions are based upon one's own point of view, and everyone's is different. We can trace this back to the beginning, when our point of view differed from God's—His was perfect Oneness; ours perfect separation. The fragmented and differentiated world that exploded from the original perception of difference is represented in all of us, since *ideas leave not their source*. We have different points of view, which change as we grow and mature. Moreover, as our needs change, so do our perceptions, values, and judgments. Therefore, the only absolute judgment is the Holy Spirit's—guilt is bad because it will hurt, and forgiveness is good because it brings happiness. That is the only valid judgment we can make.

(1:8-10) At any time the student may disagree with what his would-be teacher says about them [the above categories], **and the teacher himself may well be inconsistent in what he believes. "Good" judgment, in these terms, does not mean anything. No more does "bad."**

Another important issue raised here is the duality implicit in judgments. The concept of *good* means there is *bad*; *tall* implies *short*; *beauty* contrasts with *ugliness*. From the original dualistic belief in separation we inevitably end up with separate interests, because we have chosen between two different alternatives. These differences can be trivial—I appreciate this painting or like the weather, and you do not—but once we choose one side *as opposed to* the other, the issue becomes significant. All differences are the same for we choose between illusions; and since any concept on which we base a judgment is dualistic and relative, it cannot be of God nor His reflection. Therefore it cannot be true.

(2:1-4) It is necessary for the teacher of God to realize, not that he should not judge, but that he cannot. In giving up judgment, he is merely

giving up what he did not have. He gives up an illusion; or better, he has an illusion of giving up. He has actually merely become more honest.

Just as in the text Jesus corrects the biblical idea "judge not, that you be not judged," he tells us here: "Judge not because you *cannot* judge; you lack the ability to do so." The ego always judges between illusions, which is really a judgment of nothing. To repeat this important point, judgment came into the world when we believed we separated from God, which we re-enact over and over. Yet since the separation never happened there is no judgment, and therefore the world is just a massive game of "let's pretend." Needless to say, this does not prevent us from believing it is reality. The second characteristic of God's teachers is *honesty*, and we become increasingly honest as we acknowledge that we do not know what is right in a situation. Remember the early workbook lesson: "I do not perceive my own best interests" (W-pI.24). How could we possibly judge what ought to happen, as there is no way of knowing what is best for ourselves or anyone else? Jesus continues:

(2:5-7) Recognizing that judgment was always impossible for him, he no longer attempts it. This is no sacrifice. On the contrary, he puts himself in a position where judgment *through* him rather than *by* him can occur.

This expresses our second theme, the role of the Holy Spirit. We allow Him to judge through us by giving up the insane belief *we* can judge, thus abandoning the claim that we are right and know what is best. With this arrogance gone, the Holy Spirit's judgment shines through, which, as the text explains, is that everyone either expresses love or calls for it (T-12.I)—His *only* judgment. And whether you call for love or express it is irrelevant: if the former is the case, we naturally give love, as would a loving brother; if the latter, we naturally give love, as would a loving brother—our responses are the same for external circumstances have no bearing on them. Just as "not one note in Heaven's song was missed" (T-26.V.5:4) because of the *tiny, mad idea*, not one note in my song of love for you has changed because of something you have or have not done. This is the one justifiable judgment we can make.

(2:8-9) And this judgment is neither "good" nor "bad." It is the only judgment there is, and it is only one: "God's Son is guiltless, and sin does not exist."

Early in the manual, Jesus tells us that the core of the universal course is that "God's Son is guiltless, and in his innocence is his salvation" (M-1.3:5). He repeats the thought here—no other valid judgment is possible. A seeming attack is an expression of fear, because frightened people can be vicious and fear is a call for the love that has been denied. That is why every attack is seen by the Holy Spirit as a call for help. This judgment does not separate, differentiate, divide, oppose, or lead to conflict, for it is based on the thought we are united children of love, whether we express that truth or fear it. Therefore, our response to anyone, regardless of the verbal or physical behavior, is the same content—love—although its form can vary widely. Anything else is part of the ego illusion and does not exist. This advanced right-minded state we grow into, as we now read:

(3:1-2) The aim of our curriculum, unlike the goal of the world's learning, is the recognition that judgment in the usual sense is impossible. This is not an opinion but a fact.

Jesus is gently telling us, in effect: "Do not argue with me. This is not my opinion but a fact, and you cannot argue with facts." In the text he says that God is the only Fact (T-3.I.8:2), reflected here by stating the impossibility of judgment because of the impossibility of separation—the principle of the Atonement. This is the only authentic fact within the illusion.

(3:3-7) In order to judge anything rightly, one would have to be fully aware of an inconceivably wide range of things; past, present and to come. One would have to recognize in advance all the effects of his judgments on everyone and everything involved in them in any way. And one would have to be certain there is no distortion in his perception, so that his judgment would be wholly fair to everyone on whom it rests now and in the future. Who is in a position to do this? Who except in grandiose fantasies would claim this for himself?

In order to judge "rightly," we would have to know the entire hologram of time and the meaning of a person's actions at any given time. We would thus have to know where each behavior fits into the person's non-linear Atonement path, from the beginning—when we, as part of the one Son, chose to separate from God—to the very end—when we accept the Atonement for ourselves. If our perception were thus free of distortion, our judgments would result only in gain, no loss, and there would be only love, no specialness. However, it needs to be a perception that is totally cleansed of the ego's misconceptions: all thoughts of separation—past, present, and future. "Who is in a position to do this?" Jesus asks. Only in our insane arrogance would we answer, "We are!" Jesus kindly and gently puts us in our place.

(4:1-5) Remember how many times you thought you knew all the "facts" you needed for judgment, and how wrong you were! Is there anyone who has not had this experience? Would you know how many times you merely thought you were right, without ever realizing you were wrong? Why would you choose such an arbitrary basis for decision making? Wisdom is not judgment; it is the relinquishment of judgment.

Again, we are so sure we are right. We can all think of circumstances when we were absolutely sure of something—certain, for instance, that people hated or disliked us, only to discover they did not even know we existed; or were so sure we had a job because the interview went so well, and were not aware of the interviewer's negative impression of us; or were positive there would be a certain outcome in an election, and were mistaken. Jesus teaches that the relinquishment of judgment involves the humble admission that we know nothing, not understanding what anything means; moreover and importantly, we do not have to understand. Recall Jesus' words: "You are still convinced that your understanding is a powerful contribution to the truth, and makes it what it is" (T-18.IV.7:5). All we need understand is that whatever is going on, our response is love. Thus we need only pay attention to our interfering with its presence. This means not focusing on what others do, or the meaning of their behavior, but simply on our perceptions of what they do—the projections we place onto them.

We therefore ask Jesus for help to return to the choice point in the mind so we can choose again. We need not agonize over, nor try to figure out the meaning of anything. *Nothing here means anything*. If we think we understand how something works—the stock market, political systems, the United Nations, even our spouse or children—we will be wrong, because nothing in the world follows true rationality. Everything here is grossly distorted, as everything comes from the original gross distortion: I exist.

(4:6-10) Make then but one more judgment. It is this: There is Someone with you Whose judgment is perfect. He does know all the facts; past, present and to come. He does know all the effects of His judgment on everyone and everything involved in any way. And He is wholly fair to everyone, for there is no distortion in His perception.

Once again we hear our second theme, and the question remains: How do we get in touch with this Someone and access His Voice? The truth is that we do not have to get in touch with Him, for His wisdom and Love are already present in our minds, as is the Atonement principle. The problem is that *we* are not there. Therefore, we must move from the ego, where we chose to be, back to the right mind, where the Holy Spirit is. Giving up judgment—the perception of separate interests—is the means for attaining His distortion-free perception and accepting His Love.

(5:1-4) Therefore lay judgment down, not with regret but with a sigh of gratitude. Now are you free of a burden so great that you could merely stagger and fall down beneath it. And it was all illusion. Nothing more.

This reflects the early text statement: "You have no idea of the tremendous release and deep peace that comes from meeting yourself and your brothers totally without judgment" (T-3.VI.3:1). We are not aware of the immense burden we carry around with us: the need to judge and be right, to defend and justify our separate identities and interests. Our world and individual lives rest on judgment, because that is how they began. Our selves thus rest on the pain of believing in separation, and therefore we not only sigh in gratitude, but in relief when we change our minds.

(5:5-9) Now can the teacher of God rise up unburdened, and walk lightly on. Yet it is not only this that is his benefit. His sense of care is gone, for he has none. He has given it away, along with

judgment. He gave himself to Him Whose judgment he has chosen now to trust, instead of his own.

Jesus promises that our lives will get easier, saying we have no idea how much happier we will be when we let go of judgment. These passages nicely illustrate the blending together of our two themes. We ask for help in recognizing that our interests are the same, and this allows awareness of the Holy Spirit to grow. The more we feel His Presence, the easier it is to go to Him, which helps us let go of our misperceptions. Thus we say: "Help me learn that I am better off when I let go of being right and trying to prove You wrong, when I no longer see others as my enemies. Whatever their behavior may look like, they are my brothers."

(5:10-13) Now he makes no mistakes. His Guide is sure. And where he came to judge, he comes to bless. Where now he laughs, he used to come to weep.

That is how God "wipes away" all tears—the famous biblical verse (Isaiah 25:8; Revelation 7:17; 21:4a), quoted in the workbook (W-pII.301). *We give up the tears and hurt that come from judgment, leaving only the gentle laughter and lovely smile that look on everything as one—a shared dream of pain and suffering.*

(6:1-6) It is not difficult to relinquish judgment. But it is difficult indeed to try to keep it. The teacher of God lays it down happily the instant he recognizes its cost. All of the ugliness he sees about him is its outcome. All of the pain he looks upon is its result. All of the loneliness and sense of loss; of passing time and growing hopelessness; of sickening despair and fear of death; all these have come of it.

The cost of judgment is the central idea here. We must begin to see the causal connection between our judgments and our insistence that our interests are separate from another's, and the pain they cause: misery, depression, anxiety, and unhappiness. Recognizing the cost of judgment is what motivates us at last to let it go. Without experiencing the pain that comes from having attack thoughts—mild twinges of annoyance or raging hate—there will be no motivation to release them.

(6:7-11) And now he knows that these things need not be. Not one is true. For he has given up their cause, and they, which never were but the effects of his mistaken choice, have fallen from him. Teacher of God, this step will bring you peace. Can it be difficult to want but this?

Jesus calls us to look honestly at what we are doing, asking his help to make the choice to let judgment go. When we do, peace inevitably comes because it is already here, obscured only by our fierce need to judge.

11. HOW IS PEACE POSSIBLE IN THIS WORLD?

The theme of relying on the Holy Spirit for help is at the forefront of this section and those to follow, as is the importance of giving up of judgment.

(1:1-2) This is a question everyone must ask. Certainly peace seems to be impossible here.

Indeed, this seems to be the case more than ever these days. Jesus, however, is not only talking about world peace, but inner peace; i.e., a life without conflict, anxiety, competition, or judgment.

(1:3-5) Yet the Word of God promises other things that seem impossible, as well as this. His Word has promised peace. It has also promised that there is no death, that resurrection must occur, and that rebirth is man's inheritance.

Resurrection means awakening from the dream, which, as we will see later, has nothing to do with the so-called physical resurrection of Jesus. Likewise, *rebirth* refers to the shift from the wrong-minded birth of the ego to the right-minded rebirth of the Holy Spirit—"Christ is reborn as but a little Child each time a wanderer would leave his home" (W-pI.182.10:1). We are reborn whenever we choose the holy instant and are with Jesus. God's Word—the Atonement—promises it, and how could it not be, since we never separated from our Source?

(1:6) The world you see cannot be the world God loves, and yet His Word assures us that He loves the world.

Early in the text, Jesus quotes the well-known line from John's gospel, "For God so loved the world that he gave his only begotten Son, that whosoever believeth in him should not perish but have everlasting life" (John 3:16), saying this needs only one slight correction to be meaningful: "He gave it *to* His only begotten Son" (T-2.VII.5:14). The world to which Jesus refers is the real world, the total correction in the mind of the ego's thought system, having nothing whatsoever to do with the physical world. In point of fact, God does not "give" the real world, since He does not know about it. If God does not know about the ego's world, how could He know about a correction for it? "His Word" refers only to the Holy Spirit's Atonement path.

In saying that God loves the world, Jesus corrects the ego's vicious tale that He hates it and all it stands for. We would have to believe our Creator hates the world, and us as well, because we made it as an attack on Him (W-pII.3.2:1). The world was our way of thumbing our nose at God, sneering: "I can do you one better. I can make a cosmos—infinite, eternal, and magnificent. Beat that!" Of course God cannot, because He knows nothing of form or the "grandeur" of celestial bodies. He knows only the grandeur of His celestial Son. Jesus thus undoes the ego's prophecy that He will become as insane as we, lose His patience, and annihilate us and the world (T-26.VII.7).

(1:7) God's Word has promised that peace is possible here, and what He promises can hardly be impossible.

Peace is possible here because "here" is within the mind's Atonement principle. Being a projection, the world is also in the mind. Peace, therefore, must be possible in the world because it is within us. In fact, peace is the mind's *only* true content, being truth's reflection; everything else is illusory. The Atonement is also an illusion, yet is the final illusion because it corrects all the others (M-2.2). Since the world is nothing more than the mind's projection, and the peace of God the mind's only truth, it must be extended to the world.

This passage will make no sense if you try to understand it from the world's perspective. It is not at all unreasonable to wonder if peace is really possible when you look at current events, as I commented above. The ego thought system seems so deeply ingrained in everyone; how are billions of people going to accept the Atonement? The answer is that God's Word of Atonement has nothing to do with numbers, or time and space. It is true that there will never be peace in the world, because the world was made not to be peaceful but a place where God could not enter (W-pII.3.2:4). Peace is in the mind, and when there is inner peace—because the Atonement has been accepted—the world is gone, since there is no world outside the healed mind. This is why Jesus does not know of it. If there are only thoughts of love and peace, there is no need for a world whose purpose is defense—

nothing to defend against, no guilt to protect, no raging God to seek refuge from. Since the body was made to be a limitation on love, which you no longer choose to limit, it is unnecessary as well.

When peace is in your mind, therefore, the world is peaceful. This is why peace is not only possible in this world but a certainty. Whatever conflict or pain is experienced within the dream, including your body, you never forget its unreality. Something can affect you only if you think you are part of the dream. This means that you are never truly upset because of an impending war or cancerous growth, but only because you allowed yourself to return to unreality. No one held a gun to your mind—you entered the dream willingly because you believed it justified, protected, and sustained your existence.

(1:8-12) But it is true that the world must be looked at differently, if His promises are to be accepted. What the world is, is but a fact. You cannot choose what this should be. But you can choose how you would see it. Indeed, you *must* choose this.

For there to be peace in the world, you must look at the world differently. The world *was* made as an attack on God; the body *was* made as a limitation on love; words *were* made to keep us separate from truth—these are facts within the illusion. Remember, though, that perception is an interpretation, not a fact. The world is what it is, made to be a place where separation is the "divine" law, individuality sacred, and separate interests inevitable. Nonetheless, you can choose to look at the world differently—as a place in which you learn that you have projected onto it the ego's thought system that had been buried in your mind. In looking at the world differently, therefore, you really look at your *mind* differently—by choosing a different teacher. Thus you realize the world's only value is as a classroom in which you see your choice of teacher reflected back to you—an outside picture of your inward condition (T-21.in.1:5). The world then becomes helpful and peaceful, because it serves a peaceful purpose.

(2:1-3) Again we come to the question of judgment. This time ask yourself whether your judgment or the Word of God is more likely to be true. For they say different things about the world, and things so opposite that it is pointless to try to reconcile them.

If we are completely honest, our answer to Jesus' question about whose judgment "is more likely to be true" would be "Mine!"—because we certainly think we exist here. Yet the Word of God says we are not here. How could we be nowhere? How could we be an illusion? We need to recognize our opposition to God, the Holy Spirit, Jesus, and this course, for we continually argue with Them, whether conscious of it or not. Whenever we see differences as significant, and give power to something in this world to upset us or make us happy, we challenge Jesus and tell him we are right and he is wrong. He teaches that nothing here is significant, with power to make us happy or sad; in fact, *nothing is here*. Moreover, *A Course in Miracles* says things so opposite to what the world holds as true "that it is pointless to try to reconcile them." The world's religions, for example, attempt to reconcile mutually exclusive states—Heaven and the world, spirit and matter, God and rituals or commandments, unity and exclusion, love and attack—which is impossible. Yet the Course teaches that this is what we attempt all the time.

(2:4-5) God offers the world salvation; your judgment would condemn it. God says there is no death; your judgment sees but death as the inevitable end of life.

Our judgment sees death as the inevitable end of life because our thought system says sin deserves punishment. We hold to this because it is imperative that sin be accorded reality, for this confirms the reality of the separation.

(2:6) God's Word assures you that He loves the world; your judgment says it is unlovable.

Ideas leave not their source, and so the idea of sin and guilt has never left its source in the mind. This world—the projected ego thought—must therefore be a place of sin and guilt, and intrinsically unlovable. If we were to choose the Atonement in our minds, however, we would see it reflected in a world wherein everything would be seen differently. We would learn to love everyone and everything, not because of their form, but because we would realize their inherent unity and see them as parts of the same split-off and fragmented Sonship.

(2:7-9) Who is right? For one of you is wrong. It must be so.

If the Holy Spirit is right, there not only is no world, there is no *I*. If we are going to preserve our individual identity, therefore, it is incumbent on us to prove we are right and He is wrong. This is why we all have authority problems and stubbornly cling to our points of view. We need to convince others that we are right, whether it is about something trivial or of consequence. Our obstinacy has nothing to do with the issue at hand, but with what it *symbolizes* —the fundamental argument with God: if You are right, I cease to exist; if I am right, You disappear. The world's purpose, thus, is to provide us with ongoing opportunities to prove the correctness of our position.

(3:1-3) The text explains that the Holy Spirit is the Answer to all problems you have made. These problems are not real, but that is meaningless to those who believe in them. And everyone believes in what he made, for it was made by his believing it.

We believe in the ego thought system, the cornerstone of which is that the separation from God is real. The world is the projection of this belief, which is what makes the ego and its world so real to us. Once that belief is withdrawn, however, the thought system will disappear back "into the nothingness from which it came" (M-13.1:2). This is why the ego strategy is to keep us mindless. If we do not know we have a mind, the beliefs we have chosen remain out of awareness and we continue to believe in the ego, unable to change thought systems. It is this change we fear, and thus we tenaciously hold to our opinions and judgments, not because of them *per se*, but because of the separation they represent.

(3:4-6) Into this strange and paradoxical situation,—one without meaning and devoid of sense, yet out of which no way seems possible,—God has sent His Judgment to answer yours. Gently His Judgment substitutes for yours. And through this substitution is the un-understandable made understandable.

God's Judgment is that His Son is guiltless and innocent. Nothing has changed—"not one note in Heaven's song was missed" (T-26.V.5:4)—and the Holy Spirit is the mind's symbolic reminder of that happy Fact.

(3:7-9) How is peace possible in this world? In your judgment it is not possible, and can never be possible. But in the Judgment of God what is reflected here is only peace.

In our judgment, peace is not possible because of the thought of separation—the conflict between God and His Son. The world arose from this thought and has never ceased to be this thought. As long as we adhere to it, therefore, peace is impossible. Yet in the Judgment of God there *is* no conflict—only His Love. Hence, it is not that peace is possible; it is certain because the Atonement is certain. Indeed, God's Love is the only Certainty.

(4:1) Peace is impossible to those who look on war.

The greatest insanity of all—now and throughout history—is that peace can be attained by waging war. War merely reinforces the thoughts that caused it: separation, division, *one or the other*, victim and victimizer. Moreover, this thought system plays out again and again. This is why the peace that ends one war sows the seeds for the next, and the next after that. It will always be thus, and only the arrogant and naive believe peace is achieved through war. In point of fact, the only reason for war is to ensure that there will never be peace.

You can tell the meaning of a situation by its outcome. If war breeds conflict, hatred, and more war, we must conclude that this is why it was waged in the first place. This, then, is the crux of the ego's thought system, for it thrives on conflict and seeks to perpetuate it. This is not just the case in world affairs, but in people's personal affairs as well—as long as the mind's allegiance is with the ego. Without conflict there would be only the oneness in which all Sons are the same, and so there would be no competing interests in which one seeks to triumph over another. The resultant peace means the end of the ego.

(4:2) Peace is inevitable to those who offer peace.

If you choose peace in your mind, peace is all you offer and all you receive. Just as healing is certain and need not be repeated, peace is certain when you identify with its certainty in your mind—the presence of love that is outside time and space.

(4:3-5) How easily, then, is your judgment of the world escaped! It is not the world that makes peace seem impossible. It is the world you see that is impossible.

The world we see is impossible because it literally cannot exist: an illusory thought of separation leading to a world of separation can never be. Thus, it is not that peace is impossible; war is. Again, this makes no sense from the linear perspective of the battleground. However, it makes perfect sense when we look with Jesus from above. Through his mind's eye we have a holographic view of insanity, and perceive it is not good or bad—insanity is insanity; an hallucination is an hallucination. Whether we see a hot-fudge sundae or a nuclear war, illusions remain what they are. Looking down on this battleground, therefore, we can only smile kindly and let the mind's love extend to embrace all minds that hold thoughts of war, gently reminding them that what they see, do, and interact with has no effect—nothing has changed; nothing has hurt or destroyed love.

(4:6-9) Yet has God's Judgment on this distorted world redeemed it and made it fit to welcome peace. And peace descends on it in joyous answer. Peace now belongs here, because a Thought of God has entered. What else but a Thought of God turns hell to Heaven merely by being what it is?

The Thought of God is the Atonement, and peace belongs here because we have joined with His Judgment. Once joined, it is in the mind where it has always been, and will be extended and perceived. Jesus' point is that peace has nothing to do with the world as we judge it with our eyes, but only with how we perceive it in our minds.

(4:9-12) What else but a Thought of God turns hell to Heaven merely by being what it is? The earth bows down before its gracious Presence, and it leans down in answer, to raise it up again. Now is the question different. It is no longer, "Can peace be possible in this world?" but instead, "Is it not impossible that peace be absent here?"

These words are understandable only from within the holy instant, where we stand with Jesus outside the world of time and space, smiling at the illusion. On the battleground there is nothing to smile about, for the world is a hateful place where "starved and thirsty creatures come to die" (W-pII.13.5:1), and in the process attempt to kill off everyone else. As Jesus told Helen in the early weeks of the scribing, "the thing to do with a desert is to leave"*—not irrigate it or plant beautiful flowers. The thing to do with a battleground, therefore, is to leave, without trying to improve the world's desert by solving its conflicts with alliances, wars, and peace treaties that will never work. Instead, we go to the mind's Thought of God, in Whose perfect peace everyone's interest is the same, reflecting the Oneness of Christ's Self. From above the battleground, therefore, we look at the world through His vision, and no longer see enemies and allies, but friends calling for the love they believe they have thrown away. Our function, then, as teachers of God is to demonstrate that the love the world believes is undeserved is truly there. We thus become the living symbol of Heaven's Love, as is Jesus, and in that demonstration, peace becomes not only possible but reality.

---

* *Absence from Felicity*, p. 236.

12. HOW MANY TEACHERS OF GOD ARE NEEDED TO SAVE THE WORLD?

This section helps students get past the hundredth-monkey concept, which would mean that a certain number of people are needed to save the world. This quantifiable view of salvation can lead students to believe that the world has to be made aware of *A Course in Miracles* at the hands of proselytizing teachers and churches in a vigorous attempt to "get the word out," without realizing there is nothing out there to get the word to. It is not that you get the word out, *you accept the Word in*. The confusion between mind and body is a primary factor in this misdirected zeal, as exemplified by what we have seen of the ego's attempts to reconcile what cannot be reconciled: form with content, mind with body/world. Again, *the world does not have to be saved because there is no world*.

The answer to this question is given at the beginning—only *one* teacher of God is needed to save the world, and this one is *you*. When you have accepted the Atonement for yourself—not just an intellectual acceptance but an internal integration—there is only one Son. Not a hundred, five hundred, or six billion. *One*. Your being saved, therefore, heals the Sonship and the projected world along with it. This "one" does not exclusively mean Jesus, although he is an obvious example, but all of us. To say it another way, *A Course in Miracles* was written for one person—*you*, and when your mind is healed, the *you* becomes *You*. This section, then, returns us to the important theme of the distinction between mind and body.

(1:1-3) The answer to this question is—one. One wholly perfect teacher, whose learning is complete, suffices. This one, sanctified and redeemed, becomes the Self Who is the Son of God.

Remember, there was only one Son who believed in the thought system of separation, which was chosen instead of the thought system of Atonement. Therefore, the only valid difference in this world is between the ego's judgmental hate and the Holy Spirit's forgiving Love. Within each system all is the same, for each Son of God is the same. In the end, his sameness blends into One.

(1:4-6) He who was always wholly spirit now no longer sees himself as a body, or even as in a body. Therefore he is limitless. And being limitless, his thoughts are joined with God's forever and ever.

God's perfect Son is now outside the dream of time and space, and in the final holy instant he unites as one with the One—a "Oneness joined as One" (T-25.I.7:1).

(1:7-10) His perception of himself is based upon God's Judgment, not his own. Thus does he share God's Will, and bring His Thoughts to still deluded minds. He is forever one, because he is as God created him. He has accepted Christ, and he is saved.

God's judgment is that His Son is innocent, guiltless, and unseparated, which means He remains as God created Him. The way you "bring His Thoughts to still deluded minds" is by doing nothing. Minds are already joined, and so you do not have to bring the Thoughts anywhere. By accepting the thought of Atonement, it is carried around the world throughout the mind of God's one Son. You represent the Alternative and embody Its thought, meaning that your presence in another's dream symbolizes the same thought that is in him, asking that he make the choice you have made. Each of us has the potential to be that one teacher to each other.

(2:1) Thus does the son of man become the Son of God.

The biblical phrase *son of man* is used infrequently in the Course, referring only to the Son of God in his separated state, even though very often the term *Son of God* refers to the separated Son as well. Interestingly, the New Testament writers used *son of man* to denote Jesus. The point here is that we shift from the wrong-minded to the right-minded self, which will disappear into what always was—the one Christ.

(2:2-3) It is not really a change; it is a change of mind. Nothing external alters, but everything internal now reflects only the Love of God.

This echoes "Are Changes Required in the Life Situation of God's Teachers?" where the answer was that only a change of *mind* is needed, not

12. How Many Teachers of God Are Needed to Save the World?

anything external (M-9). The answer also reflects what Jesus teaches in the text—our purpose is not to change the world or its people, but only the way we perceive them (T-21.in.1:7). "Nothing external alters"—the curriculum of *A Course in Miracles* is not about doing things in the world, but learning to forgive. Why would we want to change illusions? We but change our teacher and the thought system we made real.

(2:4) God can no longer be feared, for the mind sees no cause for punishment.

If I am not separated I have not sinned, which means I am not guilty and do not believe I deserve punishment. Thus God is no longer perceived as the object of my sin of separation; no longer the Enemy Who will wreak vengeance on my "innocent" head. The ego's insane system simply dissolves into nothingness.

(2:5-9) God's teachers appear to be many, for that is what is the world's need. Yet being joined in one purpose, and one they share with God, how could they be separate from each other? What does it matter if they then appear in many forms? Their minds are one; their joining is complete. And God works through them now as one, for that is what they are.

There is the illusion of many because we believe God's Son is fragmented into trillions of pieces; yet we have never ceased to be His one Son. Jesus speaks in the text of the multitudinous forms of the original substitution, saying they remain the one Son who collectively believed he separated (T-18.I.4:3). What we conceive as the fragmented Sonship in the world can be compared to one huge multiple personality—split-off insane parts of one insane self. Yet as we return to the Self, we realize we are not fragmented Sons with fragmented goals. This important theme runs through the manual as a variation of our first theme of shared interests. God's Sons are one in nature and purpose, despite the appearance of differentiated selves with different needs and different pathways home. In the end, however, every message of salvation is the same: God's Son is guiltless.

Advanced teachers of God are given many names; however, in reality they are the same. As we will see much later on our journey through the manual, Jesus says Christ is known in different forms, but there remains only One (C-5.1:3-5). We have the illusion of many teachers because our needs appear different, and so God's Word comes in a form we can accept, recognize, and believe in. Yet it is not the *form* of the Word, nor the *specific* teacher that is important, but the underlying *content* of love —the Thought of Atonement.

(3:1-2) Why is the illusion of many necessary? Only because reality is not understandable to the deluded.

Reality is one. However, as we have seen, a "Oneness joined as One" cannot be understood here. Therefore, It needs to communicate in ways understandable to us: the ways of different bodies and teachings. The challenge is not to make these differences significant. Religions typically fall into that mistake, which is why they end up filled with hatred that seeks to justify itself, taking different expressions of the single message of Atonement and proclaiming them as *the* message. Recall the important statement in the manual that there are thousands of forms of the universal course: God's Son is guiltless (M-1.4:1-2;1.3:5). However those words are conveyed, we are one. Nothing has happened to change this inherent oneness and single purpose. Since we cannot understand this Oneness, we need the illusion of the many.

Now comes another humbling line:

(3:3-6) Only very few can hear God's Voice at all, and even they cannot communicate His messages directly through the Spirit which gave them. They need a medium through which communication becomes possible to those who do not realize that they are spirit. A body they can see. A voice they understand and listen to, without the fear that truth would encounter in them.

"Only very few can hear God's Voice" because only very few can be egoless. You cannot hear God's Voice if you listen to the voice of specialness, for it is *one Voice or the other*. Yet that Voice has to be expressed in a way people can understand, such as this course, Jesus' presence two thousand years ago, or that of any other advanced teacher. It is not the words, book, or body that are important, but what they symbolize. If there were no form, we would not be able to hear the Word because it is silent to us— a seemingly soundless Song, as we read:

> What answer that the Holy Spirit gives can reach you, when it is your specialness to which you listen, and which asks and answers? Its tiny answer, soundless in the melody that pours from God to you eternally in loving praise of what you are, is all you listen to. And that vast song of honor and of love for what you are seems silent and unheard before its "mightiness." You strain your ears to hear its soundless voice, and yet the Call of God Himself is soundless to you.
>
> You can defend your specialness, but never will you hear the Voice for God beside it (T-24.II.4:3–5:1).

Since we made words to keep us separate from God, the Holy Spirit has to use them to correct our mistake and return us to the wordless Presence of the One. We know we have been deceived by the ego if we think the form is holy or unholy, or if it establishes a difference between us and another, wherein interests are deemed to be separate.

(3:7-8) Do not forget that truth can come only where it is welcomed without fear. So do God's teachers need a body, for their unity could not be recognized directly.

In truth there is only one Son; a fact so fearful and terrifying—because it means the separation and its world are unreal—that it has to be presented to us in a physical form we can accept and understand. Again, do not be taken in by the external, although the universal message comes through specific bodies or teachings. If your understanding of a spiritual message leads you to make real the differences among the many forms, justifying your judgments, you know you are hearing falsely. Jesus' message only unifies, transcending differences in the many by seeing them as vehicles to the One.

(4:1) Yet what makes God's teachers is their recognition of the proper purpose of the body.

You do not deny the body, but shift the purpose your mind assigns to it. Rather than using the body to reinforce separation and justify separate interests, you use it now to learn that despite our seeming differences we are the same, sharing one interest and one goal.

(4:2) As they advance in their profession, they become more and more certain that the body's function is but to let God's Voice speak through it to human ears.

In other words, you have no investment other than getting yourself out of the way. You do not worry about the truth, you just seek and find the barriers— guilt, specialness, and sickness—you have placed between yourself and the truth (T-16.IV.6:1).

(4:3) And these ears will carry to the mind of the hearer messages that are not of this world, and the mind will understand because of their Source.

What truly attracts people to this course is not its language or even its teaching, but something immaterial, a palpable presence that comes through its pages. Many do not really understand what *A Course in Miracles* says, but nonetheless embrace and love it because they experience this egoless presence. Sometimes this same experience comes in the form of a specific person. We may not understand what is said or done, but we know there is something different about that person, and it is this we are attracted to. However, if we make that loving presence special and do not realize it is in ourselves as well, we have flown into the arms of specialness. Remember, we need the illusion of differences to learn there are no differences; the Holy Spirit needs the illusion of a separated body to teach there is no separation. We walk a fine line, for salvation can be a two-edged sword: it will save us, but if we choose the wrong teacher, distorting the meaning of salvation—confusing *form* with *content* —it will damn us.

(4:4-5) From this understanding will come the recognition, in this new teacher of God, of what the body's purpose really is; the only use there really is for it. This lesson is enough to let the thought of unity come in, and what is one is recognized as one.

Note how often the words *one* and *unity* appear, and how a common purpose underlies everything in this world.

(4:6) The teachers of God appear to share the illusion of separation, but because of what they use the body for, they do not believe in the illusion despite appearances.

Lesson 155 says you look like everyone else, the only difference being that you smile more frequently (W-pI.155.1). You dress, eat, and speak like others do, but there is an egoless peace that extends through you. You do not tell people how different you are from them, but they respond to your peace and love. You live in the body and the world, but you know you are not really there. When Jesus appeared two thousand years ago, he knew his reality was outside the world of bodies. That is why the gospel stories are essentially irrelevant, for they deal with his life here—*except he was not here*. The essence of Jesus' teachings quickly became lost in the confusion of *form* and *content*; the individual expression of truth instead of truth itself. Rather than letting the body lead them to the truth in the mind—universal and perfect oneness—the New Testament authors remained focused on the body, building religions around it. This mistake has been made by every formal religion; in fact, by everyone in the world.

To repeat, we live in the world like everyone else —looking and behaving normally—with the difference being that people perceive that the loving source of our lives is not of this world.

(5:1-4) The central lesson is always this; that what you use the body for it will become to you. Use it for sin or for attack, which is the same as sin, and you will see it as sinful. Because it is sinful it is weak, and being weak, it suffers and it dies. Use it to bring the Word of God to those who have it not, and the body becomes holy.

You *become* the purpose. If you use the body to maintain the belief that separation is real, it will be separate for you and will be seen as separate from everyone else's. *Purpose is everything.*

You are weak when you are sinful because you believe you have separated from God, Who is your only strength. Moreover, pitting yourself against the all-powerful Creator can only leave you puny and vulnerable in comparison. Believing your sin demands punishment for what you have done, you cannot but feel powerless in the face of such a threat and will ultimately suffer and die. The third chapter of Genesis graphically portrays God's punishment for Adam and Eve's original sin of disobedience: their offspring would be born in pain, suffer throughout their lives, and die. On the other hand, if the body is used to bring the Word of God to those who do not have it, it becomes holy. The body, of course, is not holy in itself—an illusion can be neither holy or unholy—but its holiness comes by serving the mind's right-minded purpose of forgiveness. *Purpose is everything.*

(5:5-6) Because it is holy it cannot be sick, nor can it die. When its usefulness is done it is laid by, and that is all.

These statements call to mind our discussion of the relationship between mind and body in the context of sickness and healing. Death is not of the body, for if something does not live it cannot die, and Jesus teaches us "There is no life outside of Heaven" (T-23.II.19:1). In our minds are both thoughts of death (we murdered God and deserve to be murdered in return) and life (the Atonement that says Life has never changed or been affected). The choice for the ego is the choice for death, mimicked by the body, the mimic of all thought. And so the body dies, for such is its source. Whether or not we believe in God, we unconsciously believe that death is our just desert because of what we have done. God will punish us; indeed, He has already punished us, for all things die, even the inanimate— rocks and wood rot over millennia, deteriorate, and end up ceasing to exist.

Yet there is another way of perceiving the body's end. When the mind is healed the body may look *as if* it were dying, but the mind has merely determined the completion of its Atonement work and the body is laid down. *The Song of Prayer* provides a beautiful account of the gentle passing into death:

> Yet there is a kind of seeming death that has a different source. It does not come because of hurtful thoughts and raging anger at the universe. It merely signifies the end has come for usefulness of body functioning. And so it is discarded as a choice, as one lays by a garment now outworn.
>
> This is what death should be; a quiet choice, made joyfully and with a sense of peace, because the body has been kindly used to help the Son of God along the way he goes to God (S-3.II.1:8–2:1).

Crucial here is the change of mind. The thought of life means God's Son is one and eternal, and so there can be no death. That healing thought teaches through us, and when teaching is done the need for the body is done as well. The world may attribute our death to physical causes, for only from above the battleground can the mind's purpose for death be understood.

(5:7) The mind makes this decision, as it makes all decisions that are responsible for the body's condition.

The mind is the decision-making agent, not the body. We do not die, therefore, because of natural laws—there are no natural laws in the world; only in the mind—the home of the Holy Spirit's Atonement that reflects Heaven's law of eternal life. We die because of an unnatural thought—the guilt that made the body mortal. Thus the myth of Adam and Eve that depicts the ego's birth, and God's as the ego's projection—a creator who believes in his creation's sin and punitively responds by destroying it, and then conceives a plan to save his children by further death. The myth's depiction of the ego's thought system explains the Bible's profound impact on the Western psyche. The biblical God's insane reactions —believing He can save His children by killing even one of them—are no different from heads of state believing they can find peace through waging war. No head of state invented such insanity, however; neither did the biblical authors. The ego did, and then invented a god to express its plan in action. Military and political leaders throughout history who thought they could bring peace through murder merely shadowed the mind's insane thought system. This is why nothing here will ever change until the ego thought changes, and only one person need do that—*you*.

(5:8-10) Yet the teacher of God does not make this decision alone. To do that would be to give the body another purpose from the one that keeps it holy. God's Voice will tell him when he has fulfilled his role, just as It tells him what his function is.

Function is *content*, but how it is expressed through us in *form* is not our concern, which is only choosing the miracle with the Holy Spirit's help. The miracle's extension, as the text explains, is not our responsibility (T-16.II.1).

(5:11-12) He does not suffer either in going or remaining. Sickness is now impossible to him.

It is neither burden or tragedy to remain here and die, because right-minded people know they are not here. In fact, they are no longer a *he* or *she*. How, then, could there be loss in remaining here?— "Sickness is now impossible to him." Physical symptoms may indeed appear, but sickness is only in the mind's belief in separation, guilt, and death.

(6:1) Oneness and sickness cannot coexist.

Now we understand why we embrace sickness, and why, as egos, we made the body to be vulnerable and mortal: to prove we are not part of God's perfect and eternal Oneness—we are right and He is wrong.

(6:2-5) God's teachers choose to look on dreams a while. It is a conscious choice. For they have learned that all choices are made consciously, with full awareness of their consequences. The dream says otherwise, but who would put his faith in dreams once they are recognized for what they are?

We are taught in *A Course in Miracles*, and it is especially clear in Lesson 136, that choices are made consciously (W-pI.136.1-6). Our being born, becoming ill, and dying are decisions of the mind, and just as quickly as they were made, we repressed our awareness because we wanted the responsibility to rest not within the mind, but in the body—ours or someone else's. The principal purpose of the Course and its miracle is to bring us back to the dream-making part of the mind—the decision maker— where we look at the dream and see it for what it is.

(6:6-11) Awareness of dreaming is the real function of God's teachers. They watch the dream figures come and go, shift and change, suffer and die. Yet they are not deceived by what they see. They recognize that to behold a dream figure as sick and separate is no more real than to regard it as healthy and beautiful. Unity alone is not a thing of dreams. And it is this God's teachers acknowledge as behind the dream, beyond all seeming and yet surely theirs.

Dreams are of separation, division, multiplicity, and differentiation, and are therefore not real. God's advanced teachers know this because their minds are outside the dream, looking back at it and seeing its absurdity. From this perspective no one could ever believe in the dream's reality, yet we need to become aware of our resistance to leaving it and returning to the mind. "Oneness and sickness cannot coexist," and we all want to be sick—after all, we are children of a god of sickness, and *ideas leave not their source*. Thinking of ourselves as egos, let alone as bodies, is a sickness, but one we eagerly choose because it keeps us from remembering our oneness—individual selves cannot exist in God's perfect Oneness.

We become advanced teachers of God when we are aware that nothing here means anything at all, as the early workbook lessons tell us. This awareness allows us to live in the world—*involved with people*—but not be affected by it. The peace and Love of God within us stand beyond all worldly events—seemingly horrific and evil—and therefore we recognize that nothing here has power over the mind. Thus we can be fully present to all people on the level of *content*, even as we relate to them on the level of *form*, for advanced teachers are aware of the mind's love beyond the body, the reflection of the reality that is outside the ego's dream of separation and hate.

13. WHAT IS THE REAL MEANING OF SACRIFICE?

Sacrifice is the bedrock of the ego's thought system, the inevitable consequence of its core principle of *one or the other*. The ego warns us that we will be forced into sacrifice and suffer grave loss if we take this journey with Jesus and practice his course: if we give up judgment we will lose; if we journey on to perfect Oneness, our very self will disappear. Our identity as individuals may indeed be a travesty of our true Identity, as we read in the text (T-24.VII.10:9), but it is *our* identity and we do not want to lose it. We thus believe in the reality of sacrifice, which Jesus now reinterprets for us:

(1:1-2) Although in truth the term sacrifice is altogether meaningless, it does have meaning in the world. Like all things in the world, its meaning is temporary and will ultimately fade into the nothingness from which it came when there is no more use for it.

Sacrifice is a meaningless term because in Heaven there is no loss. How can we lose everything when that is all there is, and we *are* everything? Sacrifice has meaning only because we think it serves the purpose of ego preservation, with which we identify. Otherwise it is nothing.

(1:3-4) Now its real meaning is a lesson. Like all lessons it is an illusion, for in reality there is nothing to learn.

Since what we learned within the illusion is wrong, we need to go through a process of *un*learning. Once this is accomplished, what remains does not have to be learned, because we will have simply remembered it.

(1:5-7) Yet this illusion must be replaced by a corrective device; another illusion that replaces the first, so both can finally disappear. The first illusion, which must be displaced before another thought system can take hold, is that it is a sacrifice to give up the things of this world. What could this be but an illusion, since this world itself is nothing more than that?

In order to learn that God is perfect Love, totally beyond the world of time and space, we first have to correct the ego thought that God is hate, fear, and vengeance. Sacrifice is such an integral part of our thought system that we cannot let it go without something first taking its place. Jesus' correction tells us that God is not angry—He loves us and loves the world. This, too, is an illusion; but it is a right-minded myth that undoes the ego's wrong-minded one, clearing the mind so the memory of God's Love can dawn upon it.

(2:1-3) It takes great learning both to realize and to accept the fact that the world has nothing to give. What can the sacrifice of nothing mean? It cannot mean that you have less because of it.

The valuelessness of the world is a familiar theme from both the text and workbook. As long as we think there is some value here, we will believe God is going to take it from us as punishment for our sin. That is what gives rise to the strange religious notion that God wants us to give up sex, certain foods, wealth, pleasure, and happiness, because these worldly things are judged as bad or sinful. Yet Jesus tells us there is nothing we need give up, because there is nothing here! Sacrifice, therefore, is the sacrifice of nothing, and how can we have less than nothing? What we give up are merely our misperceptions of guilt and separate interests. What could be of greater value than that?

(2:4-8) There is no sacrifice in the world's terms that does not involve the body. Think a while about what the world calls sacrifice. Power, fame, money, physical pleasure; who is the "hero" to whom all these things belong? Could they mean anything except to a body? Yet a body cannot evaluate.

The above quartet of items is borrowed from Freud's famous statement in his *Introductory Lectures on Psychoanalysis*: the artist is motivated by honor, power, wealth, fame, and the love of women. We could very well say we are all so motivated. Yet these things are meaningful only to a body—physical and psychological—which Jesus defines as the "hero" of every dream (T-27.VIII). However, a body cannot know what is best for itself because it does not exist, being nothing more than a puppet that carries out the dictates of the mind.

(2:9) By seeking after such things the mind associates itself with the body, obscuring its Identity and losing sight of what it really is.

Here in one sentence is a summary of the ego's strategy. The ego directs the mind to divest its identity and make itself mindless; the outcome being that we think we inhabit a body, ruled by a brain. Thus we crave the things of the body, believing it is sacrificial to give them up. In doing so we merely confirm the body's "reality," which renders the mind nonexistent. Thus, once again, if we do not have a mind we cannot change it, allowing our original decision for the ego to remain intact—what a brilliant success the ego's strategy has been!

(3:1) Once this confusion has occurred, it becomes impossible for the mind to understand that all the "pleasures" of the world are nothing.

We will not experience the world's pleasures as nothing as long as we identify with the body. Jesus is not saying we should deny pleasure, but asks only that we gently and slowly, step by step, examine the cause-effect relationship between a mind about which we still know nothing, and our bodies. He wants us to understand it is not the body that is attracted to pleasure nor feels pain, but the mind that directs the body's feelings. Our bodily identification makes resistance to taking these steps enormous, which is why the healing process needs to be gradual.

(3:2-3) But what a sacrifice,—and it is sacrifice indeed!—all this entails. Now has the mind condemned itself to seek without finding; to be forever dissatisfied and discontented; to know not what it really wants to find.

The ego's defining maxim is *Seek and do not find*—the reverse of the well-known statement in the Sermon on the Mount (Matthew 7:7-8). We want to find God—His peace and Love—but the ego has us look for Him in the body or the world, where He can never be found. However, the problem is not the world and its pleasures, enticements, or temptations—*there is no world!* The problem is in the mind's purpose of protecting, sustaining, and preserving its decision to be an ego, which our belief in the world's reality was made to serve. The decision for mindlessness is thus the problem.

(3:4-7) Who can escape this self-condemnation? Only through God's Word could this be possible. For self-condemnation is a decision about identity, and no one doubts what he believes he is. He can doubt all things, but never this.

Only through accepting the Atonement can we escape the condemnation of self-hatred, for its agony and anguish drive us into the world where we believe we truly exist. The idea that we can never doubt what we believe we are has long philosophical roots, Descartes probably being the most familiar to us. Since we do not doubt our belief in a separated self, the only reasonable approach is to make this self be comfortable, which to the ego means murder. Killing another—physically or psychologically—is the only thing we know that truly protects the self, because that is how it came into existence.

(4:1-4) God's teachers can have no regret on giving up the pleasures of the world. Is it a sacrifice to give up pain? Does an adult resent the giving up of children's toys? Does one whose vision has already glimpsed the face of Christ look back with longing on a slaughter house?

That is what Jesus thinks of this world and body of ours. As he says elsewhere, the world is a place "where starved and thirsty creatures come to die" (W-pII.13.5:1), to which we could add "come to kill," since the death of another constitutes our "life" —the only way the body lives is by ingesting something else, thereby destroying it. On both physical and psychological levels, we are all cannibals, and so were made. Indeed, the original ego thought was cannibalistic—I cannibalized the life and power of God, thus becoming God through sacrificing Him— and we are told in the text that we constantly relive that moment when terror took the place of love (T-26.V.13:1).

Who, knowing this, would want to stay here? Who would want to identify with the body, knowing it exists in a "slaughter house"? Who would want to play the sin-filled game of specialness, recognizing its harmfulness, referred to in the workbook as "sharp-edged children's toys" (W-pII.4.5:2)? The problem is we are not aware of any of this, and think life in the body is, to take Hamlet's famous words out of context, a consummation devoutly to be wished. We even think in our insanity that God is a member of homo sapiens, and that Jesus truly remains in some bodily form we can perceive. All this simply serves to justify our ego's self-perception as a body.

(4:5) No one who has escaped the world and all its ills looks back on it with condemnation.

If you have seen the world through Christ's vision, you neither hate nor love it, realizing its nothingness. How could you have a reaction to nothing? How could you be in nothing? Yet since we think we are something, this world must be something, too. That is why we need a "slowly evolving training program" to help us sever our identification with the nothingness we think is our self. What helps us do this with gentleness, kindness, and patience is shifting our perceptions of others, no longer seeing them as separate or different from us.

(4:6-10) Yet he must rejoice that he is free of all the sacrifice its values would demand of him. To them he sacrifices all his peace. To them he sacrifices all his freedom. And to possess them must he sacrifice his hope of Heaven and remembrance of his Father's Love. Who in his sane mind chooses nothing as a substitute for everything?

This is the question we need ask ourselves as we become aware of how identified we are with the world.

(5:1-4) What is the real meaning of sacrifice? It is the cost of believing in illusions. It is the price that must be paid for the denial of truth. There is no pleasure of the world that does not demand this, for otherwise the pleasure would be seen as pain, and no one asks for pain if he recognizes it.

Chapter 26 opens with "The 'Sacrifice' of Oneness"; the same sacrifice Jesus speaks of here. The real sacrifice is giving up our joy, freedom, hope, and life. By remaining with the ego, that is what we lose, and yet with Jesus we lose nothing—*literally* —for the world is nothing. Nonetheless, we continue to hold on to it, and by staying with nothing we lose Everything.

If we were really clear that holding on to judgments brings pain, and that letting go of them brings happiness, there would be no problem. The impediment is that we still believe pain is freedom because it means we exist. We do not recognize the cost to us of holding this belief, still confusing joy and pain, imprisonment and freedom (T-7.X; T-8.II). We think hating another is good and true forgiveness bad, because who would we be without our anger, judgments, conflicts, and wars? Who would we be without our bodies? And so we cling to the thought system of separate interests, and in the process sacrifice happiness and joy—not realizing the price we are paying.

(5:5-8) It is the idea of sacrifice that makes him blind. He does not see what he is asking for. And so he seeks it in a thousand ways and in a thousand places, each time believing it is there, and each time disappointed in the end. "Seek but do not find" remains this world's stern decree, and no one who pursues the world's goals can do otherwise.

The purpose of the world's goals is to reinforce the belief that the separation happened. To preserve that thought and keep it safe we have to remain in the body. Therefore, the ego has us seek for happiness, pleasure, and eternal life in the world—the attraction of the body—where we will never find them. The true meaning of sacrifice is that we give up the love Jesus holds out to us. In "The Gifts of God" (pp. 118-19), he asks us to bring to him the world's "cruel offerings" we have used to attack the Son of God, and in exchange he will give us God's gifts of love and peace. Yet Jesus cannot give us these if our hands are already filled with the ego's gifts. It is his purpose in the Course to help us realize the benefit *to us* of happily making the exchange of pain for peace, and hate for love:

(6:1-2) You may believe this course requires sacrifice of all you really hold dear. In one sense this is true, for you hold dear the things that crucify God's Son, and it is the course's aim to set him free.

A Course in Miracles does not demand that we sacrifice what we cherish and hold dear—hate, murder, specialness, loss, separation. But we believe that letting go of it will cost us, and so we need an elder brother to teach us the insanity of our thinking. The resistance to letting go of our self—the arrogant assertion that we are our bodies, strengthened by their relationships with other bodies in competition for love and attention—makes this course difficult, even though its teachings are so simple and straightforward.

(6:3-7) But do not be mistaken about what sacrifice means. It always means the giving up of what you want. And what, O teacher of God, is it that you want? You have been called by God and you have answered. Would you now sacrifice that Call?

Being called by God is not meant literally. The Holy Spirit's Presence in our minds is the meaning of "God's Call," and we have answered It to the extent to which we learn and practice this course. There is a part of us that truly wants to return home, even though we are not yet aware of what that means. That awareness is what we sacrifice by making the ego's thought system our own.

The call of the Atonement to awaken from the dream is our salvation, for this alone brings us happiness and peace. First, however, we have to be convinced that the ego's call—separation, individuality, and specialness—will not bring us anything we want. We may think we agree with this statement, and perhaps we do intellectually, but the fact that we still hold on to judgment and find practicing this course difficult—as our resistance builds—tells us there is a part of us that is still terrified. Remember, we made this world to escape from the burden of guilt in our minds. The guilt is made up, but we convinced ourselves of its reality and think if we let go of this world and are healed, we will be thrown back into the mind where an avenging God awaits us. Therefore, we have to remain in the body for protection, even though God will exact His vengeance regardless. Out of desperation we entertain the illusion that He may get us in our death, but will forgive us later because we have been good students of *A Course in Miracles*—we may die in the body, but will live on in the hereafter. All of this, of course, is the ego's subtle way of tricking us into remaining mindless and not returning to the source of the problem and its Answer.

(6:8-12) Few have heard it [the Call] as yet, and they can but turn to you. There is no other hope in all the world that they can trust. There is no other voice in all the world that echoes God's. If you would sacrifice the truth, they stay in hell. And if they stay, you will remain with them.

The underlying principle reflected here is our shared interests. If I turn away from God, I turn from everyone. That separation thought of joining with the ego reinforces every person's decision to be an ego. That is what makes special relationships so attractive. In these hymns of hate we participate in a death-filled dance in which we join together to kill the other off. Some do this over the span of sixty or seventy years of married life, reinforcing the shared belief they are unfairly-treated victims. Yet the way we see ourselves is the way we see the Sonship as a whole. Again, this does not mean our choices can affect others, but they do strengthen the choice they make. All are responsible for their own decisions, but these have no effect on those who have decided for the truth. We can strengthen that choice for others, but we must realize that what we do for one we do for all, including ourselves—the mind of God's Son is one.

(7:1-4) Do not forget that sacrifice is total. There are no half sacrifices. You cannot give up Heaven partially. You cannot be a little bit in hell.

This is a most important principle. You cannot have love and special love together, and so you cannot believe in God yet have Him believe in specialness, differences, and individuality. You cannot bring Heaven into hell, any more than you can bring hell into Heaven. However, you can bring hell *to* Heaven, which causes hell to dissolve in Its Presence. Likewise, God does not come into the world, and someone like Jesus was never truly here, even though he appeared to others who did not know the difference between mind and body. Likewise, *A Course in Miracles* did not come from this world. It appears here, but its source is the non-ego place of love outside the dream.

(7:5) The Word of God has no exceptions.

This is one line you want to remember. The Atonement excludes no one, for everyone seen through its eyes is the same—there are no exceptions to God's Love; no exceptions to the innocence of His Son.

(7:6-8) It is this that makes it holy and beyond the world. It is its holiness that points to God. It is its holiness that makes you safe.

The world is a place of separation, differences, and separate interests. The Atonement, therefore, must be outside the dream, if it is truly the correction. It is not God—because it corrects the ego's perception of separation, of which God knows nothing

—yet it reflects Heaven's Oneness. The Atonement makes no exceptions among the seemingly separated fragments—the *form*—seeing them as one—the *content*. This reflects the unity of God's one Son as spirit, in Whom there are no distinctions.

Importantly, the Atonement does not make your body safe. When you know you are not your body, what difference does the bodily state make? What makes you safe is knowing there is no sin, and therefore no punishment. Without a belief in punishment, there can be no experience of attack and suffering. The reason we suffer—and indeed why we made the body to suffer—is to prove that sin is real and does not rest in us, but in the person who inflicts the suffering. We are therefore safe within the all-inclusive holiness of Atonement because there is no sin, and so there can be no danger. Whatever seems to happen to our bodies has nothing to do with us as we truly are. That is why Christians, however sincere, began on the wrong foot when they focused on what happened to Jesus' body, not realizing it had nothing to do with him—his holiness was in his mind, united with our own. The Atonement is the journey back through the sin that never was, to the Holiness that has always been.

(7:9-13) It [the Atonement] is denied if you attack any brother for anything. For it is here the split with God occurs. A split that is impossible. A split that cannot happen. Yet a split in which you surely will believe, because you have set up a situation that is impossible. And in this situation the impossible can seem to happen. It seems to happen at the "sacrifice" of truth.

The Atonement says the separation from God—the original attack—never happened. Thus if I join with the Atonement, I cannot attack anyone. However, if I fear the Atonement—realizing I was wrong and God was right—all I need do is attack, because that attests to the reality of separation and differences: your interests are separate from mine, and therefore I am justified in attacking you, because I have no choice but to protect my self.

Therefore, truth has to be sacrificed and Oneness destroyed; God has to be extinguished if we are to exist. That is what we must see each and every time we choose the ego thought system and make judgments. Jesus asks us to consider whether we would really want our special relationship if we knew it was a triumph over God (T-16.V.10:1). If we truly recognized this each and every time we chose specialness, we would feel the horror inherent in that choice, along with its pain. This would motivate us to change our minds and let the ego go.

(8:1-3) Teacher of God, do not forget the meaning of sacrifice, and remember what each decision you make must mean in terms of cost. Decide for God, and everything is given you at no cost at all. Decide against Him, and you choose nothing, at the expense of the awareness of everything.

The importance of Jesus' words should not be overlooked. The only way we will be motivated to release the ego and take Jesus' hand is to realize the burdensome pain of holding onto our projected judgments and petty hates. Jesus urges us to see clearly the meaning of sacrifice—our willingness to throw away Heaven's Love for special love. There is no cost in deciding for God, but there is tremendous cost in deciding against Him and for the ego—we lose awareness of everything.

(8:4-6) What would you teach? Remember only what you would learn. For it is here that your concern should be.

What do you want to learn—separation or its undoing, to remain in hell or return to Heaven?

(8:7-10) Atonement is for you. Your learning claims it and your learning gives it. The world contains it not. But learn this course and it is yours.

Atonement is not for the world, nor for others; it is for *you*. When you accept the Atonement for yourself, as we have seen, the *you* becomes *You*. It is not found in the world nor its teachings, which are exclusively about separation and individuality. Learning this course thus means letting go of judgment. Twice we have been told that this is the heart of the curriculum, accomplished by realizing our cost in maintaining it. Holding on to the perception that you and I are separate has cost me the peace and Love of God. How willing am I now to make this sacrifice?

(8:11-12) God holds out His Word to you, for He has need of teachers. What other way is there to save His Son?

God does not really need teachers; the words reflect *our* need. Recall that one mind is all minds, and so when one mind is healed, the Sonship is healed. Therefore, the way I save God's Son and the world is to save myself, which I do by accepting the Atonement—God's Word. Without the belief in separation, I realize that everyone is part of the ego's insanity *and* part of the Holy Spirit's correction. Recognizing our shared mind is the requisite step for remembering we are part of the One Christ in Heaven. Thus do we teach and learn the truth of the Atonement, having unlearned the ego's meaning of sacrifice.

14. HOW WILL THE WORLD END?

In answering the question "How Will the World End?" Jesus addresses the fundamental unreality of the world. As we shall see, his primary message in this discussion is that the world can never end because it never began—the separation from God never happened, and therefore the world that appears so real must be illusory. This principle of the Atonement underlies the main objective of our work with *A Course in Miracles*—to shift our minds from seeing other people's interests as separate to seeing them as the same.

(1:1-3) Can what has no beginning really end? The world will end in an illusion, as it began. Yet will its ending be an illusion of mercy.

We see here a reference to the two levels on which the Course is written. Level One is the metaphysical —God alone is real, and everything else an illusion that does not exist because it never existed. Level Two reflects only the illusion—the right-minded correction for the wrong-minded thought system of the ego: shared interests correct the belief in separate interests. Thus the expression of mercy belongs to this second level, the home of forgiveness. The text tells us that we do not go directly from nightmares to awakening, for the ego's dreams are first replaced by the Holy Spirit's gentle dreams of forgiveness (T-27.VII.14).

(1:4) The illusion of forgiveness, complete, excluding no one, limitless in gentleness, will cover it [the world], hiding all evil, concealing all sin and ending guilt forever.

Jesus does not mean *hiding* and *concealing* in the sense that we see something terrible and pretend it is not there, or guiltily protect ourselves from shame. He means that forgiveness covers the world and so it disappears; its right-minded cover is the undoing, in contrast to the ego's cover that is denial. A key phrase here is "excluding no one"— one of the more prominent themes in *A Course in Miracles*: no one can be excluded from our forgiveness because God's Son is one. This becomes the basis of realizing that our interests and goals are the same; indeed, we *are* the same for we share the thought system of the ego, its correction by the Holy Spirit, and the power to choose between them. And so forgiveness, if it be true, must include everyone. It is that thought that heralds the end of the world, which began with the thought of separation and ends when that thought is undone. Forgiveness constitutes the gentle steps that lead us to accepting this happy truth.

(1:5-6) So ends the world that guilt had made, for now it has no purpose and is gone. The father of illusions is the belief that they have a purpose; that they serve a need or gratify a want.

Illusions serve our need to preserve the belief that we have an individual self that has separated from the Self of Christ. The world demonstrates the truth of that belief, making the self real in our experience: bodies, in which each one is separate and distinct from every other, proves the existence of the underlying thought we are separate and distinct from our Creator. That is the purpose of the world that guilt made, as Jesus points out by stating that the world is "the delusional system of those made mad by guilt" (T-13.in.2:2). Guilt drives sin into our unconscious minds, making us unaware of its presence and thrusting us into the world as protection from confronting the horror of what we believed we did to God. Guilt, thus, can be thought of as the father of illusions, insofar as it is their preserver. Incidentally, "the father of illusions" is a reference to the statement in John's gospel where Jesus refers to the Jewish people as sons of the devil, the father of all lies (John 8:44). Again, the fundamental illusion is that we have accomplished the impossible— separating from God. Sustaining that thought is the perception that we are separated from each other by separate needs. Because interests are not shared, our happiness must come at the expense of others, as must theirs at ours.

(1:7-8) Perceived as purposeless, they are no longer seen. Their uselessness is recognized, and they are gone.

Recall that purpose is everything, and as we have just seen, the purpose of illusions is to preserve our individual and special identities. The fundamental illusion as we experience it here is that we are separate from each other, and thus can attain salvation at

– 99 –

another's expense. This works not only in our world of personal relationships, but in the international arena as well where people have believed for millennia that peace is achieved through war—one wins, another loses. As previously discussed, the collective thought system of separation is the origin of this vicious insanity, for we began as one ego that fragmented, with each fragment carrying within it the principle of *one or the other*—individuality is preserved through separation from others, reinforcing our separation from God.

When we no longer share the ego's purpose, having chosen instead to share the Holy Spirit's purpose to awaken from the dream and return to the Oneness of God, illusions are unnecessary and will disappear. The illusion of a world fades because it is not the external that keeps it alive in our awareness—there *is* nothing external. The world is maintained by our belief in it, which is nourished by the underlying need to be in a world and body, for this keeps God away and preserves our individual selves.

(1:9-11) How but in this way are all illusions ended? They have been brought to truth, and truth saw them not. It merely overlooked the meaningless.

This does not mean that you deny the illusion—what your physical eyes see in the world. You deny that it has any effect on you by denying the ego's interpretation of what your eyes see. Thus you bring the illusion of separate interests to the truth of shared interests. This helps you realize how happy you become when you set judgment aside. Once again, with their purpose gone, illusions disappear as well.

(2:1) Until forgiveness is complete, the world does have a purpose.

The Holy Spirit's purpose for the world is that it be a classroom in which we learn forgiveness. The ultimate lesson is that there is no one to forgive because there is no world. In this sense, as long as we think we are here the world serves a mighty purpose: to recognize we are not separate from each other, which means we are not separate from God—His Word of Atonement.

(2:2-3) It becomes the home in which forgiveness is born, and where it grows and becomes stronger and more all-embracing. Here is it nourished, for here it is needed.

This reflects what we saw in the first paragraph—forgiveness excludes no one and embraces all. If a single person is excluded from the Sonship, all are excluded because Christ is whole. Forgiveness is nourished by the decision to have Jesus present us with the world's real purpose: to teach there is no world by denying the ego's purpose of separation.

(2:4-5) A gentle Savior, born where sin was made and guilt seemed real. Here is His home, for here there is need of Him indeed.

Forgiveness is the "gentle Savior," and its process is often expressed in the symbol of a little child or infant that needs to be nourished as it grows: e.g., "Christ is reborn as but a little Child each time a wanderer would leave his home" (W-pI.182.10:1); "here is the babe of Bethlehem reborn" (T-19.IV-C.10:8). What grows and strengthens is our commitment to the heart of the Holy Spirit's teaching: the shared interests of the Sonship.

Each time we choose the ego, we have to correct our mistake and again choose the reality of Christ. This choice is expressed in the willingness to see our interests as not separate from another's, reflecting the Oneness of our true Self.

(2:6-7) He brings the ending of the world with Him. It is His Call God's teachers answer, turning to Him in silence to receive His Word.

The silence has nothing to do with anything verbal, for it is the silencing of the ego thought system. Turning away from the ego's raucous shrieking, we hear the still, small voice of the Holy Spirit.

(2:8-10) The world will end when all things in it have been rightly judged by His judgment. The world will end with the benediction of holiness upon it. When not one thought of sin remains, the world is over.

Ending the ego's judgment—a variation of our theme of shared interests—is a returning focus of the manual, as is the all-inclusive nature of forgiveness: "not one thought of sin remains" echoes Jesus' lovely vision in the text, "not one spot of darkness still remains to hide the face of Christ from anyone" (T-31.VIII.12:5). Forgiveness thus embraces all, ending the thought of sin without which there can be no separation from God. Since the world arose from separation and has never left its source, there can be no world—forgiveness has quietly brought it to an end.

(2:11-12) It will not be destroyed nor attacked nor even touched. It will merely cease to seem to be.

Note the crucial last sentence—the world will "cease to seem to be." It never had being. The text distinguishes between *existence* and *being*, wherein the latter is of God—as spirit—and the former of the ego. The world never existed in reality; it only seemed to, and so will simply "cease to seem to be." None of this makes sense, as we have observed, from the world's perspective; i.e., trying to understand these words with a brain mediated through physical and psychological experience. This teaching is meaningful only when we are with Jesus in the mind above the battleground, looking down on the world from outside time and space, no longer bound to the body nor its needs.

(3:1-3) Certainly this seems to be a long, long while away. "When not one thought of sin remains" appears to be a long-range goal indeed. But time stands still, and waits on the goal of God's teachers.

When you identify with this worldly existence of time and space, the world's end seems almost impossible. How can billions choose to have their minds healed and let all this go? Thus Jesus says that "time stands still"—the atemporal holy instant when we choose against the ego and for the Holy Spirit.

(3:4) Not one thought of sin will remain the instant any one of them accepts Atonement for himself.

This restates one of the core themes in *A Course in Miracles*: accepting the Atonement for ourselves is our one responsibility. When we forgive totally, sin is gone and the mind is healed. There is no longer a thought of separation, which means God's Son is one—as he always was—notwithstanding the ego's mad and feverish dreams of sin. That is why only *one* teacher of God is needed to save the world—any *one* student of this course.

(3:5-6) It is not easier to forgive one sin than to forgive all of them. The illusion of orders of difficulty is an obstacle the teacher of God must learn to pass by and leave behind.

This refers to the first principle of miracles—there is no order of difficulty among them (T-1.I.1:1). All problems of sin are the same, as are all expressions of forgiveness. Thoughts come from the ego's judgment or the Holy Spirit's forgiveness, and there is no hierarchy within them—the central theme of *A Course in Miracles*.

(3:7-9) One sin perfectly forgiven by one teacher of God can make salvation complete. Can you understand this? No; it is meaningless to anyone here.

Jesus reiterates this point throughout the Course, telling us in different ways that we cannot understand his words if we seek understanding through our brains, which have been programmed by the ego to think linearly and spatially. The teachings of *A Course in Miracles* can be grasped only by transcending the intellect and going beyond the brain, looking at the world with Jesus from the atemporal and non-spatial mind.

(3:10-11) Yet it is the final lesson in which unity is restored. It goes against all the thinking of the world, but so does Heaven.

Jesus tells us tactfully we are insane because we think we are here. We think we have eyes that read words, a brain that understands, and a body that puts *A Course in Miracles* into practice. Yet all this is simply a projection of the mind's thought of separation, which can be corrected by extending the Holy Spirit's thought of forgiveness.

(4:1-2) The world will end when its thought system has been completely reversed. Until then, bits and pieces of its thinking will still seem sensible.

Thus: we can typically forgive some things, but not all; we believe in peace, but war is sometimes necessary; we love everyone, but there are certain people we cannot tolerate; if our parents had been different, we would not be in the miserable state we are today and would not need this course; nothing affects us except....

(4:3) The final lesson, which brings the ending of the world, cannot be grasped by those not yet prepared to leave the world and go beyond its tiny reach.

This includes all of us who still identify with the body, and therefore want spirituality and forgiveness to work *here*, where we want Jesus to be. Yet he tells us there is no *here*, for the world is only a projection of the thought of separation. Choosing to see our interests as separate and apart from others is the shadowy fragment of this original thought. However, asking for help to see our shared interests—for we are all in the same ego boat with the same need to leave it—reflects the Holy Spirit's Atonement principle that the separation from God never happened. Thus we realize that healing does not occur in the nonexistent world or body, but only in the mind.

(4:4-5) What, then, is the function of the teacher of God in this concluding lesson? He need merely learn how to approach it; to be willing to go in its direction.

A little willingness is all Jesus asks of us. We need not respond perfectly, but merely have the willingness to forgive and change our thinking.

(4:6-8) He need merely trust that, if God's Voice tells him it is a lesson he can learn, he can learn it. He does not judge it either as hard or easy. His Teacher points to it, and he trusts that He will show him how to learn it.

Once again we find the all-important second theme of the manual: reliance on the Holy Spirit's help. A common trap that students fall into is thinking: "This is too difficult. There is so much hatred and judgment in me and in others, how can we ever get past it?" Or students take the blissninny approach and say: "This is so easy. All I do is ask the Holy Spirit for help, and my judgments and specialness disappear." Yet Jesus cautions that we should not think of his course as hard *or* easy. We are simply to go to him every time we are tempted to see separation instead of oneness, and join his gentle smile as we remember to laugh at the *tiny, mad idea* of believing we could be separate from God or His Son.

(5:1-6) The world will end in joy, because it is a place of sorrow. When joy has come, the purpose of the world has gone. The world will end in peace, because it is a place of war. When peace has come, what is the purpose of the world? The world will end in laughter, because it is a place of tears. Where there is laughter, who can longer weep?

All this is possible because it takes place in the mind where we can choose sorrow or joy, war or peace, tears or the gentle laughter that says the ego is simply silly, with no effect upon reality.

(5:7) And only complete forgiveness brings all this to bless the world.

Complete forgiveness is the end of the learning process of seeing our interests as not separate from anyone else's. There are no true differences within the Sonship—superficial differences of *form*, yes, but none in *content*. Once again, we share the ego's insanity, the Holy Spirit's sanity, and the power to choose one or the other. When we come to recognize there are no differences among us, all judgment is gone. This complete forgiveness ends the world for us, which means the world is gone.

(5:8) In blessing it departs, for it will not end as it began.

The world began in guilt, fear, and hate, and ends as the blessing of forgiveness gently falls upon it.

(5:9) To turn hell into Heaven is the function of God's teachers, for what they teach are lessons in which Heaven is reflected.

As we saw in the opening pages of the manual, Jesus does not speak of anything behavioral, saying that his lessons are taught through the peace we have accepted within, described in "The Function of the Teacher of God" (M-5.III). We simply demonstrate the change of mind that others are free to make. Heaven's truth is perfect Oneness, reflected by not seeing differences among the Sonship, which removes all justification for anger and judgment.

(5:10-12) And now sit down in true humility, and realize that all God would have you do you can do. Do not be arrogant and say you cannot learn His Own curriculum. His Word says otherwise.

How can I not learn the truth, which is already in me? How can I not learn the truth, since it is who I am?

(5:13-15) His Will be done. It cannot be otherwise. And be you thankful it is so.

Recall again that none of what we have discussed will make sense if we reflect on it in the context of our personal and worldly experience. Jesus' teachings are meaningful only from the mind's quiet center, our home away from home. From there we look through his eyes and smile upon the ego's special world, and in his gentle kindness the world comes softly to an end.

15. IS EACH ONE TO BE JUDGED IN THE END?

God's Final Judgment is the subject of this section, and the discussion rests on the Atonement principle that says nothing happened: God's perfect Oneness has never changed, and nothing outside It exists. We share in God's Judgment by not perceiving separation anywhere in the Sonship and, as we continue to see, this theme of oneness underlies our journey through the manual.

(1:1) Indeed, yes!

Each of us is to be judged in the end, but not as the world conceives it, nor, indeed, as the Bible does; see, for example, the oft-cited parable of the last judgment when God saves the sheep and punishes the goats (Matthew 25:21-45). The final judgment Jesus speaks of here is not his return on clouds of glory to judge the living and the dead, but the judgment inherent in God's living and loving Oneness—of which we are an intrinsic part—that says: "You are still my beloved Son, for not one note in Heaven's song is missed. Nothing has changed eternal love."

(1:2) No one can escape God's Final Judgment.

This is not a threat. Discussed in both the text and the workbook (T-2.VIII.2-5; W-pII.10.3-5), this theme of God's Final Judgment holds an important place in the Course's thought system. It corrects the world's conception of the Creator that is rooted in the belief in guilt, which demands that God judge and severely punish His sinful children, a belief that Jesus gently corrects.

(1:3-4) Who could flee forever from the truth? But the Final Judgment will not come until it is no longer associated with fear.

Believing in God's avenging wrath, we fear His Love. Yet the text teaches that we are really afraid that in the redemptive Presence of His Love, our special individuality would be gone, having no place in God's Wholeness (T-13.III). Thus as long as we seek to preserve our unique self, we reinforce the belief that we have sinned against our Creator. The guilt that inevitably follows demands our punishment, and makes it impossible to think of God as a loving Father, since He is perceived as the avenging enemy. This perception is projected in the magical hope of relieving the mind's anguish, leading us to perceive that others are our enemies, too. Whether we talk about microorganisms that cause disease, or macroorganisms—governments or people in our personal life—out to hurt us, we believe that evil is intent on our destruction because we accuse ourselves of the evil intent of destroying God.

(1:5-6) One day each one will welcome it, and on that very day it will be given him. He will hear his sinlessness proclaimed around and around the world, setting it free as God's Final Judgment on him is received.

When Jesus speaks this way—"around and around the world"—he does not mean it literally since there is no world in which to go around. When we have accepted peace and love within the mind, it travels around the world because *ideas leave not their source* and the mind of God's Son is one. That is why we were with Jesus when he awakened from the dream of death (M-23.6:9-10; C-6.5:5), proclaiming the sinlessness of God's Son. The unified mind of the Sonship *is* the world, which is redeemed when we accept God's Final Judgment as the truth.

(1:7-9) This is the Judgment in which salvation lies. This is the Judgment that will set him free. This is the Judgment in which all things are freed with him.

Not some—*all*. Remember, there is no hierarchy of illusions. Everything here has become a repository for our projected guilt. *Everything.* That is why, if we have not forgiven totally and released our guilt, we will continually project the ego. We may think some people are good and others bad, but unconsciously we must hate everyone and everything as long as any hatred is retained in our minds.

(1:10-12) Time pauses as eternity comes near, and silence lies across the world that everyone may hear this Judgment of the Son of God:

> *Holy are you, eternal, free and whole, at peace forever in the Heart of God. Where is the world, and where is sorrow now?*

"Holy are you, eternal, free and whole, at peace forever in the Heart of God" is the Final Judgment;

the principle of the Atonement chosen in the holy instant. As God's one Son, we fled in fear from His Heart in the original instant, which was born of the need to preserve the individual, separated self. That is why we chose against this Judgment by choosing the ego's; namely, that we achieved the impossible and thus exist, and—through projection—it is God's fault. Jesus' words here correct the ego's insanity, because in reality God does not judge. Indeed, there is no God as we think of Him—a person Who reacts to our sin. And so to speak of God's Judgment is to correct the ego's definition, which teaches that God will destroy us for our unholiness and the only place to be safe is in the mindless world that, in answer to the above question, is truly nowhere.

(2:1-4) Is this your judgment on yourself, teacher of God? Do you believe that this is wholly true? No; not yet, not yet. But this is still your goal; why you are here.

Jesus in effect tells us: "Do not pretend you are in the real world; do not pretend you do not have an ego, for otherwise you would have no need for this course. I know you are not ready to accept God's Judgment, and so I offer *A Course in Miracles* to help you take the little steps of forgiveness that will undo your guilt, so you will finally be able to accept God's Love and return home."

(2:5-7) It is your function to prepare yourself to hear this Judgment and to recognize that it is true. One instant of complete belief in this, and you will go beyond belief to Certainty. One instant out of time can bring time's end.

It is our function to forgive, which helps us to prepare. In other words, we are asked to be aware of our need to see our interests as separate from others. We can then go to Jesus, and say and mean: "Please help me, I am looking at this wrongly because I am not seeing the Sonship as all inclusive." Jesus' response is to help us recognize that the division and judgments we have made real outside and sought to justify are projections of our self-hatred, originating in the illusion that we separated from God. It is this daily practice of bringing our illusions to Jesus' truth—one holy instant after another—that helps us walk through time to eternity, through belief to the Certainty of God.

(2:8) Judge not, for you but judge yourself, and thus delay this Final Judgment.

When we judge others and seek to justify our judgments, we but project the judgment of ourselves. Yet we will not know this because our attention is riveted on the sins of others—the "attraction of guilt" (T-19.IV-A.i). We want to see guilt in another so we do not have to look at it in ourselves. However, if we do not realize it is in *our* mind it will remain there, continuing to generate perceptions of separation, hatred, and judgment, thus preventing our hearing and accepting God's loving Judgment of our innocence.

(2:9-11) What is your judgment of the world, teacher of God? Have you yet learned to stand aside and hear the Voice of Judgment in yourself? Or do you still attempt to take His role from Him?

This is our second important theme: the role of the Holy Spirit—a role our egos patently do not like. We therefore usurp His role because we think we can do a better job of judging, a better job of saving the world and purifying it of sin. This, of course, is nothing less than the ego's strategy to have us project what we think is our darkened guilt within, see it outside, and then attack it so we do not have to deal with it in the mind, which would lead to its undoing.

(2:12) Learn to be quiet, for His Voice is heard in stillness.

This unveils the ego's reason for the mind's raucous shrieks—the chatter of our need for specialness and the hate-filled sounds of war. In fact, we are always at war—as individuals or nation states—the din of battle that drowns out the still, small Voice that speaks of the unity of God's Son. Our shared need is to learn to silence the ego's screams of hate and separate interests, which we do by recognizing the ego's caustic voice as *our* decision. Jesus lends us his ears that we may listen and choose again.

(2:13) And His Judgment comes to all who stand aside in quiet listening, and wait for Him.

Everyone has the still, small Voice within. Choose your favorite symbol of evil and know that God's Voice still speaks in that person, as It speaks in you. If you doubt this, it is only because you do not want to hear It. Denying Its Presence in another reflects your fear of hearing it in yourself. As long as you hold to your misperceptions, you will not hear God's loving Judgment, the ego's real terror.

(3:1) You who are sometimes sad and sometimes angry; who sometimes feel your just due is not given you, and your best efforts meet with lack of appreciation and even contempt; give up these foolish thoughts!

Jesus could have easily gone on to describe our addiction to specialness, but this certainly covers it. His response to our need to be unfairly treated and wear the face of innocence is that it is not sinful or evil—just foolish, for it keeps us from hearing the Voice that reminds us of God's Final Judgment. There is thus nothing to atone for or feel guilty about, and therefore no need to have a world in which to hide. To say it another way, Jesus is telling us he is not out to punish, but only love us. All other beliefs about him and God are made up.

(3:2-4) They are too small and meaningless to occupy your holy mind an instant longer. God's Judgment waits for you to set you free. What can the world hold out to you, regardless of your judgments on its gifts, that you would rather have?

Jesus says: "Do not give up these foolish thoughts because they are bad, or because I tell you to. Give them up because they are nothing—small and meaningless compared to the wonderful gift I offer you." He sets both gifts side by side for us to look at—our offerings of hate and judgment alongside his of forgiveness and love. He continually reminds us that our belief in separate interests is petty and insignificant, especially when placed by the glorious truth of our shared mind. The Oneness of God's Son is the only thought that will bring true happiness and peace, and so Jesus asks us to consider: "Who with the Love of God upholding him could find the choice of miracles or murder hard to make?" (T-23.IV.9:8). We need to realize that the thought of murder we think is justifiably directed outside is really aimed at ourselves; and so the question remains: Is this really what I want for me?

(3:5) You will be judged, and judged in fairness and in honesty.

This is a terrifying thought to the ego, because what *seems* fair and honest is that we deserve to be punished—the foundation of the ego's thought system of separation and separate interests.

(3:6-8) There is no deceit in God. His promises are sure. Only remember that.

Jesus tells us twice in the text that "the outcome is as certain as God" (T-2.III.3:10; T-4.II.5:8), and God's promise is that we are one with Him (T-28.VI.6:1-5). Again, this is meant metaphorically, since God does not make promises—perfect Oneness cannot promise anything to anyone. His "promise" is simply the creation of our one and perfect Self, and His loving Judgment reminds us that we are His Son.

(3:9-11) His promises have guaranteed His Judgment, and His alone, will be accepted in the end. It is your function to make that end be soon. It is your function to hold it to your heart, and offer it to all the world to keep it safe.

The way you keep God's Love safe within yourself is to offer it to *all* the world, not just a portion. In the inspiring final vision at the end of the text, Jesus says:

> Yet this a vision is which you must share with everyone you see, for otherwise you will behold it not. To give this gift is how to make it yours. And God ordained, in loving kindness, that it be for you (T-31.VIII.8:5-7).

To give this gift is how to make it yours—this is how you preserve it for yourself. You exclude no one from the Atonement's gift of forgiveness you have accepted, which naturally flows through the mind of God's Son, unless you interfere with it again. Thus you need to be vigilant for the ego's fear, and bring to Jesus the unholy thoughts of separation that say: "Not everyone deserves my forgiveness, or even yours." Bringing the darkness to his light guarantees acceptance of God's Judgment—for *all* the Sonship.

16. HOW SHOULD THE TEACHER OF GOD SPEND HIS DAY?

This section is paired with the following one, "How Do God's Teachers Deal with Magic Thoughts?," for both focus on magic. The first five paragraphs of this section address the structure teachers of God would introduce into their day, an indirect reference to magic. This leads to the second half that discusses magic proper, a discussion that concludes in the next section.

(1:1) To the advanced teacher of God this question is meaningless.

In discussing the characteristics of God's teachers, we saw that Jesus defined three levels of teachers. The first includes all of us who have begun the journey up the ladder. As we near the top we become advanced teachers, having let go of most of the ego's thought system and sharing the ten characteristics Jesus described in section 4. At the top of the ladder—the journey's end—we become Teachers of teachers who dwell in the real world, like Jesus.

In this first part of this section, Jesus contrasts the advanced teacher of God with the first level teacher, saying that the former do not need to be told how to spend their day—not needing form or structure, or reliance on the magic that is essential early on in the journey. This right-minded use of magic does not serve the ego's purpose of keeping us away from the miracle, but enables us to take the steps that will bring us closer to the miracle of healing.

(1:2) There is no program, for the lessons change each day.

Since the advanced teacher's ego is at a minimum, the only voice he hears is the Holy Spirit's. There is nothing he needs to undo for he follows His inner Voice, which means that whatever he says or does will be loving.

(1:3-6) Yet the teacher of God is sure of but one thing; they [the lessons] do not change at random. Seeing this and understanding that it is true, he rests content. He will be told all that his role should be, this day and every day. And those who share that role with him will find him, so they can learn the lessons for the day together.

Here again is our theme of shared interests: we learn the lessons *together*. The lessons *I* learn and teach are the lessons *you* learn and teach. These are not random because everything that occurs is used by the Holy Spirit as part of His "plan" to help us forgive. He does not choose the curriculum on the level of form, only its content of forgiveness, which corrects and undoes the ego's content of separation and judgment. God's advanced teachers thus realize that anything they say or do will express the Atonement, a way of correcting the mistaken belief in separation. Therefore, you and I may be separate in form, but not in content—our minds remain the same and therefore are at one. Our behavior has as its purpose to reflect the Atonement, in whatever form will be most helpful so that forgiveness can be taught, learned, and accepted. Since these teachers know that everyone is the same, there is no concern as each new day dawns. Regardless of external challenges, demands, or needs, advanced teachers focus on the content because they know this is everything—their sole function being to demonstrate the Holy Spirit's vision of shared interests.

(1:7) Not one is absent whom he needs; not one is sent without a learning goal already set, and one which can be learned that very day.

Every encounter is a holy encounter (T-8.III.4:1) because everything is the same. Our eyes see differences in situations, relationships, and needs, but the healed mind sees everything as the same, without exception. That is what makes the days of advanced teachers so easy, without stress or strain. They merely do whatever comes up as the day unfolds. Simply put, they just show up, and the love in their minds speaks and behaves through them. They have become an empty vessel—devoid of the ego—so they can be filled with the love that pours naturally through the mind, automatically translated into words or behavior.

(1:8-10) For the advanced teacher of God, then, this question is superfluous. It has been asked and answered, and he keeps in constant contact with the Answer. He is set, and sees the road on which he walks stretch surely and smoothly before him.

This section began with Jesus saying that the section's question was meaningless, and here he says it is superfluous. Again, having learned that interests are shared, the advanced teacher's ego has diminished sufficiently so every voice he hears is the Holy Spirit's.

The discussion now shifts to all who are at the beginning stages of the journey:

(2:1-4) But what about those who have not reached his certainty? They are not yet ready for such lack of structuring on their own part. What must they do to learn to give the day to God? There are some general rules which do apply, although each one must use them as best he can in his own way.

The curriculum is highly individualized, as Jesus will tell us later (M-29.2:6)—everyone is different, and so these general rules should be applied in the context of each person's life and specific needs.

(2:5) Routines as such are dangerous, because they easily become gods in their own right, threatening the very goals for which they were set up.

Jesus continues by elaborating on both the necessity and danger of routines. For example, we need the highly structured exercises the workbook lessons provide to correct the harsh prison of the ego's structure we have followed. This structure includes, for example, thinking of God five minutes every hour, then six, and even ten. In addition, we are asked to do the lesson fifteen minutes in the morning and again at night. As we become less fearful of the lesson, we are asked to think of it more and more frequently, and as fear of our teacher lessens, to go to him more and more as well. This learning is structured because we are still at the beginning phase of our learning. At the end of the workbook, however, Jesus tells us "this course is a beginning, not an end" (W-ep.1:1). It is meant only as a one-year training program to set us on the right path with the right teacher. As we make our way up the ladder we will need less structure, as our days become an ongoing meditation—a prayer for forgiveness. Yet to reach that level we need structured periods of training and practice such as we find in the workbook.

We are therefore asked not to forget the purpose of this structure. It is a means to an end, not the end itself. Jesus thus distinguishes between form and content, magic and the miracle, as I will explain later in this section. We need to be wary of forming a special relationship with the routine, in that if we do not do a daily meditation our day is ruined, or if we forget altogether we are bad students. On the other side, if we do the workbook perfectly we can consider ourselves perfect students, better Sons of God than everyone else—the underlying ego thought of separation and judgment. And so we should not allow our routines and structures to become gods, but to remember their content—the willingness to set aside the ego thought system and embrace Jesus as our teacher and guide.

(2:6-8) Broadly speaking, then, it can be said that it is well to start the day right. It is always possible to begin again, should the day begin with error. Yet there are obvious advantages in terms of saving time.

In "Rules for Decision" (T-30.I), Jesus says the same thing, asking us to start the day right, even though he knows that most of the time we will not succeed.

(3:1-3) At the beginning, it is wise to think in terms of time. This is by no means the ultimate criterion, but at the outset it is probably the simplest to observe. The saving of time is an essential early emphasis which, although it remains important throughout the learning process, becomes less and less emphasized.

In the text and workbook, Jesus speaks often about saving time; not because it itself is important, but because we have used it to imprison ourselves and incur pain. He therefore teaches us how time can serve a different purpose. At the beginning of our work with the Course—which could last a long time!—we experience ourselves as creatures of time and so the idea of saving it is meaningful. In fact, much of the world is geared toward this goal: instant pleasure, instant food, instant everything. Jesus thus corrects this misguided tendency. By practicing this course we, too, save time, but for an entirely different purpose. As we make our way up the ladder and become less identified with the world of time and space, choosing more and more to live in the holy instant, we realize that our reality is outside the world's dream. From that ultimate perspective, the idea of saving time is meaningless for we would be saving what does not exist.

(3:4) At the outset, we can safely say that time

devoted to starting the day right does indeed save time.

If I begin the day with Jesus, I am less likely to make mistakes later on, which means there will be less need to spend time correcting them. In this regard, Jesus had given Helen and Bill a teaching early in the scribing in which he reviewed the preceding day, explaining how much time he had to spend correcting their mistakes. If they had asked him for help *before* their errors, this would not have been necessary. This was all somewhat tongue-in-cheek, but Jesus' point was that Helen and Bill could easily have avoided the pain they brought on themselves.*

Jesus' message here is that we will save time because, by not making mistakes, we will waste less of it in undoing them: "As soon as you can on awakening, think of me and my purpose for you today—to see everything as helping you undo the ego. Thus will you have a new framework within which to experience your daily life."

(3:5-7) How much time should be so spent? This must depend on the teacher of God himself. He cannot claim that title until he has gone through the workbook, since we are learning within the framework of our course.

Jesus is addressing only students of *A Course in Miracles*. If you are not a student, the workbook would obviously not be a requirement.

(3:8) After completion of the more structured practice periods, which the workbook contains, individual need becomes the chief consideration.

At the end of the workbook, Jesus tells us that when we have completed the lessons he will place us in the Holy Spirit's hands (W-ep.4:1), which means from that point on, whatever we do during the day will be guided by Him. This does not necessarily mean we abandon all structure, but it does mean that our need guides our use. Because our needs vary, the way the Holy Spirit guides one person will differ from the way He guides another. The content is the same, but our experience of His guidance will be different because our learning needs and potential are different within the illusion. Our responsibility remains only to set our feet on the right ladder with the right Teacher.

(4:1-3) This course is always practical. It may be that the teacher of God is not in a situation that fosters quiet thought as he awakes. If this is so, let him but remember that he chooses to spend time with God as soon as possible, and let him do so.

This is another instance of Jesus' caution that we not become wedded to the form. If you wake up late or need to deal with an immediate crisis and there is no time for a meditation, simply think of God in whatever way possible at that moment. Jesus is interested in the content, not the form, as the following lines make clear:

(4:4-6) Duration is not the major concern. One can easily sit still an hour with closed eyes and accomplish nothing. One can as easily give God only an instant, and in that instant join with Him completely.

Content, not *form*; quality of time, not quantity. Jesus is not asking his students to be controlled by a watch or clock. That may be necessary and helpful at the beginning, but it can all too easily become a god in its own right, enslaving rather than freeing us. Remember, the idea is to get to the mind's content, not the body's behavior that is always the ego's goal for us.

(4:7-9) Perhaps the one generalization that can be made is this; as soon as possible after waking take your quiet time, continuing a minute or two after you begin to find it difficult. You may find that the difficulty will diminish and drop away. If not, that is the time to stop.

Jesus instructs us in a similar fashion in the workbook (W-pI.95.7-10). If you find what I am asking you to do difficult, he says, give it another minute or so, and if it still induces anxiety, fear, or depression, set it aside. Applying pressure to yourself or others is the very worst thing you can do, for you would be making the error of form real, and preventing yourself from returning to the Holy Spirit's gentle kindness. Since we are all children of guilt, we all believe we will be punished. As students of this course, we would have to believe Jesus

---

* See *Absence from Felicity*, pp. 253-58.

is a harsh teacher who will be angry if we do not do the workbook "right." Recognizing those thoughts would help us realize we are doing with Jesus exactly what we have always done—holding on to the thought system of specialness. Simply because we are students of the Course and no longer affiliated with another religious system does not necessarily mean we have let the ego go. It can still be alive and well, and as subtle and vicious as ever.

Always keep in mind the merciful love that Jesus exhibits toward everyone. Let that be your guide, both in terms of how you react to yourself as well as to others. If you are not gentle and kind, you know you have made a god of the *form* instead of focusing on the *content*.

(5:1-5) The same procedures should be followed at night. Perhaps your quiet time should be fairly early in the evening, if it is not feasible for you to take it just before going to sleep. It is not wise to lie down for it. It is better to sit up, in whatever position you prefer. Having gone through the workbook, you must have come to some conclusions in this respect.

This is the only place where Jesus says something this specific. He obviously does not want us to fall asleep, nor become slaves to ritual or to time.

(5:6) If possible, however, just before going to sleep is a desirable time to devote to God.

Jesus does not mean thinking of God in an abstract or personal sense. He means remembering the *purpose* of God, which is to accept the Atonement for yourself. Think about your purpose—of your day, sleep, and life; they are one. You do not have to say sweet and lovely things to God before you go to sleep. He hardly needs you to tell Him that you love Him. Even if He had a Self that could hear you, He would know it were not true because you are in the body, which means you must hate Him—if you truly loved Him, you would not have feared His Final Judgment and run to the body for refuge and protection. Therefore, devoting time to God means devoting time to the Holy Spirit's purpose. In "The Lessons of the Holy Spirit," Jesus tells us to "be vigilant only for God and His Kingdom" (T-6.V-C). This vigilance is really for the ego and its kingdom of guilt, hate, and judgment. Through this vigilance we are able ultimately to choose against the ego, leaving only the peace of God in our minds, as we now read:

(5:7-8) It sets your mind into a pattern of rest, and orients you away from fear. If it is expedient to spend this time earlier, at least be sure that you do not forget a brief period,—not more than a moment will do,—in which you close your eyes and think of God.

Everyone is capable of doing at least that. No matter how tired you may be, no matter what is going on in your life, before retiring you could at least think of God in terms of your purpose of awakening to Him. And then, of course, forgive yourself when you realize you have not thought about Him at all. Jesus is no fool and knows his students well, seeing how enamored they are of the individual self with which they identify, thus making forgiveness the last thing on their minds. Yet Jesus does want us to be aware of our purpose in doing his course: remembering why we are here. The ego has us come so we will never return to God, while the Holy Spirit sees our being here as a way of learning His lessons so that we return to our true home; the ego's lessons thus focus on magic, and the Holy Spirit's on the miracle.

Beginning with paragraph 6, Jesus devotes the rest of the section to the theme of magic. In the first five paragraphs, especially the last two, Jesus asked us to think as much as we could about God, which, as we have seen, means the *purpose* of God. How we live that out specifically, day in and day out, becomes the focus of the remaining paragraphs. Since the discussion revolves around *magic*, I begin by discussing its usage in *A Course in Miracles*.

Magic can be defined as *the ego's maladaptive solution to a nonexistent problem*. The *nonexistent problem* is the belief that we have separated from God, with concomitant ominous thoughts of sin, guilt, and fear, a dreadful situation from which the ego says we must escape. Yet this thought system is nothing but a myth, as indeed is everything in the hate-filled wrong mind. The ego, however, tells us this nothing is really something. In fact, it is everything, defining us as creatures of separation and sin who deserve to be destroyed because of what we have done. There is nothing we can do to change these facts, but there is a solution to our predicament: magic.

The ego's magical solution is to make up a world and body for us to hide in, preoccupying us with special relationships. We magically hope these will preserve our separate identities but lose the sin, thereby eliminating the threat of the death that is sin's inevitable consequence. We accomplish this by giving our sin to our special relationship—the ego's *maladaptive solution to its nonexistent problem*. It is maladaptive because it does not work. Dumping our sin and guilt onto others does not bring us happiness or peace. To the contrary, it instills in us a terrifyingly paranoid thought system that tells us that everyone in the world is out to get us—everyone and everything. Thus we fear the lurking germs poised to invade our physical space, the terrorists we believe are preparing to attack us, and the cruel, insensitive people—beginning with our families—who seek to steal from us our innocence and peace.

The ego has us convinced this insanity will work, which is why when anxiety begins, we run into the ego's arms of magic rather than deal with the real source of the distress, dis-ease, and depression—the belief we separated from God. The miracle shows us the problem, but we find this threatening because we know that if we accept the miracle, the nonexistent problem will disappear, leaving our individual identities behind as we disappear into the God we never truly left. The ego therefore tells us the problem is not the decision we made in our minds, but is to be found in external circumstances. Thus the temptation to return to the magic of specialness, wherein the problem and solution are seen outside the mind. The outcome is that I believe you are my problem, and the solution is to dispose of you or change you in some way; or else the problem is my body—outside the mind as well—and therefore the solution is to do something with it. These magical solutions can also be defined as the attempts to solve a problem where it does not exist—in the physical or psychological body, or in the world at large.

(6:1-7) There is one thought in particular that should be remembered throughout the day. It is a thought of pure joy; a thought of peace, a thought of limitless release, limitless because all things are freed within it. You think you made a place of safety for yourself. You think you made a power that can save you from all the fearful things you see in dreams. It is not so. Your safety lies not there. What you give up is merely the illusion of protecting illusions.

Note the word *all* in sentence 2—"all things are freed within it"—reflecting the theme of all-inclusiveness. Forgiveness embraces *all*; love excludes *no one*; there are *no exceptions* in salvation.

We think we made a place of safety for ourselves in the world and body—i.e., *magic*—believing we are not safe in the mind because God's avenging presence would destroy us. Yet the separation and its components—sin, guilt, fear, judgment, and death—are illusory, thereby requiring no protection: there is no problem in need of a solution; no need to seek refuge.

(6:8) And it is this you fear, and only this.

We are afraid that if we abandon "the illusion of protecting illusions," we abandon the belief that not only will the body save us, but that we *are* the body. In the workbook, Jesus addresses this belief that the body is salvation, and responds:

> You will identify with what you think will make you safe. Whatever it may be, you will believe that it is one with you. Your safety lies in truth, and not in lies. Love is your safety. Fear does not exist. Identify with love, and you are safe. Identify with love, and you are home. Identify with love, and find your Self (W-pII.5.5).

Magic, on the other hand, tells us the body is our home and protection, not to mention our very self.

(6:9-10) How foolish to be so afraid of nothing! Nothing at all!

Jesus means this literally. We fear the ego, the body, the world. Yet what we really fear is *a maladaptive solution to a nonexistent problem*—"the illusion of protecting illusions." To be afraid of nothing is not wicked, evil, or sinful—just silly. The world is based on this fear of nothing, and every war that has been, or will be fought; every argument we engage in; each special relationship we form; indeed, every person born into this world has arisen from this groundless fear. Thus we seek the body's nothingness to protect us from the mind's nothingness of sin, guilt, and fear.

(6:11-14) Your defenses will not work, but you are not in danger. You have no need of them. Recognize this, and they will disappear. And only then will you accept your real protection.

Defenses will not work because they "*do* what they would defend" (T-17.IV.7:1). Their purpose is to protect us from our fear, but they make us even more fearful for we would not need defenses if there were not something terrible deep within us to fear. Thus every time we engage in a defense, we but reinforce the idea that we need protection from the mind's terrible something—*defenses do what they would defend*. The bad news is that they do not work; the good news is that they do not have to—there is nothing for which we need a defense; there is no danger because there is nothing in the mind that can hurt us. The mind's only truth is the memory of God. Everything else is made up, and so we magically make a world to protect us from what never was—"the illusion of protecting illusions." Our real protection, therefore, is the truth of Atonement—the separation never happened. If it never happened we cannot be annihilated, let alone there being a God Who would annihilate us. An illusion remains an illusion.

(7:1-4) How simply and how easily does time slip by for the teacher of God who has accepted His protection! All that he did before in the name of safety no longer interests him. For he is safe, and knows it to be so. He has a Guide Who will not fail.

Having accepted the Atonement for themselves, teachers of God are no longer creatures of time and space, which are nothing but projections of the sin, guilt, and fear spawned from the separation. When we choose against the ego, therefore, time vanishes along with the separation—there is not even anything to slip by. We do not live here, though the body appears to, for we are in the holy instant in which the body does not exist (T-18.VII.3:1). Thus have all magical forms of protection—special relationships —lost their appeal and meaning. Advanced teachers of God have learned to trust only in a Power that is not of this world, the "Guide Who will not fail." "Trust" was a major focus of Jesus' discussion in section 4, and these teachers trust in the Holy Spirit's thought system that is not part of the dream, enabling them to go through their days—hour by hour, minute by minute—without fear or stress. They have ceased tilting at the ego's windmills by fighting nonexistent enemies.

(7:5) He need make no distinctions among the problems he perceives, for He to Whom he turns with all of them recognizes no order of difficulty in resolving them.

Jesus returns us to his first principle of miracles (T-1.I.1:1), around which *A Course in Miracles* is built: there is no order of difficulty in miracles. Every problem is the same, for one illusion is all illusions. Likewise, every undoing of a problem is the same, for the one solution of bringing the darkness of illusion to the light of truth—the miracle—never changes.

(7:6-9) He is as safe in the present as he was before illusions were accepted into his mind, and as he will be when he has let them go. There is no difference in his state at different times and different places, because they are all one to God. This is his safety. And he has no need for more than this.

Our fluctuating states are equally illusory—God does not know about them. A later section explains that God does not even understand words, let alone the thought system of separation that produced them. We are thus forever safe in the present—the holy instant—in which there is no separation. Without sin, guilt, and fear there can be no past, present, and future, and so we have no need for the external —the magic of specialness that was to protect us from the guilt that never existed.

(8:1) Yet there will be temptations along the way the teacher of God has yet to travel, and he has need of reminding himself throughout the day of his protection.

Jesus lets us know that he knows we will encounter problems as we go through our days—indeed, who does not have problems in this world? Simply having a body means problems—in our own and with others—and we will be tempted to go to the ego's magic for help: our "faithful" friends of separation, guilt, attack, and judgment.

(8:2-4) How can he do this, particularly during the time when his mind is occupied with external things? He can but try, and his success depends

on his conviction that he will succeed. He must be sure success is not of him, but will be given him at any time, in any place and circumstance he calls for it.

Regardless of the form our problems take, we can learn to recognize their inherent sameness: turning away from Jesus. From that thought, which reminds us of our separation from God, comes all our guilt, anxiety, and fear of punishment. That is the true source of our distress, and recognizing this allows us to choose the true source of our protection.

(8:5-7) There are times his certainty will waver, and the instant this occurs he will return to earlier attempts to place reliance on himself alone. Forget not this is magic, and magic is a sorry substitute for true assistance. It is not good enough for God's teacher, because it is not enough for God's Son.

As God's teachers we are God's Son, totally at one with our Creator and Source. This undoes all belief in magic, which the miracle helps us to understand. Jesus is not expecting us *not* to turn to magic for help; he is alerting us to the fact that is what will happen. When we get anxious and tense we forget this is all illusory. As Wordsworth said, "The world is too much with us," for it seems to impose itself upon us. We forget all that we have learned, and rely on ourselves alone—the ego—and our allies: specialness, fear, and separate interests.

(9:1-2) The avoidance of magic is the avoidance of temptation. For all temptation is nothing more than the attempt to substitute another will for God's.

The "attempt to substitute another will for God's" is the ego's original thought of magic—we will be better off outside Heaven. It is magic because it is not true, being, again, *the maladaptive solution to a nonexistent problem.* We wanted our specialness and individuality to be recognized by God. When He "refused," we took matters into our own hands, casting Him aside and establishing the world and special bodies that would give us the love He denied us. We relive this magical and insane solution over and over in our daily lives.

(9:3-4) These attempts may indeed seem frightening, but they are merely pathetic. They can have no effects; neither good nor bad, neither rewarding nor demanding sacrifice, healing nor destructive, quieting nor fearful.

Our attempts at magically replacing God's Will are simply silly, for they accomplish nothing. They are neither bad nor good; do not heal nor make us sick—nothing can only produce nothing, and with nothing. Therefore Jesus calls our attempts pathetic. Nonetheless, we keep trying and trying to find happiness, peace, and joy here—and never succeed.

(9:5) When all magic is recognized as merely nothing, the teacher of God has reached the most advanced state.

We are truly advanced when we realize all this is a dream. Since dreams are not real, nothing here can ever affect us and so we have no use for magic. Again, there is nothing wrong with taking a pill if you are sick, wanting a warm body next to you if you are lonely, or striving for money when you have none—yet none of these, or any forms of magic will bring you the peace of God. Therefore they are nothing.

(9:6-9) All intermediate lessons will but lead to this, and bring this goal nearer to recognition. For magic of any kind, in all its forms, simply does nothing. Its powerlessness is the reason it can be so easily escaped. What has no effects can hardly terrify.

This will have little meaning for us as long as we identify with the body, for bodies are highly vulnerable and in need of magical interventions in order to survive and be happy. Jesus' words are meaningful only when we recognize that our identity is not the body at all. Our true Self is love, which is not found in the world, although its reflection is present in the right mind. We thus spend our day—the subject of this section—learning how addicted we are to magic, which includes everything here we think can bring us happiness and peace.

(10:1-8) There is no substitute for the Will of God. In simple statement, it is to this fact the teacher of God devotes his day. Each substitute he may accept as real can but deceive him. But he is safe from all deception if he so decides. Perhaps he needs to remember, "God is with me. I cannot be deceived." Perhaps he prefers other words, or only one, or none at all. Yet each temptation to accept magic as true must be

abandoned through his recognition, not that it is fearful, not that it is sinful, not that it is dangerous, but merely that it is meaningless.

Since Jesus defines special relationships as substitutes for the Love of God (T-24.I), we need to see how quickly we choose them instead of love—to see separate interests and make specialness our god—and then not judge ourselves for having done so. It is important that we not try to change our specialness, but simply look and realize what we are giving up in having chosen it. Thus we come to realize the meaninglessness of substituting for what alone is meaningful in this world—learning the lessons that we are not different and separate from each other.

(10:9-10) Rooted in sacrifice and separation, two aspects of one error and no more, he merely chooses to give up all that he never had. And for this "sacrifice" is Heaven restored to his awareness.

"Sacrifice" is in quotation marks because we are truly giving up nothing. Sacrifice and separation are two aspects of the same error in the sense that once I am separate, I have sacrificed what I have separated from. Moreover, intrinsic to all separation is the core idea of sacrifice: *one or the other*; someone wins, another loses. Once I assert my existence as a separate entity, I have sacrificed the Oneness of God; once I insist I am separate from you—I am innocent and you are guilty—I have sacrificed you. Jesus asks us to see these forms of magic as what they are, for looking at them will help us realize we no longer want them because they do not make us happy.

(11:1-4) Is not this an exchange that you would want? The world would gladly make it, if it knew it could be made. It is God's teachers who must teach it that it can. And so it is their function to make sure that they have learned it.

It is our function to choose to end sacrifice, and as we learn it ourselves, to become examples for others of what they can choose. We reflect the truth that one can be happy without having to attack another, and this happiness has nothing to do with anything external. We are happy in this world because we have chosen a love and truth that is not here, reflected by our demonstration that interests are shared, not separate—we are all the same. Through the love that is unaffected by what others do, we demonstrate the Atonement truth we have learned for the world.

(11:5-7) No risk is possible throughout the day except to put your trust in magic, for it is only this that leads to pain. "There is no will but God's." His teachers know that this is so, and have learned that everything but this is magic.

Everything that is not part of God's Oneness is magic—the way we protect and preserve our separation.

(11:8) All belief in magic is maintained by just one simple-minded illusion;—that it works.

We think it works because we think we are here. That is why we resort to magic when we are upset, depressed, or in pain. And so we say: "Look—I am here, not Heaven; I am a body, not spirit. Magic works, specialness works, and our being here proves it."

(11:9-11) All through their training, every day and every hour, and even every minute and second, must God's teachers learn to recognize the forms of magic and perceive their meaninglessness. Fear is withdrawn from them, and so they go. And thus the gate of Heaven is reopened, and its light can shine again on an untroubled mind.

We are merely asked to look at our dependence on magic, not to change it; to look and realize this is not what we thought, being *a maladaptive solution to a nonexistent problem*. Magic does not work because that is how it was set up, in contrast to the miracle that always works. When we look at magic without calling it sinful or experiencing guilt or fear, it will simply disappear. Having now been made clean, our minds rest untroubled, allowing the memory of God to gently dawn upon them—the Atonement's light has been accepted at last.

17. HOW DO GOD'S TEACHERS DEAL WITH MAGIC THOUGHTS?

This section has two parts, with a closing summary. The first addresses how we deal with other people's magic thoughts after the "natural" response of anger, thus extending the previous section's discussion of magic—now that we recognize magic, how do we deal with it? The second shifts the focus from our personal experience to the metaphysical basis for this anger.

(1:1-2) This is a crucial question both for teacher and pupil. If this issue is mishandled, the teacher of God has hurt himself and has also attacked his pupil.

We mishandle the situation when we get angry at someone using magic: people taking medicine instead of healing their minds; others seeking yet another special relationship when all the past ones have failed; students who are superstitious about the Course; or world figures who wage war to achieve peace. We need to remember that anything taken seriously here is magic—whether by a public figure or someone in our personal world.

(1:3-5) This [attack] strengthens fear, and makes the magic seem quite real to both of them. How to deal with magic thus becomes a major lesson for the teacher of God to master. His first responsibility in this is not to attack it.

This applies universally, regardless of the form that magic takes—whether it is a dictator oppressing a people, a malicious boss, or an abusing parent. Jesus is addressing any situation in which the response is one of anger.

(1:6-8) If a magic thought arouses anger in any form, God's teacher can be sure that he is strengthening his own belief in sin and has condemned himself. He can be sure as well that he has asked for depression, pain, fear and disaster to come to him. Let him remember, then, it is not this that he would teach, because it is not this that he would learn.

If you are angry, it can only be because you see in another what you do not want to see in yourself. If you accuse others of anything, you should first stop and ask: "Would I accuse myself of doing this?" (W-pI.134.9:3). This does not mean you need approve of what someone does, nor that what people do is loving—needless to say, most of the time it is not. Yet, when you react in anger you have made their error real, which happens because you want to see the darkness in them and not in yourself. Recall that anger is never about what your eyes perceive, but only about how you react to what your eyes perceive.

(2:1-3) There is, however, a temptation to respond to magic in a way that reinforces it. Nor is this always obvious. It can, in fact, be easily concealed beneath a wish to help.

The temptation is to choose magic—*the maladaptive solution to a nonexistent problem* I believe to be my sinfulness, which I seek to solve by projecting it onto you and attacking you for it. This dynamic, however, can be cleverly concealed behind special love. Thus, I really hate you, but cover it with loving protestations and behavior. This magic helps me, not only because I see sin in you, but because it allows me to smugly say: "No matter what you did, I still love you and will help you." Moreover, I say: "Look, God, what a wonderful person I am. Here is this hateful person who has attacked me and others, but I am forgiving and helpful." This is the ego maneuver to which Jesus refers, and which allows us magically to demonstrate an innocence that conceals our underlying belief in sin.

(2:4) It is this double wish that makes the help of little value, and must lead to undesired outcomes.

I am clearly not helping because my help comes through magic, which reflects the wish to mask the underlying need to hate. True help comes only from my acceptance of the Atonement, for the love it releases is expressed through me and *this* is the help—not what I do or say. I simply remind you that you can make the same choice for love I have—a love that excludes no one. On the level of form we obviously cannot help everyone all the time, but on the level of thought love helps everyone because God's Son is one.

(2:5-6) Nor should it be forgotten that the outcome that results will always come to teacher

17. How Do God's Teachers Deal with Magic Thoughts?

and to pupil alike. How many times has it been emphasized that you give but to yourself?

This articulates our first theme: the oneness of God's Son. I cannot help myself without helping you, and I cannot help you without helping myself. Moreover, I cannot help you without helping the Sonship, for without that unity the Sonship ceases to be itself, and my help is not help at all. Giving and receiving are one because there are no separate givers and receivers. *Ideas leave not their source*—the idea of love never leaves its source in the mind of God's one Son; not some, but *one*, which is *all*.

(2:7-10) And where could this be better shown than in the kinds of help the teacher of God gives to those who need his aid? Here is his gift most clearly given him. For he will give only what he has chosen for himself. And in this gift is his judgment upon the holy Son of God.

God's judgment is that the holy Son of God is *one*, correcting the ego's judgment that separation is reality and interests are separate. The ego's judgment thus sanctions our giving to some and not all, giving to one person sometimes but not all the time. Jesus teaches, however, that anything other than total giving is magic, because it reinforces the idea that sin is real and therefore only certain people deserve to be helped. One of the ways we use magic to undo our belief in sin is to be helpful, so people will think of us as wonderful—loving and kind, sweet and gentle, considerate and thoughtful—when all we really do is conceal the fact that we are silent murderers seeking to have our selfish needs met, even if it means sacrificing God Himself. We will return to this dynamic in the second part of the section.

(3:1-2) It is easiest to let error be corrected where it is most apparent, and errors can be recognized by their results. A lesson truly taught can lead to nothing but release for teacher and pupil, who have shared in one intent.

Here is our first theme, stated with great clarity. Teacher and pupil, giver and receiver share one intent because there is one need, one purpose, one Son. It is not love if you do not allow it to embrace the Sonship as a whole—in *content*, not *form*. Salvation can never be achieved at someone's expense—everyone must win, otherwise no one wins; no one must lose, otherwise everyone loses. There can be no compromise in truth.

(3:3) Attack can enter only if perception of separate goals has entered.

By definition, separation is an attack, for it denies the Oneness of God, of His Son, and of Creator and creation.

(3:4-5) And this must indeed have been the case if the result is anything but joy. The single aim of the teacher turns the divided goal of the pupil into one direction, with the call for help becoming his one appeal.

Our first theme again. I change your divided goal by demonstrating the single-mindedness within myself. By choosing against the ego I have chosen against conflict, and so the Love of God that I am teaches that you were simply mistaken—not bad, evil, or deserving of punishment, but simply mistaken: God's Son has never left his Father.

(3:6-7) This then is easily responded to with just one answer, and this answer will enter the teacher's mind unfailingly. From there it shines into his pupil's mind, making it one with his.

The Oneness of God's Son, manifest in seeing shared instead of separate interests, is the one answer to everything. If I see you expressing love or calling for it (T-12.I), my only response is love. As a loving brother I can do nothing else, as I remind you that you are nothing else but that love.

(4:1-2) Perhaps it would be helpful to remember that no one can be angry at a fact. It is always an interpretation that gives rise to negative emotions, regardless of their seeming justification by what *appears* as facts.

This important paragraph is probably the clearest statement in *A Course in Miracles* of the principle that *perception is interpretation*. The objective fact within the dream is that you have done something— invaded a country, oppressed a people, fired an employee, abused a child—but my anger would be justified only if I have interpreted what you did as sinful, with terrible effects on me or on those with whom I identify.

(4:3-11) Regardless, too, of the intensity of the anger that is aroused. It may be merely slight

irritation, perhaps too mild to be even clearly recognized. Or it may also take the form of intense rage, accompanied by thoughts of violence, fantasied or apparently acted out. It does not matter. All of these reactions are the same. They obscure the truth, and this can never be a matter of degree. Either truth is apparent, or it is not. It cannot be partially recognized. Who is unaware of truth must look upon illusions.

Here we see the *all-or-nothing* principle, also exemplified in the workbook:

> You will become increasingly aware that a slight twinge of annoyance is nothing but a veil drawn over intense fury (W-pI.21.2:5).

If I am mildly annoyed or enraged, I am seeing you as separate from me—something *you* have done has had an effect on *me*. From this point of view there is no difference between mild annoyance and intense rage—there is no hierarchy of illusions, the ego's lies to the contrary (T-23.II.2:3). Jesus teaches that any perception that you are different from me, let alone that you have done or said something that has taken away my peace, is an illusion. Whether you have dropped an atomic bomb or tripped me inadvertently makes no difference. If I get angry, mildly annoyed, or simply have a startled response, I am asserting that the separation is alive and well, and is your fault—were it not for you, I would be at peace. Again, this holds regardless of the form of the accusation.

Everything here is an attack, considering that "the world was made as an attack on God" (W-pII.3.2:1). It came from an attack thought, and *ideas leave not their source*. Each attack is but the shadow of the original thought when we said to our Creator: "Your love is not enough, and so we will institute a regime change in Heaven—deposing You, we will be in charge of the Kingdom, sitting on its throne forever." We live out this usurpation each and every moment in our lives—personal and collective—accusing ourselves of this sin of "regime change." This is the source of our projected guilt, and will presently be our segue to the next part of the section.

The reason I get angry at you—accusing you of not being a good person, for whatever reason—is that I see in you the abhorrent sin I cannot tolerate in myself. Not being able to accept it, I project it onto you. This sin is the original magic thought that says I will be better off without God. *I* know the problem—my specialness is not recognized—and therefore the solution is to destroy God and establish my own kingdom in which I will be eminently special, recognized as such by *my* god. It is magical thinking because I never look at the real problem: fearing the loss of this individual self and being the Self Who is one with Its Source.

Another way of looking at our "original sin" is *selfishness*, wherein we selfishly establish our self by sacrificing God—ensuring that our own needs will be met at His expense, attacking Another so we get what we want. Our guilt over this magical act of total *self-centeredness* is enormous, and we live it out over and over again. Thus we are always on the lookout in others for the magical thought system of sin and defense, and once we see it we attack it. The ego, however, compounds our guilt for when we spot the magic, it reminds us of the same use of magic in ourselves, bringing our fear to an intolerable intensity that leads us to attack still further. Having projected our sin and attack on others as a way of getting rid of our own, our defense makes us even more fearful—recall that *defenses **do** what they would defend* (T-17.IV.7:1). In other words, we need to attack and make others the villain so God will punish them instead of us, but this very dynamic holds up a mirror that reflects back to us: "Ah, but that is what *you* really are. *You* are the evildoer, the wicked one who should be punished." Frenzied with guilt, we are driven to practice even more magic. We therefore, like experimental rats on a treadmill, go around and around this horrifically endless cycle of guilt and attack. This is the subject of the next paragraph, which makes the transition from our individual experience to the ontological thought system that is its driving force.

(5:1-2) Anger in response to perceived magic thoughts is a basic cause of fear. Consider what this reaction means, and its centrality in the world's thought system becomes apparent.

We have seen that fear is the inevitable result when we respond with anger to the magic thoughts perceived in others—I am afraid you will attack me so I attack you first, and now fear you will attack in return as we go back and forth in this cycle of attack-defense (W-pI.153.3). Jesus now explains the true nature of the situation:

(5:3-4) A magic thought, by its mere presence, acknowledges a separation from God. It states, in the clearest form possible, that the mind which believes it has a separate will that can oppose the Will of God, also believes it can succeed.

The ego says magic will help us avoid the certain punishment our guilt demands, and thus we need a world replete with bodies onto which we can project our horrendous guilt. By virtue of our conviction that we exist here as individuals, we proclaim we have indeed pulled off the impossible, despite the fact that the Oneness of God—Its very presence and Being—says separation is an impossibility. Yet the fact that *I* exist proves I have done it: "Do not tell me separation is impossible. I exist!" This means Oneness has been obliterated, and this is our secret sin.

(5:5-9) That this can hardly be a fact is obvious. Yet that it can be believed as fact is equally obvious. And herein lies the birthplace of guilt. Who usurps the place of God and takes it for himself now has a deadly "enemy." And he must stand alone in his protection, and make himself a shield to keep him safe from fury that can never be abated, and vengeance that can never be satisfied.

Here we see the unholy trinity of sin, guilt, and fear exposed in all its hideous hate. Deep within our minds is the belief we attacked God and even killed Him, and He is somehow going to rise from the grave and pursue us. All alone in our terror, we but hope we can shield ourselves from His insatiable thirst for vengeance. In painting this frightful portrait, Jesus helps us understand the psychological origin of the biblical notion of God, the figure he portrays here of an avenger that seeks to destroy anyone in its fury, even a world—and all because of what we have done. We stand alone with no help in sight, but then the ego comes to the rescue:

(6:1-6) How can this unfair battle be resolved? Its ending is inevitable, for its outcome must be death. How, then, can one believe in one's defenses? Magic again must help. Forget the battle. Accept it as a fact, and then forget it.

That is the ego's ace in the hole—the dynamic Freud called *repression*, referred to in *A Course in Miracles* as *denial*: I accept the separation, but then forget it ever happened. I bury it in my mind—the unconscious—and then strive to get rid of it, as Jesus explains:

(6:7-11) Do not remember the impossible odds against you. Do not remember the immensity of the "enemy," and do not think about your frailty in comparison. Accept your separation, but do not remember how it came about. Believe that you have won it, but do not retain the slightest memory of Who your great "opponent" really is. Projecting your "forgetting" onto Him, it seems to you He has forgotten, too.

This is the role of magic. We go to the ego and say: "Help! This vengeful, maniacal God is about to destroy us." The ego's remedy for this seemingly hopeless situation is to blot it from awareness, project it, and make a world of bodies. We continue to exist as separate entities, accepting our separation but forgetting how it really happened; forgetting, too, our having made the world. Thus do we forget our great "opponent" and magically escape His punishing wrath, hoping against hope—magically—that God has forgotten, too. Jesus now shows us how and why this magic does not work:

(7:1-2) But what will now be your reaction to all magic thoughts? They can but reawaken sleeping guilt, which you have hidden but have not let go.

Ideas leave not their source. I may have hidden the source—the idea I murdered God through selfishly sinning against Him—but that idea has not left its source in my mind, though it seems to be in you, the world of nature, or an external God. When I see you resort to magic to survive, it reminds me of the magic *I* use to survive, which means that the horror of my original sin, along with God's reaction, comes roaring back to awareness.

(7:3-4) Each one says clearly to your frightened mind, "You have usurped the place of God. Think not He has forgotten."

Our purpose in making up a world and body, thereby rendering us mindless, was to convince ourselves that God had indeed forgotten: we have forgotten, and therefore so has He. However, another's magic reminds us of our original magical belief that we would be better off not being part of God's Kingdom of Oneness, but ruler of our world of separation and exclusion. We thus can no longer escape these terrifying thoughts of sin and guilt because we see magic all around us as reminders.

(7:5-7) Here we have the fear of God most starkly represented. For in that thought has guilt already raised madness to the throne of God Himself. And now there is no hope.

Not only are we mad with guilt, God is, too. The second and third laws of chaos express the insanity of this thinking (T-23.II.4-8), wherein God has become as insane as we. We return to the beginning when, as one Son, we stood alone in our protection, knowing there was no hope. God had been made to be the maniacal murderer we accused ourselves of being—selfishly wanting only our death, because that is what we wanted of Him. Now, because of the magic thoughts of another, we are thrown back onto our own, from which we can never be extricated.

(7:7-11) And now there is no hope. Except to kill. Here is salvation now. An angry father pursues his guilty son. Kill or be killed, for here alone is choice.

This is the bottom line of *one or the other*—the metaphysical origin of the ego's principle of separate interests: I achieve salvation at your expense. Sacrifice thus becomes holy in the ego thought system (the etymological root of *sacrifice* is "to make holy"), because it makes us part of God again. God will welcome us back into His Kingdom because we are the innocent ones who have suffered at the hands of the sinful victimizer, whom God will condemn to hell. Thus we can see how our personal lives of specialness have their roots in this original thought of deriving gain at another's expense—*one or the other.*

(7:11-13) Kill or be killed, for here alone is choice. Beyond this there is none, for what was done cannot be done without. The stain of blood can never be removed, and anyone who bears this stain on him must meet with death.

Sin is real and someone must be punished for it —you or me. The stain of blood is permanent, marking someone for certain death. Jesus has here borrowed from Shakespeare's moving scene when Lady Macbeth, overwhelmed with guilt over her complicity in the regicide, hallucinates that the blood on her hands will not come off. That now is my terror: I cannot be free of the blood stain from having killed God, but magically hope that by putting the blood on your hands, mine will be clean and you will be killed instead of me. Yet seeing the sin I had put in you can only remind me that it is *my* hands that are unclean. Again, on the one hand the ego tells me magic will work—projecting my sin onto you ensures my innocence—but on the other, since *defenses do what they would defend*, my defense of attacking you simply reminds me of my sinful purpose, and I will fail as my guilt drives me even more insane.

Recall the ego's vicious circle of guilt-attack: I continually deny my guilt and attack you, which makes me guiltier. This is the reason wars are waged —by heads of state or individuals doing battle with each other. As a creature of the ego, I cannot but hate and kill—physically or psychologically. I must kill because I must try to remove the blood stain of sin from my hands. Yet the more I project, the guiltier I become, because my projections continually remind me of my secret sins and hidden hates (T-31.VIII.9:2). However, there is a non-magical solution to the problem of guilt—the *miracle*. The remaining two paragraphs tell of this happy solution.

(8:1-4) Into this hopeless situation God sends His teachers. They bring the light of hope from God Himself. There is a way in which escape is possible. It can be learned and taught, but it requires patience and abundant willingness.

As he so often does in the Course, Jesus speaks metaphorically, for we know that God does not send teachers. Nonetheless, as teachers of God we learn how to escape from the situation we believe we are in, yet this escape will not be achieved through magical means—making guilt real, and then denying and projecting it. Jesus points out that our learning requires "abundant willingness"—one of the few places where he does not say "little willingness"— because it requires great dedication. We do not undo our identification with the ego overnight. We must devote ourselves—day in and day out, hour by hour, minute by minute—to seeing how often we choose magic, and that it does not work. We need to see all magic as but *maladaptive solutions to a nonexistent problem.*

(8:5-6) Given that, the lesson's manifest simplicity stands out like an intense white light

against a black horizon, for such it is. If anger comes from an interpretation and not a fact, it is never justified.

This becomes a pivotal theme in subsequent sections of the manual. My anger is not justified because you have never done anything to me. Your body might certainly have done something to mine, but I am not a body any more than you are. My right-minded thought of Atonement cannot be assailed by anything you do, but only by my mind's decision. Therefore, you can have no effect on me unless I give you that power—this realization is the basis of forgiveness.

(8:7-9) Once this is even dimly grasped, the way is open. Now it is possible to take the next step. The interpretation can be changed at last.

Since the problem is not others or what they have done, we do not have to be concerned about changing *them*. Aware that the decision maker is the problem, we can do something about the mistake. This is the willingness to open the mind's door to Jesus' light, allowing it to shine on the ego thought system and expose it, gently laughing with him at the silliness of thinking that we ever could have chosen something so insane. Forgiveness thus welcomes the Atonement's shining through the darkened corners of our guilt-ridden minds that are filled with hate and judgment.

(8:10-11) Magic thoughts need not lead to condemnation, for they do not really have the power to give rise to guilt. And so they can be overlooked, and thus forgotten in the truest sense.

"Forgotten" in the ego sense means first to make the thoughts real and then deny them. Magic thoughts are "forgotten in the truest sense" when we realize they were never necessary—the separation never happened and God is not angry. They therefore fade into their own nothingness—the past dissolving into the eternal present—and nothing really changes except my earlier decision for madness, as we see:

(9:1-2) Madness but seems terrible. In truth it has no power to make anything.

The thought I could destroy God, establish a self independent of Him and a world in which that self lives, is madness—a *tiny, mad idea* that has had no effect on reality. Thus a thought that does not exist needs no protection through the magic of defense.

(9:3-5) Like the magic which becomes its servant, it neither attacks nor protects. To see it and to recognize its thought system is to look on nothing. Can nothing give rise to anger?

The theme of nothingness that appeared in the preceding section returns. When we look at the wrong mind from the perspective of the right mind —with Jesus' love beside us—we see that nothing is there, literally: no sin, guilt, or fear of punishment. Since nothing happened, there is nothing to defend against—the end of magic.

(9:5-7) Can nothing give rise to anger? Hardly so. Remember, then, teacher of God, that anger recognizes a reality that is not there; yet is the anger certain witness that you do believe in it as fact.

I believe my sin is real, and having projected it, I believe the sin I perceive in you is real, too. I therefore believe my anger is justified. I see you as sinful because I see myself that way; and it is much easier to confront and punish your sin than mine, which my anger reveals to you and to the world.

(9:8) Now is escape impossible, until you see you have responded to your own interpretation, which you have projected on an outside world.

This section is an especially powerful depiction of the dynamics of the ego thought system. We make the sin of separation real, and overwhelmed with guilt, we project it onto the world, magically hoping to be free of it. A careful look within the mind, however, reveals its deep despair, for in the end everyone dies. Given its source in the ego thought system, the world holds out no real hope of lasting peace and happiness, and so there is no point in trying to change it. This use of magic only roots our attention here, reinforcing our sense of hopeless despair. Our true hope lies in changing our minds. That is the function of the miracle—to bring our attention back within, where we can then correct our mistaken decision.

(9:9) Let this grim sword be taken from you now.

It is taken from us, of course, only when we give it to Jesus—he cannot take it as long as we withhold it. This sword of anger and judgment is relinquished simply by our looking at what we believe the ego has done and giving it no power over our peace.

(9:10-12) There is no death. This sword does not exist. The fear of God is causeless.

Fear was caused by the belief in sin, which asserts our separation from God. Yet since it never happened and God's Oneness is a Fact, there is nothing we need feel guilty about; no need to project sin and fear punishment—*the fear of God is causeless*.

(9:13) But His Love is Cause of everything beyond all fear, and thus forever real and always true.

God's Cause and Love is in our right minds, held there by the Holy Spirit's Atonement principle that says we have not separated from our Source, and therefore not from anyone else—we are one. All projections of sin and guilt are unjustified because their source is unreal. Recognizing this is how we remember the Love that is our true Cause and Identity.

18. HOW IS CORRECTION MADE?

We now descend from the metaphysical heights of the previous sections, which spoke of the unreality of the world and our distorted relationship with God, to the basic thrust of *A Course in Miracles*—relationships. The next three sections deal specifically with the theme of judgment and anger, the ego's primary way of reinforcing its belief in separate as opposed to shared interests.

This section thus picks up where the last one left off—how we deal with magic thoughts. Its focus is the same as "The Correction of Error" (T-9.III), which is our reaction to people who make mistakes. If, for instance, you are teaching arithmetic and a child adds 3 and 4 and gets 9, you clearly need to correct the error. The issue, however, is not what you do on the level of form, but content—the source of the real error that we believe we are separate. The error's correction is that we are *not*. As long as we remain right-minded—the Holy Spirit's content—whatever we do behaviorally to correct people's mistakes will be done lovingly and kindly, without reinforcing separation through attack, embarrassment, or humiliation.

(1:1) Correction of a lasting nature,—and only this is true correction,—cannot be made until the teacher of God has ceased to confuse interpretation with fact, or illusion with truth.

Jesus does not speak of teaching people how to add numbers or solve problems, but about correction that will last. This, ultimately, is our acceptance of the Atonement, exemplified by demonstrating to others that our interests are not separate from theirs. Recall our discussion in the last section, where Jesus made the point that anger is always an interpretation, never an objective perception. In other words, I can observe you doing something harmful to another, but I do not have to give an attacking interpretation to what I observed. Thus, I do not overlook what my eyes see, but I do try to choose against the ego's interpretation of what they see. I thus need to be alert to my continual tendency to confuse interpretation with fact, or illusion with truth. The illusion is that you are doing this to *me*—that you are an evil person who deserves to be punished for your sin. The truth is, however, that you are doing this only to yourself, and if I am feeling affected by what you do, it is because I have made the choice to let you affect me. The ultimate truth is that we are one, a oneness that can never be split apart.

(1:2) If he argues with his pupil about a magic thought, attacks it, tries to establish its error or demonstrate its falsity, he is but witnessing to its reality.

It is one thing to disagree with someone during a discussion of politics or religion, for example, but quite another when it ends up as an argument because of the investment in proving the other person wrong. On the level of form, people naturally disagree about many things. However, when you need to prove the other person wrong and yourself right, you know the ego has taken over. Keep in mind that *A Course in Miracles* never speaks of form—only the mind's content. No two people will ever agree on everything. Yet they can always agree on the level of content, because on that level there are no differences, unless they choose to put them there.

Therefore, if I see disagreement it is because I have chosen to see it—*that* is the problem. If I react to your magic thought—a silly or terrible thing you said or did—*I* am the one who is sick. It has become my problem for I have allowed you to disturb my peace and destroy the love within me. Whether or not you have a problem, therefore, is irrelevant. Whenever I have an investment in proving the other person wrong, *I* am wrong. This goes back to what we tried to do with God in the beginning—prove Him wrong and ourselves right. God said we do not exist as individuals, for our Self is within Him. We countered by saying: "You are wrong. I exist as an individual, and the fact that I am speaking to You proves it!" The ego was thus born when we sought to prove God wrong to establish our individual identity. That became the template for our lives as bodies, and is why we have such a need to be right. Our form indeed may be right, but our content is certainly wrong if we are invested in the form, since such investment always supports separate interests—for me to be right, another has to be wrong. Behind this is our burning need to say the same to God, the tragic mistake we relive over and over again.

(1:3) Depression is then inevitable, for he has "proved," both to his pupil and himself, that it is their task to escape from what is real.

"Proved" is in quotation marks to let us know it is not genuine proof, for an illusion can never be proven true. However, depression is the inevitable outcome of the mind's belief in separation, having nothing to do with what goes on between you and me, but only with my ego's choice to be right. That is why Jesus repeatedly tells us his course is simple, for everything comes down to the same thing. If I choose him as my teacher, regardless of external events, I will be peaceful and happy because I have been wrong. If I choose the ego, whatever happens or whatever lies I tell myself, I will never be at peace, even though I may delude myself into thinking I am happy because I am right and got what I wanted. Yet my ego will warn me that others will take it from me, just as I took it from them. Recall that the principle of *one or the other* pervades the ego's thinking. If I am happy, you cannot be. Moreover, if I am happy it has come at your expense, which is why you are not happy. Since I made you in my image—a thief, liar, and murderer—you must be the same, a fact I conveniently forget. Rather than see my self-accusation, therefore, I see only the thief in you, out to get what you want at my expense.

My life, therefore, will inevitably be filled with tension, for I must always be on my guard, preparing my defense. The hopelessness of this situation —the ego's attack-defense cycle ensures I will never feel safe—inevitably leads to depression. This is the case whenever I attack your magic thought and prove you wrong. Jesus says in the text that if a brother asks you something outrageous, do it (T-12.III.4). Yet if you experience a quick reaction not to do the outrageous thing, which you perceive as magic, you are making the same mistake he is. The other person believes salvation lies in your doing the outrageous thing, while you believe salvation lies in not doing it. This makes you equally wrong, because salvation lies only in accepting the Atonement. This does not mean you always do the outrageous thing—as Jesus clarifies later: "But be certain that this does not mean to do a foolish thing that would hurt either him or you" (T-16.I.6:5)—but if you experience a quick opposition, you know the ego has succeeded in making you as insane as the one you are accusing.

(1:4) And this can only be impossible.

In other words, we cannot escape from what is real. Once we establish sin's reality, how could we escape from it? Even in the ego system we do not escape, for in the end God will avenge sin with our death. When the ego wrote its script, it made the body mortal because death is the final proof our punishment is deserved. Even though we cannot escape the body's mortality, we magically hope that by projecting our guilt onto others we will live on in Heaven. Yet is our fate sealed, for sin and guilt remain—*ideas leave not their source*—and we believe our projections will creep back into our minds (T-7.VIII.3:11). This means we believe others will attack us as we attacked them. Since it is all our dream, governed by the ego's thought system of sin and guilt, this fear is inevitable unless we change teachers. Only then can there be meaningful change in how we feel.

(1:5-6) Reality is changeless. Magic thoughts are but illusions.

Two lovely sections in the text reflect this truth: "The Changeless Dwelling Place" (T-29.V) and "Changeless Reality" (T-30.VIII). The ego's heaven is based on change: the Son did not like God's Kingdom, and so changed it and made himself ruler of his own. However, the Atonement principle remains true: reality cannot be changed—"not one note in Heaven's song was missed" (T-26.V.5:4). God has never ceased being God, and His loving Oneness has never ceased being what it is. Our magical illusions to the contrary, we have remained God's one Son, a perfect part of His perfect Love.

(1:6-7) Magic thoughts are but illusions. Otherwise salvation would be only the same age-old impossible dream in but another form.

Jesus here takes a swipe at formal religion, specifically Christianity. The salvation that Christianity has offered is nothing more than the ego's plan for salvation, where sin is first made real, and escape from it accomplished through atonement and suffering, as exemplified in the biblical account of Jesus' sacrificial death. Yet, once sin is established as real, it cannot be escaped, and the idea that salvation comes from anything other than a change of teachers is the Course's understanding of magic. As discussed above, *magic is a maladaptive solution to a nonexistent problem.* Vicarious salvation—achieved through Jesus' death on the cross—is the Bible's maladaptive solution, the attempt to solve the nonexistent problem of sin by turning God into the mad sinner who believes that sacrificial murder is the way to attain salvation. The principle that the end justifies the means is always a dangerous principle to follow.

The biblical plan for salvation is thus no different from any other ego plan. True salvation looks at the error and realizes it never happened, while the ego establishes sin as real and devises a strategy to do something about it, as if something actually happened that had to be undone. What does need to be undone however, is our mistaken choice. In other words, we look at the illusion and affirm it is not reality. And it is gone. Recalling our discussion of "How Will the World End?" (M-14), the world will end as it began—an illusion—when we look at its underlying thought and simply say: "This is unreal, and thus has no effect upon the truth."

(1:8-9) Yet the dream of salvation has new content. It is not the form alone in which the difference lies.

In *A Course in Miracles*, salvation is a dream, as is forgiveness. However, these are right-minded dreams that undo the ego's nightmares. Forgiveness is thus not only different in form, but in content. The content of the ego's plan for salvation, once again, is that sin is real and needs to be atoned for. The Holy Spirit's content is that sin is *un*real; therefore nothing need be done—the basis of "I Need Do Nothing" (T-18.VII). I need do nothing because there is no problem that has to be solved. Jesus is not referring to the behavioral level, where we obviously have problems to be solved, but to the mind, where the belief in the nonexistent problem of separation can be undone.

Correcting someone's mistakes is a wonderful way of expressing love, *when the correction is made without attack.* This, of course, is how Jesus and his course correct mistakes. To be sure, he does not hesitate to point out our mistaken thinking, but never in the spirit of attack or punishment; nor does he demand anything of us. He simply says: "You made a mistake, and these are its consequences. But if you look at this mistake through my non-judgmental eyes, it will be undone along with its consequences, and you will be supremely happy." That is all. Jesus does not choose for us, and does not demand we choose differently. He merely shows us both choices, stripping away the veils the ego used to keep its plan concealed so we would never even know it had a plan. True correction thus occurs when our eyes open, allowing us to choose freely the love that undoes the ego's choice for hate.

(2:1) God's teachers' major lesson is to learn how to react to magic thoughts wholly without anger.

Not *partially* without anger; *wholly* without anger. This is what establishes us as advanced teachers of God. Keep in mind that anger, as with everything in *A Course in Miracles*, is not meant behaviorally but only on the level of the mind. Even when someone may *appear* to be angry, when such response is appropriate to a situation, there is no loss of peace and no need to prove the other person wrong.

(2:2) Only in this way can they proclaim the truth about themselves.

The truth about ourselves is that we are God's innocent and sinless Son, unseparated from our Creator and therefore unseparated from the Sonship. My anger affirms separation: I am a self who is justified in attacking your self, perceived outside me, and I am justified in attacking because you attacked me and took away my peace. This but upholds the ego's "fact" of separation, belying my true Identity as God's undivided Son.

(2:3) Through them, the Holy Spirit can now speak of the reality of the Son of God.

We are not the ones who speak of the reality of God's Son; the Holy Spirit does. He is the mind's Thought or Memory of God's Love that automatically "speaks" through us when we abandon the interferences to it—our investment in specialness, separate interests, and upholding the principle of *one or the other*. Since I believe I am a body, and everyone believes likewise, God's Love will take shape in words and deeds. Yet the content alone is important. As Jesus states of the miracle:

> Miracles as such do not matter. The only thing that matters is their Source, which is far beyond evaluation.
> Miracles occur naturally as expressions of love. The real miracle is the love that inspires them (T-1.I.2:1–3:2).

(2:4) Now He can remind the world of sinlessness, the one unchanged, unchangeable condition of all that God created.

Sinlessness in *A Course in Miracles* refers to our unseparated condition. As God's teachers, we demonstrate that we believe in shared rather than separate interests. We cannot get angry at one perceived to be like us, but when we listen to the ego's interpretation and judge others to be different, anger is inevitable. Bodies differ, as do nationalities, religions, and opinions, but God's Sons are not different. Thus do we exemplify what we wish to learn.

(2:5-7) Now He can speak the Word of God to listening ears, and bring Christ's vision to eyes that see. Now is He free to teach all minds the truth of what they are, so they will gladly be returned to Him. And now is guilt forgiven, overlooked completely in His sight and in God's Word.

Note that Jesus says *all* minds—how often that occurs in his teaching! You cannot teach *some* minds, because all minds are joined. By choosing against guilt, the love in your mind automatically flows through the Sonship as one, because the mind of God's Son is one. Thus, what allows the Holy Spirit's Love to guide your words and actions is the simple decision to get the ego out of the way by looking at it, saying: "I no longer want this. Separation brought me only an illusion of peace and happiness, and it is true peace I want." To the extent we mean these words, we will live them and gladly release our judgments, grievances, and petty thoughts of anger.

(3:1) Anger but screeches, "Guilt is real!"

When I am angry, I say you deserve to be judged: "Look at what you have done! You should feel guilty because of your selfishness and loveless insensitivity." My anger thus points an accusing finger, behind which is the silent hope that God will be listening and agree with me: "Yes, *there* goes the sinner I will punish; not you."

(3:2) Reality is blotted out as this insane belief is taken as replacement for God's Word.

God's Word, the Atonement principle, says the separation never happened, and so there is no sin, guilt, or fear of punishment. Anger says the opposite: separation is a fact, caused by sin, for which punishment is justified. We believe this because it preserves our self—the miscreation of separation and sin.

(3:3-5) The body's eyes now "see"; its ears alone can "hear." Its little space and tiny breath become the measure of reality. And truth becomes diminutive and meaningless.

As the text says, we have chosen the grandiosity of the ego over the grandeur of God (T-9.VIII), the littleness of the ego's thought system over the magnitude of Heaven's. Thus we made the body to see sin in another—the attraction of guilt (T-19.IV-A.i). I need there to be a *you* onto whom my guilt can be projected, and so I made my body with eyes and ears to see and hear your body demonstrate my secret sin, justifying my attack on you.

(3:6-8) Correction has one answer to all this, and to the world that rests on this:

> *You but mistake interpretation for the truth. And you are wrong.*

As the text says: "And God thinks otherwise" (T-23.I.2:7). Again, Jesus is quite clear in the Course in telling us we are mistaken, but the crucial point is that he does not attack us. There is nothing wrong in telling people they are wrong. Indeed, many times this is the most helpful thing to do. But the challenge is to do it with Jesus and not the ego, which means correcting kindly with the purpose of helping, not humiliation or attack.

> **(3:9-12) But a mistake is not a sin, nor has reality been taken from its throne by your mistakes. God reigns forever, and His laws alone prevail upon you and upon the world. His Love remains the only thing there is. Fear is illusion, for you are like Him.**

Nothing happened. I just dreamt I could murder God and abolish His regime, establishing my own kingdom with myself on the throne. Yet that was only a dream, and nothing changed in truth. Thus in my right-minded relationship with you I demonstrate that my love is unchanged, despite what you may have done or said; unconditional love is not contingent upon behavior or personality. I may think what you are doing is a mistake, but I know this has nothing to do with who you truly are. I know, too, that if I attack your mistake, I would be making real our joint belief that separation is reality.

(4:1) In order to heal, it thus becomes essential for the teacher of God to let all his own mistakes be corrected.

Not *your* mistakes, *mine*. As taught in the *Psychotherapy* pamphlet, healing occurs through the healing of the *therapist*, whose misperceptions alone have to be healed:

> The therapist sees in the patient all that he has not forgiven in himself, and is thus given another chance to look at it, open it to re-evaluation and forgive it (P-2.VI.6:3).

Interestingly, nothing is said in the pamphlet about healing the patient directly, because the patient is not the real concern. It is the therapists who are the problem, and if their minds are healed of guilt, thus undoing their projections onto the patient, the Love of the true Therapist flows through them, healing therapist and patient alike. Thus healing, by removing the blocks to our awareness of its presence, is the result of demonstrating to each other that we are not separate.

(4:2) If he senses even the faintest hint of irritation in himself as he responds to anyone, let him instantly realize that he has made an interpretation that is not true.

I should always be vigilant for God and His Kingdom by being vigilant for my ego. Whether I am looking at a news broadcast, am at work, with my family, or merely thinking of someone, I simply watch my thoughts. If I find even the slightest hint of irritation or anxiety, I know immediately it is my problem, regardless of the external circumstance. I now need to ask Jesus for help to look at this person differently, to look at my investment in seeing us as separate and not the same.

(4:3-4) Then let him turn within to his eternal Guide, and let Him judge what the response should be. So is he healed, and in his healing is his pupil healed with him.

Our two major themes are here stated side by side. I learn to see you as having the same interest as me by asking Jesus to help me see through his eyes. As I am healed of my belief in separation, so are you; as you are healed of your belief in separation, so am I—it is impossible that healing occur to one without the other: "When I am healed I am not healed alone" (W-pI.137). If we are of one mind and thus the same, what occurs to one must occur in the other. This, needless to say, is true only for the mind, not the body.

(4:5) The sole responsibility of God's teacher is to accept the Atonement for himself.

This theme recurs constantly. Accepting the Atonement for myself in the context of our relationship means I do not see your interests as apart from mine. If I am happy, *you* must be; if you are happy, *I* must be. It is not *one or the other*, but "together, or not at all" and "the ark of peace is entered two by two" (T-19.IV-D.12:8; T-20.IV.6:5). I cannot be in the ark without you, a fact that corrects the ego's attitude that seeks to exclude you, onto whom I have projected the dark spot of sin I do not want to acknowledge in myself. I can tell immediately when I have followed the ego by noting my irritation, anger, annoyance, depression, anxiety, or fear.

(4:6) Atonement means correction, or the undoing of errors.

This is why it is important to realize the error is not in the body but the mind—the place of Atonement—and why it is a mistake for students of *A Course in Miracles* to attempt to bring Jesus or the Holy Spirit into the dream and ask Them to fix things there. The world is not only not the problem, there is no world—the central lesson the Course attempts to teach (W-pI.132.6:2-3). The mind's *mist*-houghts that lead to the world and body are the errors that need to be undone, and these arise when we choose the wrong teacher, easily corrected by choosing the right One.

(4:7-10) When this has been accomplished, the teacher of God becomes a miracle worker by definition. His sins have been forgiven him, and he no longer condemns himself. How can he then condemn anyone? And who is there whom his forgiveness can fail to heal?

Forgiveness heals everyone. This makes no sense if we identify with the body and try to comprehend it from the world's perspective. It makes sense only when we realize everything is played out in the mind—*everything*. The world, therefore, is literally a dream. The contents of our sleeping dreams are a product of our thoughts, which we understand when we awaken. While asleep, however, the dream seems real indeed—the people we are with, events and places, physical and psychological sensations—and we have no idea this exists only in the mind. Correspondingly, when we awaken from the ego's sleep of separation by looking through Christ's vision at the dream that is the world, we realize His truth. We are brought to this happy realization by asking Jesus, our teacher and guide, for help to see another's interests as our own—the two themes that carry us along as we gladly journey home with him and all our brothers.

19. WHAT IS JUSTICE?

As we go through this section, we will find Jesus teaching the same ideas as before, but in a different form. *Justice* as presented here corrects the belief in separate interests, the meaning of *injustice* that rests on the belief that you and I are separate, with my happiness coming at your expense. Jesus helps us realize our interests are one—we have the same wrong and right minds, and the same need to exercise our decision-making power to choose between them. Since we would have no need for justice if injustice did not exist, Jesus states that justice is unknown in Heaven because there is nothing there to be undone.

(1:1) Justice is the divine correction for injustice.

The divine truth is our inherent oneness as God's Son, reflected within the illusion as justice—we share the same interest and need; the same insanity and sanity.

(1:2) Injustice is the basis for all the judgments of the world.

All judgments come from the belief in separation: You are separate from me, which means if I am innocent—my goal—you must be guilty. However, if you are innocent, I must be guilty, and thus I am compelled to do everything possible to judge against you and prove your guilt.

(1:3) Justice corrects the interpretations to which injustice gives rise, and cancels them out.

The interpretation is that we are separate individuals who are attacked, thus justifying our anger toward the attackers and our demand that they be punished. Justice reminds us that nothing has been done to us personally. Its interpretation of attack is that it was a call for help that mirrors our own; and therefore if we attack another we but attack ourselves, ensuring we will never awaken—the goal for which the ego continually strives.

(1:4) Neither justice nor injustice exists in Heaven, for error is impossible and correction meaningless.

This is a common theme found throughout *A Course in Miracles*; for example,

God does not forgive because He has never condemned (W-pI.46.1:1).

Our Creator knows nothing of sin, so there is nothing to forgive. In the ego's plan for salvation, however, sin is quite real, which finds expression in the biblical religions: God sees sin and does something about it. Yet all He really does is make things worse, because His response justifies persecution, suffering, sacrifice, and murder, which explains why Western religions have been fraught with persecution, suffering, sacrifice, and murder. None of this, however, has meaning in Heaven, where sin and attack do not exist.

(1:5-7) In this world, however, forgiveness depends on justice, since all attack can only be unjust. Justice is the Holy Spirit's verdict upon the world. Except in His judgment justice is impossible, for no one in the world is capable of making only just interpretations and laying all injustices aside.

Keep in mind that *unjust* is synonymous with *separate interests*, and *justice* with *shared interests*. The Holy Spirit's "verdict upon the world" is that no one is separate. There is no good and evil, or sinner and sinned against—only innocence, shared equally by all God's Sons. How silly to believe that part of God could wrench itself from perfect Oneness! To see separation as silly means there is no justification here for being angry, anxious, enraged, depressed, guilty, or retaliatory.

"Except in His judgment justice is impossible": This parallels a statement early in the text that love without ambivalence is impossible in this world (T-4.III.4:6). Since love is perfect oneness, bodies—the embodiment of separation—cannot love, nor express justice. We can only choose to learn the Holy Spirit's justice, and when our minds are healed of ego thoughts we are just, because we no longer see anyone as separate.

(1:8-9) If God's Son were fairly judged, there would be no need for salvation. The thought of separation would have been forever inconceivable.

Because we do not judge God's Son fairly—we attack him in ourselves and everyone else—we need to be saved. That is why we have *A Course in Miracles*, and why we need such symbols of God's Love as Jesus or the Holy Spirit. As long as we think we are bodies, we need a correction that meets us on our own terms. Justice, then, has meaning for us as the correction for the lies the ego told us were true.

(2:1-2) Justice, like its opposite, is an interpretation. It is, however, the one interpretation that leads to truth.

In other words, justice is an illusion; a benign interpretation that reflects Heaven's Love.

(2:3-4) This becomes possible because, while it is not true in itself, justice includes nothing that opposes truth. There is no inherent conflict between justice and truth; one is but the first small step in the direction of the other.

What opposes truth? Separation. What opposes truth in relationships? Separate interests. Justice acknowledges that people may be separate in form, but not content. It therefore does not oppose the truth because it reflects its oneness in the dream. Justice becomes the first small step—along with its sisters forgiveness, salvation, and vision—that leads to truth. When Jesus says, "Do not deny the little steps He [God] asks you take to Him" (W-pI.193.13:7), he refers to these small steps we practice day in and day out. Now to the lovely lines that end this paragraph:

(2:5-6) The path becomes quite different as one goes along. Nor could all the magnificence, the grandeur of the scene and the enormous opening vistas that rise to meet one as the journey continues, be foretold from the outset.

We may be at the journey's beginning, but at least it is the right journey with the right Guide, Who leads us along the different path of learning we are not different from each other. We have no way of knowing how wonderful this will be, echoing Jesus' words from the text:

> You have no idea of the tremendous release and deep peace that comes from meeting yourself and your brothers totally without judgment (T-3.VI.3:1).

We begin to give up judgment, realizing how costly it is to see people as either enemies or saviors—we need not hate them nor have them love us—and replace this specialness by the recognition that we are the same. Again, Jesus is telling us we have no idea of our happiness when we shift our thinking. Yet as splendorous as even this will be, it pales before the Heavenly beauty still to come:

(2:7) Yet even these, whose splendor reaches indescribable heights as one proceeds, fall short indeed of all that wait when the pathway ceases and time ends with it.

Two lovely sections in the text—"The Forgiven World" and "Where Sin Has Left" (T-17.II; T-26.IV)—describe in beautiful and moving words our perception of the world when we release our hatred, grievances, and stubborn insistence on being right—wonderful beyond anything we can imagine. Yet again, the beauty of the real world cannot hold a candle to the radiance of Heaven and its love, which we are not yet ready to hear about.

(2:8-9) But somewhere one must start. Justice is the beginning.

We have a long way to go, but let us set our feet on the journey. As we proceed, we lose our sense of time and impatience because we begin to realize the wonders of the path, which only increase in experience when we release our guilt, hatred, and judgment. Depression lifts and anxiety dissipates, and all that is necessary for this to occur is that we look within for the Teacher Who shows us that our problems are within, where they can be undone. Thus are we relieved of the unbearable burden of trying to correct the world, let alone everyone in it.

(3:1) All concepts of your brothers and yourself; all fears of future states and all concerns about the past, stem from injustice.

Jesus refers to the ego's unholy trinity of sin, guilt, and fear. We apply these concepts of God's Son to what the ego tells us is the guilt-ridden present, the fearful future, and the sin-filled past, all of which stem from the injustice of separation.

(3:2) Here is the lens which, held before the body's eyes, distorts perception and brings witness of the distorted world back to the mind that made the lens and holds it very dear.

This theme is found throughout—the body brings to the mind what the mind sent it to find: sin, guilt, and justifications for hate. Once we accept the thought of separation—the basis of all injustice—everything we perceive is distorted, for our bodies see everyone as separate. Sin and guilt are perceived around us, but never within—the purpose of projecting a world of bodies. This basic injustice, and the world that arose from it preserve our insignificant self and make us think it is wonderful, even divine. Thus we hold it dear and cherish its very existence.

(3:3-5) Selectively and arbitrarily is every concept of the world built up in just this way. "Sins" are perceived and justified by careful selectivity in which all thought of wholeness must be lost. Forgiveness has no place in such a scheme, for not one "sin" but seems forever true.

The purpose of perceiving sin is to banish the thought of wholeness, the dynamic we preserve by projecting the mind's thought of separation and making a world of sin. As egos, it is incumbent upon us to seek and find sin in everyone else, and destroy it there. Our magical hope is that by obliterating the "bad guy" out there, we have ensured our innocence. This explain why governments wage war and citizens support it—we all have the magical hope that once we find and destroy the enemy, we are free: *it is not us*, to contradict Pogo; *it is them*. Having destroyed the enemy, we have a brief and ecstatic moment of elation: I am free; I am saved! And then the anxiety begins anew, because the guilt in the mind has never been undone, and so we always need an enemy—"Another can be found" (W-pI.170.8:7). In addition, when the ego made the world, it made everyone different in order to justify a hatred based on these differences—gender, race, religion, nationality, and political and economic beliefs. *Vive la différence* (*long live the difference*), to borrow the French expression again, is the ego's cry because this establishes that my difference from God is real—again, the basic injustice. It goes without saying that forgiveness has no place here, unless it is the ego's forgiveness-to-destroy.

(4:1-2) Salvation is God's justice. It restores to your awareness the wholeness of the fragments you perceive as broken off and separate.

Salvation does not bring the fragments back, nor does it unite them. It merely restores to our awareness the truth that no fragmentation occurred. It is important to understand that forgiveness and salvation do nothing; neither does justice. They but remind us of the wholeness that is already there, covered by layers of hatred, division, and judgment. Our job is simply to remove these layers by asking Jesus' help us look at them differently, thereby learning how painful they have been to us. Once these covers are gone, what remains is the memory of our wholeness as God's Son. We had perceived the Sonship as broken off and separate, but it never ceased being unfragmented and whole.

(4:3) And it is this that overcomes the fear of death.

Why? Because the fear of death comes from guilt, and guilt comes from separation and injustice. If I undo separation, I undo guilt and injustice as well. Moreover, since guilt demands punishment, even unto death, if there is no guilt there can be no death, and obviously nothing to fear. Undoing death does not mean making us immortal by some magical transformation, but by undoing the *thought* of death that is our inevitable punishment for sin. Thus we joyously exclaim with the *Bhagavad Gita*: "How can the immortal die?" (T-19.II.3:6). We realize our immortality, not as body but spirit—part of the living and eternal God.

(4:4-5) For separate fragments must decay and die, but wholeness is immortal. It remains forever and forever like its Creator, being one with Him.

The separate fragments that decay and die are manifest in the body. Yet Jesus teaches that in the holy instant—free from separation or guilt—there is no body (T-15.IX.7:3), which means there is nothing to decay and die.

(4:6) God's Judgment is His justice.

God's Judgment is that we are still His holy Son (W-pII.10.5:1)—nothing has changed. The Atonement is the principle of changelessness within the dream, just as separation is the principle of change that establishes the dream and keeps us asleep. Yet God's justice reflects the truth that we remain awake and have not changed Heaven.

19. What Is Justice?

(4:7-9) Onto this,—a Judgment wholly lacking in condemnation; an evaluation based entirely on love,—you have projected your injustice, giving God the lens of warped perception through which you look. Now it belongs to Him and not to you. You are afraid of Him, and do not see you hate and fear your Self as enemy.

Jesus' reference is to the biblical God, because He judges in a way totally unlike what Jesus presents in his course. The Judaeo-Christian God judges good *and* evil, and the latter naturally deserves His punishment. History has shown how individuals, generals, and world leaders have used the Bible as the basis for justifying hatred of others. After all, God hates and judges, and so they speak on His behalf and kill as He does. Inspired by His judgment, they determine the evildoers and punish them. Again, projecting onto God justifies their hatred and need to condemn: one lives, another dies—*one or the other*. And very few realize it is but their image they see in the deity.

However, Jesus tells us this has nothing to do with the true God, Who only loves His Sons equally. When Jesus says that all his brothers are special (T-1.V.3:6), he negates the meaning of *special*. We are all the same, and God does not see separate Sons—only *one*. It is thus easy to see how the world has misinterpreted Him, for judgment of any kind is unjustified if it separates. The Holy Spirit's judgment alone is justified, for it says we are not different from each other. As we have seen, people either call for love or express it, and it is irrelevant to our response which it is, for we respond only one way—lovingly. It would therefore be helpful to go through the day seeing how prone we are to fall back on magical thoughts of attack, believing it is our prerogative—given us by God—to correct the error and prove another wrong. Sin is thus made real, but not in the mind. Having given "God the lens of warped perception"—separation and injustice—we now see everything through this distorted lens: hating and fearing our Self, we hate and fear everyone else. We repeat the last two sentences:

(4:8-9) Now it belongs to Him and not to you. You are afraid of Him, and do not see you hate and fear your Self as enemy.

Projection enables us to deny that *we* set up the divine plan for salvation. After all, the Bible asserts it is God's plan: someone wins, another loses; sin is real and has to be paid for, and those who fall short will be destroyed. Because it is God's plan, we are justified in fearing Him. Yet the truth is that we want to fear and hate God so we do not discover that what we really fear and hate is our Self. The individual self that we name, and has a past and a future, cannot exist in the state of perfect Wholeness that is the Self of Christ. Therefore, that Self is the enemy, and is the meaning of Jesus' words in the text:

> You are not really afraid of crucifixion. Your real terror is of redemption (T-13.III.1:10-11).

We fear remembering Who we are as Christ, and since the Holy Spirit reminds us of this Self we need to blot Him out and destroy His Thought of Atonement. Feeling guilty over this "sin," we project the guilt so we are now justifiably afraid of the enemy outside—a person in our life, a country, or God Himself. The injustice is now perceived in "them" and not us, concealing its true source in the mind.

(5:1) Pray for God's justice, and do not confuse His mercy with your own insanity.

The mercy of God, as seen by the world, falls upon some people, but not all. That is why Jesus asks us not to confuse true mercy—as all-inclusive as is God's Love—with the insanity that seeks to separate. When we pray for God's justice, the person we pray to is ourselves, that we recognize we lack nothing. As Jesus tells us:

> The only meaningful prayer is for forgiveness, because those who have been forgiven have everything (T-3.V.6:3).

We pray to our decision-making self, asking Jesus to help us remember that true justice is in the mind. This thought, equated with Atonement, is what we truly want. We thus do not pray to some external agent—divine or otherwise—who magically dispenses justice or grants miracles. Since we separated from God's Love, only we can choose to return to it. Our joining with Jesus, who symbolizes God's justice, returns his loving sanity to our insane and frightened minds.

(5:2-4) Perception can make whatever picture the mind desires to see. Remember this. In this lies either Heaven or hell, as you elect.

This reflects one of the Course's central themes: *projection makes perception*. The mind decides what it wants—the hell of the ego's separation or the Heaven of the Holy Spirit's Atonement. Once the decision is made, I will see either an attacking world that causes pain, or a world reflecting back to me the oneness in my mind. I see the same world an ego sees, but the interpretation differs markedly. My eyes see fear, viciousness, and pain, yet this does not justify perceptions of attack but calls for help, as I remember that these calls echo mine, for there is no difference between others and me.

(5:5-6) God's justice points to Heaven just because it is entirely impartial. It accepts all evidence that is brought before it, omitting nothing and assessing nothing as separate and apart from all the rest.

"*Entirely* impartial"—God's justice makes no distinction in what is without distinction, for the Holy Spirit sees God's Son as one. Thus we see the all-inclusive nature of Jesus' thinking: "omitting nothing and assessing nothing as separate and apart from all the rest." To repeat this important point, everything the Holy Spirit sees expresses love or calls for it. The former comes from the right mind, the latter from the wrong mind, and since we all share the same split along with the ability to choose between them, there is no difference among us.

(5:7-8) From this one standpoint does it judge, and this alone. Here all attack and condemnation becomes meaningless and indefensible.

It would be impossible to justify attack when everyone is the same. Needless to say, God cannot be blamed for attack when He does not see differences —He knows only His Self and Its perfect Love and Oneness.

(5:9-11) Perception rests, the mind is still, and light returns again. Vision is now restored. What had been lost has now been found.

We did not find light in the world, nor through attack, but in the mind where it patiently awaited our return. We had mistakenly looked elsewhere— the meaning of magic. Sane once more, we have chosen the justice of the right mind, and our perception rests in the quiet Love of Christ. Through the Holy Spirit's kind perception we see all as one, for as we share the same physical equipment of arms, legs, etc., we share the same mental equipment of judgment and forgiveness. Recognizing this inherent sameness of God's Son gives rise to vision, which gently corrects the ego's misperceptions of separation and differences.

(5:12-13) The peace of God descends on all the world, and we can see. And we can see!

We note once again Jesus' use of the word *all*. The peace of God descends on all the world; otherwise it is not His peace, the subject of the next section. Since true peace embraces all people, war can never truly succeed because the peace that follows falls only on the winners, whose victory, in the world's insane perception, establishes them as good and righteous, separated from the losers whose evil brought about their defeat.

The repeated rhythm of the phrase "and we can see" is a familiar one in *A Course in Miracles*. At the end of "For They Have Come," for example, Jesus exclaims exultingly: "For They have come! For They have come at last!" (T-26.IX.8:8-9). When God's peace and love descend on all people, we will have seen through Christ's vision in which His Son is recognized in everyone, without exception.

20. WHAT IS THE PEACE OF GOD?

The ego's greatest fear is our choosing the peace of God, for as a dimension of His Love, peace is all-inclusive, and so separation cannot exist in its presence. The discussion thus focuses on judgment and attack—the ego's life-blood—for they are the impediments to the experience of this peace.

(1:1) It has been said that there is a kind of peace that is not of this world.

This calls to mind St. Paul's statement, "the peace of God, which passeth all understanding" (Philippians 4:7), as well as Jesus' words in the gospel, "my peace I give unto you, not as the world giveth" (John 14:27).

(1:2-5) How is it recognized? How is it found? And being found, how can it be retained? Let us consider each of these questions separately, for each reflects a different step along the way.

These three questions form the basis of Jesus' discussion.

(2:1-5) First, how can the peace of God be recognized? God's peace is recognized at first by just one thing; in every way it is totally unlike all previous experiences. It calls to mind nothing that went before. It brings with it no past associations. It is a new thing entirely.

The peace we are most familiar with does not last, nor embrace all people. This is certainly evident in international relations, as a study of history readily confirms, where peace embraces the victors and quickly vanishes as the vanquished rise to destroy it. True peace, however, Jesus tells us, has nothing to do with what the world has known or seen, or what we have experienced in our individual lives.

(2:6-7) There is a contrast, yes, between this thing and all the past. But strangely, it is not a contrast of true differences.

The Holy Spirit teaches through contrast: His thought system with the ego's—joy and pain, freedom and imprisonment, forgiveness and grievances. Yet there can be no real difference between truth and illusion because they are mutually exclusive. For there to be a meaningful discussion of difference, there need to be two reasonably valid points of view. The peace of God and the world's version of peace do not reflect equal dimensions of reality—only one is true. This is but another way of saying that *A Course in Miracles* is not a dualistic thought system in which exist both good and evil, spirit and matter, God and the world; the only reality is God, which is why we speak of it as a *non*-dualistic system. The duality reflected in the Course deals only with the illusion, within which Jesus contrasts the wrong– and right-minded thought systems. There can be no real contrast between truth and illusion, however, because there is no illusion—by definition.

(2:8-11) The past just slips away, and in its place is everlasting quiet. Only that. The contrast first perceived has merely gone. Quiet has reached to cover everything.

You do not correct the past, fight against it, or defeat it. You simply shine truth's light and watch the past gently disappear—there can be no darkness in the presence of light; no hate, fear, or division in the presence of love; no perception of separate interests in the presence of shared interests.

Peace in this world is always thought of within a dualistic framework, as the opposite of war or conflict. The peace of God, however, has no opposite. It is what remains when belief in opposition and separation is withdrawn, for without belief the ego's thought system disappears, having been upheld only by belief. Thus, our focus should not be on correcting error on the level of form, but by shining the Holy Spirit's truth of shared interests on the ego's illusion of separate interests. Again, all that then remains is peace, because conflict is gone.

The belief in conflict, represented by anger, has a purpose: to banish peace from awareness. Yet its presence has not left the mind, which is how the peace of God differs from everything else. It is not part of the world's dream, as is the ego's version of peace: conflict, war, and peace, and then more conflict, war, and peace; personal disagreements, handshakes, and all is well, and then more disagreements, and on and on and on. True peace transcends distinctions and differences, which is how we discern it comes from Jesus, for it reflects the love that embraces all people as one.

Now the second question:

(3:1-2) How is this quiet found? No one can fail to find it who but seeks out its conditions.

This echoes Lesson 131: "No one can fail who seeks to reach the truth" (W-pI.131). Its conditions are the negation of the ego thought system, and so we find its peace and sublime quiet by releasing our anger and judgments, our belief in separate interests and the value of specialness. The positive in *A Course in Miracles* is the undoing of the negative; thus peace is found by undoing the barriers to it—an echo of Jesus' reminder in the text that our task is not to seek for love, but to seek and find the barriers we placed between ourselves and love (T-16.IV.6:1).

The peace of God, born of the thought of the mind's oneness, lies just beneath the ego's layers of judgment, anger, and obsession with being right. When we withdraw these veils, peace remains, as the lesson assures us: "The peace of God is shining in me now" (W-pI.188). Clouds may block the sun's rays, but the sun shines nonetheless. God's peace is the sun in our minds, but its light is blocked from awareness by the darkness of our decision for the ego. Peace is therefore found by looking at the negative, and beyond it to the light. This is what distinguishes the Course from other spiritual paths. Jesus helps us not by granting wishes or fixing things here, or even by loving us—his love is too threatening. His help comes from sharing his vision, that we may look at the ego through his non-judgmental eyes, acknowledging that it never gave what we truly wanted. Finding the light of peace is thus inevitable.

(3:3-5) God's peace can never come where anger is, for anger must deny that peace exists. Who sees anger as justified in any way or any circumstance proclaims that peace is meaningless, and must believe that it cannot exist. In this condition, peace cannot be found.

I choose anger because I am afraid of peace, for within the peace of God this self I think I am is meaningless. Identified therefore with the ego, I am compelled angrily to exclude people from my forgiveness; otherwise, my guilt would remain within as a source of extreme and perpetual torment. I need an object onto which I can project my guilt so I can be free of it, which means I need people whom I can perceive as different from me, especially in the role of enemy. In God's peace there are no differences, a fact my ego perceives as profoundly threatening. If I can find no one to blame, I am thrown back onto myself—the sinful, guilt-ridden self that deserves to be punished by God. Thus peace is threatening, despite our belief that we want it above all else.

We are, however, quite comfortable with a dualistic peace—the world's version that is forged between two disputing parties. Our egos will never accept the non-dualistic peace that undoes the mind's conflict when we choose Jesus as our teacher. There is a major difference between the two. True peace is not achieved by making peace between you and me, because our seeming conflict is a smoke screen concealing the true conflict that emanates from the instant we chose against God, and then appeared to be locked in eternal battle with Him. Since the decision-making mind is the source of all opposition and conflict, this is where they must be undone if genuine peace is to be found. Thus the ego tells us that anger and judgment will protect us from peace, which is why we are always in a state of war. Part of the mind knows that once we accept the Atonement, the peace that is born of oneness will naturally follow, in which there is no argument, conflict, or war, but only God's one and undivided Son.

(3:6) Therefore, forgiveness is the necessary condition for finding the peace of God.

Forgiveness undoes the ego thought system of attack by forgiving others for what they have *not* done. Regardless of their behavior, people are not the problem; we are not in conflict with them but ourselves. Yet the external conflict can be used by Jesus as the means of returning to the conflict within. When we ask his help with an external conflict—whether within our body, or between ours and another's—his help lies in explaining that *projection makes perception*: the external conflict is an "outside picture of an inward condition" (T-21.in.1:1-5). The external problem represents the conflict in the mind, and is easily resolved once we look at the ego with Jesus and say: "I do not want you any more. You lied, and did not bring the peace and happiness you promised. I have received only pain and suffering from your teachings." This negative response to the ego's negation is what Jesus means when he says that "yes" means "not no" (T-21.VII.12)—we decide we no longer want the ego's negation of truth. This, then is the condition of forgiveness: undoing the ego by looking at it without guilt.

(3:7) More than this, given forgiveness there *must* be peace.

As the condition for attaining peace by undoing all interferences to it, forgiveness makes peace inevitable. It removes the veils of darkness and lets the peace of God shine as it always has. It is our fear of this peace, as we have seen, that explains why it is so difficult to let go of judgment. Even though we may be committed and dedicated students of this course, intent on giving up attack thoughts, we still find ourselves holding onto grievances in opposition to Heaven's condition, serving the need of preserving our separated self.

(3:8-12) For what except attack will lead to war? And what but peace is opposite to war? Here the initial contrast stands out clear and apparent. Yet when peace is found, the war is meaningless. And it is conflict now that is perceived as nonexistent and unreal.

This important statement tells us why the peace of God is outside the ego's dream and within the right mind. Once you believe in attack—the original thought of separation—you must believe you are at war. Thus the psychological law: when you attack, guilt will follow, and through projection you will believe people are out to attack you. You will have conveniently forgotten that you made the first attack in your mind, and therefore must believe that others are treating you unfairly, justifying your going to war. Every head of state, as well as every individual follows this pattern of the *face of innocence* (T-31.V.2-4)—someone made me do it.

Peace is the opposite to war because war dissolves in its presence. Remember, war is dualistic by definition; the peace of God is non-dualistic by definition—it does not see opposition or separation, but oneness, reflected here by the right-minded perception that our interests are the same. Once you have accepted peace instead of war, you look on the battleground and see nothing here as real. You merely perceive one figment of your imagination fighting with another in a make-believe world—literally, for we *make* ourselves *believe* in what we "see."

Now the third question, with Jesus essentially repeating what he said in the answer to the previous one:

(4:1-3) How is the peace of God retained, once it is found? Returning anger, in whatever form, will drop the heavy curtain once again, and the belief that peace cannot exist will certainly return. War is again accepted as the one reality.

We have often encountered the idea that everything in *A Course in Miracles* is to be understood within the framework of purpose—know what something is for and its meaning will be clear. Therefore, once we recognize the purpose anger serves, the reason for its prevalence will be evident: to drop a veil so we no longer experience the peace and Love of God, which our egos fear more than anything. Most people cannot conceive of themselves without anger—who would they be without it? Indeed, our birth is forged out of anger, and sustained by dependence on those who are not always there for us. This is intrinsic to our scripts that were written at the beginning, and are re-experienced throughout time. It is a cosmic setup, designed by the ego so we would always feel justified in the rage that truly makes the world go round. Anger thus was chosen by the mind to keep our identities intact, banishing peace and establishing permanent liberation from oneness, the great threat to our individual existence.

(4:4-5) Now must you once again lay down your sword, although you do not recognize that you have picked it up again. But you will learn, as you remember even faintly now what happiness was yours without it, that you must have taken it again as your defense.

We are not aware of having intentionally taken up the sword of judgment (T-31.VII.9; W-pI.190.9). Yet, as Lesson 136 explains, it was not done unconsciously. Once the mind decided to attack, it was repressed almost as quickly as the decision was made. We are therefore not aware of having chosen to feel angry, sick, or unfairly treated (W-pI.136.3-4). Jesus repeatedly asks us to contrast how we feel holding the cruel sword of judgment over someone's head, let alone our own, with the peace and joy that comes when we lay it down. If we want peace to return, we need to look at our anger and understand why we chose it. We need to see how we deceive ourselves into thinking it arose out of nowhere, or, for example, that it erupted because of an hormonal imbalance. The truth is that we chose to be angry because we feared the peace and Love of God, in Whom there are no distinctions.

(4:6-8) Stop for a moment now and think of this: Is conflict what you want, or is God's peace the better choice? Which gives you more? A tranquil mind is not a little gift.

This is the bottom line. *A Course in Miracles* is about having us look at, evaluate, and contrast the ego's thought system with the Holy Spirit's, seeing the cost to us of choosing conflict in terms of losing our happiness and peace. Jesus thus presents the choice to us, and asks us not to underestimate the magnitude of the peace of God and the quiet joy of being without conflict: "A tranquil mind is not a little gift."

(4:9) Would you not rather live than choose to die?

Recall the familiar biblical passage that those who live by the sword will die by it (Matthew 26:52); those who live by attack will believe they will be attacked in return. Since everyone attacks, the ego connects its dots and tells us we die because we have attacked and sinned, death being our justified punishment; thus we all believe we are separate, have attacked, and will die. Yet Jesus teaches that we transcend death and resurrect our minds—as we will see in section 28—by choosing a different Teacher who leads us through His happy dreams of forgiveness, awakening us from the nightmare of death unto everlasting life.

(5:1-3) Living is joy, but death can only weep. You see in death escape from what you made. But this you do not see; that you made death, and it is but illusion of an end.

We see in death escape from what we made, for it marks the end of the body's suffering. Moreover, since we made sin and believe we deserve punishment, death absolves us of sin and, hopefully—*magically*—God will reward us by letting our penitent selves remain with Him. That is why we need the concept of an afterlife: hell for the evildoers and Heaven for us. Thus we escape from sin by paying God back through suffering and death, proving our innocence so He would recognize we deserve an eternally blessed life. We maintain that we suffered because others mistreated us, and therefore we were justified in being angry and hateful, dying at the sinful hands of others. Yet we do not realize that death is not a natural law and has nothing to do with God. It is of *our* making, an intrinsic part of the ego thought system and inevitable conclusion to a self that was forged in sin and separation. In truth, however, death is only an illusion of an end—nothing happened then, nor happens now.

(5:4-6) Death cannot be escape, because it is not life in which the problem lies. Life has no opposite, for it is God. Life and death seem to be opposites because you have decided death ends life.

In "The Laws of Chaos," Jesus says "there is no life outside of Heaven" (T-23.II.19:1). What we consider life is part of a dualistic thought system—life *and* death. In fact, the meaning of death is that I was first alive, and the inevitable conclusion of life is that I die. Nonetheless, this definition has nothing to do with God, in Whom life is eternal and unchanging. Spirit neither lives nor dies; it is not born, nor develops or evolves. Life simply *is*. Death is therefore not the escape, because life is not the problem—sin is. Jesus tells us further "there is a risk in thinking death is peace" (T-27.VII.10:2). Death is not only not the answer, but is a *maladaptive solution to the nonexistent problem* of separation and sin.

(5:7-10) Forgive the world, and you will understand that everything that God created cannot have an end, and nothing He did not create is real. In this one sentence is our course explained. In this one sentence is our practicing given its one direction. And in this one sentence is the Holy Spirit's whole curriculum specified exactly as it is.

This is a variation of the lines that introduce the text: "Nothing real can be threatened. Nothing unreal exists. Herein lies the peace of God" (T-in.2:2-4; italics omitted). You learn this curriculum when you forgive the world the projections of your secret sins and hidden hates, the guilt buried deep within that you cast onto the world. When you forgive your projections they are gone; and when gone outside, they must also be gone inside because inner and outer are one. Having thus forgiven the world, you see clearly from above the battleground that everything of God is life, and nothing exists beyond that. You understand that the battleground—the world of time and space—is made up, not to mention the little things that go on within it and seem so important: our petty dreams and cherished fantasies. All are shabby substitutes for the Love of God, and with Jesus beside us we clearly recognize the distinction between the two.

(6:1-3) What is the peace of God? No more than this; the simple understanding that His Will is wholly without opposite. There is no thought that contradicts His Will, yet can be true.

The simplicity of this statement is why this is a non-dualistic thought system. There is no opposite to God, the principle reflected in the world by our learning we are the same. What are the same cannot be opposites. Therefore I would be mistaken in perceiving you as different from me. My innocence does not depend on your guilt, and it is impossible that you have something I lack—content, not form—which is another state of opposites. Separation and anger are thoughts that contradict His Will, but so, too, does the idea that peace and forgiveness are between two people—*there are no people here*. Conflict is thus not between persons, countries, or competing interests, for these are only shadowy fragments of the mind's illusory conflict between God and the ego. Moreover, this war that rages within is illusion, because God knows nothing about it.

(6:4) The contrast between His Will and yours but seemed to be reality.

Seemed to be reality, yet on that seeming an entire universe of mind and bodies was made: sin, guilt, and fear; and time and space. And all this because we believed we were at war with God over the separation.

(6:5-8) In truth there was no conflict, for His Will is yours. Now is the mighty Will of God Himself His gift to you. He does not seek to keep it for Himself. Why would you seek to keep your tiny frail imaginings apart from Him?

God is one with you. Why would you not accept that you are one with Him? Such acceptance means you see that your tiny frail imaginings—fantasies, hopes, and dreams of specialness—cannot hold a candle to God's Love. Why, then, would you want them? That is Jesus' perennial question to us, and one we repeatedly have to ask as we watch ourselves choose the world's version of peace and love over God's.

(6:9-10) The Will of God is One and all there is. This is your heritage.

This is the state of perfect Oneness, in which there is no differentiation, fragmentation, or distinction—nothing except the single truth that we reflect by seeing the Sonship with shared rather than separate interests. To state it again, we all share the insanity that drove us here, and the need to awaken from the ego's dream of madness.

(6:11) The universe beyond the sun and stars, and all the thoughts of which you can conceive, belong to you.

Jesus is not speaking of another galaxy. The universe "beyond the sun and stars" is spirit—the home of Christ.

(6:12-13) God's peace is the condition for His Will. Attain His peace, and you remember Him.

The basic formula of *A Course in Miracles* is that you see the face of Christ in your brother and remember God. You forgive, and as the veils of specialness are lifted, the memory of God dawns on the mind that was always its home. Thus, if you want to remember God and His peace, and your Identity as His one Son, you choose to forgive and not see separate interests. When you choose otherwise, it is because you want to remember neither your Source nor your Self. Remember that purpose is everything, and anger is purposive to the ego's goals, as forgiveness is for the Holy Spirit's.

21. WHAT IS THE ROLE OF WORDS IN HEALING?

We leave the theme of anger and return to the power of decision in the mind—not the body—which ultimately is the decision to see our interests either as separate from, or shared with each other.

(1:1) Strictly speaking, words play no part at all in healing.

Healing is not the result of prayers, blessings, laying on of hands, or saying or doing anything at all, because it is not the body that is sick. This returns us to another of our important themes: the relationship between mind and body. The body's symptoms are the shadows of the sickness of guilt, and so it is the mind's thoughts that need healing. Words, therefore, have no healing power in and of themselves.

(1:2-4) The motivating factor is prayer, or asking. What you ask for you receive. But this refers to the prayer of the heart, not to the words you use in praying.

Jesus uses the traditional spiritual term *prayer of the heart*, although he is really referring to the prayer of the *mind*, since in the Course *heart* is synonymous with *mind*. He essentially asks: Do you pray to the ego or the Holy Spirit?; do you want its gifts or His?; does your mind seek to make the error of separation real by making bodily sickness real, or to learn that error is unreal because the separation from God never happened? Healing, therefore, consists in recognizing the truth of the Atonement—nothing has changed the unity of Father and Son. Yet you will receive what you pray for—"the prayer of the heart"—because it is your dream.

(1:5-6) Sometimes the words and the prayer are contradictory; sometimes they agree. It does not matter.

Sometimes you sincerely want the peace of God and that is what you pray for. However, at other times your prayer reflects the ego's wishes—the glorification of differences; anything *but* the peace of God. And thus, for example, you practice what *The Song of Prayer* calls "healing-to-separate" (S-3.III), wherein you see yourself as the one who heals, separate from the one in need of healing. You pray to God, the Holy Spirit, or Jesus to heal the body, contradicting the healing the mind truly wants, for healing-to-separate is the prayer to have separation reinforced. Therefore, when you believe the body is in need of healing, it is your mind that needs to be healed because the body is not sick. Believing someone or something has to be healed—an investment in having an external problem solved—means you believe the ego is right. You then magically use the external to solve a nonexistent problem, ensuring that the illusory separation will still be real to you. Inevitably, then, you suffer the consequences of pain, misery, suffering, and death.

(1:7) God does not understand words, for they were made by separated minds to keep them in the illusion of separation.

This very important statement repeats Jesus' point from the workbook (W-pI.183.7:3-5). God does not understand words because they were made to keep us separate, and how can He "hear" His Son be other than Himself, united with Him? To be sure, Jesus uses words—Part II of the workbook consists of one wonderful prayer after another directed from us to God the Father—yet their purpose is to correct the specialness with which the ego prays. Remember that Jesus addresses his course to little children, and so he tells us fairy tales and sings nursery rhymes because that is the level of our spirituality. However, his words are benevolent and kind, in contrast to the ego's songs and tales of suffering and hate. To summarize, Jesus teaches us that God cannot understand words, as His perfection is beyond all duality. Nonetheless:

(1:8) Words can be helpful, particularly for the beginner, in helping concentration and facilitating the exclusion, or at least the control, of extraneous thoughts.

This parallels "How Should the Teacher of God Spend His Day?" (M-16), where Jesus distinguished between the advanced and normal teacher. The former needs no structure, but as little children beginning the journey, we most certainly do. Again, that is why we have the prayers in the workbook. As we grow and make our way, our need for structure diminishes and we will no longer need words to correct the ego's words, but simply to reflect the

21. What Is the Role of Words in Healing?

Love of God. And then our need for words is gone forever—we will have become the Word itself.

(1:9-10) Let us not forget, however, that words are but symbols of symbols. They are thus twice removed from reality.

This is borrowed from Plato, who in the *Republic* (596c-602b) discussed this very topic. For example, from the Holy Spirit's point of view, the reality is God's Love, which we symbolize in the image of a loving Father, which, in turn, is symbolized by words such as a *loving Father Who is lonely without us and weeps over our separated condition.* Thus the words are symbols of the symbol of God's Love, which symbolizes Its reality. The same is true of the concept of *forgiveness*, the reality within the right-minded dream. This is symbolized by two people in conflict who join together in a shared interest. *A Course in Miracles* then uses words to describe the two people in conflict—the symbol of a symbol. The words are therefore "twice removed from reality."

The significance of this passage is that Jesus is telling us not to pay attention to the literal meaning of his words, saying to us, in effect: "Let the words speak to you and take you to the place beyond them." Recall the wonderful section "Beyond All Symbols" (T-27.III)—God is beyond symbols, as is truth. Yet as long as we think we are here, identified with the body, we need symbols and words. Jesus is therefore not saying we should abandon them, but that our focus should be on reaching the reality beyond them. As symbols, words are illusions, and at the beginning of the clarification of terms he tells us that his "course remains within the ego framework" (C-in.3:1), meaning it utilizes symbols, concepts, and words. And so, the words we made to keep us separate, Jesus uses to bring us together. The words themselves are not holy, but the love that inspired them most certainly is.

(2:1-3) As symbols, words have quite specific references. Even when they seem most abstract, the picture that comes to mind is apt to be very concrete. Unless a specific referent does occur to the mind in conjunction with the word, the word has little or no practical meaning, and thus cannot help the healing process.

Jesus says to us in the text:

You cannot even think of God without a body, or in some form you think you recognize (T-18.VIII.1:7).

The reality of God is that He is abstract and non-specific—beyond concepts and symbols. Yet when we use the word *God*, no matter what our intellects may understand, an image will be generated by the brain. We need these words and concepts to correspond to the physical concept of ourselves, which is why Jesus speaks of God as "Father"—a masculine Parent—even though he teaches that God's reality is beyond all form.

While letting us know that we need symbols as stepping stones on our journey, Jesus nonetheless does not want us to be wedded to or dependent on them. We therefore make our way from a symbol to that which it symbolizes, until we reach reality —the experience of God's Love that is not of this world. Helping us along the way is learning to relate to others in the context of shared versus separate interests. *Shared interests* are words symbolizing our oneness of purpose that represents the reality of God's Oneness, as *separate interests* are words symbolizing our separate purposes that represent the "reality" of the ego's separation. We thus have words that describe a concept that symbolizes a reality—from both right- and wrong-minded perspectives.

(2:4-6) The prayer of the heart does not really ask for concrete things. It always requests some kind of experience, the specific things asked for being the bringers of the desired experience in the opinion of the asker. The words, then, are symbols for the things asked for, but the things themselves but stand for the experiences that are hoped for.

There are two experiences—peace and love, conflict and hate—that denote the ego's and Holy Spirit's thought systems. If I want the ego's conflict, I will pick a fight to prove that you are wrong and I am right; if I want to prove the separation real, I will see you as sick and I the healer who can help you—or you, the benighted student and I the teacher who can instruct you in wisdom. If, however, I want to prove the truth of the Atonement, I will see our relationship—regardless of its form— as an opportunity to learn forgiveness. Thus I first want the experience, and then use the world's symbols to bring the experience I desire.

"The words, then, are symbols for the things asked for, but the things themselves but stand for the experiences that are hoped for." Again, if I want to prove God is wrong and I am right—"the desired experience"—I may ask to win the lottery, or that this relationship or job work out. But what I really pray for is to prove either that God is wrong and I am right, or I am wrong and God is right—that separation or Atonement is true—using the things of the world to prove the underlying content. Returning to the decision-making mind—the level of content—is therefore of the essence.

(3:1-3) The prayer for things of this world will bring experiences of this world. If the prayer of the heart asks for this, this will be given because this will be received. It is impossible that the prayer of the heart remain unanswered in the perception of the one who asks.

It is my dream. If I want to prove the ego is real, I need to prove the world is real, which I do either by your giving me what I want (special love) or depriving me (special hate). My decision maker, joined with the ego, chooses the life I will lead, and the ego does not care whether I am "happy" or "unhappy," as long as my life is one of specialness. I have made the world real through pleasure or pain, and that is what I pray for because I want the experience of saying to God: "You were wrong and I am right." Since the inner and outer are one, what is given is what is received—guilt and pain, or forgiveness and joy.

(3:4-8) If he asks for the impossible, if he wants what does not exist or seeks for illusions in his heart, all this becomes his own. The power of his decision offers it to him as he requests. Herein lie hell and Heaven. The sleeping Son of God has but this power left to him. It is enough.

We all have asked for the impossible in our dreams. We wanted to have what does not exist, and we know this is so because we think we are bodies. The prayer of our hearts was answered—not by God, but by ourselves, for it is our dream. Wanting to prove that separation is the reality and oneness the illusion, we made a world in which everyone is separate, we suffer at the hands of others, and our needs are met (or unmet) by the world. However, whether positive or negative, we get what we ask for. If we *feel* unfairly treated, we have no one to blame but ourselves. We *want* to feel this way because that allows us to point an accusing finger and say: "Behold me, brother, at your hand I die" (T-27.I.4:6). It is your fault and God will punish you. I will certainly die, but God will reward me and condemn you in the hereafter because of your sin against me, proven by my suffering and pain. This, then, is what we desire, and therefore no one here is truly an innocent victim. The mind's decision maker chooses to be victimized in the dreams we call our lives, and that is the prayer of the heart: to prove we are right and God is wrong, which our world makes manifest. Yet though asleep, our minds still have the power to choose hell or Heaven, sleep or awakening.

(3:9-10) His words do not matter. Only the Word of God has any meaning, because it symbolizes that which has no human symbols at all.

Our words make no difference; only our purpose. Do I want to prove God right? Then I will see a world that reflects His Oneness. Do I want to prove God wrong? Then I will see a world of separation and specialness. The power is mine alone because it is my dream, just as I am responsible for my dreams at night.

People often ask for things that seem to be holy, especially if they are religiously inclined. Yet they are not aware of the prayer of the heart that says they want to prove the separation real, as is the world of separate interests—they have the truth and others do not. However, the only meaningful choice is for God's Word of Atonement, for it symbolizes the love and unity that is beyond the world entirely, the reality behind all dreams.

(3:11-12) The Holy Spirit alone understands what this Word stands for. And this, too, is enough.

We need not know what love is—what God's Word stands for—but we do need to know that we want to return home. The means of our return is seeing shared instead of separate interests—the meaning of forgiveness.

(4:1-2) Is the teacher of God, then, to avoid the use of words in his teaching? No, indeed!

21. What Is the Role of Words in Healing?

Back to the practical. Earlier in the section, Jesus said that words are irrelevant and were made to keep God away (M-21.1:7). Yet, as with the body and the world, they can serve a holy purpose. Everything we made to separate and kill can now be used to teach the opposite. The ego speaks first, writes its script, makes up a world, and establishes a curriculum of hate. When we change our minds and reject the ego, Jesus transforms its curriculum to one of forgiveness, and for this we need to use the world's symbols and words.

(4:3-5) There are many who must be reached through words, being as yet unable to hear in silence. The teacher of God must, however, learn to use words in a new way. Gradually, he learns how to let his words be chosen for him by ceasing to decide for himself what he will say.

At the journey's end we have no need for words, as Jesus reflects at the close of the workbook: "Our use for words is almost over now" (W-pII.14.2:1). Until then, however, words are necessary, and so God's teachers speak as others do, but with a different purpose, for their words come from a different Source—teachers of God know they are not the author of the words they use.

Importantly, Jesus is not saying to ask the Holy Spirit what to say, even though his words sometimes seem to suggest that. Helen once received an important message from Jesus on this very subject. When asking him what she should say to help someone, Helen heard that this was the wrong question; she should instead be asking his help to remove the judgments from her mind.* At that point, whatever she said would come from Jesus and be loving. In other words, our job is to remove the ego's veils of specialness, our investment in hearing the static. When we withdraw this investment in the ego's raucous shrieks, they will disappear. Without the interference, love's signal comes through loud and clear as it flows through the mind, behaviorally expressed in words and deeds. Thus, we do not have to ask the Holy Spirit what to say, but simply beseech His help to remove what *we* want to say—anything that reinforces specialness. What remains is the thought of love, gently transformed into words of kindness and peace.

(4:6) This process is merely a special case of the lesson in the workbook that says, "I will step back and let Him lead the way."

This is the heart of the matter. As you step back from the ego, God's Love leads the way (W-pI.155). "Stepping back" is simply another way of referring to lifting the veils—being vigilant for the ego and *its* kingdom, because that is how we return to God and *His* Kingdom. Remember, salvation's "yes" is "not no": saying "yes" to Jesus means looking at the ego and affirming your choice against it. If you want to say words that are helpful, get yourself out of the way. Say "no" to the ego and love will inevitably come through. You need not think about it, for you will not be truly speaking. Your mouth may open and close, but the loving content of the words will not come from you, its source being the right-minded *you* that is shared with everyone.

(4:7-9) The teacher of God accepts the words which are offered him, and gives as he receives. He does not control the direction of his speaking. He listens and hears and speaks.

Giving and receiving are the same. When I am out of the way, the Love of God within me, now accepted by having removed the obstacles in its path, is received by me. Because I have accepted it, I give it, for it flows through me of itself. Love's natural extension is like a horse that runs gracefully and freely without a rider, needing no direction or guidance. We therefore "listen" by *not* listening to the ego. As the text says:

> What answer that the Holy Spirit gives can reach you, when it is your specialness to which you listen, and which asks and answers? (T-24.II.4:3)

The voice of specialness drowns out the Holy Spirit's still, small Voice. Since we do not experience His peace, we become creatures of specialness. When we stop listening to the ego's voice, however, we hear only the Holy Spirit and whatever we speak is not of us. What we say or do will thus be helpful to all people, without exception. It may be directed in *form* to one person or to a particular group, but if our words and behavior come from love, they must embrace the entire Sonship in

---

* *Absence from Felicity*, pp. 381-82.

content, for its seemingly separate parts share the same need and purpose—to return home.

(5:1-3) A major hindrance in this aspect of his learning is the teacher of God's fear about the validity of what he hears. And what he hears may indeed be quite startling. It may also seem to be quite irrelevant to the presented problem as he perceives it, and may, in fact, confront the teacher with a situation that appears to be very embarrassing to him.

Although this was meant specifically for Helen, it has obvious application for all of us. Helen would sometimes hear Jesus and second-guess what she heard, a practice that was pointless because she had nothing to do with the process. Again, if we truly come from a non-ego space, whatever we say will be helpful. Our challenge is to be in touch with the ego and our need to be special, because that is the problem. We may think we come from love, and yet are hateful. Consider Christianity's history, up to and including the current century. How many Christians sincerely believed they were hearing God's Voice direct them as they waged war, led crusades, and conducted inquisitions—all with their banner of Jesus held high. This could happen only because they were unaware they had an ego, which is why this course focuses almost exclusively on undoing it.

Therefore, the only way you can hear the Voice for God is to choose It over the ego. The workbook says "God's Voice speaks to me all through the day" (W-pI.49), yet Jesus never says in the lesson that we *hear* It throughout the day. The Holy Spirit continually speaks to us because He is always present in our minds. The problem is that we choose not to hear. Thus we have a text, workbook, and manual—a complete course—to help us choose again. *A Course in Miracles* is therefore not about love, but about the miracle that undoes the interferences to love. To say it differently, this is a course in recognizing guilt and undoing it by choosing against it, realizing at last that it will not give us what we want.

When the guilt and its veils of darkness are gone, the peace of God shines through your mind. You know you are following the right teacher when you have no investment in the form this peace takes, as you realize it makes no difference—*form* is nothing; *content* is everything. You have done your part by accepting the Atonement for yourself, denying the reality of guilt. Remember that Atonement is correction (M-18.4:6). You correct an error, not the truth, and so the Atonement is involved only with correcting the mind's mistaken choices. If you focus on your wondrous words of wisdom, all the people you help and all you think you do in Jesus' name, realize as quickly as you can that you but listen to the voice of specialness. Jesus does not care about the world. How could he? There is no world! It is thus not the world that needs saving, but *you* when you think there is a world out there, and one that needs your help. We have seen that this is magic, which protects the underlying magical thought that we exist by having separated from God. It is this belief, and this belief alone, that needs correction.

(5:4-5) All these are judgments that have no value. They are his own, coming from a shabby self-perception which he would leave behind.

This self-perception thrives on specialness. I want to be important, well-liked, and admired; I want to be helpful so people will think I am wonderful. The ego's shabby, little self is in constant need of approval, without which it could not exist. When you are in a non-ego state, however, what is there that needs approval? You are already aware of Who you are as God's Son, identified with the love that flows through you. You do not give a second thought to what you do or say, for you know you have brought the ego's illusions to the truth, which now is freed to speak through you.

(5:6-7) Judge not the words that come to you, but offer them in confidence. They are far wiser than our own.

You offer words in confidence because you are confident of their source, which is the memory of God's Love in the mind; confident because you no longer have an investment in being right and proving God wrong. This confidence leads to the quiet joy that comes from realizing that you and everyone else walk home together, sharing the same interest and goal. Despite our separated detours, we all return as one—"the outcome is as certain as God" (T-2.III.3:10).

(5:8-9) God's teachers have God's Word behind their symbols. And He Himself gives to the words they use the power of His Spirit [the Holy Spirit],

raising them from meaningless symbols to the Call of Heaven Itself.

Words are inherently meaningless because they were made to keep us from the Meaningful. Yet they can become symbols of the Atonement, which symbolizes the reality of God's Oneness and Love—the Call of Heaven Itself. Serving a different purpose, our words are the vehicle through which the Love of God speaks. Our task is not to be involved with the Call or Its words, but to release the interferences that would keep Their love out of awareness. Love does the rest as we gently awaken from the dream and know that Heaven's Call is our Self.

22. HOW ARE HEALING AND ATONEMENT RELATED?

This section picks up from the previous one regarding the role of words in healing, and the relationship between mind and body, one of the significant variations on our theme of shared versus separate interests, reflecting the comparison of oneness with the ego's belief that we are separated from God and from each other. In what follows, Jesus makes it clear that healing and Atonement are identical; moreover, he states that healing, Atonement, forgiveness, and the miracle are the same. This is particularly interesting in light of his early statement in the text that distinguishes among healing, Atonement, and the miracle, saying that the Atonement is the principle, the miracle is the means, and healing is the result. And then he adds that we should not confuse the miracle and healing, and therefore should not talk about a "miracle of healing" (T-2.IV.1:2-5). The point, again, is that the miracle is the means and healing is the result. However, elsewhere in the text, and also in this section, Jesus does indeed use the term *miracle of healing*, an example that points out the inconsistency in the Course's language (the *form*), even though the teaching (the *content*) is strictly consistent. The explanation for this language discrepancy is that early on, Jesus is teaching the specific parts of the healing process. Once this teaching has been established, however, he can use the terms more loosely in the spirit of poetic license. Thus Jesus equates healing, Atonement, forgiveness, and the miracle—we could actually include other terms as well: the holy instant, the holy relationship, salvation, and redemption—for these are but differing ways of referring to the correction of the error, or the undoing of the blocks we placed within ourselves that prevent us from recognizing love's presence.

We can therefore see that the task of God's teachers is not to teach in terms of form—not to save the world or heal the sick—but to accept the Atonement for themselves. Undoing the belief in the reality of guilt—the ultimate sickness—allows the love of Jesus to flow through their healed minds. Since minds are joined, the world is healed as well. This is a familiar and significant theme running through the manual, and we will return to it again and again in the sections to come. We also revisit here the discussion in section 5 on the role of sickness in the ego's plan, which has its locus in the mind, the body merely being the projection of the mind's sick thought of guilt.

(1:1-2) Healing and Atonement are not related; they are identical. There is no order of difficulty in miracles because there are no degrees of Atonement.

Thus the equation of healing, Atonement, and miracles—different terms to express the ego's undoing. Despite the myriad number of forms in which the error is expressed, there is but one—the belief we are separate from God. Therefore, there is no order of difficulty in healing, miracles, or Atonement. The correction remains the same: we return to the place in our minds where we—the decision maker—chose wrongly, and correct our mistake by choosing Jesus as our teacher instead of the ego. This simplicity is the core of Jesus' discussion in this section.

(1:3) It is the one complete concept possible in this world, because it is the source of a wholly unified perception.

Once again we find the central theme of unity. Atonement is a "unified perception" because all is seen the same way, regardless of what our sensory organs report. Everything that occurs here symbolizes calls for love or expressions of it; and regardless of which it is, our response is the same: love. This is the ever-present response to calls for help in the world at large or in our personal worlds. There can be no exceptions; otherwise the perception is not unified. Their single-minded focus on shared interests is *the* way teachers of God grow in their function.

(1:4) Partial Atonement is a meaningless idea, just as special areas of hell in Heaven are inconceivable.

Jesus made this same point in the section on sacrifice, telling us there cannot be a little bit of hell in Heaven, or a little bit of Heaven in hell (M-13.7). It must be *one or the other*—we are either separated or one with God, and there is no in between. That is why there is no partial Atonement. *All* sources of distress and upset in this world—personal and collective—are due to the mistake of listening to the ego's voice telling us we are separated.

(1:5-6) Accept Atonement and you are healed. Atonement is the Word of God.

Our sole responsibility as miracle workers is to accept the Atonement (T-2.V.5:1), a theme repeated throughout the text and workbook, and appearing again here. We heal the world by healing our minds, accepting Jesus as our teacher by realizing the ego is not to be trusted.

(1:7) Accept His Word and what remains to make sickness possible?

This makes no sense if you identify with the body—what does acceptance of the Atonement have to do with catching a cold, having cancer, or being wounded in a war? Yet it makes perfect sense when you recognize that the mind is the only level of sickness, which is impossible once the mind is healed of its belief in guilt. Sickness therefore is the choice for separation over oneness, hate over love, the ego over the Holy Spirit. The belief in guilt is not only the sickness, but is what gave rise to the phenomenal universe. Moreover, it is what drove us—as one Son—to be born, and continues to sustain what we think of as our physical lives.

(1:8) Accept His Word and every miracle has been accomplished.

The term *miracle* should always be understood as *correction*, a shift in perception or in teachers. It corrects the fundamental error we made as one Son, and continually reflect in our everyday lives—choosing the ego as teacher instead of the Holy Spirit.

(1:9-12) To forgive is to heal. The teacher of God has taken accepting the Atonement for himself as his only function. What is there, then, he cannot heal? What miracle can be withheld from him?

We again see forgiveness equated with healing, the miracle, and Atonement. Through the miracle of forgiveness we fulfill our only function—accepting the Atonement for ourselves. Our function is not to teach *A Course in Miracles*, heal others or the world, bring peace, or do anything but heal ourselves by accepting the Atonement. Asking Jesus to be our teacher, we deny the reality of separation, guilt, and specialness, and once the ego's thought system is gone, God's Love flows through our minds, taking whatever form will be most helpful. Therefore, when the Course speaks of teachers of God, it refers only to those who have accepted their function of forgiveness. They have set their feet on the right ladder, allowing Jesus to be their guide as they gently make their way home.

(2:1) The progress of the teacher of God may be slow or rapid, depending on whether he recognizes the Atonement's inclusiveness, or for a time excludes some problem areas from it.

These important words are another variation of the manual's fundamental theme of shared interests. The all-inclusiveness of the Atonement is what makes it a true correction. If I forgive every person except one, I have forgiven no one; if I ask Jesus to help me look at every problem in the world except one, I have asked him for nothing. Remember that the Atonement's all-inclusiveness is the healer, and the core of the healing process is whether we choose separation or oneness. No area of our fantasies, problems, or unforgiveness can be excluded from God's healing Love, for if we do, we exclude the universe because it is all or nothing. That is why healing and Atonement, miracles and forgiveness are related, and why there is no order of difficulty among them.

(2:2) In some cases, there is a sudden and complete awareness of the perfect applicability of the lesson of the Atonement to all situations, but this is comparatively rare.

Be wary of those who tell you they have had "a sudden and complete awareness of the perfect applicability of the lesson of the Atonement to all situations," for this is indeed rare. Jesus is speaking of a *total* acceptance of the Atonement, which means you are in the real world, a state of mind in which you know that your reality is outside the ego's thought system and its world of time and space. Almost always the attainment of the real world is a slow process, as we have discussed (M-9). It is thus much more helpful to see the journey as steady and gentle so you will not be tempted to deny your resistance and fear of the truth. By accepting resistance rather than denying or fighting it, bringing fear to Jesus' love, you allow his gentleness to heal it.

(2:3-4) The teacher of God may have accepted the function God has given him long before he

has learned all that his acceptance holds out to him. It is only the end that is certain.

Sentences like these are helpful because they teach that we need not feel guilty because of our fear. We may realize this course is our path and its teachings true; we may have accepted forgiveness as our function and want to devote our lives to asking Jesus' help in shifting our perceptions of the world; yet resistance is great and we are terrified to continue on. Thus we may be on the right ladder with the right teacher, but hesitate to climb to the top for we know it would mean the end of our individual and special self.

Being aware of our fear and resistance is also helpful because we will then be less tempted by the ego's arrogance and false holiness, and more open to learning what it means to be truly gentle and respectful of our fear. We cannot be gentle with others if we are not gentle with ourselves, which means giving ourselves permission to be afraid, respecting that we still choose the ego, even though another part of the mind knows that what we are choosing is false. It is not a sin to fear losing one's identity. Feeling guilty about it, however, is—but only in that it is so silly. The name of the ego's game is *guilt*, the reason we are here. The last thing we want to do is deny or reinforce the guilt by feeling bad because we are not more spiritually advanced—whatever that term means to us.

(2:5) Anywhere along the way, the necessary realization of inclusiveness may reach him.

At any time on the journey we may become aware that our identity—the physical/psychological self—is an illusion. This realization comes by understanding the all-inclusive nature of the correction. Every aspect of the material universe is made up. Since none of it is real, none of it should be taken seriously in the sense of having power to affect our peace of mind. Guilt, fear, and specialness all express how we make the world of bodies real. Yet when we remember the world's illusory nature, we realize that nothing here can make us happy or sad. How can nothing have effects?

(2:6) If the way seems long, let him be content.

Do not overemphasize the duration of the journey, for it is long only in dreams. If you become upset about how long forgiveness is taking you, or how long it seems to be taking the world to wake up, you have made the error real. This means you have forgotten that your only function is to accept the Atonement. Nothing but that.

(2:7-9) He has decided on the direction he wants to take. What more was asked of him? And having done what was required, would God withhold the rest?

The answer, of course, is "no," although God does not withhold or grant anything. The truth is that we *have* everything, for we *are* everything. And what we *have* and *are* cannot be diminished or increased. Making our way up the ladder is therefore an illusion: "a journey without distance" (T-8.VI.9:7). As long as we believe we are here we will believe we are on a journey, and we will need the help of One wiser than ourselves—the Holy Spirit or Jesus—to guide us gently along the path through illusions to the truth.

(3:1) That forgiveness is healing needs to be understood, if the teacher of God is to make progress.

Forgiveness undoes the guilt I projected onto you by bringing it back to my mind, where I can look at it and let it go. This guilt is the sickness, and therefore what has to be healed is not a physical or psychological condition, but the mind's belief in guilt's reality.

(3:2-3) The idea that a body can be sick is a central concept in the ego's thought system. This thought gives the body autonomy, separates it from the mind, and keeps the idea of attack inviolate.

The attack I keep inviolate is the belief I attacked God. This is the source of my guilt that I project onto others, forgetting that I made the first attack in my mind. Perceiving only their attack justifies my counter-attack in self-defense. This is the argument every head of state uses to justify war, because every ego uses it—attack is what makes us what we are, and projection protects us. Yet guilt over our initial attack on God remains the true sickness, which, again, has nothing to do with my body. Similarly, my anger has nothing to do with your body since it involves only what I *believe* you have done. This effectively conceals my secret belief that *I* am the sinner and therefore the one who deserves punishment.

(3:4-5) If the body could be sick Atonement would be impossible. A body that could order a mind to do as it sees fit could merely take the place of God and prove salvation is impossible.

The Atonement says the separation never happened, while the body's existence affirms the separation as a fact, witnessed to by sickness—bodies feel pain, get feverish, develop cancer or upset stomachs, age, and die. Thus do they witness to the insanity that we have usurped God's place and sit on the throne of creation. We have now become God, and the Atonement—the correction for the ego's mad belief in separation—must be a lie.

(3:6-9) What, then, is left to heal? The body has become lord of the mind. How could the mind be returned to the Holy Spirit unless the body is killed? And who would want salvation at such a price?

This is yet another place in *A Course in Miracles* where Jesus points a gentle finger at Christianity's errors. Its theology tells us the body is the problem—we will find peace only in the body-less afterlife because the body is the locus of sin. This justifies people's attempts to take their own life—"Life is terrible, but when I leave the body I will be free." We thus regard the body as a jailer or prison, and so liberation comes when we escape the prison by killing the jailer. The Churches gave theological justification to this insanity of future salvation through death by placing the ego's thought system in the Mind of God. Thus the Course emphasizes the *now* of salvation, as discussed in "The Immediacy of Salvation" (T-26.VIII). We need not wait for release in the future—there *is* no future. We need not wait to be outside the body—we were never *in* the body. Salvation is immediate in the mind's holy instant when we choose against the ego and accept Jesus instead.

(4:1-5) Certainly sickness does not appear to be a decision. Nor would anyone actually believe he wants to be sick. Perhaps he can accept the idea in theory, but it is rarely if ever consistently applied to all specific forms of sickness, both in the individual's perception of himself and of all others as well. Nor is it at this level that the teacher of God calls forth the miracle of healing. He overlooks the mind *and* body, seeing only the face of Christ shining in front of him, correcting all mistakes and healing all perception.

Recall Lesson 136 in the workbook, "Sickness is a defense against the truth," where this dynamic of sickness as a decision is explained in great detail.

Beginning with sentence 3 and on to the end of the section, note how many times Jesus uses the concept *all* or *inclusiveness*. No matter what the form of physical or psychological dis-ease, or social or international distress, the problem remains simple: we chose the wrong teacher. This wrong choice is the sickness, while healing, or the Atonement, is choosing correctly—applied to all specific forms of distress. Choosing the Holy Spirit's forgiveness overlooks the body *and* mind—the sick, evil, sinful body; the guilt-ridden, evil, and sinful mind—and leads us to the right mind where the Holy Spirit's vision sees the face of Christ—the symbol of the innocence of God's Son—in all His brothers. We do not skip steps, but move slowly from the world to the mind that made it, and then to the decision-maker that corrects its mistaken choice and happily chooses again.

(4:6-9) Healing is the result of the recognition, by God's teacher, of who it is that is in need of healing. This recognition has no special reference. It is true of all things that God created. In it are all illusions healed.

The *who* in need of healing is ourselves, which embrace the Sonship because it is one. We are all sick—the evildoers and their innocent victims, the physically well and physically ill. *Specialness* is Jesus' term for the thought system that says we are different and unique; some are good, others bad; some meet our needs, others do not; some are sick, others well. Yet he teaches that healing has no special reference because sickness has no special reference. We all share the sick belief we inhabit real bodies because we all believe guilt is real. Remember that we separated from God as one Son, and will return as one—healed and whole.

(5:1-2) When a teacher of God fails to heal, it is because he has forgotten Who he is. Another's sickness thus becomes his own.

Recalling the principle that *perception is interpretation*, if I interpret you as sick, meaning I see you as different for you have a sickness I do not, I am the one who is sick. Your sickness is separation, and so is mine because I see you as separate from me and from others. It makes no difference whether I see you as physically or morally sick; I am seeing the Sonship as fragmented—divided into sick and well, evil and good—and so at that moment *I* am the one who is sick.

(5:3-4) In allowing this to happen, he has identified with another's ego, and has thus confused him with a body. In so doing, he has refused to accept the Atonement for himself, and can hardly offer it to his brother in Christ's Name.

How can I be an instrument of peace if I am not peaceful, which is the case when I see the Sonship divided into separate categories? I must thus recognize *my* sickness, and as quickly as possible ask the inner Healer for help to understand the situation—my fear of oneness, leading me into the arms of separation and specialness. That is the problem, and because it was my choice I will suffer. What motivates me to return to the decision-making part of my mind and choose again is wanting to be free of pain, realizing that my discomfort and dis-ease—physical or emotional—are not caused by external circumstances, but from my decision. Thus we again and again see Jesus focusing on our two basic themes: 1) oneness versus separation, shared versus separate interests; and 2) choosing correctly by going within and asking the Holy Spirit for help.

(5:5) He will, in fact, be unable to recognize his brother at all, for his Father did not create bodies, and so he is seeing in his brother only the unreal.

People frequently ask where does *A Course in Miracles* say God did not create the world or the body? Here is one of those many places.

(5:6) Mistakes do not correct mistakes, and distorted perception does not heal.

As almost every national leader has failed to learn, peace is not attained through waging war. Peace cannot be found in any kind of situation—international or personal—through attack, which simply compounds the mistake because it teaches: "Yes, the ego is right. Attack is how you get what you want; becoming free of guilt by attacking others is how you find peace." This distorted perception sees separate interests, while healed perception is the vision of Christ that sees only shared interests, reflecting the inherent sameness of God's one Son.

(5:7-10) Step back, now, teacher of God. You have been wrong. Lead not the way, for you have lost it. Turn quickly to your Teacher, and let yourself be healed.

"You have been wrong," Jesus says. That others are wrong is irrelevant. *You* are wrong, because you perceive incorrectly by perceiving separation. No matter how you may try to justify, rationalize, or spiritualize your perceptions, you are seeing separate interests. It therefore makes no sense to teach others, or try to solve their problems because you are now the problem and in need of help. Whenever you perceive evil versus good, or sick versus well—selective rather than all-inclusive perception—you know your ego has been your guide, which is the signal to go within and ask the Holy Spirit for help.

(6:1-3) The offer of Atonement is universal. It is equally applicable to all individuals in all circumstances. And in it is the power to heal all individuals of all forms of sickness.

In these three short sentences are *six* references to the Atonement's all-inclusive nature, illustrating the centrality of this concept to the Course and the importance of remembering that perception is not what the sensory organs report. In the world there are indeed differences, but Jesus refers to the ego's judgmental interpretation of these physical and psychological distinctions, for they truly separate the Sonship and deny the truth of the Atonement.

(6:4-5) Not to believe this is to be unfair to God, and thus unfaithful to Him. A sick person perceives himself as separate from God.

Who is not included in this category? As long as we think we are bodies, studying *A Course in Miracles,* for example, we must believe we are separate from God. In Heaven there is no Course, no people with eyes to read the printed word or ears to hear a speaker, no brain to interpret what is seen and heard. Jesus thus addresses all people—for everyone here is sick—and teaches that to reject the all-inclusiveness of the Atonement is to be unfaithful to the Oneness of God, which is His reality and our own as His Son.

(6:6-7) Would you see him as separate from you? It is your task to heal the sense of separation that has made him sick.

The way we heal the sense of separation is to heal it in ourselves. This is not something we can do alone, however, but there is a Healer within to Whom we can go. In fact, turning to Him *is* the healing.

(6:8-11) It is your function to recognize for him that what he believes about himself is not the truth. It is your forgiveness that must show him this. Healing is very simple. Atonement is received and offered.

We have seen this over and over in *A Course in Miracles*, especially in "The Function of the Teacher of God" (M-5.III). Our function is to heal, but not by our hands or words. We heal through the gentle reminder that the peace within us offers to someone who is not peaceful: "My brother, you can choose again, as I did." Thus I do my part, and the love of Jesus does its part through me. I have become an empty vessel through which his love flows, taking whatever form is most needed.

(6:12-14) Having been received, it must be accepted. It is in the receiving, then, that healing lies. All else must follow from this single purpose.

Note our subtheme that giving and receiving are the same. Since we are one, I give only to myself: what I give, I receive. What I give to you, you receive because we are one. Having received it, you must share it. Yet it is not we who do the sharing or giving. Our part is but to ask for help in getting our egos out of the way, allowing love to flow through us and to us—"To give and to receive are one in truth" (W-pI.108).

(7:1-4) Who can limit the power of God Himself? Who, then, can say which one can be healed of what, and what must remain beyond God's power to forgive? This is insanity indeed. It is not up to God's teachers to set limits upon Him, because it is not up to them to judge His Son.

Our function is not to limit love's flow by deciding who is worthy of our forgiveness, but by deciding to accept the Atonement for ourselves we undo the barriers we made to keep love hidden and unavailable.

(7:5-6) And to judge His Son is to limit his Father. Both are equally meaningless.

God's Son is perfectly one within himself and at one with His Creator—*ideas leave not their source*. Since we are an idea in the Mind of God and have never left our Source, to attack any fragment of the Sonship is to attack the whole, which means to attack its Creator.

(7:7-8) Yet this will not be understood until God's teacher recognizes that they are the same mistake. Herein does he receive Atonement, for he withdraws his judgment from the Son of God, accepting him as God created him.

Our first theme: God's Son is one, for that is how He created Him. Since we are all part of that oneness, we need to withdraw the judgment we placed upon His Son. You may recall that Jesus summarizes psychotherapy by saying that healing occurs when therapists forget to judge their patients (P-3.II.6:1). When they cease to judge, therapists and patients are jointly healed of their belief in separate interests. The therapist, therefore, becomes the expression in form of the Atonement that says the separation never happened.

(7:9-10) No longer does he stand apart from God, determining where healing should be given and where it should be withheld. Now can he say with God, "This is my beloved Son, created perfect and forever so."

This is taken from the gospel scene when the heavens open and God's voice speaks about Jesus, who has just been baptized by John in the river Jordan: "This is my beloved Son in whom I am well pleased" (Matthew 3:17). Thus John the Baptist is not the beloved Son, nor are the others in the water—only Jesus. In *A Course in Miracles* this statement becomes all-inclusive: we are all God's beloved Son. Our task is to become aware of the desire to exclude—through judgment and attack—certain parts of the Sonship from His Love. It is to undo this wish—through forgiveness—that we ask for help, the means of becoming an advanced teacher.

23. DOES JESUS HAVE A SPECIAL PLACE IN HEALING?

This section is the only one in the manual where Jesus speaks about himself,* and, interestingly, it is in the third person, in contrast with the first person references throughout the Course. One should not make too much of this *stylistic* difference, however, as if Helen were listening to more than one voice. To paraphrase the famous Hindu saying: the Voice is one, but listeners call it by many names.

Jesus is described here as our Western world's greatest symbol of what it means to know the Sonship as a unity. He is thus a shining example of what we all wish to become: one who has accepted the Atonement for himself—seeing everyone's interests as shared—and helping others become what he is. Borrowing a phrase from the workbook, at the same time he stands atop the ladder, he leads us there: he the end we seek, and he the means by which we come to him (W-pII.302.2:3). The following section illuminates this lovely truth.

(1:1-3) God's gifts can rarely be received directly. Even the most advanced of God's teachers will give way to temptation in this world. Would it be fair if their pupils were denied healing because of this?

Jesus tells us we need not be perfect here, but need only ask the help of one who *is* perfect within the dream: himself. Yet the fact that we are not perfect does not suggest we cannot be helpful—readiness does not mean mastery (T-2.VII.7; M-4.IX.1:10). A later section (M-26) returns to the first sentence.

(1:4-6) The Bible says, "Ask in the name of Jesus Christ." Is this merely an appeal to magic? A name does not heal, nor does an invocation call forth any special power.

Although asking in the name of Jesus Christ is not "an appeal to magic," it has been used that way. The point is not to use these words as a magical means of solving problems, but rather as symbols that will take us to the decision-making place in the mind where we can choose the love that Jesus represents. We thus do not simply invoke his name, magically hoping everything will be all right, saying: "Please help me, Jesus, and take away my problems." Instead, we see his name symbolizing the mind's loving presence of Atonement, to which we bring our illusions of fear, hate, judgments, and pain. When we misunderstand this, calling on his name is only "an appeal to magic"—another way to conceal our egos. It makes no difference whether we do this as biblical Christians, students of *A Course in Miracles*, or followers of another spiritual path. The principle is to bring illusion to truth; not truth to illusion.

(1:7-9) What does it mean to call on Jesus Christ? What does calling on his name confer? Why is the appeal to him part of healing?

These three questions will now be answered:

(2:1-2) We have repeatedly said that one who has perfectly accepted the Atonement for himself can heal the world. Indeed, he has already done so.

Jesus teaches that when we heal the world through accepting the Atonement, there is no longer a world to be perceived. When the mind is healed—the Atonement having been accepted—the mind is restored to its original unity with the Sonship, which means the Sonship's mind is healed as well. That is how we "save" the world, not by doing anything external—there is nothing external to do—but by saving ourselves from our wrong choices. Again, when we choose correctly it is not the individual mind that is healed—there is only an illusion of an individual mind—but the mind of God's Son. We then truly know the separation never happened, and the unity of the Sonship has not been fragmented. Since the world is the projection of the thought of separation, when that thought is undone, so is the world. Recall Jesus' emphatic statement:

> There is no world! This is the central thought the course attempts to teach (W-pI.132.6:2-3).

There is no world because the thought that made it is gone:

> This world was over long ago. The thoughts that made it are no longer in the mind that thought of them and loved them for a little while (T-28.I.1:6-7).

---

* Jesus is, however, discussed again in two sections in the clarification of terms: "Jesus – Christ" and "The Holy Spirit."

23. Does Jesus Have a Special Place in Healing?

This means that in the instant the thought of separation seemed to arise, it was undone. The physical universe thus appeared to arise in one instant, and was gone the next. Thus is the world healed. However, we still believe we live in what is already gone, the point of "The Present Memory" (T-28.I).

(2:3-4) Temptation may recur to others, but never to this One. He has become the risen Son of God.

"One" is capitalized because it refers to the Son of God Who has become Christ. Jesus is a symbol of one who has arisen from the ego's grave. In a later section, in fact, he defines *resurrection* as awakening from the dream of death (M-28), but as discussed previously, this has nothing to do with a body rising from a tomb. How can a body that does not exist rise or be resurrected? What *is* resurrected or reborn is the decision-making part of the mind that awakens from its dream of separation, crucifixion, and death.

(2:5-6) He has overcome death because he has accepted life. He has recognized himself as God created him, and in so doing he has recognized all living things as part of him.

Note the word *all*—again. This is the theme we have followed throughout the manual—recognizing that our interests are one. We share the need to awaken from the ego's dream, for as we are one in Heaven we are also one in hell.

(2:7) There is now no limit on his power, because it is the power of God.

The "power of God" is the love in our split minds, reflecting the Love of God in Heaven.

(2:8) So has his name become the Name of God, for he no longer sees himself as separate from Him.

Lessons 183 and 184 talk about the Name of God, but nowhere in those lessons is it ever given, for the simple reason that it does not exist. The "Name of God" is a symbol for Oneness, Love, or God Himself; but there is no real Name, because there is nothing specific in Heaven.

If you accept the Atonement, you no longer see yourself as separate from your Creator and Source because you no longer see yourself as separate from anyone—our interests are the same. If you attack one person, you have attacked the Sonship. It does not matter whether you are furious at an entire nation, race, group, or individual. If you see separation in one place, you have made it real in all places, for the whole is found in every part. Consequently, you will believe you have separated yourself from God. This is so important that we need to be constantly reminded: *The way we awaken from the dream of separation and death is to realize we are the same.* The practice of forgiveness thus consists of bringing to Jesus the temptation to make differences significant, and when we truly know we are part of one insane dream, and our reality abides outside it, we have accepted the Atonement. The world is then healed, and we have become an example of this truth: "When I am healed, I am not healed alone" (W-pI.137).

(3:1-4) What does this mean for you? It means that in remembering Jesus you are remembering God. The whole relationship of the Son to the Father lies in him. His part in the Sonship is also yours, and his completed learning guarantees your own success.

When you read lines like these—and there are many similar passages in the Course—you need to forget everything you ever thought about Jesus, read in the Bible, or heard from others. Set aside all misconceptions and projections, for none of them is relevant to the person spoken of here—one who knows the world is an illusion, the body is not the Son of God, and healing is not making a mud patty out of spittle and putting it on a person's eyes, as one biblical account attests Jesus did. Healing has nothing to do with sin, the body, or the world, but only with the gentle acceptance of the Atonement's truth. In that quiet instant the world is healed. Nothing more need be done—there is no sacrifice, suffering, death, or healing in physical terms—for the world is undone because it never was. All this Jesus represents to us—the shining symbol of what it means to be outside the dream, and therefore not taking anything seriously within it. That is why he does nothing in the world—does not intervene, bring peace, or heal cancer. He but gently calls to us to leave the dream with him and enter the real world.

(3:5-7) Is he still available for help? What did he say about this? Remember his promises, and

ask yourself honestly whether it is likely that he will fail to keep them.

His promise is: "I am always with you." He tells us that throughout the Course, as he repeatedly told Helen. He is always here, regardless of circumstances, or our feelings about him or anyone else. His loving presence shines in our minds, and that simple presence calls to us to bring our illusions, problems, pains, and judgments to his truth. This takes place in the mind, because there is nothing else. Being a teacher of God, therefore, has nothing to do with the external; it is not attained, for example, by teaching *A Course in Miracles* through the spoken or written word. God's teachers live Jesus' message, and by doing so they demonstrate its truth. The love that is in Jesus is in each of us; a love we allow to breathe free, and which gently calls to everyone to step out of the dream with us.

(3:8-9) Can God fail His Son? And can one who is one with God be unlike Him?

Our first theme, again. Remember, the theme of shared interests reflects the Oneness of God that undoes the belief that we are separate from Him. The truth is that we are one with our Source and with the Sonship.

(3:10-11) Who transcends the body has transcended limitation. Would the greatest teacher be unavailable to those who follow him?

The answer of course is that Jesus is always available, because he is in our minds. Again, Jesus is not the only symbol of the Love of God, but he is that for us. We will see the importance of *symbol* in the rest of this section.

(4:1-4) The name of Jesus Christ as such is but a symbol. But it stands for love that is not of this world. It is a symbol that is safely used as a replacement for the many names of all the gods to which you pray. It becomes the shining symbol for the Word of God, so close to what it stands for that the little space between the two is lost, the moment that the name is called to mind.

If Jesus is not a meaningful symbol for you, and you have no unforgiveness toward him, use any symbol—this is not a course in spiritual specialness —that represents for you a love and truth that is not of this world. When we do not ask that egoless presence for help—regardless of its form—it is only because we do not want the love that undoes the world's special love. We have chosen instead fragmentation and separation—good versus evil, winners and losers—and we want our judgments to be justified.

In view of this, it is helpful to be aware that when you judge yourself or others, it is because you do not want to hear the non-judgmental voice that reflects Heaven's Love. Your ego thus demands a different symbol, which leads you to make a Jesus who will justify your belief in specialness and separate interests. Calling on a non-special Jesus for help, therefore, means calling on the name that says the separation is not true. Try, therefore, not to make the symbol a judgment of others or yourself. Rather, let it be a way of moving beyond your petty judgments, secret sins, and hidden hates to the one whose love speaks salvation's Word.

(4:5-7) Remembering the name of Jesus Christ is to give thanks for all the gifts that God has given you. And gratitude to God becomes the way in which He is remembered, for love cannot be far behind a grateful heart and thankful mind. God enters easily, for these are the true conditions for your homecoming.

When we do not feel grateful to Jesus, it is because we do not want to come home. Jesus tells us here that gratitude is the way we will return, and elsewhere that love is the way we walk in gratitude (W-pI.195). It goes without saying that it is difficult indeed to be grateful to someone we believe is a threat, who will take away our individuality and specialness, our cherished hatred, judgment, and self-righteousness. When we do not feel grateful for this course, its teachings of forgiveness, and its teacher, it is only because we do not want to learn its lessons. It is essential, though, that we not judge ourselves when we realize our lack of gratitude. We need simply be aware of what is going on—that we do not want to be at peace, and we know this for a fact. Choosing to exclude certain people, we cherish petty annoyances, anger, and justified wars. We want them instead of the vision that sees all people as one —as part of us as we are part of them. Therefore, how could we be grateful to a teacher who represents this non-ego perception? Once again, we need to see our decision for the ego as helpful information, but nothing for which we should feel ashamed or guilty.

(5:1-2) Jesus has led the way. Why would you not be grateful to him?

We do not want to be grateful to Jesus because we do not want his way; we want *ours*—the way of specialness and exclusion.

(5:3-4) He has asked for love, but only that he might give it to you. You do not love yourself.

You cannot love yourself and be here, for it is your self-hatred and guilt that has driven you into the world.

(5:5-6) But in his eyes your loveliness is so complete and flawless that he sees in it an image of his Father. You become the symbol of his Father here on earth.

What Jesus loves in us he loves in himself—love is one and does not see separation. At the journey's end, Jesus disappears, too, as does our individual self. Yet within the illusion of separation, he is the shining and radiant symbol of the Self we remember when we awaken from the dream.

(5:7-11) To you he looks for hope, because in you he sees no limit and no stain to mar your beautiful perfection. In his eyes Christ's vision shines in perfect constancy. He has remained with you. Would you not learn the lesson of salvation through his learning? Why would you choose to start again, when he has made the journey for you?

Jesus asks us why we would ever want to do this without his help. And, indeed, while he does not say it here, it is clear that we cannot do it without his help (or that of any other symbol). This, then, is Jesus' plea to us: that we take his hand, learn what he is teaching, and ask to look at the world through his eyes. Most importantly of all, we need to be aware of how much we do not want to look, and then accept his forgiveness of our fear.

(6:1) No one on earth can grasp what Heaven is, or what its one Creator really means.

So often Jesus tells us that we cannot understand oneness, but we can understand shared interests. Thus he would say to us: "When you learn the lesson of shared interests—we are all the same—you will come to understand that this reflects your Oneness as Christ, totally at one with God."

(6:2-4) Yet we have witnesses. It is to them that wisdom should appeal. There have been those whose learning far exceeds what we can learn.

Just as Jesus is a witness for us, he asks us to be a witness to others. We all have the same need, are on the same journey, and share the same insanity and sanity—no one here is without the ego and the Holy Spirit. Our recognition of this unity becomes the witness to the oneness of creation, the prerequisite for becoming a Teacher of teachers, whom Jesus talks about in a later section.

(6:5) Nor would we teach the limitations we have laid on us.

We all have limitations and that is not what we would teach, for our right mind desires only the truth of God's Love that lies beyond them. We cannot teach Its oneness, but we can reflect it by not reinforcing perceptions of ourselves as separate from anyone else.

(6:6-7) No one who has become a true and dedicated teacher of God forgets his brothers. Yet what he can offer them is limited by what he learns himself.

To be a true teacher of God means we have learned that we are not separate from each other, for we are all part of the one Sonship. How, then could we forget anyone? Yet the love we offer each other is limited by the extent to which we have accepted love within ourselves. We thus need to be aware of the limits we have placed on our openness to love, of the fearful part within us that is resistant to the vision of all-inclusiveness. Only then can we be aware that *we* need help, as Jesus reminds us:

(6:8-10) Then turn to one who laid all limits by, and went beyond the farthest reach of learning. He will take you with him, for he did not go alone. And you were with him then, as you are now.

In a later section, Jesus reiterates our oneness by reminding us we were with him when he arose; i.e., when he awoke from the dream of death (C-6.5). Recall that Jesus' rising from the dead has nothing to do with a physical resurrection, as depicted in the Bible. When he awoke from the dream of death we were with him, because when he was healed he was not healed alone. When one Son is healed, the entire Sonship is healed.

Remember, these ideas are difficult to grasp and cannot be understood within the linear framework we use to understand the world and our lives. They are understandable only from an atemporal and non-spatial perspective, in the part of the mind where healing abides. Jesus asks us to seek his help, because he symbolizes the Atonement we wish to accept. We cannot achieve this without him, because to attempt this alone would be the same mistake as feeling we can find love without God, or get to Heaven by ourselves—*that* heaven is really specialness, which means it is hell. In the end, however, we recognize that by asking Jesus for help we ask but our decision-making selves, because love is one.

(7:1-4) This course has come from him [Jesus] because his words have reached you in a language you can love and understand. Are other teachers possible, to lead the way to those who speak in different tongues and appeal to different symbols? Certainly there are. Would God leave anyone without a very present help in time of trouble; a savior who can symbolize Himself?

The importance of these statements is that Jesus is letting us know that the content remains the same, even when its forms of expression differ. Thus, in terms of *form*, this course is Western in its conceptual thinking and Christian in statement. It is but one specific form of the universal course—not the only form, of which there are many thousands (M-1.4:1-1). That is why we need to guard against forming a special relationship with the Course's *form*. It is its *content* of love we want; the song of love itself, not its parts (S-1.I.3). Again, Jesus tells us his course has come to us in a form we can love and understand, and which will help us on the journey. Yet it is not for everyone, as he reiterates:

(7:5) Yet do we need a many-faceted curriculum, not because of content differences, but because symbols must shift and change to suit the need.

We find again the thematic variation of form and content. The content never changes, for how can love be different? God's Son is forever guiltless because the separation never happened. Yet has this single content been taught in many ways throughout the ages. Therefore, again, Jesus urges us not to develop a special relationship with him or the form of his teaching: "It is the content of love you want," he reminds us, "and what keeps you focused on your goal is seeing the right-minded choice for shared interests. Thus you will not give anything here the power of specialness to separate you from anyone else."

(7:6-8) Jesus has come to answer yours [your need]. In him you find God's Answer. Do you, then, teach with him, for he is with you; he is always here.

Once more, Jesus is not the only symbol of the Atonement, and as we will see in the clarification of terms, the man Jesus was an illusion (C-5.2:3)—a most helpful one, to be sure, for as a symbol of the Love of God he leads us to the place beyond all illusions: the real world that is the journey's end. Until we arrive there, however, we need help. For so many of us in the West, Jesus is the shining figure that will take us home. And so, while cautioning us not to misuse him by turning his love into an object of special love or hate, he nonetheless urges us not to deny the true help he can be, for he is our Atonement answer to the ego's thought system of separation and hate.

24. IS REINCARNATION SO?

In the previous section, Jesus spoke about the misuse of symbols. We will see that theme extend to the subjects of this and the next section—reincarnation and psychic powers—which alert us to the temptation of using symbols in the service of specialness and separate interests. These twin sections also address the important distinction between mind and body.

The notion of reincarnation is prevalent throughout *A Course in Miracles*, many times in the form of a subtle suggestion that this is not the only time we have been here in the dream. In addition, Jesus spoke personally with Helen and Bill about their past lives together. Yet he tells us in this section that belief in the concept is irrelevant to our salvation, which can occur *now* when we accept the Atonement. It thus makes no difference whether we believe we come into this world once or hundreds of times. Since time is not linear and is inherently illusory, the concept of reincarnation itself is inherently meaningless.

(1:1-3) In the ultimate sense, reincarnation is impossible. There is no past or future, and the idea of birth into a body has no meaning either once or many times. Reincarnation cannot, then, be true in any real sense.

The concept has meaning only within the dream. Since there is no body, how can we incarnate once, let alone many times? This was the basis of Jesus' comment on the biblical teaching of the incarnation of Christ: "The Word was made flesh and dwelt among us" (John 1:14). "Strictly speaking," he tells us in the text, "this is impossible" (T-8.VII.7:2). The Atonement—the Word or Thought of Love—cannot be made into flesh that is an illusion. Indeed, the world itself is an illusion, and so the concept of reincarnation ultimately has no meaning. Nonetheless, Jesus continues:

(1:4-7) Our only question should be, "Is the concept helpful?" And that depends, of course, on what it is used for. If it is used to strengthen the recognition of the eternal nature of life, it is helpful indeed. Is any other question about it really useful in lighting up the way?

We have seen this theme of purpose many times already in the manual. In the text, Jesus says the only question we should ask of anything is "What is it for?" (T-4.V.6:8-11). It is the same question here. Believing in reincarnation, therefore, can serve either the wrong or right mind. *Purpose* alone is what is important, not the belief itself—*what is it for?* The belief in reincarnation is helpful if it sparks a recognition that the body is not our identity and our lives are not as they appear. However, Jesus cautions us:

(1:8-11) Like many other beliefs, it can be bitterly misused. At least, such misuse offers preoccupation and perhaps pride in the past. At worst, it induces inertia in the present. In between, many kinds of folly are possible.

The belief in reincarnation often leads to preoccupations with one's past, many times evoking a sense of pride in earlier lives: I was a pharaoh in Egypt or an ancient priestess, Plato or Aristotle, Mary Magdalene or St. Peter, Shakespeare or Goethe. In the early years of the Course, I remember no fewer than four people proclaiming to us they were St. Paul. This arrogant misuse always expresses some degree of belief in separation. For example: I am better than you because of who I was, and in this life I continue the extremely important work I did not quite complete in a previous lifetime. On the other hand, there are those who feel a kind of inertia, having concluded there is no hope in this life because of their terrible karma.

All such uses of reincarnation focus on the world and body, instead of the mind's single thought: the decision to side with the ego, which now has to be undone by choosing the Holy Spirit. This alone should be our focus, and the right-minded use of belief in past lives helps us return our attention to the mind. The belief, again, is bitterly misused when it supports the ego's strategy of keeping us mindless, focusing only on the separate body. The word itself contains the meaning of body: *incarnate*.

(2:1) Reincarnation would not, under any circumstances, be the problem to be dealt with *now*.

– 161 –

The keyword is *now*, an emphasis carried throughout the manual, workbook, and text—the holy instant in which there is no past or future: no sinful past for which we need atone; no guilty present that makes us feel unworthy and in fearful anticipation of future punishment. There is only *now*, and the world becomes the means—with Jesus as our teacher—to lead us back to the mind where we recognize the body as a projection, as are our past, present, and future lifetimes. At any given moment, therefore, we can say to the ego: "I no longer want you as my teacher." In this holy instant of salvation we say to Jesus: "Help me see the situation as you do—not through the eyes of specialness or judgment, but through the eyes of shared interests." This is the unified perception of the Holy Spirit that truly saves us from the ego's endless cycle of deaths and rebirths.

(2.2-3) If it were responsible for some of the difficulties the individual faces now, his task would still be only to escape from them now. If he is laying the groundwork for a future life, he can still work out his salvation only now.

Whether you believe you are a product of your upbringing in this lifetime, or of what happened to you several lifetimes before, it makes no difference to your salvation. If you are unhappy now, it is because you made a decision now; your past being irrelevant to the decision. This applies equally to the belief that your present life is preparing you for some future state. People might think, for example: "I have to forgive these abusing people because that will free me later on. I will become holy in a future life because of the work I am doing now." Yet this misses the point, for not only does it focus on the future, but it assumes that time is linear, wherein we work out our bad karma in the present so we will be liberated in the future. Yet time is non-linear or holographic, and so there is no past to work out, for everything occurs together in the time-less mind. What is important is using our current experience as a vehicle to return to the true *now*—outside time and space—where we can correct our choice for the ego by choosing the Holy Spirit as our Teacher.

(2:4-6) To some, there may be comfort in the concept, and if it heartens them its value is self-evident. It is certain, however, that the way to salvation can be found by those who believe in reincarnation and by those who do not. The idea cannot, therefore, be regarded as essential to the curriculum.

Jesus reiterates the irrelevancy of the concept of reincarnation. The Course's curriculum embodies two central thoughts: accepting the Atonement and asking the Holy Spirit's help to forgive. Thus, I ask Him to help me look at the world through the eyes of shared interests—the nature of the miracle, forgiveness, healing, and Atonement.

(2:7-8) There is always some risk in seeing the present in terms of the past. There is always some good in any thought which strengthens the idea that life and the body are not the same.

We see here how the thought of reincarnation is a two-edged sword. It can be helpful because it gets us beyond a slavish dependence on the body that never questions its existence. However, the concept can also lead us to bypass responsibility for decisions we are making *now*. Again, whether we attribute our present condition to our upbringing or a past life makes no difference, although this could at least help us recognize that the ego is always doing the same thing. It would be truly helpful, therefore, if the belief in reincarnation helps us to choose *now*. In summary, then, reviewing our personal as well as distant pasts can be helpful, but only as it would reveal the sameness of the ego, and that its thought system of time is a trap to avoid taking responsibility for our lives.

The ego would therefore have you believe that if you are unhappy, it is not because of a decision you are making in the present, for all you seem to be aware of is that you are the innocent victim, the helpless effect of decisions made by others or yourself in a distant past, over which you now have no control. It is helpful, again, to see the larger picture and realize that every problem is the same. The problems you had when you were three, five, and ten years old are the same as you experience as an adult, or when you were in Greece, Atlantis, or living as a prehistoric creature—the problem of separation shared with everyone, its universality being the cannibalism of dog-eat-dog, *one or the other*. If believing in a past life helps you reach this level of insight, that is its value. This includes recognizing that you can do what we all need to do, whether we believe in the concept or not: decide for God *now*.

(3:1-4) For our purposes, it would not be helpful to take any definite stand on reincarnation. A teacher of God should be as helpful to those who believe in it as to those who do not. If a definite stand were required of him, it would merely limit his usefulness, as well as his own decision making. Our course is not concerned with any concept that is not acceptable to anyone, regardless of his formal beliefs.

This last sentence should bring a smile to students' faces, because there obviously is much in this course that people would find unacceptable, such as that the world is an illusion and God did not create it. However, Jesus is speaking of moving beyond the form to the content, and not letting any specific teaching of *A Course in Miracles* get in the way of its message: asking help of our Teacher to perceive shared interests. To accomplish this it makes no difference what we *believe* about the world, psychic abilities, or reincarnation, for we can always ask Jesus to help us see our special love and hate partners as not separate from us. Salvation comes only through forgiveness, chosen in the present.

Thus we need not get stuck on metaphysical, theological, or New Age concepts, nor use them as a means of making ourselves separate from those who do not believe as we do. We can practice this course on forgiveness *perfectly* and not believe it nor understand its metaphysics. We can practice this course *most imperfectly* and believe everything it says and be able to quote chapter and verse where it says it. What alone is important is practicing our two themes: turning to the Holy Spirit for help in shifting our perceptions of others so we no longer see their interests as separate from our own. This *content* is what Jesus addresses here. Anything else is a distraction from our purpose.

(3:5-6) His ego will be enough for him to cope with, and it is not the part of wisdom to add sectarian controversies to his burdens. Nor would there be an advantage in his premature acceptance of the course merely because it advocates a long-held belief of his own.

Do not follow *A Course in Miracles* simply because you like its metaphysical teachings about the illusory world or its implied statements of reincarnation. What should attract you to it is that it will get you home. Period. Jesus also cautions against using the Course's concepts as a club against others—"You cannot come to my group unless you swear on a stack of Courses that God did not create this world!" Students have done that—perhaps not quite that explicitly, but something akin to asking people to pledge allegiance to the Course "creed"; otherwise Jesus will not welcome them into his "church." Thus he makes it clear that he does not want us using his course as a weapon against others. Its content alone is important—the common theme of forgiveness that holds God's Son together as one, and helps us progress on the journey.

(4:1) It cannot be too strongly emphasized that this course aims at a complete reversal of thought.

The complete reversal of thought is moving from separation to oneness, separate to shared interests, the world and body to the mind. Crucial here, however, is not intellectual understanding, but experiencing ourselves as the same—in the insane separation of *one or the other*, and in the healing sanity of Atonement.

(4:2-4) When this is finally accomplished, issues such as the validity of reincarnation become meaningless. Until then, they are likely to be merely controversial. The teacher of God is, therefore, wise to step away from all such questions, for he has much to teach and learn apart from them.

Our need is to teach and learn we are not separate. Any thought of separation as real and valid is our call for help. We need to go to the Holy Spirit, asking that our perceptions of a fragmented Sonship be corrected, along with our justified thoughts of hate, judgment, and even murder—all of which we hold as proof that we were right and the world wrong, behind which stands God, the true object of our attack.

(4:5) He should both learn and teach that theoretical issues but waste time, draining it away from its appointed purpose.

A Course in Miracles has a theology like every other religion or spirituality; and Jesus is cautioning us against using it to reinforce separation. Successful learning of this course has nothing to do with mastering its theoretical principles, but with living its truth and demonstrating we are not separate, that no one and nothing in this world have power to take away the Love and peace of God within us. This is the goal of our learning and what we wish to have taught through us. All people fall into the trap of believing that others have the power to make them happy or sad, and that their interests are not the same. Thus we need to remember daily that everyone, including ourselves, shares in the ego's insanity of separation and specialness.

(4:6-8) If there are aspects to any concept or belief that will be helpful, he will be told about it. He will also be told how to use it. What more need he know?

As long as you have an investment in the ego, Jesus cannot "tell" you what you should teach or whether a concept will be helpful. You need first to bring to him the blocks within you—your desire for specialness and separation—for they will interfere with your hearing his gentle guidance. This hearing does not necessarily mean a voice *per se*, the way Helen "heard" one. There is more often than not a quiet knowing that what you are saying and doing is helpful, loving, and kind; a knowing that comes when you eliminate the interference of your need to be right. Thus, Jesus is not saying *not* to teach or talk about the concepts in *A Course in Miracles*, but he is asking us to be wary of misusing these ideas by seeing them as means of reinforcing separation, rather than undoing it.

(5:1-4) Does this mean that the teacher of God should not believe in reincarnation himself, or discuss it with others who do? The answer is, certainly not! If he does believe in reincarnation, it would be a mistake for him to renounce the belief unless his internal Teacher so advised. And this is most unlikely.

Jesus does not care what you believe. Every belief is a lie anyway. As stated in the *Psychotherapy* pamphlet, belief in God is a meaningless concept, "for God can be but known" (P-2.II.4:4). The only value a belief holds is its purpose—*what it is for*. If it is meant to lead beyond belief—which always separates—to the experience of oneness, it is valuable indeed. On the other hand, if it reinforces separation, it is valueless. It is therefore not the belief in and of itself that is the problem, but the way it is used. In God, however, there is no belief, only the non-dualistic experience of His Love since there is no *I* to have such an experience. In Heaven we *are* the experience, for we *are* love.

Belief did not come into the picture until after the separation. Just as we made words to keep us in the illusion of separation from God (M-21.1:7), we also made beliefs to serve the same purpose; and certainly, as the history of the world attests, we made beliefs to keep us separate from each other. Students of *A Course in Miracles* are unfortunately not exempt here. However, once beliefs were made, we can choose to have them serve a different purpose, helping us realize there is a reality within the dream that reflects the reality in Heaven—the reflection that teaches us our interests are one.

(5:5-6) He might be advised that he is misusing the belief in some way that is detrimental to his pupil's advance or his own. Reinterpretation would then be recommended, because it is necessary.

Again, belief itself—regardless of its subject—is not the problem; misusing it is, since this always means employing the belief in the service of specialness. In the three chapters in *The Song of Prayer* on prayer, forgiveness, and healing, Jesus first discusses their misuse by students before he talks about their true forms. The misuse is always a shadow of the ego, and whether we are praying for specifics, forgiving-to-destroy, or healing-to-separate, we are engaged in the practice of separation and separate interests. Thus Jesus asks us to be vigilant for the ego's purpose in these beliefs—in reincarnation or in anything else.

(5:7-10) All that must be recognized, however, is that birth was not the beginning, and death is not the end. Yet even this much is not required of the beginner. He need merely accept the idea that what he knows is not necessarily all there is to learn. His journey has begun.

Jesus repeats the point he made at the end of paragraph 2—there is always some good in a thought that weakens the equation of life with the body. Here he wants us to recognize that birth is not the beginning and death is not the ending. The body is simply a "hero" in the ego's dream (T-27.VIII) that begins with birth and ends with death, with a possibility of further life beyond the body. Thus Jesus urges us to be humble in saying: "I do not understand what the body is for, nor the purpose of the Course; I do not know my own best interests." Thus, if you do not understand the Course's purpose of forgiveness, how can it help you? You may know there is something in it that will help, but as long as you think you know your problem you will not recognize the answer in the mind. Yet all you need realize is that *A Course in Miracles* will teach you what you need to learn, and there is a Teacher within to guide you according to His principle of shared interests. Nothing more than that recognition is required for the journey.

(6:1-2) The emphasis of this course always remains the same;—it is at this moment that complete salvation is offered you, and it is at this moment that you can accept it. This is still your one responsibility.

There is no past, future, or guilt-ridden present; only the holy instant in which I learn I made a mistake that can be undone. I realize this by asking Jesus to help me look at how I perceive another, how I use my special relationships as shadows of the past (T-17.III): "I do not relate to you as you are, but as I have made you out to be; an image based on a past that was also made up." And so I learn to see my current experiences—especially relationships—as the means used by Jesus to return me to the mind: the source of the problem. This problem is not with you, nor is it between you and me as interacting bodies, but with my mind's decision for the ego. Salvation is nothing more than understanding the true nature of the problem, which allows me finally to resolve it.

(6:3-8) Atonement might be equated with total escape from the past and total lack of interest in the future. Heaven is here. There is nowhere else. Heaven is now. There is no other time. No teaching that does not lead to this is of concern to God's teachers.

At any given moment I can awaken from the dream. All I need do is look through Jesus' eyes—the vision of Christ—and see everyone as the same. If I could truly know this vision from within, there would be no justification for the perception of differences. The separation would be undone, for I would have accepted the Atonement for myself. Therefore the teaching I want is what will return me to the decision-making power in the mind. I thus bring my daily experiences of the unholy instant to the holy instant, which undoes my mistaken choice.

(6:9-10) All beliefs will point to this if properly interpreted. In this sense, it can be said that their truth lies in their usefulness.

No belief is true, for beliefs were made to keep truth away. Yet they can now serve a different purpose. Thus Jesus reminds us: "My body is a wholly neutral thing" (W-pII.294). Even though the body was made as a limitation on love, and therefore is an attack, it can be used to serve either the ego's purpose to reinforce that attack, or the Holy Spirit's purpose to undo it. Once again, the belief in and of itself is irrelevant. People have killed and fought wars over beliefs, not realizing these were not the problem. Yet they can be used to undo the problem of guilt, reinforcing the truth of shared interests instead of the illusion of separate ones.

(6:11-13) All beliefs that lead to progress should be honored. This is the sole criterion this course requires. No more than this is necessary.

Once again, purpose is at the core of the Course's teachings. It is not a belief, ability, or anything else that is important, not even *A Course in Miracles* itself. It is the *purpose* for which we use them that provides their meaning. People have done with the Course what has been done with the Bible—using it as a means of separation, attack, and specialness, rather than as a means of correcting these thoughts. To change the purpose, therefore, means using the Course as you would anything in the world—as a way of returning to the mind and choosing again.

25. ARE "PSYCHIC" POWERS DESIRABLE?

The main point here is that psychic powers in and of themselves are neutral. They can be used to service the ego's need for specialness and separation, or the Holy Spirit's purpose of undoing the ego through forgiveness. Needless to say, psychic powers can be and have been bitterly misused.

(1:1-2) The answer to this question is much like the preceding one. There are, of course, no "unnatural" powers, and it is obviously merely an appeal to magic to make up a power that does not exist.

Magic sees a nonexistent problem somewhere in the body or world, and then uses itself as a way to undo, heal, or fix it. However, the real issue is the ego's magical solution to move us from the mind to the body, which sets up its attempts to solve the projected problem. Yet underlying all perceived problems is the mind's decision for separation. This is the *only* problem, and it calls for the *only* solution—the Atonement.

There are no unnatural powers because the reality is that we are all part of one natural Mind (or spirit). The unnatural, separated mind, wherein we share the same capacity to choose between magic and the miracle, is an illusion. This universality of mind, albeit unreal, should nonetheless be our reference point in relating to one another. The ego uses anything to keep us separated, and on the bodily level we can easily define differences among people, but when we perceive others as separate from us because of these differences, we fall into the trap of making separation real. In our right minds, however, we do not deny the differences our eyes and ears report, but these no longer make a difference to us. The only valid distinction to be made in this unreal world is between the ego's and Holy Spirit's perceptions—the contrast between illusion and truth. All other differences are meaningless.

(1:3-4) It is equally obvious, however, that each individual has many abilities of which he is unaware. As his awareness increases, he may well develop abilities that seem quite startling to him.

Helen is an example of these abilities. The period after she joined with Bill to find another way stunningly contained many psychic experiences, and she was cautioned by herself, as well as Jesus, not to overemphasize them. To her credit, she never did. What alone was important was how she used the abilities, and their major purpose was to prepare her for bringing forth the Course.*

(1:5) Yet nothing he can do can compare even in the slightest with the glorious surprise of remembering Who he is.

Borrowing again from the poetic teaching of *The Song of Prayer*, we do not want the parts of the song, no matter how beautiful or inspiring they may be, but the song itself—the *content* of love's remembrance, not the *form* of psychic ability (S-1.I.2-4).

(1:6) Let all his learning and all his efforts be directed toward this one great final surprise, and he will not be content to be delayed by the little ones that may come to him on the way.

This is the awakening from the dream. When you cross over to the real world, as Jesus says in the text, "you will think, in glad astonishment, that for all this you gave up *nothing!*" (T-16.VI.11:4). Your individual self was nothing; the world was nothing. But the experience of the total inclusiveness of God's Love is everything—the great, final, and glorious surprise. Knowing that this is what awaits you, Jesus is saying, why accentuate your psychic abilities, or any ability for that matter? You do, however, want to accentuate where these abilities will take you—out of the dream—if they are used for that purpose. This explains why anything you make important that establishes a separation between you and others must be of the ego. If you use different abilities and powers—psychic, physical, intellectual, artistic—to accentuate differences and erect altars to yourself or others, you know for certain you have bought into the ego's specialness and misused the power of your mind. Thus you need always to keep the end of the journey in sight. Focusing on an ability, experience, or personality trait will root you on the ladder of specialness, to shift

---

* See my *Absence from Felicity*, Chapter 5.

metaphors, and you will never achieve the goal of returning home.

(2:1-4) Certainly there are many "psychic" powers that are clearly in line with this course. Communication is not limited to the small range of channels the world recognizes. If it were, there would be little point in trying to teach salvation. It would be impossible to do so.

There is nothing wrong with psychic experiences as such; for instance, if you are in touch with someone who is not physically in your presence. Jesus is merely urging you not to place undue emphasis on it. Thus, he would ask you, as an example, not to boast about it, nor think you are specially blessed because of it. Having the same mind, everyone has the same potential.

(2:5) The limits the world places on communication are the chief barriers to direct experience of the Holy Spirit, Whose Presence is always there and Whose Voice is available but for the hearing.

Our two great themes are again intertwined. The world places limits by imposing separation, thus establishing separate interests as reality. However, when we ask help of the Holy Spirit, Who is equally in everyone, we recognize we are the same. We do not deny our special identities, nor our abilities, potentials, or experiences—we deny the ego's use of them. Above all, we do not compare ourselves with others. "Love makes no comparisons" (W-pI.195.4:2) because love comes from perfect Oneness, in which God's Son finds his Self, without distinctions.

(2:6) These limits are placed out of fear, for without them the walls that surround all the separate places of the world would fall at the holy sound of His Voice.

The "walls" are bodies, including the ways we use them to reinforce separation. Turning to the Holy Spirit's Call in the mind dissolves the body, as Jericho's walls fell at the sound of Joshua's trumpets (Joshua 6:20).

(2:7-8) Who transcends these limits in any way is merely becoming more natural. He is doing nothing special, and there is no magic in his accomplishments.

What is truly natural is that we are one, reflecting spirit's natural state of oneness; the unnatural is that we are separated. However, we share not only one Self, but the unnatural qualities of the illusory split mind as well—the ego's separation and the Holy Spirit's Atonement.

Jesus' use of the word *special* is important here, connoting anything that accentuates separation, differences, or exclusion. We clearly do not speak of *form* but *content*, for we cannot physically be with everyone all the time.

(3:1-2) The seemingly new abilities that may be gathered on the way can be very helpful. Given to the Holy Spirit, and used under His direction, they are valuable teaching aids.

Do not deny your special abilities, nor fear being successful in the world. We are all prone to denying our gifts because of past guilty associations with misuse and sin. Denying them, however, is the same mistake as flaunting them. When we go to Jesus the guilt is undone, freeing us to be helpful because these abilities can now serve a different purpose. Rather than being used to aggrandize the ego and keep us separate from each other, they can be used to diminish our specialness and remind us that God's Sons are one.

(3:3-6) To this, the question of how they arise is irrelevant. The only important consideration is how they are used. Taking them as ends in themselves, no matter how this is done, will delay progress. Nor does their value lie in proving anything; achievements from the past, unusual attunement with the "unseen," or "special" favors from God.

We need always remember the journey's purpose, and seeing our inherent sameness and shared interests moves us steadily forward. If we keep in mind that attaining our goal of becoming ego free will make us happy, we will not build altars of specialness to ourselves or to others. We should try not to forget that the ego seeks to reinforce the separation that gave birth to it, tempting us to see people as better or worse than we, or as having special gifts. Helen was always clear about this when students tried to venerate her, insisting that they could do what she did. Indeed, it cannot be otherwise, for that would make this course in undoing specialness a lie.

(3:7-8) God gives no special favors, and no one has any powers that are not available to everyone. Only by tricks of magic are special powers "demonstrated."

This reminds us why we left God and continue to hate Him—the all-inclusiveness of His Love was not acceptable to us, as He did not grant the specialness we demanded (T-13.III.10:1-4). And so we are continually tempted to demonstrate the unique powers we may have, which maintain the specialness of separation that belies God's perfect Love.

(4:1-4) Nothing that is genuine is used to deceive. The Holy Spirit is incapable of deception, and He can use only genuine abilities. What is used for magic is useless to Him. But what He uses cannot be used for magic.

What deceives is my believing I have a special ability that sets me off from you—or seeing you with an ability that sets you off from me. At this point Jesus cannot be of help, and therefore that ability would inevitably be used on behalf of the ego. Magic separates; the Holy Spirit's miracle embraces all as one.

(4:5-7) There is, however, a particular appeal in unusual abilities that can be curiously tempting. Here are strengths which the Holy Spirit wants and needs. Yet the ego sees in these same strengths an opportunity to glorify itself.

Jesus reinforces the idea that an ability is of value when it helps us realize we are the same, and that the power lies in the mind not the body. However, because the need to be special is so strong, it is all too tempting to make the ability into something important and spiritual, forgetting that the meaning of anything rests in its purpose, not in the ability itself. Nothing is spiritual here other than awakening to the happy fact we are not here.

(4:8-9) Strengths turned to weakness are tragedy indeed. Yet what is not given to the Holy Spirit must be given to weakness, for what is withheld from love is given to fear, and will be fearful in consequence.

When we withhold from the Holy Spirit, we reenact our withholding from God—the source of separation, guilt, and fear. Jesus wants us to heed his cautions, for they are essential to our spiritual progress. Anything that reinforces separation keeps us separate from God, him, and the ultimate purpose of this course. When we withhold love we fall into the arms of projection, and blame everyone else for our sins, slipping quickly into building idols of specialness in ourselves and others. All this because we refuse to learn the simple lesson of our oneness —sharing the need to leave the world of bodies and return home.

(5:1) Even those who no longer value the material things of the world may still be deceived by "psychic" powers.

The split mind is not inherently spiritual, not being of God, yet we still believe psychic powers are spiritual. Recall that the word *spiritual* comes from *spirit*—our reality that is not of this world. The only spiritual thing we are capable of here is the right-minded purpose of asking Jesus to be our teacher, that he use our experiences as the means to awaken us from the dream. In and of themselves, psychic abilities are nothing. Indeed, we used these abilities of the mind to make up a world. That is why the mind is guilty and we strive so mightily to avoid it.

One way we deal with guilt is believing the mind to be wonderful—holy and powerful—impressed by what it can do. We cover our guilt with specialness, which breeds further guilt and leads to the inevitable misuse of the mind. Rather than being the means of breaking identification with the body, and therefore specialness, the mind reinforces them. That is why Jesus cautions us against being deceived by psychic power. The only true power is our choice—for or against the ego. Everything else is a vehicle for having us forget the power of the mind to choose.

(5:2-4) As investment has been withdrawn from the world's material gifts, the ego has been seriously threatened. It may still be strong enough to rally under this new temptation to win back strength by guile. Many have not seen through the ego's defenses here, although they are not particularly subtle.

This is the same caveat we find in the text, where Jesus wants us to be aware that as we walk with him on the journey and identify with the Holy Spirit's evaluation of us, the ego becomes retaliative and vicious (T-8.V.5:4-6; T-9.VII.4). As we withdraw identification from the body, having accepted its nothingness, our fear becomes so great that we now identify with the special mind. There really is no difference, however, between identifying with a special body or special mind, but we do not see this because we do not want to, as we now read:

(5:5) Yet, given a remaining wish to be deceived, deception is made easy.

Deception pervades our world in so many ways; to name but two: we believe peace is gained by waging war, and love can be attained through seduction. The deception is rather obvious when we look at it with open eyes, but not so when we are in the midst of it because we want to be in the middle of specialness and attack. Yet it remains true that whatever separates us from anyone else must be of the ego.

(5:6-7) Now the "power" is no longer a genuine ability, and cannot be used dependably. It is almost inevitable that, unless the individual changes his mind about its purpose, he will bolster his "power's" uncertainties with increasing deception.

You must always be clear about your purpose. Following the Holy Spirit, your purpose is to awaken from the dream of differentiation, exclusion, and specialness. Anything in the body's world —any ability or gift—can be used to help you return to the mind to make another choice. That gives the ability true power, regardless of how the world sees it. Since what reinforces your differences from others keeps you in the dream, it is necessary to be aware of the part of the mind that wants to be deceived and remain asleep.

(6:1-2) Any ability that anyone develops has the potentiality for good. To this there is no exception.

Any ability. And it need not be something the world reveres or admires. We all have abilities and, once again, it is not the ability itself that is important, but to what it is devoted. Even though we are much different on the bodily level, we are the same in purpose—the ego's or the Holy Spirit's. To say this one more time, it is important that we not deny our various abilities and gifts—psychic, psychological, or physical—but simply to deny the ego's use of them.

(6:3) And the more unusual and unexpected the power, the greater its potential usefulness.

If we have an ability that shows others that the mind transcends the body, that can be helpful indeed. It points to the fact that things are not what they appear to be—the body is not lord of the mind, but the mind is the cause of everything physical. Again, without being aware of our proclivities for specialness, we will leap into the ego's arms in which abilities become special, something to take pride in or to admire in others, ruing the day that deprived us of them.

(6:4-8) Salvation has need of all abilities, for what the world would destroy the Holy Spirit would restore. "Psychic" abilities have been used to call upon the devil, which merely means to strengthen the ego. Yet here is also a great channel of hope and healing in the Holy Spirit's service. Those who have developed "psychic" powers have simply let some of the limitations they laid upon their minds be lifted. It can be but further limitations they lay upon themselves if they utilize their increased freedom for greater imprisonment.

The world would destroy the mind's ability to choose, while the Holy Spirit restores to the mind the ability the ego sought to obviate. Psychic powers can help turn us in the mind's direction, but if they are used for specialness, we are once more in the ego's magical embrace. Repeatedly, Jesus cautions us not to deny our abilities and gifts, but to be clear about our purpose in using them. His purpose, which he gladly shares with us, is Atonement, not glorification; remembering the power of God's Love, not attaining worldly power; awakening us to oneness, not maintaining the dream of separation. If we are clear about this purpose, we will not overemphasize a psychic ability or any ability. We will not be guilty because of a self-accusation of misuse; nor will we try to destroy the gift. At the same time we will not revel in it, but will treat it as neutral— to serve the mind's purpose of separate or shared interests, specialness or Atonement, imprisonment or freedom.

(6:9) The Holy Spirit needs these gifts, and those who offer them to Him and Him alone go with Christ's gratitude upon their hearts, and His holy sight not far behind.

The key idea is "offer them to Him." They are our gifts, but it is His purpose we gratefully want. Christ, of course, is not grateful, but the Sonship is—in gratitude that we are finally choosing to return home. The "holy sight" of Christ's vision sees only the unified Sonship, and gives no power to anything to separate us. As the Course says, what God has joined as one remains one (e.g., T-8.VI.9:4; T-22.V.3:5), referring to the famous biblical statement: "What therefore God hath joined together, let not man put asunder" (Matthew 19:6).

In summary, then, the purpose any ability serves reflects the teacher we choose. If we are clear about why we climb the ladder—awakening from the dream and returning home—we will see everything here, whether dramatic or uninspiring, as having the potential to serve our holy purpose.

26. CAN GOD BE REACHED DIRECTLY?

This is the only place in the manual where Jesus talks about Teachers of teachers, the third of the categories of teachers he described earlier. To review, the first is the basic teacher of God, which includes all of us; next is the advanced teacher, who possesses the ten characteristics we discussed in section 4; lastly, there is the Teacher of teachers. Like Jesus, these Teachers are in the real world, the state of mind in which all illusions have been recognized for what they are. Teachers of teachers are therefore no longer truly here within the dream—although their bodies may still be seen—but their names remain a shining symbol of the Atonement.

(1:1) God indeed can be reached directly, for there is no distance between Him and His Son.

Jesus is saying God can be reached directly because we are one with Him. The ego would tell us we cannot reach God because of the separation. Yet in point of Fact, we are already united with Him, and so not only *can* we reach Him, we *are* with Him, as the following discussion explains:

(1:2) His awareness is in everyone's memory and His Word is written on everyone's heart.

Even on the level of our dream of separation, God's Presence is in all of us. We not only share the wrong-minded thought system of guilt, fear, and hate, but the right-minded Atonement, the Word that is in everyone's mind as a memory, calling us back to the Heart we never left.

Note Jesus' double use of the word *everyone*. No matter how villainous others may be in our estimation, God's memory is as present in them as in ourselves. Otherwise, it can be in no one. That memory is of our oneness as God's Son, excluding no one. We can thus all reach God, because that thought linking us to Him is in everyone, awaiting only our decision. Indeed, the purpose of *A Course in Miracles* is to help us remove the interferences to the truth so we can remember God's Word. The instant we do, we become the Word and awaken from the dream to remember our unity with the God we never left: "You are at home in God, dreaming of exile" (T-10.I.2:1). Thus we are part of God's living Oneness, yet insanely dreaming of separation and alienation. Jesus' course enables us to change our minds, teaching us how happy we will be when we finally awaken to His Word.

(1:3) Yet this awareness and this memory can arise across the threshold of recognition only where all barriers to truth have been removed.

All illusions are the same. If you exclude one from the truth, you make all illusions true. At the end of the text is this wonderful statement: "Not one spot of darkness still remains to hide the face of Christ from anyone" (T-31.VIII.12:5). *Not one. All* illusions, *all* barriers have been brought to the truth, in which they gently disappear.

(1:4-6) In how many is this the case? Here, then, is the role of God's teachers. They, too, have not attained the necessary understanding as yet, but they have joined with others.

Our first theme is restated: God's teachers do not see their interests as separate from anyone else's. This establishes them as teachers, placing them on the right ladder with the right teacher learning the right lessons. The ego's ladder is one of specialness, on which we are perceived as different from each other. This theme returns in almost every section, addressed to all students of *A Course in Miracles*—i.e., teachers of God. Perhaps we have not climbed very far, but we are at least on Jesus' ladder because in one holy instant we did not see our interests as apart from another's. We may not have generalized to the entire Sonship and to all difficult situations, but we have begun to learn we are happier when we release our grievances and do not see someone as separate from us.

The ladder thus symbolizes the process of learning to generalize the lesson of shared interests. It is learned by gradually identifying less with the body and more with the mind. This subtheme of mind and body is a variation of the theme of separate versus shared interests, for the decision to see others as separate occurs in the mind, as does the decision to see them as one in purpose. Generalizing, we recognize that people's behavior is immaterial. We learn that the situation does not matter—the stock market, the weather, a war—for we remain at peace whenever we so choose. If we are not peaceful, it is not due to external situations, but because of the mind's decision to be in conflict.

(1:7-8) This is what sets them apart from the world. And it is this that enables others to leave the world with them.

Jesus is not talking about leaving the world or the body, as in death, because we have never been in the world or the body. His point is leaving the ego's thought system that gave rise to the world, a thought system predicated on the separation that began with the judgment that our selfish interests are more important than God. This original thought —I do not care about my Creator but only my needs—becomes the core of the ego thoughts in the mind of each fragment of the Sonship, and therefore the basis for all experience in the world.

(1:9-10) Alone they are nothing. But in their joining is the power of God.

This does not refer to the body, nor joining with other Course students. Jesus speaks only of our thoughts—the belief that salvation comes at another's expense, and that our individual experiences of love are important. We have no recognition that such thinking precludes our happiness and peace. Jesus' point, therefore, is that love cannot be genuine if it does not—in the mind—embrace everyone. There can be no judgment or specialness in the Presence of God's Love, and in realizing that our interests are not apart from someone else's, we undo the separation that was the barrier to our awareness of the power of God and the experience of His Love.

(2:1-3) There are those who have reached God directly, retaining no trace of worldly limits and remembering their own Identity perfectly. These might be called the Teachers of teachers because, although they are no longer visible, their image can yet be called upon. And they will appear when and where it is helpful for them to do so.

This describes anyone who physically has transcended the ego. To be a symbol of the Atonement and the Love of God, a Teacher of teachers need not necessarily be dead, although it is almost impossible, as paragraph 3 will explain, to remain here in that state without some kind of limitation. Present bodily or not, these Teachers remain thoughts in the mind, available whenever we call for help. Thus, for example, since we are still identified with the physical, it is helpful to call upon Jesus' "body" as friend and brother.

(2:4-7) To those to whom such appearances would be frightening, they give their ideas. No one can call on them in vain. Nor is there anyone of whom they are unaware. All needs are known to them, and all mistakes are recognized and overlooked by them.

The mind of God's Son is one. There is one mistake, not thousands; there is one need, not thousands. The mistake was choosing the ego's separation over the Holy Spirit's Atonement, and the need is to correct the mistake. Jesus speaks of many mistakes and needs because our separated experience is that we have made multiple mistakes and have multiple needs, and so he uses words and concepts that we can accept without fear. The content, however, is beyond our dreams of separation and the dualistic world of time and space. The point is that the Atonement is abstract and non-specific, as is the idea of the Holy Spirit. Yet since we identify with a specific body, personality, and self, we need specific representations of the mind's abstract presence of the Atonement. Jesus is but one of these symbols, as we have seen; and there have been countless others throughout history. Yet as Western students of *A Course in Miracles*, our symbol of God's Love will most likely be the one we know as Jesus.

(2:8) The time will come when this is understood.

We cannot understand these teachings now, which is why Jesus speaks in dualistic terms. It is important to remember that his words are symbols pointing to a reality beyond themselves. Their full meaning will be comprehended when we are no longer bound to the world, because we will know we exist outside the dream. As we increasingly let go of judgments, and as we have more and more experiences of being beyond the ego, we will come to find that the Course's words we have read for years will suddenly leap off the page, as we exclaim: "So *that* is what it means!" It is not necessary, however, to understand their full meaning at this stage in our learning, but it is necessary to know that we do not understand, yet recognize that we progress on the journey to the extent to which we can ask for help in perceiving everyone as one, walking the same journey—not *one or the other*, but *together, or not at all*.

26. Can God Be Reached Directly?

(2:9) And meanwhile, they give all their gifts to the teachers of God who look to them for help, asking all things in their name and in no other.

Jesus may be thought of in this context. His gift of love comes to us in whatever form we can accept. But his gift is maximal, as we have seen earlier in the manual, referring back to the first miracle principle: "All expressions of love are maximal" (T-1.I.1:4). Love is thus expressed in many forms, *A Course in Miracles* being one of them. However, it is not the expression we really want, but its use as a means to move beyond it to the love that is its source. At that point all will be understood, because truth will have become our experience. Thus we use the different forms and symbols, but are not taken in by them.

(3:1-2) Sometimes a teacher of God may have a brief experience of direct union with God. In this world, it is almost impossible that this endure.

In the experience of direct union with God, referred to as *revelation* early in the text (T-1.II.1:5), we pay no attention to the body. Therefore, Jesus will speak of Teachers of teachers working through those who still have limitations that keep them anchored here.

(3:3-6) It can, perhaps, be won after much devotion and dedication, and then be maintained for much of the time on earth. But this is so rare that it cannot be considered a realistic goal. If it happens, so be it. If it does not happen, so be it as well.

In other words, Jesus is saying not to place undue emphasis on experiencing direct union with God, nor to strive to have this mystical experience, for it alone will not bring you home. What will awaken you, however, is the daily work of undoing guilt through forgiveness. If you have such an experience of union, that is fine; if you do not, that is fine, too. Either way, you need to practice your daily lessons—both in the workbook and the ongoing situations of your life—of asking for help in looking at relationships differently. Again, the experience of unity "is so rare that it cannot be considered a realistic goal," and it is not the purpose of *A Course in Miracles* to evoke this experience in its students.

That is why Jesus tells us in the text that its goal is not knowledge or Heaven:

> Forget not that the motivation for this course is the attainment and the keeping of the state of peace. Given this state the mind is quiet, and the condition in which God is remembered is attained (T-24.in.1:1-2).

Peace is achieved, in the context of this course, through the forgiveness that is to be our central focus.

(3:7) All worldly states must be illusory.

Not some. *All.*

(3:8-10) If God were reached directly in sustained awareness, the body would not be long maintained. Those who have laid the body down merely to extend their helpfulness to those remaining behind are few indeed. And they need helpers who are still in bondage and still asleep, so that by their awakening can God's Voice be heard.

The presence of Jesus in our minds is too threatening. That is why we have built barricades of guilt —the special love and hate relationship—to block his love from awareness. Although this course comes from love's purity, it cannot be its pure expression, for it consists of concepts, symbols, and words that, we were told earlier, were made to keep God separate (M-21.1:7). That is why Jesus says his "course remains within an ego framework" (C-in.3:1). The *content* of its teaching is perfect, but not its *form*; and so it is the love we want, not its expression. Yet we need the indirect, dualistic form to offset our fear of the direct, non-dualistic experience of the content. Thus duality serves the holy purpose of helping us—kindly and gently— accept the love that is our non-dualistic reality.

(4:1-3) Do not despair, then, because of limitations. It is your function to escape from them, but not to be without them. If you would be heard by those who suffer, you must speak their language.

These lines parallel the statement in "The Little Willingness," where Jesus tells us not to be disturbed by the shadows, for that is why we came (T-18.IV.2:1-5).* His meaning is that we should not

---

* These themes are developed in my *Forgiving Our Limitations*, the second volume of *The Healing Power of Kindness*. See ordering information at the end of the book.

be disturbed by our egos, for we are here to *un*learn all the ego taught us once we chose to listen to it rather than the Holy Spirit. Within the context of his teaching in this passage, however, the message is different. In view of the feelings of guilt and despair over our limitations, Jesus asks us to look at them in a more positive light—to think of the possibility that they could be vehicles through which the Holy Spirit teaches His Love. Consider that if you were to be ego-free, no one could stand to be in your presence. What the world calls limitations can thus become helpful expressions of love in forms people can accept without fear. That is why in Lesson 155 Jesus says that we should be normal and look like everyone else, differing only in the sense that we would smile more frequently (W-pI.155.1). Therefore, someone like a Helen Keller would be born with severe physical limitations, but through overcoming the handicaps becomes a shining example that inner peace is not dependent on external circumstances.

The idea is not to have a perfect body—that is an oxymoron. Besides, why would anyone want one? What you want is a perfect mind. Thus, do not despair because of limitations, because they can become ways of love teaching through you—and also ways of teaching *you*. Limitations are almost always thought of in a pejorative sense: there is something wrong with you because… And students are tempted to think if they get this course right, their problems would disappear. Yet this is exactly what the ego wants—having you focus on the body rather than the purpose the body can serve: reinforcing the ego's separation or undoing it through the Holy Spirit's forgiveness. When you focus on your failures, the ego is jubilant. Instead, accept your body as it is, but escape from the burden of guilt your ego has placed on it. Rather than harbor self-blame (or blame) for a life of scarcity, for instance, you could surmount your painful circumstances by learning that feelings of self-worth are not contingent on meeting the world's criteria of success, but on recognizing that the mind is the source of all scarcity and abundance —and what you experience is your choice.

Thus Jesus says: "It is your function to escape from them, but not to be without them." In other words, there is nothing wrong with having ego thoughts, as long as we do not put them front and center in ourselves. There is nothing wrong with having a body, whether it works well or not, as long as we do not make it our primary focus. It is our function to escape from the guilt we put on the limited body, but not necessarily to be without it, for the body's limitations can become a way in which God's Love, so terrifying to the world, is expressed in a more manageable way. Again, "if you would be heard by those who suffer, you must speak their language." Theirs is the language of limitation and duality, and so, as teachers, it is ours as well.

To make the point again, we do not want to change our personalities or our bodies, but only the purpose we have given them. Instead of seeing them as hellish prisons from which we yearn to escape, they become classrooms in which we learn, and through which we teach, Heaven's lessons of Atonement. This is the right-minded reason for being here. The importance of this shift cannot be overstated, for as we look at limitations differently, the shift in perception will help us become more gentle toward ourselves, and therefore more gentle toward others. It does not matter whether these limitations are physical, emotional, social, or moral— whether we believe war will bring peace, conflict tranquility, or specialness happiness—we will see them as limitations from which we want to escape guilt's burden. By our peaceful and defenseless examples, therefore, we will help others forgive their guilt. Once more, the goal is not to be without limitations, but to become free of the ego's purpose of guilt it had assigned to them.

(4:4-6) If you would be a savior, you must understand what needs to be escaped. Salvation is not theoretical. Behold the problem, ask for the answer, and then accept it when it comes.

The effectiveness of this course is based upon understanding where and what the problem is: the mind's decision to identify with the grandiosity of the ego's littleness rather than the grandeur of Christ's magnitude. That mistake is the source of limitation, not the world of bodies. Two sections in the text speak of this: "Littleness versus Magnitude" and "Grandeur versus Grandiosity" (T-15.III; T-9.VIII). We thus see the limitations in the world of form as reflections of the mind's mistaken choice. Once we understand the nature of the problem, we can do something about it with Jesus' help. In turn, his love helps others through us by our example. And so, the presence or absence of limitations—the world's or our own—will make no difference to us, for we will demonstrate only peace, gentleness, kindness, and love.

(4:7-8) Nor will its coming be long delayed. All the help you can accept will be provided, and not one need you have will not be met.

Since the answer is already present in the mind, all we need do is accept it. Again Jesus speaks to us on the level we think we are in, wherein we have a multitude of needs. However, he so often reminds us there is only one need. As there is only one prayer —for forgiveness—because we have everything (T-3.V.6:3), we need only awaken from the dream of lack by letting the wrong teacher go and identifying with the right One.

(4:9-11) Let us not, then, be too concerned with goals for which you are not ready. God takes you where you are and welcomes you. What more could you desire, when this is all you need?

One more word of caution: we should have as our immediate goal only the next rung of the ladder, without becoming caught in counting the rungs still ahead. We need focus on where we are now, watching what upsets us and not worrying about having a direct experience of God. We should ask instead for a direct experience of how good it feels to forgive and let go of judgment, at the same time being aware of how much we still fear that next step.

27. WHAT IS DEATH?

This section goes hand in hand with the one that follows: "What Is the Resurrection?"—both are wonderful summaries of many of the themes found not only in the manual, but in the text and workbook as well. Parallels to this present section may be found in the text's "The Attraction of Death" (T-19.IV-C) and workbook lessons "There is no death. The Son of God is free" and "There is one life, and that I share with God" (W-pI.163; W-pI.167).

(1:1) Death is the central dream from which all illusions stem.

This returns us to the mind-body issue, an important variation of our major theme. We think of death as of the body, as we do life, pleasure, and pain. The thrust of *A Course in Miracles* is to shift our attention to the mind, so we—the decision maker as observer—may understand that choosing the ego brings pain, regardless of the pleasure it seems to afford us, and choosing the Holy Spirit brings true pleasure—"all real pleasure comes from doing God's Will" (T-1.VII.1:4)—which comes from removing the pain that inevitably follows the choice for separation.

Death is "the central dream from which all illusions stem" because the ego's thought system begins with the death of God. The sin and guilt that erupted from that seeming act led to the terrifying prospect that God would destroy us. We escaped from this battleground of certain death by making up a world and hiding in a body. Yet our bodies die in the ego's vicious circle that goes nowhere. We can thus understand why Jesus teaches that death is the central concept in the dream. It is clearly not physical death to which he refers—what does not exist cannot die—but to the *thought system of death* that begins with the idea that in the choice between God's Self and our own we chose ours, meaning that the Self of God had to be sacrificed.

(1:2-5) Is it not madness to think of life as being born, aging, losing vitality, and dying in the end? We have asked this question before, but now we need to consider it more carefully. It is the one fixed, unchangeable belief of the world that all things in it are born only to die. This is regarded as "the way of nature," not to be raised to question, but to be accepted as the "natural" law of life.

It is absolutely insane, Jesus is saying, to equate death with a body and think it is real, not to mention thinking that God had something to do with it. That everything here dies is a fact of what we call life in the dream. Even inanimate objects "die," since over eons they will deteriorate, decompose, and disappear.

(1:6-7) The cyclical, the changing and unsure; the undependable and the unsteady, waxing and waning in a certain way upon a certain path,—all this is taken as the Will of God. And no one asks if a benign Creator could will this.

The Introduction to Chapter 13 also depicts the insanity of this world; and at the end of the description Jesus says: "If this were the real world, God *would* be cruel" (T-13.in.3:1). Here, too, he is making it clear that our Creator and Source has nothing to do with what is not perfect, eternal, and changeless, thus dismissing the thought that the cosmos is divine.

(2:1-2) In this perception of the universe as God created it, it would be impossible to think of Him as loving. For who has decreed that all things pass away, ending in dust and disappointment and despair, can but be feared.

The ego wants us to be afraid of God; and so it makes up a world of pain and suffering, as well as theologies that tell us how and why God did this. The Adam and Eve story is a prime example. The Bible teaches that having inherited Adam and Eve's sin, we are justified in believing our Creator would sin against us by causing us to suffer and die. Who would not be afraid of a god like this? Constantly reminding us that God is to be feared is an important part of the ego's strategy to keep us mindless. It would do anything to prevent us from returning to our minds; and this includes making a cosmos and body in which we live and die. Yet we never question this insanity. Having blocked out the world's origin, we remain in a mindless state because we are terrified of the wrathful Presence within. This is so, even though God's anger is an illusory defense against our choosing the Atonement, which contains the memory of the true God Who only loves us and knows of nothing else. Jesus' point is that no one really asks how a loving God could act in such a way. Yet there is a simple explanation—*He doesn't*. Our all-loving Creator can have nothing to do with a dream.

(2:3-4) He holds your little life in his hand but by a thread, ready to break it off without regret or care, perhaps today. Or if he waits, yet is the ending certain.

In the text, Jesus speaks of two layers of the illusion: the secret dream and the world's dream. The latter is of

> an ancient enemy, a murderer who stalks you in the night and plots your death, yet plans that it be lingering and slow…(T-27.VII.12:1).

This emanates from the secret dream of guilt demanding punishment. The more brutal the punishment in the world, the better the ego likes it, as is obvious from world events.

(2:5-6) Who loves such a god knows not of love, because he has denied that life is real. Death has become life's symbol.

Jesus refers here to our true life in Heaven, which we have denied. Followers of religions that preach such a god—and Western religions are not alone in this—cannot know of love. That is why they hate, persecute, and kill—all in the name of a loving Deity. Life has thus come to signify death, which means there once was physical life.

(2:7-8) His world is now a battleground, where contradiction reigns and opposites make endless war. Where there is death is peace impossible.

That is why there is no peace in the world. Every time a country wages war it prevents peace, for its decision for war is based on a thought system that reinforces the thought of war—and it recycles endlessly. If you truly want to help in bringing peace to the world, choose to end conflict in your mind—the source of war. From that conflict-free place of peace, love will flow and guide your words and behavior. Regardless of the form, whatever you express will embrace—*in content*—all people without judgment. Without such content, peace will never be possible here, for it is inconceivable as long as there is a belief in death—"the central dream from which all illusions stem."

(3:1-2) Death is the symbol of the fear of God. His Love is blotted out in the idea, which holds it from awareness like a shield held up to obscure the sun.

The ego made an insane and vicious nightmare of sin, guilt, and fear—we sinned against God and our guilt demands He punish us—its motivation being to make us so frightened we would voluntarily leave the mind, become mindless, and never return to the place where we chose to believe the ego. Therefore, the problem is not *what* the ego tells us, but that we *believe* what it tells us—a critical distinction. The ego thought system of hate, hate, and still more hate would have no effect if we did not invest it with reality. We call the part of the mind that did so *the decision maker*, the true power within the dream. We therefore have to return to the mind where the wrong decision was made and correct it. This has been blotted out by fear and our desire to hold onto the thought system of separation. In the workbook, Jesus speaks of a double shield of oblivion (W-pI.136.5:2)—the first is the guilt that leads us to believe there is a vengeful God in our minds, and the second is the world that protects us by rooting our awareness outside the mind, so we will never have to confront the terrifying presence of God's wrath.

(3:3-8) The grimness of the symbol is enough to show it cannot coexist with God. It holds an image of the Son of God in which he is "laid to rest" in devastation's arms, where worms wait to greet him and to last a little while by his destruction. Yet the worms as well are doomed to be destroyed as certainly. And so do all things live because of death. Devouring is nature's "law of life." God is insane, and fear alone is real.

This is the world that people venerate, seek to preserve, and kill for—and most insanely of all, believe God has created. Yet the world "He" created is only about death. "Devouring is nature's 'law of life,'" because that is the ego's origin. In our insane dream we believed we devoured God—convinced we could get away with murder—and then possessed His power, creative life, and love. Moreover, since we got everything by devouring, we believe we can keep it only by devouring those who would seek to take it from us, but in the end, we are devoured as well—when the body dies it is eaten by worms, which are in turn eaten. This gruesome passage is actually borrowed from an even more gruesome passage in *Hamlet* (IV,iii), where the prince offers some cynical observations about death to his uncle, whom Hamlet is sure has killed his father. Hamlet presents this same idea of worms eating worms—the underside of life we do not want to see. In defense we strive to make the body sacred, but the horror is not really what worms do, or what people do to each other. The horror is what our minds believe we did to God. This places the onus firmly on the belief that comes from the decision-making mind—the source of everything in the dream—which begins and ends with death. Thus does one organism devour another, recycling life—a thought that is renewed by continually reinforcing its seeming reality through our bodily experience.

(4:1-2) The curious belief that there is part of dying things that may go on apart from what will die, does not proclaim a loving God nor reestablish any grounds for trust. If death is real for anything, there is no life.

The subject here is people's belief in the existence of a soul that lives on after the body's death. However, life, being of God, is eternal: "There is no life outside of Heaven" (T-23.II.19:1). Thus there is no life here at all, for as part of God, life does not change, grow, or diminish; it does not die, nor is it born. Indeed, Jesus is emphatic in teaching us that the living God has nothing to do with death.

(4:3-5) Death denies life. But if there is reality in life, death is denied. No compromise in this is possible.

This is an uncompromising course. It is *one or the other*: spirit or flesh, oneness or separation, the eternal Christ or the moribund Son.

(4:6-10) There is either a god of fear or One of Love. The world attempts a thousand compromises, and will attempt a thousand more. Not one can be acceptable to God's teachers, because not one could be acceptable to God. He did not make death because He did not make fear. Both are equally meaningless to Him.

Sin, guilt, and the world are not only meaningless to God; He does not even see them because they do not exist. The world, however, is quite adept at compromise, maintaining that both life and death are real. Thus we kill some people so that others will have a better life. That is total insanity, as is our belief that God created us so we would die, only to be saved later—*though not all of us*. We thus attempt thousands of compromises over the issue of life *and* death.

(5:1-3) The "reality" of death is firmly rooted in the belief that God's Son is a body. And if God created bodies, death would indeed be real. But God would not be loving.

This accounts for our making such a big deal about death. We do not fear it but are attracted to it—the third obstacle to peace (T-19.IV-C). Death means there was life as the body must have lived, the fact that establishes as real the thought of separation that made it. Thus the world's worship of the Bible, which proclaims God as the creator of the world and body. Yet Jesus teaches us that God would not be loving if this were true.

(5:4-5) There is no point at which the contrast between the perception of the real world and that of the world of illusions becomes more sharply evident. Death is indeed the death of God, if He is Love.

If God is Love—perfect, changeless, and eternal—and death is real, then the body must be real as well. But then God would no longer be perfect, changeless, and eternal. This reasoning is also found in Lesson 190, "I choose the joy of God instead of pain," where Jesus says: "If God is real, there is no pain. If pain is real, there is no God" (W-pI.190. 3:3-4). If pain or death is real, God cannot exist, because the true God knows nothing of this. This explains why as a society, let alone as individuals, we are obsessed with death, not to mention birth. They focus on the body, fulfilling the unconscious wish to prove God wrong, for separation and oneness cannot coexist—if our separate bodies are real, God's one spirit cannot be. And from the belief in death comes the specialness that maintains our separate existence, for which someone else is responsible.

(5:6-10) And now His Own creation must stand in fear of Him. He is not Father, but destroyer. He is not Creator, but avenger. Terrible His

27. What Is Death?

Thoughts and fearful His image. To look on His creations is to die.

This is the God we must believe in, whether consciously or not. Insofar as we think we are here, this belief is in our minds because the secret thought underlying life in the body is that we tauntingly thumb our nose in God's face, derisively exclaiming: "You were wrong. You said I could never do this; that there could not be life outside of Heaven. Well, I showed You. Here I am. Do something about it!" As part of the ego's strategy, the ego's god does indeed do something about it, as recounted in the Bible. He smites us, sends plagues, and does all kinds of unconscionable things that culminate in His taking back from us the life we stole from Him. Needless to say, the true God is totally unaware of this insanity. Jesus therefore wants us to become aware of our belief system. We do not have to change what we believe, but it is important that we not feel guilty about it.

(6:1-2) "And the last to be overcome will be death." Of course!

Jesus is quoting St. Paul's famous statement (1 Corinthians 15:26), but with a meaning different from the traditional understanding. The overcoming of death is not accomplished through the resurrection of Jesus' body, but the overcoming of the *thought system* of death. If the ego's existence begins with the death of God, this is the last thing to be overcome. The key element here, as always, is separate interests: mine come before God's—I selfishly care only about my own needs and goals, even if God has to suffer and die as a result. However, I need not be in touch with that original thought, for I relive it over and over in my special relationships. I only have to see *how* I relive it. In other words, I need to focus on my need to push you away. I may not be thinking of killing you physically, but psychologically I definitely want you out of the picture. Thus your interests are secondary to mine, and my only concern is that I get what I want. This is something with which we can all identify, and thus choose against.

(6:3) Without the idea of death there is no world.

If there is no world, there is no *I*. Therefore, in self preservation, I cling to the ideas of the body's life and death.

(6:4-8) All dreams will end with this one. This is salvation's final goal; the end of all illusions. And in death are all illusions born. What can be born of death and still have life? But what is born of God and still can die?

We see again the repetition of the word *all*. Remember, this is an uncompromising course. Nothing born of God can die, because what is born of Him is life, and life is eternal.

(6:9) The inconsistencies, the compromises and the rituals the world fosters in its vain attempts to cling to death and yet to think love real are mindless magic, ineffectual and meaningless.

So much for the thought systems of the world, and certainly its religions—attempts to compromise truth and illusion by making truth part of the illusion. Thus are these attempts but mindless magic: *doing* nothing for they *are* nothing. They appear to be effective, but only because we believe in them. If we withdraw our belief, they disappear back into nothingness.

(6:10-11) God is, and in Him all created things must be eternal. Do you not see that otherwise He has an opposite, and fear would be as real as love?

Thus we speak of *A Course in Miracles* as a *nondualistic thought system*. There is God, Oneness, and Love, and nothing else. Most religious systems in the world, especially in the West, are dualistic—meaning there is an opposite to God: the material world of good and evil.

(7:1) Teacher of God, your one assignment could be stated thus: Accept no compromise in which death plays a part.

This line is extremely important. Many years ago, I gave a workshop based on this sentence and changed the word *death* to *duality*: "Accept no compromise in which duality plays a part."* Anything that is dualistic is an illusion. There are indeed right-minded illusions that will lead us to the truth, such as forgiveness and the miracle, yet they are

---

* "Duality as Metaphor in *A Course in Miracles*," available on CD. See ordering information at the end of the book.

still part of the dream. We need to pay attention to how we attempt to bring together mutually exclusive concepts like love and hate, peace and war, God and judgment, Heaven and hell, life and death.

(7:2-4) Do not believe in cruelty, nor let attack conceal the truth from you. What seems to die has but been misapprehended and carried to illusion. Now it becomes your task to let the illusion be carried to the truth.

Rather than have the body—which we thought was real—brought to the illusion of death, we now want the thought system of illusion and death brought to the truth of Atonement.

(7:5-6) Be steadfast but in this; be not deceived by the "reality" of any changing form. Truth neither moves nor wavers nor sinks down to death and dissolution.

This will help you learn the lesson of not taking anything in the world seriously, whether it affects your body or that of a loved one. You learn not to take things seriously because they have no effect on your inner peace. This should not be taken to mean, however, that you deny fear or anxiety, for example. Simply try to accept that the problem is not what you think it is—not what is happening to bodies, but that your mind chose the teacher of death instead of the Teacher of life.

Looking at the ego will at least help you become more honest, because you will realize, again, that the problem is not external. Death is not a problem to be overcome, nor are sickness, war, or loss. They are but part of the same problem of the mind's belief in separation, which you undo by looking at it with the love of Jesus beside you.

(7:7-10) And what is the end of death? Nothing but this; the realization that the Son of God is guiltless now and forever. Nothing but this. But do not let yourself forget it is not less than this.

Jesus returns to the beginning of the manual, weaving together the ways in which he speaks of the universal course, with its thousands of different forms. Its theme is that "God's Son is guiltless, and in his innocence is his salvation" (M-1.3:5). In other words, we are not separate—without sin and guilt, we are without the belief in separation—and so the Self God created remains perfectly one, united with Its Creator and Source, without differentiation or distinction—only the Everything of God and Christ.

Again, we need not have the experience of oneness, but it is important that we understand the reflection of that truth. If God's Son is guiltless, it means *you* are guiltless; the *you* being anyone we blame for our condition, anyone we say has power to take God's Love from us. If God's Son is guiltless, nothing has happened. It is not necessary that we stay focused on the Course's metaphysics or an intellectual understanding of this principle, but we do need to bring it down to our current experience, watching how we give away our power and then blame others for taking it from us. Death, then, becomes the epitome of the ego's selfishness—*one or the other*—concluding with: "I will gladly kill you if it means I can survive, and I will see to it that I survive and you do not."

I repeat those final lines:

(7:7-10) And what is the end of death? Nothing but this; the realization that the Son of God is guiltless now and forever. Nothing but this. But do not let yourself forget it is not less than this.

This kind of construction is occasionally found in *A Course in Miracles* (e.g., T-21.in.1:1-3). The end of death—the end of the Atonement path—is nothing more or less than understanding that the Son of God is guiltless, as he has always been, and will always be. A simple statement, and yet it expresses the All of God's Love. You need, however, to see the specific application of that principle in your everyday life, and allow no compromise to interfere —"Accept no compromise in which death plays a part" (7:1). Death is the origin of the thought system that says it is *one or the other*. Again, watch how you live that out daily. Do not try to change the ego, feel guilty about it, or judge yourself for it. But do watch it and see the perniciousness of its thoughts that will never bring you happiness or peace, and will never bring you home. That realization will motivate you finally to let them go.

28. WHAT IS THE RESURRECTION?

As I said above, this is the twin of the preceding section "What Is Death?"—death is the problem, and resurrection is the answer. Recall that in *A Course in Miracles*, resurrection, as with death, has nothing to do with the body. It is important to keep in mind that the Course's purpose is to move us from our identification with the body to the decision-making mind, wherein is found the power to choose between the thoughts of death and resurrection: death keeps us asleep, mired in the thought system of guilt and hate; resurrection awakens us by freeing us from guilt and hate, thus returning us home. This final section of the manual, preceding the epilogue "As for the Rest…," sums up the journey by describing its glorious end.

(1:1-2) Very simply, the resurrection is the overcoming or surmounting of death. It is a reawakening or a rebirth; a change of mind about the meaning of the world.

One could not ask for a clearer statement about the meaning of *resurrection*: "a change of mind about the meaning of the world." The ego said the world was a place of safety, a haven that would protect us *from* guilt, although it is actually a haven *for* guilt. The world was supposed to protect us from fear, suffering, and certain death at the hands of a vengeful God, yet we end up in a fearful body in which we inevitably suffer and die. Because this is the meaning the ego gave the world, the early workbook lessons focus on its meaninglessness. The Holy Spirit's meaningful correction is that the world is a classroom in which we learn His lessons of forgiveness, which culminate in our resurrection.

(1:3) It is the acceptance of the Holy Spirit's interpretation of the world's purpose; the acceptance of the Atonement for oneself.

Our second major theme—the need to rely on the Holy Spirit, Whose purpose for the world is to teach that what we have experienced outside is a picture of the illusory world of guilt we made real inside. Thus we learn there is no world. The world, therefore, is inherently meaningless, but given to the Holy Spirit it has a mighty meaning.

(1:4-5) It is the end of dreams of misery, and the glad awareness of the Holy Spirit's final dream. It is the recognition of the gifts of God.

Jesus speaks of the real world, which we attain when we realize that the ego's gifts of hate and fear, specialness and death are no longer what we want. Once and for all we say "no" to the ego's negation of God, and "yes" to His gifts of eternal life and perfect love. This, then, is the resurrection: "the glad awareness of the Holy Spirit's final dream."

(1:6) It is the dream in which the body functions perfectly, having no function except communication.

This does not necessarily mean that the body functions perfectly on the physical level. It functions perfectly only in the sense that it is no longer the ego's slave, used for suffering that inflicts the pain of guilt on others: "Behold me, brother, at your hand I die" (T-27.I.4:6). The perfect body now serves as a reminder that it was made by the ego to shield us from the mind's guilt, which shields us from choosing the Atonement. Yet whatever it does, whatever its limitations, the body can serve the purpose of forgiveness. Remember that this is not understandable from the perspective of the battleground that *is* the world and body, where we judge and seek to understand through the lens of our limited and distorted perception. Jesus' teachings make sense only above the battleground—the mind looking at the world from outside the dream, wherein it sees everything through the forgiving light of Christ's vision.

(1:7) It is the lesson in which learning ends, for it is consummated and surpassed with this.

Learning ends when we awaken from the dream. It brings us to Heaven's gate and thus is consummated, followed by the experience of love and awakening. Learning thus takes us only so far, which is why this is a course in miracles, not in the resurrection that follows the completion of the Holy Spirit's curriculum: accepting the Atonement by correcting all mistaken decisions, which reflected the mind's original decision for the ego.

(1:8) It is the invitation to God to take His final step.

God's "final step" is a metaphor for what follows when we reach the top of the ladder, which disappears as we rejoin formlessness and disappear into the Heart of God. Since perfect Oneness does not take steps, this is a poetic way of describing to us—still on the ladder—what happens: the wrong mind disappears because there is no longer an ego; the right mind disappears because there is no longer anything to correct; the decision maker disappears because there is no longer anything to decide. All that remains is the memory of God's Love. In that final holy instant we disappear into His memory and become His Love—God's last step.

(1:9-10) It is the relinquishment of all other purposes, all other interests, all other wishes and all other concerns. It is the single desire of the Son for the Father.

Jesus tells us in the text that he "will come in response to a single unequivocal call" (T-4.III.7:10). He says the same thing here. Since our single purpose is to return home and awaken from the dream of separation, hate, and death, we see everything in our day as helping us reach that goal. That single-mindedness allows us to ascend the ladder quickly, for nothing remains to hold us back. All other concerns, wishes, and purposes are gone, no longer attractive to us. Thus we say and mean: "I am not interested in specialness, for I know there is nothing here for me. How can I desire what does not exist? Moreover, the *I* that would desire it does not exist either." We have thus recognized that nothing here works, for nothing here *can* work. Only the Atonement principle heals, because that alone leads us home—the awakening from the dream of death that is the meaning of resurrection. And if death, as we have seen, is the beginning and end of the ego thought system, when the ego ends, nothing is left but the Love of God that encompasses everyone. Remember, love does not know of duality, differentiation, or distinction.

(2:1) The resurrection is the denial of death, being the assertion of life.

This is because resurrection emanates from the Atonement principle that says nothing has changed: separation never happened; life has never been compromised.

(2:2-3) Thus is all the thinking of the world reversed entirely. Life is now recognized as salvation, and pain and misery of any kind perceived as hell.

Everything in the world has served the ego's purpose of keeping us in hell—the ego's heaven. Yet all that is reversed is our choice to deny the ego thought system of death, recognizing that everything here is an illusion—good and bad, holy and unholy, life and death—because only God is true. Compromise is no longer an option.

(2:4) Love is no longer feared, but gladly welcomed.

This is the single desire of the Son for the Father. We no longer fear God's Love because we realize how painful it is to be separate from Him, how painful to be a separate and special entity. We therefore remember the happiness and joy that is ours when we leave the ego behind, and really mean it when we say we welcome only the truth.

(2:5-8) Idols have disappeared, and the remembrance of God shines unimpeded across the world. Christ's face is seen in every living thing, and nothing is held in darkness, apart from the light of forgiveness. There is no sorrow still upon the earth. The joy of Heaven has come upon it.

Everything in the ego system goes—all the idols that are our special love and hate objects. Once we have withdrawn our judgments from the Sonship, the memory of God "shines unimpeded across the world." This is in the mind because there is nowhere else—the world has never left its source. Since the mind of God's Son is one, minds are already joined, and when we lift the veils of darkness, hate, and guilt—put in the mind to impede remembering our Creator's Love—His light shines in everyone's mind, as did the light in Jesus' mind when he awoke. This is the world—the inner world—God's Love shines upon, as all pain and sorrow end. We have separated ourselves from the thought of death, having joined at last with the resurrected thought of life.

"Christ's face is seen in every living thing, and nothing is held in darkness"—our theme of shared interests: we all return to Heaven, or none of us does. In my mind, if I am to awaken from the dream I cannot exclude anyone—a public figure or one in my personal life. I thus need to watch how quickly I forget when I turn on the news, walk into my office, or think of a family member.

(3:1-3) Here the curriculum ends. From here on, no directions are needed. Vision is wholly corrected and all mistakes undone.

Note again Jesus' use of the word *all*, for there can be no exceptions to our forgiveness. The Course's curriculum thus ends when we have forgiven every last vestige of guilt in ourselves, but what happens beyond vision is not our concern, for when the ladder disappears, God takes the last step as we enter into His Heart of Love.

(3:4-5) Attack is meaningless and peace has come. The goal of the curriculum has been achieved.

Recall Jesus' statement that the goal of his course is not knowledge, but peace (T-24.in.1:1), which comes when you no longer hold any grievances against yourself or anyone else. Again, be aware of how quickly you fall into the arms of separation, judgment, and conflict. This includes those you love to hate as well as those you think you love. Recognize the distinctions within the Sonship you strive to make real and justify, and then let them go.

(3:6-8) Thoughts turn to Heaven and away from hell. All longings are satisfied, for what remains unanswered or incomplete? The last illusion spreads across the world, forgiving all things and replacing all attack.

In this world there are many different longings, yet in the end there is but the longing to return home. Once again we see the emphasis Jesus places on the theme of shared interests—"forgiving all things." Our forgiveness is the final illusion, elsewhere referred to as a "happy fiction" (C-3.2:1)—a fiction because it is still an illusion, but happy because it leads us beyond the world's pain to the joy of Heaven.

(3:9-10) The whole reversal is accomplished. Nothing is left to contradict the Word of God.

The "Word of God" is the Atonement that says the separation never happened. Thus no perception of separate interests remains—the reversal is *whole*, not *partial*. Remember that perception is not what our sensory organs tell us, but the mind's interpretation of what they tell us. Despite the seeming differences in the world, we will no longer perceive ourselves separate from anyone or anything, for we share the single purpose of forgiveness.

(3:11-13) There is no opposition to the truth. And now the truth can come at last. How quickly will it come as it is asked to enter and envelop such a world!

Opposition is over because we no longer accept compromises in which death plays a part (M-27. 7:1). Love is the only reality, and within the dream there are only reflections of love or calls for it. Truth comes because all obstacles have been undone, and so it envelops the mind that is no longer projected as a world.

(4:1) All living hearts are tranquil with a stir of deep anticipation, for the time of everlasting things is now at hand.

This refers to the Christian notion of eschatology —the end times. The "everlasting things" are at hand, but not externally as depicted in the Bible. This is the time of the mind's resurrection, the awakening from the ego's dream of death.

(4:2-6) There is no death. The Son of God is free [Lesson 163]. **And in his freedom is the end of fear. No hidden places now remain on earth to shelter sick illusions, dreams of fear and misperceptions of the universe. All things are seen in light, and in the light their purpose is transformed and understood.**

Again, "not one spot of darkness still remains to hide the face of Christ from anyone" (T-31.VIII. 12:5). These hidden places are the pockets of hate and guilt in our minds, which we keep hidden because they protect us from love. We are protected even more by projecting our hatred onto others. All fear and hate are gone when we remember our single desire for the Father: we want to return home, and want nothing else. Thus we understand the purpose of everything—not to exclude us from God, but to remind us that our only purpose is to return to Him.

(4:7-8) And we, God's children, rise up from the dust and look upon our perfect sinlessness. The song of Heaven sounds around the world, as it is lifted up and brought to truth.

The "song of Heaven that sounds around the world"—the same idea as "across the world" (2:5)—is the inner world of the mind. It is not really a song, for it has but one note. I choose this one when I let go of the ego's dissonant sounds of guilt and hate. Accepting the soundless song for myself, I have accepted it for the Sonship.

(5:1-2) Now there are no distinctions. Differences have disappeared and Love looks on Itself.

The illusion of separate existence began with the belief in distinctions and differences: I was distinctively different from God, and in order for me to exist He had to be sacrificed. We re-enact this insanity over and over—*ad infinitum, ad nauseam*—making ourselves sicker and sicker, as individuals and as a society, because we believe that exclusion, attack, and hate will get us what we want. Yet, they merely reinforce the ego's thought system of sickness and separation.

Love looks only on Itself. That is why we became angry at God in the beginning. We demanded special attention, but Love looked only on Itself and did not see a separated Son, nor spoiled brats having temper tantrums and screaming: "Pay attention to me, Daddy." Since God saw only Himself, we made up a world of distinctions and differences and a god who sees them, so we *would* be paid attention to.

(5:3-5) What further sight is needed? What remains that vision could accomplish? We have seen the face of Christ, His sinlessness, His Love behind all forms, beyond all purposes.

Once the ego is gone and we have seen the sinlessness of Christ, we no longer need the correction of vision. Every instance in our lives—every person and every thing our perception fell upon—has offered us the opportunity of choosing vision and remembering God's Love. Yet His Love is not within a form—this is not pantheism—for it is behind them all, reflected through the holy purpose of forgiveness.

(5:6-9) Holy are we because His Holiness has set us free indeed! And we accept His Holiness as ours; as it is. As God created us so will we be forever and forever, and we wish for nothing but His Will to be our own. Illusions of another will are lost, for unity of purpose has been found.

This lovely passage is reminiscent of the prose poem "The Gifts of God:"

> Holy are we who know our holiness, for it is You Who shine Your light on us, and we are thankful, in Your ancient Name, that You have not forgotten. What we thought we made of You has merely disappeared, and with its going are the images we made of Your creation gone as well (*The Gifts of God*, p. 119).

No longer accepting the unholiness of the ego, we welcome the holiness of our Identity as Christ: "we wish for nothing but His Will to be our own." This, again, is the single desire of the Son for the Father, in which everything becomes unified in the purpose of remembering Who we are. As God's true Son, how could I perceive anyone as separate from me, or more or less holy? Thus my daily purpose is to look at the impediments to recognizing we are one. I watch my judgments and special needs, without fighting against my ego nor striving to let it go, fully aware that I am choosing a thought system of death—yours and mine, because if it happens to you, it must happen to me, as well as to God. Yet the still, small Voice lovingly whispers in my ear: "Is this really what you want?" When I see clearly what I am doing—moment by moment, hour by hour, day by day—and how painful it is, this will motivate me to ask: "Why would I throw away the Love of God for *this*? Why would I hold onto these mean judgments and cruel thoughts, let alone behaviors, when I can experience His Love instead?" We therefore bring the illusion that our judgments will bring us happiness to the joyful truth that says: "I no longer need this. It is not a sin to let go of judgments and be happy." Thus we begin to experience the "Love behind all forms, beyond all purposes."

(6:1) These things await us all, but we are not prepared as yet to welcome them with joy.

These things await *all* of us, not just some. And so we need to focus on how we want to exclude, and not see another's purpose as one with ours. We resist this because from the moment we see shared interests we would not attack, judge, or condemn, but only understand. This means the end of life as we have known it, and it is this fear we need to look at so we may release it.

The above is a comforting line, for Jesus is telling us not to panic: we do not have to do this today. Indeed, he knows we are *not* going to do it today, but he does want us at least to be aware of *what* we will not do, and *why*.

(6:2-3) As long as any mind remains possessed of evil dreams, the thought of hell is real. God's teachers have the goal of wakening the minds of those asleep, and seeing there the vision of Christ's face to take the place of what they dream.

Jesus returns once again to our first theme, as he will at the very end of the manual. Our function is not to save the external world, but the inner world of our minds. By choosing truth in the holy instant, it will blaze across the world and heal it—*in the mind*. Restated, our function is to have Christ's face—the vision of innocence, the guiltlessness of God's Son—replace the world's dream of sin and guilt.

(6:4-5) The thought of murder is replaced with blessing. Judgment is laid by, and given Him Whose function judgment is.

The Holy Spirit's judgment is not condemnatory, but one that reflects the inherent sameness of God's Son. Some within the dream express love, while others are calling for it. Yet as children of love, our response is always the same: love, to those expressing love; love, to those who call for it.

(6:6) And in His Final Judgment is restored the truth about the holy Son of God.

God's Final Judgment, as you recall, is that we are still His beloved Son—a happy Fact that will never change.

(6:7-8) He is redeemed, for he has heard God's Word and understood its meaning. He is free because he let God's Voice proclaim the truth.

"God's Voice proclaims the truth," not in words or through an amplifying system. His truth is in all of us, and when we choose to hear the Voice of Atonement we will have chosen for everyone, because God's Son is one.

(6:9) And all he sought before to crucify are resurrected with him, by his side, as he prepares with them to meet his God.

All those I had judged, wanted to kill, and whose interests I did not see as my own are now forgiven. The veils of specialness that separated me from my brothers are gone. As I have parted these veils and accepted the Atonement for myself, I have done it for all of us, for we are one in resurrection as we had been one in crucifixion. Recall once again that from the battleground, on which we all stand separately, this oneness makes no sense. However, above the battleground we understand there is only one Son and one thought of separation, and, in the end, we realize the separation never happened—we forever remain as God created us: one Son, one Will, one Love.

29. AS FOR THE REST…

During my classes on the text of *A Course in Miracles*, I spoke of the musical form called the coda, the concluding part of a larger work that introduces new material that is yet related to the music preceding it. Beethoven, for example, was a master of this. Both the ending of the text and this section, "As for the Rest"—which is similar to an epilogue—can be thought of as musical codas. Along with introducing new ideas, Jesus here concludes his book by bringing back the manual's two major themes: not seeing another's interests as separate from our own—the prerequisite for being a teacher of God—and our need to ask the Holy Spirit for help.

(1:1-3) This manual is not intended to answer all questions that both teacher and pupil may raise. In fact, it covers only a few of the more obvious ones, in terms of a brief summary of some of the major concepts in the text and workbook. It is not a substitute for either, but merely a supplement.

Here, as well as elsewhere in the manual and workbook, Jesus stresses the idea of a unified curriculum—when the text was taken down, the other two books of course did not exist. We need them all, and none of the three should be taken as substitute for the other two, for each has a different focus. The manual's purpose is to provide a brief summary of some important concepts from the text and workbook, as well as focusing on what it means to be a teacher of God, or student of *A Course in Miracles*. However, it is not meant to replace the theory in the text, or the mind-training exercises in the workbook.

(1:4) While it is called a manual for teachers, it must be remembered that only time divides teacher and pupil, so that the difference is temporary by definition.

The manual began with this idea that teachers and pupils are the same. While there is surely a difference in form and time, these are illusory. Teachers learn what they teach, and pupils teach what they learn—in content.

(1:5-7) In some cases, it may be helpful for the pupil to read the manual first. Others might do better to begin with the workbook. Still others may need to start at the more abstract level of the text.

This is Jesus' way of telling us there is no right or wrong way of doing his course. However, he does mean for us at some point to work with all three books.

(2:1-6) Which is for which? Who would profit more from prayers alone? Who needs but a smile, being as yet unready for more? No one should attempt to answer these questions alone. Surely no teacher of God has come this far without realizing that. The curriculum is highly individualized, and all aspects are under the Holy Spirit's particular care and guidance.

This reflects our second theme, the role of the Holy Spirit. We should not attempt to understand or seek to solve a problem without first asking His help. In saying the "curriculum is highly individualized," Jesus alerts us to a trap that many students and would-be teachers of *A Course in Miracles* fall into, believing there is only one way of doing this course, and thus pressuring people into doing it that way—*their* way. Jesus thus gently corrects this error by reminding us there is only the Holy Spirit's way. Since He is abstract and non-specific, He does not care how you study and practice, as long as you forgive and allow His Love to inform your thoughts and flow through you. You *will* be told the particular way you can best learn the curriculum, but this would not necessarily come through words—without an ego investment, you would simply know how to proceed. It is important, again, to recognize that a certain practice that works for you may not necessarily work for another, especially when Jesus teaches there is no right or wrong way of proceeding with the Course.

(2:7-10) Ask and He will answer. The responsibility is His, and He alone is fit to assume it. To do so is His function. To refer the questions to Him is yours.

Remember what asking means: bringing the impediments to our hearing to His loving Presence. When we relinquish our specialness, the blocks disappear and we can hear, though not necessarily in words. This "hearing" can be a quiet recognition in which we know the most loving way to respond, whether it be to an external situation, or how to work with *A Course in Miracles*. There can thus be no mistake in what Jesus is saying: we are to bring our illusions to the Holy Spirit's truth, but that is *all* we are supposed to do. As the text tells us, our function is only to choose to forgive, to choose the miracle of Christ's holiness over the ego's unholiness. Thus the extension of forgiveness, the miracle, and holiness in form is not our concern (T-22.VI.9; T-16.II.1). If we identify with their form of expression, thinking, for example, we are doing holy work as a student/teacher of this course, we are back in the throes of the ego's specialness. The only holy work is to bring our guilt to His love. Nothing more than this.

(2:11-14) Would you want to be responsible for decisions about which you understand so little? Be glad you have a Teacher Who cannot make a mistake. His answers are always right. Would you say that of yours?

Jesus said the same thing in his earlier discussion of judgment (M-10)—we judge what we know nothing about, and thus are always wrong. Our limited egos can never understand the meaning of things or what is in our best interests, let alone the world's. We cannot even understand how this course is to operate in the world. To think we do is the height of arrogance; yet that is exactly the ego's plan—to have us think we understand. We believe we live in a spatial/temporal universe, yet fail to recognize that *A Course in Miracles* is outside time and space, as, in fact, is the ego itself. How could we, children of time and space, comprehend a dimension totally beyond our capacity? Indeed, the brain was programmed not to recognize the existence of the mind, and with these limitations how could we possibly understand the meaning of anything here? Yet we *can* understand the need to ask Jesus' help to see shared instead of separate interests. That alone is our responsibility.

Jesus now brings to our coda the manual's first expression of the following thought:

(3:1-7) There is another advantage,—and a very important one,—in referring decisions to the Holy Spirit with increasing frequency. Perhaps you have not thought of this aspect, but its centrality is obvious. To follow the Holy Spirit's guidance is to let yourself be absolved of guilt. It is the essence of the Atonement. It is the core of the curriculum. The imagined usurping of functions not your own is the basis of fear. The whole world you see reflects the illusion that you have done so, making fear inevitable.

This world began when we said: "I can live without God." When the Holy Spirit arose as the memory of God's Love in our minds, we said the same thing to Him: "I can live without You." Finally, when Jesus appeared within the dream, we said once again: "I can live without your loving and wise presence in my life." Indeed, each and every time we express this thought to anyone, we re-enact the original moment when we told God we would make our own kingdom and definition of love, and would thus be happy. The ego called that thought sin, leading to guilt, followed by fear of God's retaliation. Therefore, to ask the Holy Spirit for help is to end the belief that we know better. This is the means of absolving ourselves of guilt, and is the essence of the Atonement that says the separation from God never happened. I am not separate because in asking God's Voice for help, I call upon His memory to remind me of what I had chosen to forget.

Because the world we see reflects the illusion we have usurped God's role, we read:

(3:8-9) To return the function to the One to Whom it belongs is thus the escape from fear. And it is this that lets the memory of love return to you.

God is no longer perceived as the enemy, nor is the Holy Spirit experienced as God's general dispatched into the mind to destroy us. Our minds are thus no longer perceived as battlegrounds, and so is fear escaped.

The ego made up its tale of sin, guilt, and fear as a means of blocking the memory of God's Love from our awareness. When we withdraw our belief in it—simply recognizing we were wrong and there is Someone within us Who is right, the One to Whom we go for help—the ego's thought system is undone. The memory of this Love inevitably returns, because nothing remains to impede its flow through the mind.

(3:10-11) Do not, then, think that following the Holy Spirit's guidance is necessary merely because of your own inadequacies. It is the way out of hell for you.

When we first begin climbing Jesus' ladder, we will be tempted to ask for specific help, recognizing we cannot make the journey by ourselves. The bottom rungs indeed involve asking for specifics, as the first two sections of *The Song of Prayer* tell us (S-1.I,II), but as we make our way up the ladder, we begin to understand that we are really asking for help in undoing the mind's thought system. We thus realize this is not about getting a better job or relationship, a healthier body, or achieving world peace. We ask for help only to make shared interests important. As we make our way up the ladder, therefore—from hell to Heaven—we shift from asking for specifics to being reminded of our oneness: we walk together with our brothers because we and our brothers are one.

(4:1-5) Here again is the paradox often referred to in the course. To say, "Of myself I can do nothing" is to gain all power. And yet it is but a seeming paradox. As God created you, you *have* all power. The image you made of yourself has none.

We let go of the power we thought we had, and accept instead the power of God that is the Holy Spirit's truth in our minds.

(4:6-8) The Holy Spirit knows the truth about you. The image you made does not. Yet, despite its obvious and complete ignorance, this image assumes it knows all things because you have given that belief to it.

We—the decision-making self in the mind, not the body—have given that belief to the ego, the image we made of sin, guilt, and fear. We arrogantly think, for example, that this self is so wise in studying, understanding, and practicing this course. That merely shows how little we truly understand. In the text, Jesus asks the question: "Who is the 'you' who are living in this world?" (T-4.II.11:8). There *is* no "you" living in this world. What we experience is simply a false image in the mind, while Jesus is speaking only of, and to, the decision maker.

(4:9-12) Such is your teaching, and the teaching of the world that was made to uphold it. But the Teacher Who knows the truth has not forgotten it. His decisions bring benefit to all, being wholly devoid of attack. And therefore incapable of arousing guilt.

We want to grow up and become like Jesus, with no guilt or attack thoughts in our minds, only the love of the Atonement. As we accept it for ourselves, it automatically extends through us and embraces *all* (not some) people, for the Atonement is *wholly* (not partially) without separation.

(5:1) Who assumes a power that he does not possess is deceiving himself.

That is what we did at the beginning, assuming that the power we stole from God was ours, and we could do with it what we wished. We do this in our personal lives as well, but through denial are unaware of our arrogance. The power we think we have is nothing, because it is only the power to make illusions. Thus when Jesus speaks of the ego's "dynamics," he puts the word in quotes (T-11.V)—being nothing, the ego has no dynamics or power.

(5:2-3) Yet to accept the power given him by God is but to acknowledge his Creator and accept His gifts. And His gifts have no limit.

We must recognize that we have thrown away the unlimited gifts of our Creator, accepting in their place the puny and limited gifts of the ego. Seeing clearly what we are doing motivates us, finally, to let them go.

(5:4) To ask the Holy Spirit to decide for you is simply to accept your true inheritance.

Asking the Holy Spirit does not mean He will tell us what stocks we should buy or sell. He is concerned only with reminding us of our true inheritance and treasure as God's Son.

(5:5-10) Does this mean that you cannot say anything without consulting Him? No, indeed! That would hardly be practical, and it is the practical with which this course is most concerned. If you have made a habit to ask for help when and where you can, you can be confident that wisdom will be given you when you need it. Prepare for this each morning, remember God when you can throughout the day, ask the Holy Spirit's help when it is feasible to do so, and

thank Him for His guidance at night. And your confidence will be well founded indeed.

Jesus is not advocating a simplistic approach to asking, where you do absolutely nothing before consulting the Holy Spirit, which would put the emphasis in the wrong place: asking help for what you should do behaviorally, rather than for releasing your mind's interference. Thus you want His help to be as aware as possible of your thoughts of specialness and separate interests, orienting each day toward fulfilling the single purpose of returning home. This means approaching every circumstance as the means by which you will awaken from the ego's dream of death, an opportunity to acknowledge how mistaken you have been, having built an illusory kingdom of guilt, hatred, and judgment. You realize that you no longer wish this, even though a part of you still wants to remain in the ego's world. You therefore ask for help to recognize how often you choose the ego, and how quickly you justify or spiritualize your behavior. Looking with Jesus, you look without judgment, bringing the pain of what you have chosen to the happiness that is yours when you let specialness go. Thus you become aware of both sides of the split mind by bringing the illusion of separation to the truth of Atonement.

(6:1-2) Never forget that the Holy Spirit does not depend on your words. He understands the requests of your heart, and answers them.

This calls to mind our discussion of the section "What Is the Role of Words in Healing?" (M-21). The request of the heart is for one of the mind's two choices: to remain in the ego's dream of specialness, or to awaken from it.

(6:3-8) Does this mean that, while attack remains attractive to you, He will respond with evil? Hardly! For God has given Him the power to translate your prayers of the heart into His language. He understands that an attack is a call for help. And He responds with help accordingly. God would be cruel if He let your words replace His Own.

In "The Judgment of the Holy Spirit" (T-12.I), Jesus explained that the Holy Spirit always sees a call for help behind attack; a teaching he repeats here.

Our words replace God's in awareness, but not in reality. His Words—the Answer of Atonement reflected in Jesus' love—are in our minds, regardless of the veils of hate, judgment, and specialness with which we cover them. Love, peace, and joy remain there, and so whenever we have an attack thought, Jesus reinterprets it as a call for love, responded to with love. He does nothing else, for his is only a presence of light and love, to which we bring our thoughts of darkness and hate. To the extent to which we lay them at the altar, we accept his gifts that have waited for us.

(6:9-11) A loving father does not let his child harm himself, or choose his own destruction. He may ask for injury, but his father will protect him still. And how much more than this does your Father love His Son?

This is a metaphorical way of telling us that God is not the monster we made Him out to be. His Love knows nothing of the dream, and His judgment remains constant: we are His beloved Son, forever at one with Him. Nothing happened to affect this—"Not one note in Heaven's song was missed" (T-26.V.5:4). Thus we bring our nightmare world of sin, guilt, and vengeance to the simple truth in which Jesus says: "My brother, choose again. Your life is only a bad dream, and nothing has changed Heaven's Love."

(7:1) Remember you are His completion and His Love.

That is Who we are, what the Atonement reminds us of, as does the end of the workbook:

> I am God's Son, complete and healed and whole, shining in the reflection of His Love. In me is His creation sanctified and guaranteed eternal life. In me is love perfected, fear impossible, and joy established without opposite. I am the holy home of God Himself. I am the Heaven where His Love resides. I am His holy Sinlessness Itself, for in my purity abides His Own (W-pII.14.1; italics omitted).

(7:2-5) Remember your weakness is His strength. But do not read this hastily or wrongly. If His strength is in you, what you perceive as your weakness is but illusion. And He has given you the means to prove it so.

Near the end of the text, Jesus says we always choose between our weakness and the strength of Christ in us (T-31.VIII.2:3): the weakness of the ego's selfish interests of *one or the other*, as opposed to the strength of Christ's vision that sees God's Son as sharing one interest and one goal. Recognizing our weakness and releasing it through forgiveness allows Christ's strength to rise in our awareness.

(7:6-8) Ask all things of His Teacher, and all things are given you. Not in the future but immediately; now. God does not wait, for waiting implies time and He is timeless.

This is a variation of the theme of God's living Oneness, beyond time and space. Therefore nothing has to be done now to gain something in the future. We simply accept Heaven's Oneness in the world through its reflection: the decision to see shared interests.

"Ask all things of His Teacher, and all things are given you" means bringing our concerns and judgments to His Love. All things will then be given us, because all things are truly one thing—the peace that surpasses all worldly experience; the peace that is beyond all conflict and duality.

(7:9) Forget your foolish images, your sense of frailty and your fear of harm, your dreams of danger and selected "wrongs."

Jesus speaks of forgetting them because we have remembered them, such as the ego's image of being attacked by God, Whose fearful memory is in our wrong minds. Thus the ego causes us to forget the memory of God's Love, and remember instead the lies it tells us—tales of hate and war, frailties and vulnerabilities, and fearful "dreams of danger and selected 'wrongs'." Whenever, therefore, we draw closer to the truth, beginning to release our guilt, we hear the ego's voice of hate whispering in our ears: "Do not forget your friends that protect you—sin, guilt, fear, and death" (see T-19.IV-D.6:1-3). Suddenly we become ill, anxious, obsessing about nothing, or angry as we recall past grievances and hurts. All these rise up as if they were real and present, and Jesus asks us now gently to let them go.

(7:10-11) God knows but His Son, and as he was created so he is. In confidence I place you in His Hands and I give thanks for you that this is so.

Jesus closes with a poem, as he closed the text with a prayer, beginning:

> I thank You Father, for these holy ones who are my brothers as they are Your Sons (T-31. VIII.10:1).

This was the Course's answer to what is known in Catholic circles as Jesus' priestly prayer (John 17), where he prays to God on behalf of his disciples, whom the Church later interpreted to mean his priests. The mistake here, from the point of view of *A Course in Miracles*, is that this prayer was meant only for the special, not for all people as is the prayer at the conclusion of the text.

At the end of the manual, Jesus does something similar. In the synoptic gospels—Matthew, Mark, and Luke—Jesus sends his disciples into the world, exhorting them to convert the unbelievers. Here, too, Jesus sends us into the world, but not to change it or preach to it the good news of forgiveness, but to demonstrate that the right-minded shift has been accomplished in us. Thus is the world changed, because the world is us.

> **(8)** And now in all your doings be you blessed.
> God turns to you for help to save the world.
> Teacher of God His thanks He offers you,
> And all the world stands silent in the grace
> You bring from Him. You are the Son He loves,
> And it is given you to be the means
> Through which His Voice is heard around the world,
> To close all things of time; to end the sight
> Of all things visible; and to undo
> All things that change. Through you is ushered in
> A world unseen, unheard, yet truly there.

29. As for the Rest…

> Holy are you, and in your light the world
> Reflects your holiness, for you are not
> Alone and friendless. I give thanks for you,
> And join your efforts on behalf of God,
> Knowing they are on my behalf as well,
> And for all those who walk to God with me.

AMEN

And so the manual closes as it began, with Jesus asking us to be the means that will bring comfort and peace to a world that winds on wearily, lacking all hope. This, once again, is not about doing anything external, nor changing our lives or anyone else's, but changing our minds. In this way we "close all things of time," "end the sight of all things visible," and "undo all things that change." We change ourselves by seeing everyone's interests as one, realizing not only that we walk the final journey with Jesus, but with all our brothers. We have learned that if we do not walk with all people, we do not walk with him. Thus the world changes—the good news that makes the Holy Spirit's Voice heard around the world, lighting up a world that heretofore knew only the darkness of guilt and hate. This is joyously accomplished by making our single purpose the vision to see everyone's journey as our own, regardless of its form. Only then can we truly mean it when we say to Jesus: "Help me awaken from these dreams of hate to your happy dreams of forgiveness and love."

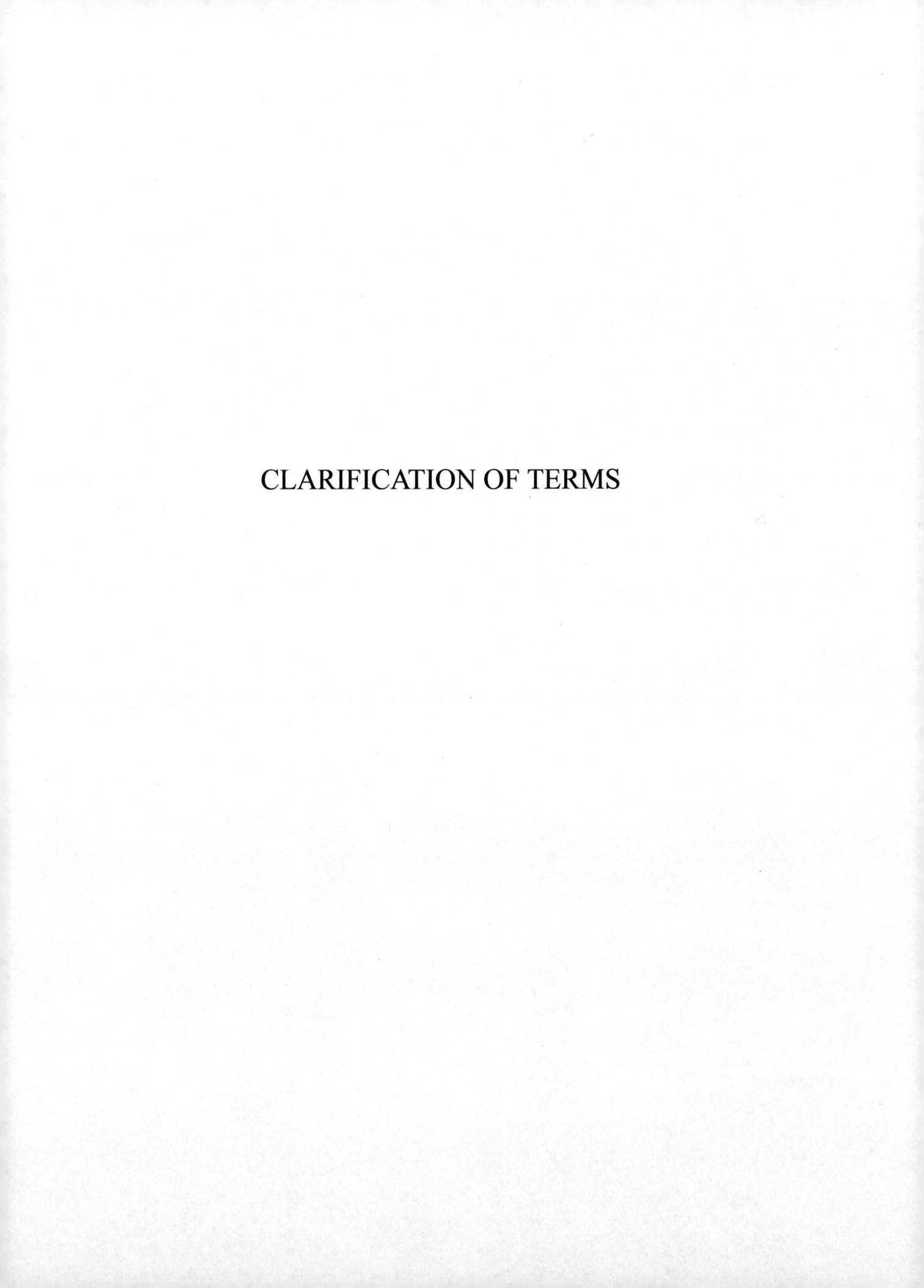

CLARIFICATION OF TERMS

GENERAL INTRODUCTION

In times past, when concert attendees liked a particular movement or work, they would almost demand that it be repeated. The audience would cry out "Encore!" which in French means "Again!" Today, however, orchestras or recitalists do not repeat music, but at the close of a performance, in acknowledgment of the audience's appreciation, they will frequently perform a new piece—almost a standard practice in recitals. In a sense, we could look at the clarification of terms as Jesus' encore for *A Course in Miracles*, as it was not originally part of it. In the late summer and early fall of 1975, when the final editing of the Course was completed and the manuscript in its final form, we made 300 photo-offset copies. Subsequently, several people came to Helen and asked if she would take down a glossary or definition of terms, because so many words are used differently in the Course from the way they are used in popular or religious speech. In fact, I recall Helen and I sitting on her couch, making up a list of words and terms we thought might require formal definition. Needless to say, most of these did not make their way into the actual work. They did, however, become the basis for my *Glossary-Index*, which I published in 1982.

Later that fall, therefore, Helen took down what is now known as the clarification of terms, the purpose of which was to describe or explain several of the key terms used in the Course. We were not sure what to do with it, but Helen, who sometimes received messages through pictures, saw the teacher's manual with the clarification of terms at the end. Thus, when the books were finally printed in 1976, it was included in the volume containing the teacher's manual, although it does not formally belong to it—it is more like an appendix.

The clarification of terms has eight sections: an introduction and epilogue, and six intervening sections that are the heart of the piece, which compare terms used in the Course: mind and spirit; ego and the miracle; forgiveness and the face of Christ; true perception and knowledge; Jesus and Christ; and the final section, the Holy Spirit. Unlike the three main books, the clarification of terms is not developed in a musical or symphonic way. Yet it does have a theme that runs throughout its pages: *form and content*, or the use of symbols. This will be discussed quite specifically in the Introduction, and I will return to this idea as we go through each section. Its importance lies in helping students of *A Course in Miracles* avoid the trap of confusing form and content, symbol and source, as well as the trap of taking things literally that are meant metaphorically.

The material did not come through with a title. I recall writing "Use of Terms" at the head of the initial draft, taken from a line at the end of the Introduction, but that did not seem to fit. We ultimately gave it its current name, since the word *clarification* occurs twice in the opening pages. Finally, if you consult this to find out how *A Course in Miracles* defines certain words—like *miracle, ego,* or *forgiveness*—you will be disappointed, for though it describes them, often in poetic ways, it does not really define them. However, once you are familiar with *A Course in Miracles*, reading through the clarification of terms can be most helpful. It does provide, moreover, one of the clearest discussions of the nature of Jesus and the Holy Spirit, which is only implied in the Course itself.

INTRODUCTION

(1:1) This is not a course in philosophical speculation, nor is it concerned with precise terminology.

Jesus immediately alerts us to the fact that this will not be a standard dictionary or glossary. He is interested in the content, not the form or the specific way words are used. Thus he says in the very next line:

(1:2) It is concerned only with Atonement, or the correction of perception.

It is the Course's message that is important, not its presentation. *A Course in Miracles* is not meant to be an alternative theology, even though it certainly is one. Jesus does not want his students to fall into the same trap that has befallen Christians for over two thousand years, where they would argue relentlessly, if not viciously, over the meaning of specific words and terms—like *Jesus, the Holy Spirit, salvation*—sparking endless controversies, if not wars. Therefore, Jesus urges us not to make that mistake, as the purpose of his course is to restore awareness of our underlying unity. Thus it should not be used to engender even more division among the Sonship; rather than divide or separate through specialness, its goal is to unite through forgiveness.

Jesus therefore sets the tone for what follows. As in *Psychotherapy* and *The Song of Prayer*, he amplifies some of the core teachings of the Course, while at the same time alerting his students to the perils of spiritual specialness so they would clearly understand his purpose of reminding them of their unity as God's one Son. To use the Course's language to place a gap between one student and another, or between students of *A Course in Miracles* and followers of other spiritualities, would be directly antithetical to its underlying purpose: the change of mind that is the Atonement—the correction for the perception of separate interests.

(1:3) The means of the Atonement is forgiveness.

We will see in these pages that Jesus uses these words interchangeably: *correction, forgiveness, Atonement, miracle, salvation, true perception, face of Christ*—different terms depicting the same content of correcting wrong-minded thinking. This thinking becomes right-minded when we choose the Holy Spirit as our Teacher, which is what these terms reflect. Since Jesus does not bind himself to form, he does not want us to bind ourselves to technical definitions of his words. By using them loosely and interchangeably, and sometimes inconsistently, he inspires us to move beyond the symbol to the underlying content. For example, when you read a great poem or novel, you use the language to lead to an experience, for which you do not need to analyze the author's use of words. Similarly, in expressing his vision of the Atonement and truth Jesus is like an artist, and our desire should be to learn his message and gain the experience to which his course gently leads us.

(1:4) The structure of "individual consciousness" is essentially irrelevant because it is a concept representing the "original error" or the "original sin."

Individual consciousness is the split mind. Early in the text, Jesus says that consciousness was the first split introduced into the mind after the separation (T-3.IV.2:1); it is thus part and parcel of duality, wherein *we* are conscious of *something*. In Heaven, the non-dualistic Mind of Christ is not conscious of anything, being undifferentiated reality. Jesus tells us here he is not interested in studying the structure of the split mind. When we speak of a wrong mind, right mind, and decision maker, we intend them as symbols that point to an experience beyond the words themselves. The difficulty comes when we attempt to depict in linear form a mind that is inherently illusory. Indeed, everything we speak about is symbolic, for God is the only Fact (T-3.I.8:2). All else either reflects this blessed Fact—forgiveness—or denies it—the thought system of separation.

Therefore, to analyze the split mind is to analyze nothing, and so Jesus' goal is to move us beyond the split mind; to correct perception, not analyze it. The only analysis Jesus asks us to do is of the purpose our misperceptions serve—to prevent our awakening from the dream. The original error is the *tiny, mad idea* of separation taken seriously, from which arises our split mind or individual consciousness. We are asked only to undo the mind's original decision to make this *tiny, mad idea* real. Forgiveness is the means of undoing, and specific analyses would simply lead us astray, for they do not correct, as we now read:

(1:5-6) To study the error itself does not lead to correction, if you are indeed to succeed in overlooking the error. And it is just this process of overlooking at which the course aims.

This course is not intended to be a study of the ego; its purpose is to move us beyond the ego, not to become masters of it. This last refers both to an intellectual understanding of the ego's thought system, as well as to becoming so enamored of its specialness that we remain enmeshed in it. We need to look at the ego only to understand why we have chosen it, and the painful cost of choosing guilt over forgiveness. Overlooking the error does not mean not seeing it, but looking beyond it, which motivates us no longer to choose it. We thus look beyond the ego in the sense of correcting our faulty decision. The ego itself does not need to be corrected—an illusion needs no correction—we simply choose not to believe in it anymore.

We see again that Jesus hopes to keep us from falling into the ego's trap. He wants us to study the text in order to learn the foolishness of identifying with a thought system of separation and specialness. Only then can we move beyond it and find the peace of God—our true goal.

(2:1) All terms are potentially controversial, and those who seek controversy will find it.

We can make a problem of anything, and Course students, like all others, have done just that. You can argue about a word, for example—why does Jesus say one thing in the text and something contradictory in the workbook? Remember, purpose is everything, and the ego's underlying purpose is to make trouble—between yourself and Jesus, between yourself and others, between yourself and yourself. If you want to find error, you will; if you seek controversy, it will be there. *A Course in Miracles* is written as a work of art, not a scientific treatise. Words and concepts are used loosely, but understanding its message and underlying thought system will prevent you from falling into the ego's trap. When you become one with the artist's vision, whatever the work of art—words, images, or music—you will understand it intuitively, without conceptual analysis. In effect, Jesus says the same thing here: "I do not want you to study this as a treatise. Let the words work within your heart; it is the experience of love I want you to have, not intellectual understanding."

(2:2-3) Yet those who seek clarification will find it as well. They must, however, be willing to overlook controversy, recognizing that it is a defense against truth in the form of a delaying maneuver.

If you want to understand *A Course in Miracles*, you will. Yet if you stick to its symbols without moving beyond them, you will find only controversy and conflict. Remember that Jesus speaks solely of purpose. We would seek and find fault with the Course because of its language in order to use it as a defense against its truth, which lies beyond all words. Defending against truth is an important theme in the Course, but here Jesus articulates it in a specific context—the Course itself.

(2:4) Theological considerations as such are necessarily controversial, since they depend on belief and can therefore be accepted or rejected.

We all have known Christians who demand we believe what they do—their particular understanding of the Bible, the purpose of Jesus' life, the meaning of salvation, etc.—going so far as to kill in the name of upholding the truth of their beliefs. You can almost hear Jesus pleading with us not to do this with his course, not to use it as a weapon against others who do not agree with us. We are asked to agree on only one thing: we are one in purpose. Whether or not we agree on the meaning of a particular passage or teaching in the Course is irrelevant to the fulfillment of that one purpose. *This is not a course to be believed, but experienced.* The experience of love comes when we forgive, which means setting aside separate interests—anything that would divide us from others. We all walk the same journey, and while we do not have to agree with what another says or does, this does not mean making the disagreement the foundation of attack. Different opinions are natural here, yet these do not have to make a difference in the sense of impeding Christ's vision that sees all God's Sons as one.

(2:5-6) A universal theology is impossible, but a universal experience is not only possible but necessary. It is this experience toward which the course is directed.

In Heaven, this universal experience is love, and in the world it is love's reflection—forgiveness—that undoes the ego's thoughts of separation, divisiveness, and specialness. It is impossible to have a universal belief system because everyone's beliefs differ. Yet such differences are meaningless, for *all* can serve the single purpose of moving us beyond the form to the universal experience of love. You do not have to subscribe to another's belief system or understanding of the Course, but you can nonetheless use the differences as a classroom in which to learn that although you may differ on the level of form, your content remains the same. Therefore Jesus tells us his is a course in cause not effect (T-21.VII.7:8), content not form. Specialness, on the other hand, is the triumph of form over content (T-16.V.12:2), which indeed describes most religions. In fact, the paragraph in which that passage appears is a subtle refutation of Christianity, which has substituted the rituals of love for its true experience. When rituals are revered by believers as sacred, they become divisive, because not everyone is included. God's Love, however, is universal, and it is that universality that Jesus asks us to practice with this course.

(2:7) Here alone consistency becomes possible because here alone uncertainty ends.

This course is consistent only on the level of content—love, because love alone is constant. Once into form—theology or belief—you introduce uncertainty, because not everyone will agree. Brains will differ, but the mind is one—both the wrong-minded ego and the right mind of the Holy Spirit.

(3:1) This course remains within the ego framework, where it is needed.

This is an important statement. This course is not truth, because it consists of symbols, concepts, and theories; likewise, it has a mythology, theology, Christology, cosmology, and eschatology, as do other religious thought systems. All these are of the ego, and Jesus tells us this is the framework in which he presents his universal message. As we recall from the beginning of the manual, *A Course in Miracles* is only one form among many thousands of the universal course (M-1.4), which is the unity of the Atonement—the separation never happened, God's Son is guiltless, and sin does not exist. This content alone is consistent.

In this world, speaking and writing require words, which are "but symbols of symbols.... twice removed from reality" (M-21.1:9-10). In light of this, once again, we should use the Course's symbols only as a means of moving beyond them. If we do not, we will inevitably find ourselves stuck in separation and judgment. This course is mainly meant for a Western audience—thus its form. For better or for worse, the Western world's thinking has been dominated by Christianity, and the Course's point of view is that it has been "for worse": a message of love and unity displaced by specialness and divisiveness. Jesus' original message—whose purpose was to help us leave the ego's thought system and awaken from the dream—turned into one that made the dream world real, from which we can never escape, for we simply substitute another special dream for our current one that is failing.

The content of correction, therefore, comes in form, because that is our world, and thus Jesus uses predominantly Christian words, but with different meanings. However, he does not want us trapped by them, such that the Course's definitions—*sin* or *forgiveness*, *Jesus* or *Christ*, for example—become weapons to be used against Christians who have understood them differently. What alone is important is the unity of love beyond all form.

(3:2) It is not concerned with what is beyond all error because it is planned only to set the direction towards it.

Recall the conclusion of the workbook: "This course is a beginning, not an end" (W-ep.1:1). The purpose of the workbook—indeed, of the Course itself—is to set us on the right road with the right teacher, following the right principle. We then spend the rest of our lives continuing on the journey with Jesus, practicing daily his principle of forgiveness that will get us home. *A Course in Miracles* does not focus on love or knowledge, as its goal for us is peace (T-8.I.1:1-2), that we take the steps that will awaken us from the dream. The Love of God beyond the dream is therefore not our concern, and this key theme is expressed throughout the clarification of terms.

(3:3) Therefore it uses words, which are symbolic, and cannot express what lies beyond symbols.

Introduction

In "Beyond All Symbols" (T-27.III), Jesus says that God and truth are unknowable here. What can be taught and learned, however, are truth's reflections—through forgiveness. The Oneness of God and Christ cannot be understood, yet we can learn we are truly bound, not by hate or separate interests, but by forgiveness and shared interests. Jesus uses words to help us learn the content, but the words themselves are irrelevant to the underlying message, being but a framework within which it is placed. Therefore, it is the message we want, not the words, concepts, or theory that express it.

(3:4) It is merely the ego that questions because it is only the ego that doubts.

All questions, then, are of the ego, for only the ego can doubt—Christ is certain. In "The Quiet Answer" (T-27.IV), Jesus says questions are really expressions of hate, because they are based on the ego's idea that we live in a dualistic condition in a dualistic world, where we ask questions about something for which there can be no true answer. In Heaven, the only truth, there are neither questions nor answers; no one who asks, no one who answers. When we ask a question, we come from separation. Within that context, of course, there are wrong-minded or right-minded questions; but asking still remains part of the illusory world and thus come within an ego framework. However, like everything we made, the Holy Spirit can use them for another purpose, and so we should not refrain from asking. After all, *A Course in Miracles* itself came as an answer to Helen's and Bill's question about "the other way."

(3:5) The course merely gives another answer, once a question has been raised.

The Course tells us the ego speaks first, is wrong, and the Holy Spirit is the answer (T-5.VI.3:5; 4:2). First, a question is raised or a problem expressed, and then the answer follows. Again, this course came as an answer to a problem—Helen and Bill's relationship, and theirs with others: their plea for another way and their determination to find it. *A Course in Miracles* is the other way, not only for them but for all of us plagued by special relationships. Our lives within the ego's world are based on special needs, wherein we seek for answers in the world, none of which works. The Course is one answer that does work, however, which is Jesus' point here.

(3:6-7) However, this answer does not attempt to resort to inventiveness or ingenuity. These are attributes of the ego.

The world's answers are ingenious, complicated, and convoluted, because they seek to answer a question without truly answering it—the question of who we are. If this were truly answered, the world would disappear, including the one who asked the question. Thus the world—the shadow of our secret thoughts and wishes—was made never to answer meaningful questions, appearances to the contrary. Indeed, some answers to this fundamental question can be brilliant. The greatest brains in history have given answers, or have attempted answers to that question to ease our self-doubts, but none has provided a truly valid answer. And so Jesus says:

(3:8-9) The course is simple. It has one function and one goal.

This function and goal is to answer the question, "What am I?"—the question posed near the end of the workbook (W-pII.14). The world constitutes the ego's answer: "I am a body—separated, special, and unfairly treated." The Course exposes the falsity of the ego's words, and questioning the ego is the only right-minded question—raising it to awareness so it can be looked at. We then realize the ego is not who we are, and with the interference gone, "What you are will tell you of Itself" (T-31.V.17:9)—the true Answer. However, the Course is not concerned with *What* we are, but merely in eliminating the ego's *what*. This one function and one goal is why *A Course in Miracles* is so simple.

(3:10) Only in that does it remain wholly consistent because only that can *be* consistent.

If you read this carefully, you will see that Jesus is telling you his course is not consistent on the level of form: symbols, concepts, and words. Its consistency lies in its content of forgiveness: undoing our belief in separate interests. To repeat, Jesus' plea to us—explicit and implicit—is that we not identify with the Course's theory and theology, but that we use them as means to experience the inherent unity of God's Son. We thus all share the same degree of judgment and hate, forgiveness and love, and the mind's power to choose between them.

This, then is where the Course leads us: to uncover the ingenious—not to mention grandiose—ways in which we seek to distract ourselves from the ego's fundamental purpose of making ourselves and others unhappy. It is within this function of undoing —content, not form—that the Course's consistency is found. To revisit this essential caveat, do not let your understanding of *A Course in Miracles* drive a wedge between you and others, whose understanding may differ from yours. Again, you need not agree with what they say, but you do not have to see them as enemies. Above the battleground, where the content is one, you realize we are all in the same boat of separation, an awareness that is the condition for our return home.

(4:1) The ego will demand many answers that this course does not give.

Typical examples of such demands are: How could the separation happen? How could a part of perfect Oneness be separate from Itself? How can individuals exist when they are part of God's One-mindedness? Jesus will provide the best answer—albeit a non-intellectual one—to these questions:

(4:2) It does not recognize as questions the mere form of a question to which an answer is impossible.

In other words, concealed behind *all* questions is a statement: I believe the ego, separation, and individual consciousness are real, and I want you to explain how they happened. Therefore, the "question" is an attempt to seduce another to come into the questioner's web of separation and answer the question, thereby affirming the underlying statement. The only way truly to answer the question is to have your answer come from love, which means not seeing a difference between yourself and that person. Thus your answer will be the perfect answer, expressed in whatever form the questioner can accept without fear.

Yet underlying the ego's purpose for the question is this fervent plea: "Please help me realize that the separation is not real and I am wrong. The only way I can hear this is if you answer me without judgment, anger, or impatience." If you hear this underlying plea you cannot but give the right answer, and thus will always find the right answer in this course: its answer in form will mirror the one content, for all questions are the same, coming from the same ego statement and representing the same call for help.

(4:3-5) The ego may ask, "How did the impossible occur?", "To what did the impossible happen?", and may ask this in many forms. Yet there is no answer; only an experience. Seek only this, and do not let theology delay you.

There is no intellectually satisfying answer to the question—only an experience—because it is not a real question, as we have just seen. When you hear the call for help behind the question, you will give the right answer in the form that will best suit the questioner's need. The experience, born of your loving content, will answer the questioners by moving them beyond the question to what is truly being asked: "Please show me I am wrong—the separation is not reality, love has not been destroyed, and I deserve to be loved." That is everyone's plaintive cry.

Jesus is therefore telling us that this experience of forgiveness is what we truly want: "Seek only this, and do not let theology delay you." Again, while this course has a theology—and do not let anyone tell you it does not—Jesus yet says: "What difference does it make? Do not use this as a weapon against those who believe in other thought systems. Your true desire is for the love uniting us all."

(5:1-2) You will notice that the emphasis on structural issues in the course is brief and early. Afterwards and soon, it drops away to make way for the central teaching.

By "structural issues" Jesus means the structure of the mind. The early pages of the text refer to the wrong and right minds, the One mind, wrong-mindedness, right-mindedness (miracle-mindedness) and One-mindedness. "Afterwards and soon" comes the "central teaching" of forgiveness, at which point the aforementioned terms are dropped. Jesus described the structure of the mind at the beginning because it was needed—remember that Helen and Bill were psychologists—however, he wants us ultimately to move beyond the split mind to the Mind of Christ.

(5:3) Since you have asked for clarification, however, these are some of the terms that are used.

In this, Jesus' encore performance, he in effect says to us: "Since you asked for this, I will provide it. However, it will not be in the form you thought you wanted, because it is not what you are truly asking for." In clarifying these terms, therefore, he cleverly gives us the answer we secretly desire, for in these beautiful and inspiring passages we find the answers to the request for a glossary or dictionary, yet beyond them is his true answer in the form we can accept without fear, infused with the content of love.

1. MIND – SPIRIT

This first section deals with mind and spirit, and thus Jesus speaks of the wrong, right, and One minds.

(1:1-2) The term *mind* is used to represent the activating agent of spirit, supplying its creative energy. When the term is capitalized it refers to God or Christ (i.e., the Mind of God or the Mind of Christ).

We will see in this section that Jesus is somewhat inconsistent in his use of words, illustrative of his explanation in the Introduction. He uses words here slightly differently from their use in the Course itself, thus teaching us to pay attention to the content, not the form. In describing mind as the "activating agent of spirit," Jesus implies a difference between the two terms. This, of course, is not so in Heaven, where we are spirit *and* mind, the two being synonymous. To get a sense of Jesus' meaning here, think of a fountain: the mind is the engine that drives the fountain, and spirit is the water that flows through it. Yet these are but symbols for something beyond comprehension in our separated state.

Typically in *A Course in Miracles*, however not exclusively, when the word *mind* is lowercased it refers to the split mind, but when capitalized it always refers to the Mind of God or the Mind of Christ, which *is* the equivalent of spirit.

(1:3-4) *Spirit* is the Thought of God which He created like Himself. The unified spirit is God's one Son, or Christ.

S*pirit*, then, as we see in this first paragraph, is our true Self—the unified spirit being God's one Son.

(2:1-3) In this world, because the mind is split, the Sons of God appear to be separate. Nor do their minds seem to be joined. In this illusory state, the concept of an "individual mind" seems to be meaningful.

We appear to be different and separate, which is what our bodies were designed to demonstrate. Therefore, because we think we are individuals, Jesus addresses us as if we have individual minds. This is not the truth, he is telling us, but he will use words that are appropriate for our experience.

(2:4) It is therefore described in the course *as if* it has two parts; spirit and ego.

Jesus now uses *spirit* differently—as a synonym for the right mind, and *ego* for the wrong mind. This interchange of meanings illustrates the folly of attempting to analyze the precise meanings of these words and terms. Thus at the end of the first paragraph, Jesus speaks of the unified spirit, which is Christ, and here—and only here—*spirit*, again, is equated with the right mind.

(3:1) Spirit is the part [the right mind] **that is still in contact with God through the Holy Spirit, Who abides in this part** [the right mind] **but sees the other part** [the wrong mind] **as well.**

It would be more technically correct to say that the *reflection* or *memory* of spirit is in the right mind.

(3:2) The term "soul" is not used except in direct biblical quotations because of its highly controversial nature.

This is also not an absolutely accurate statement. The word *soul* is not used very often; but when it is used in the text, it *almost* always is in a biblical quotation—the devil asking us to sell our soul to him, for instance. However, there are a couple of places where Jesus uses the word to talk about the religious notion of the soul continuing on after death. In this context, *soul* is equated with the individual mind.

Again, on the form level this is not a technically and perfectly consistent text at all, yet it is consistent in content. Jesus' point is that he does not want to use the word *soul*, for it may foster theological controversy—a point he made in the Introduction. In New Age circles, *soul* means one thing; in Christian theology another; in Judaism, still another. In *A Course in Miracles*, *soul* can be understood as the equivalent of spirit—our nature as Christ:

(3:3) It [soul] **would, however, be an equivalent of "spirit," with the understanding that, being of God, it is eternal and was never born.**

Jesus returns to *soul* as unified spirit, while just before he equated spirit with the right mind, which contains the memory of our reality as spirit.

(4:1) The other part of the mind is entirely illusory and makes only illusions.

Jesus refers to the ego thought system. Here, in the clarification of terms, he does not go into any detail about that thought system, which is amply covered in the text.

(4:2) Spirit retains the potential for creating…

Since true spirit is always creating, Jesus is again referring to the right mind because he speaks of spirit having the *potential* for creating. Our mind has this potential while we sleep, for we are not in touch with the Mind's power to create.

(4:2) …but its Will, which is God's, seems to be imprisoned while the mind is not unified.

The key word here is *seems*. It *seems* that our true Self as spirit is imprisoned. In reality, nothing has happened.

(4:3-5) Creation continues unabated because that is the Will of God. This Will is always unified and therefore has no meaning in this world. It has no opposite and no degrees.

We think Heaven and Christ have changed, or that we have destroyed Them. Yet our insane dreams have had no effect on changeless reality. It is because this is a world of change that we know the Will of creation is not present here. The Will of God—God and Christ—is totally unified, with no opposites or middle ground between them. Being non-dualistic, God's Will has no consciousness, differentiation, or distinction, and therefore has no meaning in our dualistic universe. The right mind, however, contains the memory of this Oneness and the unified nature of the Sonship. In this world, unity is grasped by way of its reflection—our joint purpose of forgiveness. At the end of the text we read: "For we are one in purpose, and the end of hell is near" (T-31.VIII.10:8). Hell is having separate purposes, and it ends—our awakening from the dream—when we recognize our shared purpose. Yet in Heaven there can be no shared purpose, since there is only the Oneness of Christ.

(5:1) The mind can be right or wrong, depending on the voice to which it listens.

Jesus is talking about the decision maker, without naming it specifically. The *it*—"depending on the voice to which *it* listens"—is the decision-making part of the mind that can listen to the ego or the Holy Spirit. This reflects what Jesus means by "structural issues." When we speak of the split mind having the voice of the ego, the Voice of the Holy Spirit, and a part that chooses, we refer to a structure, yet this is of a split mind that does not exist. These, then, are mere symbols, meant to approximate our experience in the world of "hearing" two voices or thought systems: I can release this grievance and be happy, or hold onto it and be miserable—and I am aware of both possibilities.

(5:2) *Right-mindedness* listens to the Holy Spirit, forgives the world, and through Christ's vision sees the real world in its place.

The real world is referred to quite often in the clarification of terms, but it is not one of the terms to be clarified. We see here the equation of right-mindedness with Christ's vision, forgiveness, the Holy Spirit, and the real world—different ways of expressing the Atonement.

(5:3-4) This is the final vision, the last perception, the condition in which God takes the final step Himself. Here time and illusions end together.

The end of learning to forgive is that we awaken from our sleep. We recognize that everything here is a dream, governed by the principles of separate interests: *one or the other*—someone wins, another loses. Outside the dream, we know we are one and no longer part of the ego's world. There may be a figure or body that people identify as us, but we remain aware that this self is not who we are. Such awareness is the vision of the real world—the final vision—in which time and illusions are one. In fact, the world of time and space is the projection into form of the fundamental illusion that we are separate from God. The dream of separation began as a thought and never ceases to be one, yet we believe it can be projected to make a world. All this, however, gently disappears when we forgive and release our illusions of specialness. What remains is the memory of God.

On the other hand:

(6:1) Wrong-mindedness listens to the ego and makes illusions; perceiving sin and justifying anger, and seeing guilt, disease and death as real.

This is the world we love, because we cherish the thought system of sin, guilt, fear, punishment, and death that gave rise to it—the foundation of our individual existence.

(6:2) Both this world and the real world are illusions because right-mindedness merely overlooks, or forgives, what never happened.

Later on, Jesus describes forgiveness as "a kind of happy fiction" (C-3.2:1), the final illusion, the culminating happy dream. It is an illusion, yet is happy because it leads beyond all misery and pain, which were born of our guilt. To say we forgive what never happened is another way of saying what the Course teaches: we forgive our brothers for what they have not done. They have done nothing to us for they have not taken us from Heaven, nor seized the peace of God from our minds. God's Love and peace are totally present within us, regardless of what others have or have not done. Moreover, as we forgive them their "sins," we forgive ourselves for the same accusation we had projected.

(6:3) Therefore it [right-mindedness] is not the *One-mindedness* of the Christ Mind, Whose Will is one with God's.

This completes the structure of the mind: the split mind consists of wrong and right-mindedness (and an implicit decision maker that chooses between them), while the Christ Mind is One-mindedness—the state of wholly undifferentiated and unified being.

(7:1) In this world the only remaining freedom is the freedom of choice; always between two choices or two voices.

A Course in Miracles revolves around this key concept of our power of decision. Again, without using the term, Jesus is speaking of the mind's decision maker that chooses between the ego and the Holy Spirit.

(7:2) Will is not involved in perception at any level, and has nothing to do with choice.

True or unified spirit is not involved in perception at all, nor is God—in Heaven, there is nothing to choose between or among.

(7:3-6) *Consciousness* is the receptive mechanism, receiving messages from above or below; from the Holy Spirit or the ego. Consciousness has levels and awareness can shift quite dramatically, but it cannot transcend the perceptual realm. At its highest it becomes aware of the real world, and can be trained to do so increasingly. Yet the very fact that it has levels and can be trained demonstrates that it cannot reach knowledge.

We are aware that we go back and forth between insanity and sanity, choosing the lower level of the wrong mind or the higher level of the right mind. Both levels are part of the perceptual world, which means they are illusory. As the Atonement is accepted—the right mind having corrected the wrong mind—both disappear, as does the decision maker, for there is nothing left to choose between. We remain but an instant longer in the real world before God reaches down and lifts us back unto Himself: the One-mindedness of Christ we never truly left.

This attainment of the real world is the ultimate goal of *A Course in Miracles*, and the workbook specifically trains our minds to choose for the Holy Spirit and against the ego. The remainder of the clarification of terms deals with the process of forgiveness, which awakens us to the real world and then to knowledge.

2. THE EGO – THE MIRACLE

The writing now becomes more poetic than in the Introduction and first section. Yet only this section and the Epilogue are written entirely in blank verse; the others are part verse and part prose. What follows is an example of our previous discussion—the purpose of the clarification of terms is not so much to explain the terms, as it is to describe them poetically. Thus, no definition of the ego is really given; instead we find a more poetic rendering of the ego's illusory nature.

(1:1-3) Illusions will not last. Their death is sure and this alone is certain in their world. It is the ego's world because of this.

In the ego's world—both its thought system and the world that arose from it—everything changes and comes to an end, and therefore nothing here can be certain. This, in fact, is Jesus' argument for why the world could not have been created by God. In the case of minerals and inanimate objects, it may take millions of years for the end to come, but everything in form will change, decompose, and eventually cease to exist, whereas Heaven is changeless and eternal. Jesus uses this criterion to distinguish Heaven from earth and God from the ego, which also establishes why God would have—and could have—nothing to do with the ego's thought system of separation, nor with its world. Thus Jesus teaches that only God is certain, and when we chose the ego we chose the path of uncertainty, rather than the Holy Spirit's certainty that takes us home.

(1:4-5) What is the *ego*? But a dream of what you really are.

Here is where one would expect Jesus to define the ego, but he does not. The ego's dream is of a separated, split-minded self, which substitutes for the One-minded Self we really are. In the Course, Jesus uses words like *parody* and *travesty* (T-24.VII.1:11; 10:9) to describe the ego and body—travesties or parodies of spirit, the Christ that God created as Himself.

(1:6) A thought you are apart from your Creator and a wish to be what He created not.

This is all the ego is: a thought that we could be separate from our Creator and Source. It comes from a wish to be other than what God created—a Self at one with Him. This Self is not a *part* of totality, but Christ *within* His totality. Thus, when the *tiny, mad idea* seemed to arise within the mind of God's Son, it arose because of this wish: "I want to be more than everything, with a self separate from God, a self He notices." This wish—the ego—gave rise to the thought that not only do I want to be apart from God; I *am* apart from Him. If you will pardon the play on words, I am no longer *a part* of God, I am *apart* from Him.

In truth, however, there can be no wish. *A Course in Miracles* distinguishes between wishing and willing. The ego's wrong mind wishes, as does the right mind. Yet Heaven—the One-mindedness of Christ—only wills, for God's non-dualistic Will cannot wish. The very fact we have a wish to be separate and different is the illusion. Once we entertained that thought, or believed we could entertain that thought, it became real for us. However, it was reality only for our deranged minds, as the next sentence makes clear:

(1:7) It is a thing of madness, not reality at all.

Madness in *A Course in Miracles* is a synonym for *insanity*, its core being the belief that we could exist apart from God—the thought that a part of Him could wrench itself from His living and loving Oneness, declaring its independence and existing within its own kingdom. We all subscribe to this madness, which is why Jesus tells us we are mad: we literally see and hear what is not there, thinking the unreal is reality—the characteristics of psychosis.

(1:8-9) A name for namelessness is all it is. A symbol of impossibility; a choice for options that do not exist.

The ego is something that does not exist. What makes this so difficult to understand, however, is that *we* are the thing Jesus says does not exist—a body governed by a brain that thinks about words like these. This difficult position can be called the mother of all paradoxes: Jesus speaking to a brain that thinks it exists, telling it that it is nothing more than a name for namelessness, and thus is not real.

(1:10) We name it but to help us understand that it is nothing but an ancient thought that what is made has immortality.

We are told in *A Course in Miracles*, and in a particularly beautiful passage in the workbook, that what God created can never *not* be immortal and eternal (W-pII.13.5:4). Yet the ego is a thought system that says what it has made—a self of individual consciousness and the world that arose from it—is indeed immortal. Thus, it would follow that if the ego's world, thought system, and self are always here, God's Self and His Kingdom cannot be. Oneness and separation, reality and illusion, love and hate, light and darkness are mutually exclusive states that cannot coexist except in an insane mind that dissociates them.

Following from the Introduction—"This course remains within an ego framework, where it is needed."—Jesus names this "ancient thought" to help us understand his teaching, and also to help us get in touch with the part of us that believes we exist. This part is illusory, but it would not help us progress in this course if Jesus kept telling us we do not exist. He tells us often enough as it is, but we usually gloss over those references, pretending he does not really mean it. More often than not, however, he talks about us as if we were here, addressing the decision maker and urging it to choose the right over the wrong mind, even though, again, he has also made it clear that the entire split self is non-existent. Thus his authoritative teaching remains gentle, kind, and patient. He meets us where we think we are, gently leading us to where we truly are.

(1:11) But what could come of this except a dream which, like all dreams, can only end in death?

The ego begins with a thought of death, because it is the thought that it attacked and destroyed life. The ego camouflages this thought, saying it is really a thought of life, for it gives us a body that lives and interacts with other living bodies. Yet the fact of the matter is that everything that emanates from the ego is tinged with death, as we read from the text:

> And death is the result of the thought we call the ego, as surely as life is the result of the Thought of God (T-19.IV-C.2:15).

This is Jesus' meaning when he says of death: "do not confuse symbol with source" (T-19.IV-C.11:2). The symbol of death is the body's demise, yet the body cannot die for it never lived. The fact that the body seems to die within the ego's dream is because it comes from a thought, which is its source. Thus Jesus asks us not to pay attention to the body, but to return to the mind's thought of death that is the problem. In other words, Jesus helps us move from symbol to source, body to mind, form to content. And so we come to understand that the ego's dream world must end in death because it came from death: *ideas leave not their source*.

(2:1-2) What is the ego? Nothingness, but in a form that seems like something.

Here again Jesus gives us a description, not a definition. We know the ego seems like something, because we think *we* are something—living in a world that seems to be something. Yet that cannot change the ego's inherent nothingness.

(2:3) In a world of form the ego cannot be denied for it alone seems real.

We made a world of form because within it the ego's thought system of separation seems real, thereby making God unreal—the world's purpose. In the world of bodies the ego seems very much alive and well, and God an impossibility:

> The world was made as an attack on God.... [and] meant to be a place where God could enter not... (W-pII.3.2:1,4).

Therefore, when the ego speaks of God, Heaven, and spirituality, it speaks only on behalf of itself, for its dualistic theologies—wherein God creates the world—reflect the seeming reality of separation and sin. Thus the importance of this next statement, reflecting the Holy Spirit's answer:

(2:4) Yet could God's Son as He created him abide in form or in a world of form?

Throughout the Course—we will see another reference later—Jesus explains how the true God has nothing to do with the physical universe.* How could God's Son, who is spirit, possibly live in a world of bodies? Thus, for example, this is not a course that reflects holistic health—the unity of mind, body, and

---

* See, for example, T-8.VI.1-3; T-11.VII.1; T-13.in.2:2–3:1; and my *Glossary-Index* for a more complete list.

2. The Ego – The Miracle

spirit—for Mind and spirit have nothing to do with mind and body. Recall that this is a non-dualistic thought system. We can, of course, dream that we abide in form, but dreaming does not make reality. Nonetheless, we can live in this world as a reflection of Heaven's love—where we truly abide. Section 6 below speaks of our being Jesus' manifestation in the world, as he is the Holy Spirit's, and so we are asked to reflect the thought system of Atonement that Jesus and the Holy Spirit represent: shared instead of separate interests.

(2:5) Who asks you to define the ego and explain how it arose can be but he who thinks it real, and seeks by definition to ensure that its illusive nature is concealed behind the words that seem to make it so.

Continuing his discussion from the Introduction, Jesus turns to the second part of his answer to the question of how the illusory ego could have arisen from reality. His point is that whoever asks for a definition of the ego and explanation of its origin, clearly thinks it is real. Engaging in such discussion thereby ensures that the ego's illusory nature will be hidden behind the words and theories. Thus the ego loves theology, philosophy, ontology, and all the speculative disciplines, because they study the original error as if it were actually there to study. Instead, Jesus asks us to understand the purpose the ego serves, not the ego itself.

We move away from the ego by understanding that the mind chose it out of fear of love's all-encompassing nature, and thus we recognize that each time we indulge a specialness thought, have a pain, become angry, or feel unfairly treated, there is a purpose behind such insanity, a method in the ego's madness: attack truth by proving there is no truth. *That* is what Jesus wants us to understand—not the ego itself, which cannot be understood. Thus Jesus does not define the ego but simply describes it, as would an artist. Through his words, he provides us with an experience of the ego's nothingness that can engender great anxiety: "If what Jesus says is true, I do not exist here, but in the Heart of God."

(3:1-5) There is no definition for a lie that serves to make it true. Nor can there be a truth that lies conceal effectively. The ego's unreality is not denied by words nor is its meaning clear because its nature seems to have a form. Who can define the undefinable? And yet there is an answer even here.

No matter how much you seek to study, describe, explain, analyze, or define something, you cannot make it what it is not. Yet we arrogantly insist that by defining the ego we can in fact change illusion into truth. We all are fooled by this, because we try to establish this self as reality. However, in the end, lies will not work and truth will always emerge. There is an answer to the ego but not to the question, What is the ego and how did it arise? The answer is to the *problem* of the ego, which, of course, is the *miracle*, as we now see:

(4:1-4) We cannot really make a definition for what the ego is, but we *can* say what it is not. And this is shown to us with perfect clarity. It is from this that we deduce all that the ego is. Look at its opposite [the miracle] and you can see the only answer that is meaningful.

This goes to the heart of the undoing process of *A Course in Miracles*. We cannot say what love is, but we can say what it is not. Special love is dualistic and exclusive—hating, bargaining, manipulating. By looking at the ego's special love, therefore, we realize that real love cannot be involved.

(5:1) The ego's opposite in every way,—in origin, effect and consequence—we call a miracle.

The ego is the heart of the wrong-minded system, as the miracle is of the right-minded system. The ego is the problem; the miracle the correction. The ego's thought system of separation, division, and exclusion takes us from the mind to the body; the miracle returns us to the mind where we chose to be separate, so we can happily choose again and see differently.

(5:2-3) And here we find all that is not the ego in this world. Here is the ego's opposite and here alone we look on what the ego was, for here we see all that it seemed to do, and cause and its effects must still be one.

The world is the effect, the ego thought system the cause: *ideas leave not their source*. The idea of a separated self and world cannot leave its source in the mind. Thus the physical world has never left its source—the mind's thought of separation—though it *seemed* to. Cause and effect are one, as are source and idea—the *content* of hate and separation is one with the *form* of hate and separation. The miracle helps us understand this causal connection.

(6:1-7) Where there was darkness now we see the light. What is the ego? What the darkness was. Where is the ego? Where the darkness was. What is it now and where can it be found? Nothing and nowhere.

These words makes perfect sense when read with the heart and not the brain, where they can infuriate because they seem not to say anything. Yet they are not supposed to, because there is nothing meaningful to say about the ego itself. Yet Jesus exposes the lie of its illusory nature through evoking contrast: once you have an experience of truth, you will understand the ego's nothingness; once you know what it means to see someone as one with you, you will understand the meaning of specialness; once you have an experience of the mind's light, you will understand the ego's darkness and know it is not understandable.

Therefore, it is the contrast between the ego and the miracle that shows the ego's true nature, not studying, analyzing, or explaining it. Understanding of the ego comes when you step beyond it—again, the contrast between the ego's hate-filled darkness and the Holy Spirit's love-filled light—for the ego cannot be understood from within its thought system but only from an experience outside it. Thus the miracle leads us to the right-minded self that observes the wrong-minded self, and gently smiles its darkness away.

(6:8-18) Now the light has come: Its opposite has gone without a trace. Where evil was there now is holiness. What is the ego? What the evil was. Where is the ego? In an evil dream that but seemed real while you were dreaming it. Where there was crucifixion stands God's Son. What is the ego? Who has need to ask? Where is the ego? Who has need to seek for an illusion now that dreams are gone?

This, then, is Jesus' answer. When we experience true forgiveness, the ego is no longer a concern because it is gone. In the holy instant we understand what the ego was—pain, misery, depression, unhappiness, loneliness, fear, and guilt. Our experience now is only the peace and Love of God that embraces all people as one. Because we have received the answer there is no point in asking questions. And so we again see a wonderful expression of Jesus' explanation from the Introduction: when we experience love the hate is gone, as is our need to analyze. The dream has ended; what else is there to know?

(7:1-3) What is a *miracle*? A dream as well. But look at all the aspects of *this* dream and you will never question any more.

The point of *A Course in Miracles* is to end our questioning. At their core, again, questions seek to substantiate the thought system that gave rise to both the question and the questioner. Within the miracle that leads to the experience beyond all asking, questions disappear, for they were born of self-doubt that disappears in the presence of love. Knowing the love you are—not cognitively or intellectually, but through experience—you include the entire Sonship in this love. Dreams remain because there is yet a sense of self, but it is an all-inclusive self that does not perceive separate interests—the condition for awakening from the dream.

(7:4) Look at the kindly world you see extend before you as you walk in gentleness.

The world itself does not change, but we have become kind and gentle as the duplicity of specialness—its neediness and hate—is gone. From forgiving thoughts of gentle kindness we look kindly and gently on the world, for the outer is a projection of the inner, and it is the content, not the form that is our new focus.

(7:5-6) Look at the helpers all along the way you travel, happy in the certainty of Heaven and the surety of peace. And look an instant, too, on what you left behind at last and finally passed by.

We take one final look, smile gently, and say: "I was truly insane because I believed the ego, living by its laws of specialness—competition, gain, and loss—yet it brought me nothing except misery." Suffering is gone because we realize it was simply a mistaken choice. We do not dwell on the error, but look at it one last time with gratitude, because it was the stepping stone that led us home.

(8:1) This was the ego—all the cruel hate, the need for vengeance and the cries of pain, the fear of dying and the urge to kill, the brotherless

illusion and the self that seemed alone in all the universe.

This graphically sums up the ego, yet when the miracle is chosen, everything changes in our perception and experience.

(8:2-4) This terrible mistake about yourself the miracle corrects as gently as a loving mother sings her child to rest. Is not a song like this what you would hear? Would it not answer all you thought to ask, and even make the question meaningless?

Why would you seek to ask a thousand questions and receive a thousand answers when you can ask but one, have it be answered, and all pain be undone? This one question comes in different forms—why would I choose the ego over the Holy Spirit, hate over love, specialness over Christ's vision?—but in Atonement's gentle song all concerns disappear in the single answer of love.

(9:1) Your questions have no answer, being made to still God's Voice, which asks of everyone one question only: "Are you ready yet to help Me save the world?"

We do not save the world by our deeds, but by healing the inner world we made to be a place of hate. Since minds are joined, when we choose to be healed the mind of the Sonship is healed. As the world comes from the mind and has never left its source, it must be healed as well, shining with the Holy Spirit's forgiveness.

(9:2) Ask this instead of what the ego is, and you will see a sudden brightness cover up the world the ego made.

In other words, stop worrying about the ego and analyzing it, trying to understand it and the world. Seek only the experience of light, which forgiveness brings about through the Holy Spirit.

(9:3) No miracle is now withheld from anyone.

This is an important statement and its content recurs throughout the Course. The love we experience within ourselves embraces all people, *without exception*; otherwise, it cannot be love. This all-inclusiveness of the miracle undoes the ego's thought system of specialness.

(9:4) The world is saved from what you thought it was.

You thought the world was a place of hell, pain, and death, yet it was only a projection of an illusory thought. By undoing this thought—choosing Jesus' miracle instead of the ego's judgment—all suffering is gone.

(9:5) And what it is, is wholly uncondemned and wholly pure.

The world is wholly uncondemned and wholly pure, not because anything has changed on the level of form, but because the world of thought has been transformed. Forgiveness and innocence have replaced judgment and sin, and nothing now remains but the shining peace of God that embraces the Sonship as one.

(10:1-3) The miracle forgives; the ego damns. Neither need be defined except by this. Yet could a definition be more sure, or more in line with what salvation is?

When you damn, you affirm separation by saying: "You lose and I win. You deserve to be condemned because of your sin, and I am without it because it is now in you." This practice of separate interests defines the ego system. On the other hand, the miracle forgives because it undoes the barriers of separation that existed between you and me, and between me and the world.

The miracle forgives, the ego damns; the miracle joins, the ego separates; the miracle sees shared interests, the ego separate interests. One brings joy, the other pain—we need know nothing else. Our understanding of why things do or do not happen, or how to make them happen, is not necessary. This greatly simplifies our lives, for we need only understand the choice between illusion and truth, the ego and the miracle.

(10:4) Problem and answer lie together here, and having met at last the choice is clear.

We have brought damnation to forgiveness, crucifixion to resurrection, darkness to light. The ego's defense of dissociation is thus undone, for when brought together, Atonement gently corrects separation and nothing is left but Heaven's blessing of love.

(10:5) Who chooses hell when it is recognized?

Recall the line from the text:

> Who with the Love of God upholding him could find the choice of miracles or murder hard to make? (T-23.IV.9:8).

With this Love upholding us, from outside the dream, we see the difference between the thought systems of hate and murder, and forgiveness and love. Once seen, the choice is obvious, and the Course's purpose is to make it obvious. When we recognize the contrast—between the ego's darkness and the miracle's light—we understand the darkness was nothing and the miracle everything.

(10:6) And who would not go on a little while when it is given him to understand the way is short and Heaven is his goal?

When we recognize that the miracle is the way we are led home, we could not but ask for help each time we are tempted to judge, condemn, damn, and separate. When the choice is clear, how could we not choose again? Once the experience of peace comes, we have a standard against which we can measure all other experiences. We have learned that when we choose the ego, we choose the darkness of despair, guilt, hate, and fear; and when we choose the miracle, we choose joy, happiness, and peace, with Heaven not far behind.

3. FORGIVENESS – THE FACE OF CHRIST

This section focuses on two important terms in *A Course in Miracles*: *forgiveness* and *the face of Christ*. The face of Christ is not meant to be taken literally, as if you were to see something with your eyes. And it certainly does not mean the face of Jesus. Rather, the face of Christ symbolizes total innocence, the Course's great symbol of forgiveness. When you withdraw the projections of hate you placed on your brother, what remains is the innocence of God's Son—in him, in you, and in the Sonship as a whole. The real world is also mentioned in this section, as well as in the one that follows—the culmination of the journey we walk with each other.

(1:1) *Forgiveness* is for God and toward God but not of Him.

Forgiveness has nothing to do with God: "God does not forgive because He has never condemned" (W-pI.46.1:1). Forgiveness is a correction, but God sees nothing to correct because there is no problem—the separation never happened. This is the Atonement's answer to the ego's wrong-minded questions, which but affirm itself.

(1:2) It is impossible to think of anything He created that could need forgiveness.

God created His Son perfect, changeless, and pure, and so nothing in Heaven needs to be forgiven. It is the illusion of God's Son that needs forgiveness —the illusions we have about our special hate and love partners: the enemies we attack, and the people we cannot live without. When Jesus tells us that true learning is *un*learning (M-4.X.3:7) he is describing forgiveness, which withdraws our projections of guilt onto others. In that sense forgiveness is nothing positive, for it simply undoes the ego's negation of truth.

(1:3-4) Forgiveness, then, is an illusion, but because of its purpose, which is the Holy Spirit's, it has one difference. Unlike all other illusions it leads away from error and not towards it.

Forgiveness is illusory because *everything* here is. However, unlike the things of the world that keep us believing in what was made up, forgiveness leads us beyond the illusion to what was created, which we did not make. This awakening from the ego's illusory dreams of attack is its single purpose.

(2:1) Forgiveness might be called a kind of happy fiction; a way in which the unknowing can bridge the gap between their perception and the truth.

The symbol of a bridge is often used in the Course. Sometimes the Holy Spirit is referred to as the bridge between perception and knowledge, as is the real world, bridging illusions and God's truth. Other times, *bridge* refers to the shift from the ego's wrong-minded thought system to the Holy Spirit's right-minded truth.

(2:2) They cannot go directly from perception to knowledge because they do not think it is their will to do so.

The reason we unknowing ones do not suddenly awaken from the ego's dream to God's reality is not that we cannot do so, but that we do not believe we can, or even that we should. We are terrified of knowledge because the ego taught us—and we learned the lesson very well—that if we take Jesus' hand, walk the pathway of the miracle and awaken from the dream, we will disappear into oblivion. Thus, *our* will is to remain in perception in order to keep our self intact.

This is a journey from the wrong-minded self, through the right-minded self, to the One Self that shines away individual identity: the heart of what the ego told us at the beginning when it wove its tale of sin, guilt, and fear, teaching us to be afraid of Heaven's love. In God's Presence, the ego warned, the individual self would be annihilated. The truth, however, is that in His Presence it would simply disappear back into its own nothingness. As long as we identify with the physical, psychological self we think we are, we will fear that disappearance. Our ego will not see it as the self gently melting into the Self, but rather its own catastrophic destruction. Thus we need the little steps—the happy dreams— that will heal our misperception of God from a hateful father to a loving One. In the end, of course, God is no Father at all, yet because we believed the ego's lies, we first need a happy fiction that speaks of our Source as a loving Father. As we increasingly identify with His Love and less with the ego's projected hate, we learn to transcend both the love and hate we experience from an outside source, and realize that God's Love is our Love, His Self is our Self, and individuality and hate are the lie. So again:

(2:3-4) This makes God appear to be an enemy instead of what He really is. And it is just this insane perception that makes them unwilling merely to rise up and to return to Him in peace.

Thus Jesus speaks of forgiveness as a process. As we saw in section 4 of the manual, there are six stages in the development of trust. It is a process, not because it need be, but because our fear of love dictates it be so. We proceed slowly because this fear is great, and so before we lose all sense of self, we first must correct our wrong-minded self by recognizing our right-minded one. Yet we still have a self, with an image seen daily in the mirror. Yet this is a self that embraces all people as part of the Sonship, on the same journey. Only at the end do we realize this self was an illusion, too, for the reflection of Oneness has become what it reflected: Oneness Itself.

(3:1-5) And so they need an illusion of help because they are helpless; a Thought of peace because they are in conflict. God knows what His Son needs before he asks. He is not at all concerned with form, but having given the content it is His Will that it be understood. And that suffices. The form adapts itself to need; the content is unchanging, as eternal as its Creator.

Jesus tells us once more what he told us in the Introduction: his course comes in a specific form. The content of love is one, but because of our fear, we need its answer expressed in forms we can accept. It is far less fearful to accept the concept of a God Who loves us than a God Who does not know we exist; the concept of a helper named Jesus is more acceptable than the idea that there is no helper, because there is no one to be helped. We can accept the indirect concept of forgiveness because we fear the direct love that forgiveness reflects. We thus need the symbol—what Jesus gives us here—of a God Who knows what we need, until we are able to accept the truth of a God Who does not know our needs because He does not know our separated selves.

Again, Jesus urges us to see the content, which adapts to whatever form is needed. Ultimately, we are the ones who adapt the form. Our minds take the abstract experience of love and transform it into something specific to which we can relate. Those forms include a concept of a God Who knows what we need, a Jesus who guides us, *A Course in Miracles* to teach us the message of seeing shared instead of separate interests. All these, however, reflect the non-specific content of love and truth, which, again, is always adapted to a form we can accept.

Remember, it is not the form we want but the content. The world has always fallen in love with symbols, and then worshipped them. It has built altars and churches to the symbol so it could never reach the content. It was said of Jesus that he pointed a finger to the truth, and then everyone worshipped the finger. That is the point he is making here: "I am pointing a finger to the truth, which is what you want. Do not worship me, this course, or its message. Do not worry about the concepts, theories, or words, but let them—symbols of what you really want—be the means of your return home."

(4:1) *The face of Christ* has to be seen before the memory of God can return.

This is the formula of salvation given us by *A Course in Miracles*: we see the face of Christ in our brother and remember God. Seeing Christ's face in another means seeing it in ourselves, for forgiveness ultimately means undoing our guilt. Once the ego and its dreams of judgment are gone, all that remains is God.

(4:2-4) The reason is obvious. Seeing the face of Christ involves perception. No one can look on knowledge.

We are terrified of what lies beyond forgiveness, which is why this is not a course in knowledge or love, but in learning to choose their reflections.

(4:5-8) But the face of Christ is the great symbol of forgiveness. It is salvation. It is the symbol of the real world. Whoever looks on this no longer sees the world.

When you look on the world, you look through the eyes of separation and guilt. It is not only that your eyes see separation—they will always see separation—but your mind will interpret it: good versus evil, innocence versus guilt. You will see differences on the level of form—gender, weight, skin color, culture, nationality, religious and political belief—and accentuate what your eyes perceive as differences. We therefore need a corrected perception that sees differences, but recognizes that they make no difference. Underlying differing forms is the content of the one split mind—hate, love, and the power to choose between them. Recognizing the mind's oneness welcomes the face of Christ, because we no longer make superficial differences the cause of attack. Recall that the face of Christ is a symbol of innocence, which undoes separation, sin, guilt, and blame: "Whoever looks on this no longer sees the world."

(4:9-12) He is as near to Heaven as is possible outside the gate. Yet from this gate it is no more than just a step inside. It is the final step. And this we leave to God.

Beyond the gate of Heaven is perfect Oneness, and the real world is just this side of Heaven's gate. In its reflected light of truth we are aware of the dream, but know it is a dream of which we are no longer a part. Having attained the real world we have totally forgiven, and thus the right mind has corrected the wrong mind. The final step now occurs as the right and wrong minds disappear, as does the decision maker, leaving only the One-mindedness of Christ.

(5:1) Forgiveness is a symbol, too, but as the symbol of His Will alone it cannot be divided.

Forgiveness is not the Will of God, which is total oneness, but reflects that Will because it sees that you and I and everyone are the same—the vision of Christ. This is what it means to see the face of Christ in your brother, where the right mind no longer interprets the body's differences as meaning anything at all.

(5:2-3) And so the unity that it reflects becomes His Will. It is the only thing still in the world in part, and yet the bridge to Heaven.

That describes forgiveness—it is not Heaven, love, or oneness, but the means by which the thought of oneness is returned to our awareness.

(6:1-4) God's Will is all there is. We can but go from nothingness to everything; from hell to Heaven. Is this a journey? No, not in truth, for truth goes nowhere.

In the text, Jesus says this is "a journey without distance to a goal that has never changed" (T-8.VI.9:7). In truth, we go from nothing to everything; but it is that very truth that so frightens us. Therefore, we need intermediate steps—happy dreams—that represent the Atonement principle in less threatening forms.

(6:5-9) But illusions shift from place to place; from time to time. The final step is also but a shift. As a perception it is part unreal. And yet this part will vanish. What remains is peace eternal and the Will of God.

The final step is also a shift—from perception to knowledge. However, since there is no world of perception, there can be no real shift. This inherently unreal process begins from the *tiny, mad idea* and descends the ladder of separation into the world of special relationships. It then reverses itself through the Holy Spirit's forgiveness that returns us home. We make our way up the ladder by daily practice, asking Jesus to correct the ego by helping us think of God as a loving Father. We thus become less and less involved with the world and more and more involved with the mind, until we realize, finally, that there is no world or mind, for all this is an illusion. It has therefore been a journey from Everywhere to nowhere, back to Everywhere; a journey that does not occur over time and space, but as long as we believe we are temporal-spatial creatures, we believe we make the journey.

In the next paragraph, Jesus again contrasts *wish* and *will*:

(7:1) There are no wishes now for wishes change.

There are no more wrong-minded wishes—hate and exclusion—and no more right-minded ones—forgiveness and inclusion. Only the Will of God remains.

(7:2-3) Even the wished-for can become unwelcome. That must be so because the ego cannot be at peace.

If the "wished-for" is based on a separated world, it still comes within an ego framework and so we inevitably become afraid. We choose forgiveness, and then find it unacceptable because we fear what it represents. This experience is unknown in Heaven where there is no welcoming of truth—we *are* the truth. Yet as long as our identity is based on the ego thought system, on which we are dependent, we will be afraid of the Will beyond our wishes.

(7:4-8) But Will is constant, as the gift of God. And what He gives is always like Himself. This is the purpose of the face of Christ. It is the gift of God to save His Son. But look on this and you have been forgiven.

I look on the innocence of my brother—by withdrawing my projections—and recognize the innocence in myself, to be described beautifully in the next section. I take back what I put from myself onto you, and bring it to my mind. Thus I acknowledge that the guilt is not in you but in me, realizing that my guilt defended against the innocence that is my true reality. By the day-to-day practice of changing my mind about you, I learn to change my mind about me, reflecting the change of inner teacher from the ego to the Holy Spirit.

(8:1) How lovely does the world become in just that single instant when you see the truth about yourself reflected there.

The world does not change. You could be in Auschwitz, have your mind healed, and be in the real world. The scent of death will be as strong as it was before, but you will not smell it. Your body might, but *you* will not, because your healed mind will perceive only expressions of love or calls for it. You will realize that everyone has the same love and call for love, for underlying the ego's hate we are the same. That is what makes everything lovely. "Seek not to change the world," the text says. "but choose to change your mind about the world" (T-21.in.1:7). When you thus change your mind—choosing innocence instead of guilt—everything becomes beautiful in your perception.

(8:2) Now you are sinless and behold your sinlessness.

You do not see sin in anyone. Remember that sin separates—there is a sinner and a sinned against. If you are the sinner, I am sinless, expressing the ego's principle of *one or the other*. When, however, I see only the sinless in me and realize nothing has changed perfect love, I cannot see sin in another. *Projection makes perception*—if there is no sin in me, I cannot see it anywhere in the Sonship.

(8:3) Now you are holy and perceive it so.

Perceiving holiness in myself, I naturally extend it and perceive it all around me—*ideas leave not their source*. The idea of holiness and sinlessness has never left the mind, which means that is what I perceive. This corrects the mistaken idea that when I see sin inside, it must be outside as well.

(8:4) And now the mind returns to its Creator; the joining of the Father and the Son, the Unity of unities that stands behind all joining but beyond them all.

I am no longer *reflecting* the unity of God and Christ—seeing the Son with one split mind—for I have *become* the unity that had been reflected.

(8.5-6) God is not seen but only understood. His Son is not attacked but recognized.

As Jesus says at the end of Chapter 19:

> Together we will disappear into the Presence beyond the veil, not to be lost but found; not to be seen but known (T-19.IV-D.19:1).

That is the very end of the journey, when we disappear as one into the Heart of God. Jesus continues with this theme in the next section, and will take it one step further when he speaks of the worlds of true perception and knowledge.

4. TRUE PERCEPTION – KNOWLEDGE

The previous section dealt with forgiveness and culminated with our attainment of the real world—"How lovely does the world become in just that single instant"—closing with God's final step. At the beginning of this beautiful section, Jesus continues his description of the real world and speaks more extensively of how true perception corrects false perception. When the correction is complete, both perceptions disappear and only knowledge remains.

(1:1-2) The world you see is an illusion of a world. God did not create it, for what He creates must be eternal as Himself.

Many students have taken the first part of this passage out of context and used it to buttress their view that *A Course in Miracles* teaches that God created the phenomenal or perceptual universe, but not its ego aspects—suffering, hate, war, etc. It is quite clear, however, both from this passage as well as dozens and dozens of others, that this is not what Jesus means at all. Rather, he literally means that God did not create the physical universe. As in many other places, including section 1 above, he explains why:

(1:2-5) God did not create it, for what He creates must be eternal as Himself. Yet there is nothing in the world you see that will endure forever. Some things will last in time a little while longer than others. But the time will come when all things visible will have an end.

This is the identical argument found—in more poetic language—in "Forgiveness and the End of Time" (T-29.VI). The world of perception cannot have been created by God, the Creator of knowledge, because He is changeless, eternal, and perfect. Here, however, everything changes, for nothing lasts forever and is certainly not perfect. Thus Jesus advances his thesis that the true God had nothing to do with the material world, which means the cosmos is an illusion. Although that same principle is found in the higher teachings of Hinduism and Buddhism, *A Course in Miracles* extends the discussion by explaining the purpose the world serves: to be a block standing between ourselves and God, proving the separation actually happened. Thus, we think we are in a body, with sensory apparatus that seems to confirm we are here, and which also proclaims that God is not. In fact, not only is God not here, He can no longer exist because in the ego system it is *one or the other.*

A Course in Miracles thus teaches not only that the world is illusory, but unveils its purpose: why the world was made, why we are born into it, why we so steadfastly choose to be here, and why the world's religions bring God and His spokespeople into it. If the world is real, so am I; if it is an illusion, I—an integral part of the perceptual world—must be an illusion, too.

(2:1-2) The body's eyes are therefore not the means by which the real world can be seen, for the illusions that they look upon must lead to more illusions of reality. And so they do.

The real world is the state of the separated mind—not Heaven's One Mind—that is healed of all thoughts of separation and guilt. We are therefore aware that this world is a dream, and that the Self—our true Identity—is outside it. When Jesus was *in* the world, he was not really here for he knew he was not *of* it. He was perceived as a body with a personality, but he knew this was not Who he was, an awareness he now helps us to reach.

The ego made eyes and other sensory organs so that the world would witness to its "reality"; consequently, the real world cannot be perceived by the body. Thus the Course contrasts the vision of Christ with the ego's seeing. The former occurs in the mind, and only in the mind, while the latter typically refers to our physical eyes. Yet the body remains an illusion looking upon an illusion, reacting to an illusion it has made real. We can, however, with Jesus' light showing the way, look beyond the body to the truth within the mind, patiently awaiting our decision.

(2:3) For everything they see not only will not last, but lends itself to thoughts of sin and guilt.

All worldly things lend themselves to thoughts of sin and guilt because we project the mind's sin and guilt onto them, seeing the ego's separation everywhere. These objects and people are neither sinful nor sinless—they are nothing. However, the mind's wrong-minded thoughts must go somewhere, because the mind's pain and anguish are intolerable. They therefore are projected, landing on everyone and everything indiscriminately. Since the ego is a thought of death—the belief it destroyed life—it made up a world that is a place of death: *ideas leave not their source*. The ego is also a thought of change—the original change from Christ to the ego—and so everything it sees will change: *ideas leave not their source*.

(2:4) While everything that God created is forever without sin and therefore is forever without guilt.

This is another way of saying that nothing here is of God. The very fact that we perceive each other as separate and different, regarding these perceptions as meaningful, tells us we believe in illusion. The fundamental difference on which the ego bases everything—whether we are conscious of it or not—is that others are sinful and we are sinless: they have the sin we have projected. Following the fourth law of chaos, if they have it, we do not (T-23.II.9-11). We therefore walk this earth from birth to death, desperately trying to demonstrate that the world is responsible for how terrible we and others feel. This is the world of sinners and sinned-against, victimizers and victims; yet in truth we are one.

(3:1) Knowledge is not the remedy for false perception since, being another level, they can never meet.

This idea is found in the text as well, where Jesus comments on the famous biblical statement: "The Word was made flesh, and dwelt among us…." (John 1:14). (In the gospel, *Word* refers to Jesus, the cosmic Christ). He says:

> Strictly speaking this is impossible, since it seems to involve the translation of one order of reality into another (T-8.VII.7:2).

The Word—the Thought of God—cannot be made flesh, because thought and flesh are on mutually exclusive levels: reality and illusion. So much, then, for the Incarnation of Jesus.

Thus, "knowledge is not the remedy" because it cannot correct what it does not know. False perception is corrected by true perception, which gently melts into knowledge. Nothing in true perception opposes knowledge, while everything in the ego's perception opposes it, and so they never meet.

(3:2-4) The one correction possible for false perception must be *true perception*. It will not endure. But for the time it lasts it comes to heal.

True perception is of course perceptual, which means it is an illusion. Jesus tells us in the text: "that is why visions, however holy, do not last (T-3.III.4:6). No matter how holy the visions of the world's mystics and spiritual teachers, they remain perceptual—something seen or heard. They are but symbols, and spiritual aspirants have often mistakenly built shrines, altars, and churches on "sacred" places where "sacred" people had their "sacred" experiences. Yet, since the visions are perceptual, again, they cannot last. Knowledge alone endures.

Therefore, the only shrine to be built is in the *mind* of God's united Son. This is the altar at which we seek to worship, for it is the mind that had the vision. If it is a true vision of God's Love—whatever the form—it must be of the One Mind that is shared by all of us: the altar on which we want to place our devotions.

(3:5-6) For true perception is a remedy with many names. Forgiveness, salvation, Atonement, true perception, all are one.

Jesus runs through the various terms that are so important in the Course—different symbols of the right mind's correction. We could have added others, too: *the face of Christ, vision, the miracle*. We look at the ego's thought system of separation and specialness, and say: "I do not want this any more." That is the single correction.

(3:7) They are the one beginning, with the end to lead to Oneness far beyond themselves.

They share a oneness here, in that this is the single vision that sees everyone as the same. These visions and experiences thus become the stepping stones that lead us to the non-dualistic awareness of perfect Oneness.

(3:8-9) True perception is the means by which the world is saved from sin, for sin does not exist. And it is this that true perception sees.

True perception does not see sin and then forgive or atone for it; it looks at sin and sees beyond it, because nothing is there. This is another major difference between the Jesus of *A Course in Miracles* and the Jesus of the Bible. The biblical figure, without question, saw sin. Indeed, he was sent into the world because his Father saw it, too. In *A Course in Miracles*, Jesus does not see sin for he could not see what never happened.

This, then, is how the world is saved. True perception looks at what the world calls sin, and says: "What sin?" In the dream, all that is real is a call for help. Yet it is not just one person's call, but everyone's. Indeed, all who think they are here plead for help: "Please tell me I am wrong. I do not know where home is, but tell me this world is not it. This world, void of hope, is a place of misery, loss, and death. Please show me there is somewhere else." While we are not yet ready to learn of the "somewhere else"—our true home—we are at least ready to learn there is another way of being here: looking through the eyes of Christ instead of the ego's; the eyes of shared rather than separate interests.

The point, therefore, is not to change the world, others, or ourselves, but to change the eyes through which we look at the world, others, or ourselves, culminating in true perception. We thus look through the mind's eye—to use Hamlet's phrase—not the body's. Our physical eyes, however, also look through the mind's eye, but it is the ego's mind of separation. Thus we are asked to shift our interpretation of what the body's eyes see.

(4:1) The world stands like a block before Christ's face.

The *face of Christ* is a symbol for the innocence of Christ, the innocence we share as God's Son. The world of separation and perception is the world of winners and losers—*one or the other*—born of separate interests that veil Christ's face, preventing His Love from being known.

(4:2-3) But true perception looks on it as nothing more than just a fragile veil, so easily dispelled that it can last no longer than an instant. It is seen at least for only what it is.

The world is no more than this fragile veil, having no power to keep away the light. "The Two Worlds" describes guilt as a "fragile veil," a "bank of low dark clouds…. [not] strong enough to stop a button's fall, nor hold a feather" (T-18.IX.5:4; 6:1,4). What seems to be a solid wall, a "granite block of sin" (T-22.III.5:6) that keeps us from the Love of God is nothing but this flimsy veil. When we look at it with Jesus, our eyes look through it and beyond, for his is the loving presence that helps us look at the block in our minds and realize it is not a block at all. In other words, we understand that nothing happened; no barrier exists between our self and Christ. His light streams through, and as we identify less with the individual self and more with the light, true perception fulfills its function and our eyes open at last.

(4:4) And now it cannot fail to disappear, for now there is an empty place made clean and ready.

The world must disappear, for what upheld it was the wish to have it block our innocence. The world thus demonstrates our guilt, and everyone else's. This establishes sin's reality—God is not real, and the ego identity alone is true. Therefore we all have a tremendous investment in seeing the world of specialness, differences, and judgment. True perception looks through it all, however, leaving behind a place made clean and ready for the Love of God. As we slowly waken, the memory of God dawns upon our mind, with His Love an instant behind.

(4:5) Where destruction was perceived the face of Christ appears, and in that instant is the world forgot, with time forever ended as the world spins into nothingness from where it came.

This last phrase is almost word for word what Jesus said in the manual (M-13.1:2). What prevents our forgetting is the recognition, on some level, that if the world is nothing, we are nothing, too. We do not want to spin into nothingness or disappear into the Heart of God, and so the ego makes up its horror stories of sin and vulnerable bodies in need of protection. We project this sin onto others, therefore feeling we have to protect our vulnerable selves from their attack. Thus our egos rest easy once again, as the world has served its unholy purpose.

Destruction is cherished in the ego system because it means sin is real. I destroyed Heaven; now I fear it will rise up and destroy me. Once I find myself in a body—where both Heaven and the ego's distorted heaven are distant memories—I believe everyone is out to destroy me. In the text, Jesus explains that when we project, we fear that our projections will return to hurt us, elsewhere described as the attack/defense cycle (W-pI.153.2-9):

Believing they have blotted their projections from their own minds, they also believe their projections are trying to creep back in (T-7.VIII.3:11).

All this is gone the instant we let go of the ego and our belief in conflicting interests. This is the holy instant in which there is no thought of separation or the body—only the real world, as Jesus now describes:

(5:1-4) A world forgiven cannot last. It was the home of bodies. But forgiveness looks past bodies. This is its holiness; this is how it heals.

In saying that forgiveness looks past bodies, Jesus does not mean for us not to see them, but to look past the ego's purpose for the body—keeping sin and separation real. We do not accomplish this by denying what our eyes see, or that we have a body that breathes and eats. Rather, we see bodies as frames that conceal what we believe to be a wretched picture of guilt and hate. Behind this, however, is a picture of light, and this is what we now see, looking past the body to the thought of the body—guilt—and on to the Thought of Atonement: guilt covers Atonement, as the body and world cover guilt. Forgiveness undoes all this and takes us to the wrong decision that is the source of the problem. Now we make a better one—for the transcendent beauty of "the forgiven world" (T-17.II).

(5:5) The world of bodies is the world of sin, for only if there were a body is sin possible.

The body is the embodiment of the ego thought system (W-pI.72.2:1-3), built on a foundation of sin that causes us to use our bodies lovelessly. Even when we think we are being loving, the body is used to attack ourselves and others by our seeing it either as an idol of pleasure or source of pain. Either way, bodies are made real, which means we have made sin real.

(5:6-7) From sin comes guilt as surely as forgiveness takes all guilt away. And once all guilt is gone what more remains to keep a separated world in place?

Sin and guilt are twin thoughts, for there cannot be one without the other. Moreover, Jesus teaches that guilt keeps the world in place. The world and body are but shadows of the mind's guilt, made to keep the guilt hidden (T-18.IX.4-5). Our lives are continually dictated by guilt, with no awareness that the mind is its source. We think our behavior comes from instincts, impulses, memories, desires, or the world at large—none of which is true. Everything the body does, thinks, or feels comes from guilt. Remove the guilt, and the body has no other purpose.

(5:8) For place has gone as well, along with time.

Time and place are also shadows of guilt. The ego's projection of sin, guilt, and fear gave rise to a linear world of time—past, present, and future: we sinned in the past, experience guilt now, and fear the future because of our inevitable punishment. Similarly, the world of space is the projection of separation. When these thoughts are gone, the world spins back into its own nothingness.

(5:9-10) Only the body makes the world seem real, for being separate it could not remain where separation is impossible. Forgiveness proves it is impossible because it sees it not.

The eyes see the body, but perception in *A Course in Miracles* is interpretation—the mind interpreting what the eyes see. They see differences because that is the nature of the perceptual world. Yet the interpretation given to those differences varies, depending on our choosing the ego or the Holy Spirit as our teacher. The ego uses perceptions to prove the reality of differences—some good, some bad. The Holy Spirit uses what we see to teach us that everyone is the same—behind the form is one content; beyond the symbol is one call for help.

(5:11) And what you then will overlook will not be understandable to you, just as its presence once had been your certainty.

Once we let the ego go, it disappears. Not only will we not understand it, we will not remember it. What holds memories in place is guilt, without which there is no memory or past, for guilt's purpose is to prove there *is* something to remember—something happened, and it happened to me. This defends against the fact that *I* am the one who did the something. Thus, when the ego is gone we will have only what Jesus calls "the present memory" (T-28.I)—the awareness that we are a child of God, held for us by the Holy Spirit.

Paragraph 6 is a lovely summary of what elsewhere I have called *the three steps of forgiveness*.

(6:1) This is the shift that true perception brings: What was projected out is seen within, and there forgiveness lets it disappear.

When I ask Jesus for help with a difficult situation or relationship, he tells me that what I see outside is a picture of an inward condition (T-21.in.1:5). The first step, therefore, is recognizing that my anger against you is made up, having nothing to do with you, regardless of your behavior: my judgments were projections of my guilt. The second step recognizes that the guilt I brought back to my mind is also an illusion. Just as I chose hate to conceal my mind's guilt, I chose guilt to conceal love's memory—our first two steps of forgiveness. Jesus continues:

(6:2) For there the altar to the Son is set, and there his Father is remembered.

The *altar* in *A Course in Miracles* means the place in our minds where we choose either the ego or the Holy Spirit. At last, our decision maker has chosen forgiveness, the means of remembering our Father.

(6:3) Here are all illusions brought to truth and laid upon the altar.

This is the culmination of the Course process of bringing illusions to the truth, not truth to illusions. We bring our guilt to the forgiveness within: the darkness of our hatred of others to the darkness of our hatred of ourselves. All this we bring to the love Jesus holds out to us: the light of truth that says the darkened thoughts of hate and self-hate are mere defenses against our Identity as children of light.

(6:4-6) What is seen outside must lie beyond forgiveness, for it seems to be forever sinful. Where is hope while sin is seen as outside? What remedy can guilt expect?

Thus we made a world, and, again, Jesus reminds us of its purpose: to keep us mindless. If I see the problem outside, it cannot be forgiven or undone, because the solution is within. By leaving my mind, I see the problem and solution where they are not: I would be happy if only I made more money, if only my body were healed, if only this relationship would work out. Yet this game will never work, as everyone who has played it knows—and we all are masters of the game of specialness. Even when we get what we think we want it is never enough, because it is not the real source of our unhappiness, which lies only in the mind's choice for guilt.

Therefore there is no hope in the system because "what is seen outside must lie beyond forgiveness." This means it must lie beyond correction. Jesus cannot help us when we tell him there is a problem out there for which we need his help. In conceiving of ourselves and him that way, we have done a remarkable job of rendering him powerless. The problem is inside, which is why we keep projecting it outside and dragging Jesus, the Holy Spirit, and God into the world to fix what does not exist. Thus the problem can never be resolved outside, which is why there is no hope, as the beginning of the manual states:

> …time…winds on wearily, and the world is very tired now. It is old and worn and without hope (M-1.4:4-5).

The world *is* hopeless, but not just because of current crises. There has never been any hope, for we look in the wrong place. Wars will never be resolved externally, or by a change of leadership on either side of a conflict, but only by returning to the root of the problem: the war we fight inside ourselves, against ourselves.

(6:7-10) But seen within your mind, guilt and forgiveness for an instant lie together, side by side, upon one altar. There at last are sickness and its single remedy joined in one healing brightness. God has come to claim His Own. Forgiveness is complete.

This is forgiveness' third step. Jesus teaches that the first two steps are our responsibility; the third is the Holy Spirit's (W-pI.23.5). We do our part by bringing illusions to the truth—bringing the outside guilt within, letting it go by learning it is only a defense. Forgiveness has caused guilt to fade away, and now, having completed its function, it fades away, too. Everything is gone but the memory of God, which dawns in our awareness.

We come now to the final paragraphs, which beautifully describe this gentle dawning.

(7:1-6) And now God's *knowledge*, changeless, certain, pure and wholly understandable, enters its kingdom. Gone is perception, false and true alike. Gone is forgiveness, for its task is done. And gone are bodies in the blazing light upon the altar to the Son of God. God knows it is His

Own, as it is his. And here They join, for here the face of Christ has shone away time's final instant, and now is the last perception of the world without a purpose and without a cause.

The world had a mighty purpose from the ego's point of view: to keep its thought system alive. It had a mighty purpose from the Holy Spirit's point of view as well: to undo the ego. Now both purposes are gone in the blazing light of forgiveness in which guilt is undone.

(7:7) For where God's memory has come at last there is no journey, no belief in sin, no walls, no bodies, and the grim appeal of guilt and death is there snuffed out forever.

Sin, guilt, and death have a definite appeal, as long as we wish to preserve our identity as an individual self. When that need is gone, so is the appeal of guilt and death. All that remains, then, is the light of Christ.

(8:1) O my brothers, if you only knew the peace that will envelop you and hold you safe and pure and lovely in the Mind of God, you could but rush to meet Him where His altar is.

Jesus pleads with us like this often in his course: "If you only knew how much happier and more peaceful you would be when you let go of judgment, hatred, and specialness! Why delay one instant longer the wonderful joy of knowing you are forgiven?" The problem, however, is that we steadfastly resist what he is saying because we do not want to lose our self.

(8:2-3) Hallowed your Name and His, for they are joined here in this holy place. Here He leans down to lift you up to Him, out of illusions into holiness; out of the world and to eternity; out of all fear and given back to love.

Note the reference to the Lord's Prayer, where it is only God's Name that is hallowed. Here, His Name and ours are the same. Thus does the journey end that began with the thought They were different. We have come to understand the ego's purpose for our identification with it, learning at last the pain of our decision to separate. As we practice forgiveness, recognizing that what we perceive outside is a projection of what we have made real inside, we are convinced by Jesus we will be happier when we let these projections go. And we do. The darkness of guilt fades away, leaving only the light that welcomes us into itself—our self merging into Self.

5. JESUS – CHRIST

The last two sections of the clarification of terms differ in tone from the preceding four, as they deal specifically with Jesus and the Holy Spirit. It is interesting that of the six sections, two are devoted to Them, and it is clear they have been given to help Course students avoid the specialness that is almost inevitable in relating to our inner Teachers. The key to understanding how to ask Jesus or the Holy Spirit for help is recognizing the difference between symbol and source, form and content, perception and knowledge. Knowledge is what we ultimately want—the non-specific, abstract presence of love. Yet its specific expressions are needed as long as we consider ourselves to be specific expressions of hate, and we know we do because we think we are here. Just as forgiveness is erased once it erases guilt, so, too, are expressions of love dissolved when they dissolve expressions of hate. If we hold on to the expression—form or symbol—we end up with nothing. One final point, similar to "Does Jesus Have a Special Place in Healing?" (M-23), the third person voice here does not mean Helen was listening to a *second* voice. These two sections, as in the manual, come from the same inner voice as found in the rest of the Course, though presented differently for stylistic reasons.

(1:1) There is no need for help to enter Heaven for you have never left.

Thus Jesus explains that help is an illusion. However, as long as we have the illusion of needing help, we need the illusion of releasing our old helper—the ego—and choosing a new one. Keep in mind that all this takes place only within the realm of illusion.

(1:2) But there is need for help beyond yourself as you are circumscribed by false beliefs of your Identity, which God alone established in reality.

We will see this same construction in the next section on the Holy Spirit. God alone knows Who we are, which means *we* do not know. This course does not aim at teaching this Identity, but does emphasize our looking at who we think we are—our ego identity—which we must then let go. Remember, when the right-minded self corrects the wrong-minded self, *both* disappear; guilt and forgiveness for an instant lie side by side on the altar, and then are gone in a blazing light (C-4.6:7-8). What follows that light we need not know, and the Course does not tell us, but gently points us toward it.

(1:3) Helpers are given you in many forms, although upon the altar they are one.

There is only one content—love—but it is expressed in many forms. More specifically here, the content is the Atonement principle: the separation from love never happened.

(1:4) Beyond each one [form] there is a Thought of God, and this will never change.

This is the Thought of Atonement that reflects the Love of God within the mind's dream.

(1:5) But they [these forms] have names which differ for a time, for time needs symbols, being itself unreal.

It is too overwhelming for us to be in the Presence of God's Love, so we need It to be expressed in a form we can relate to without fear. These forms are the helpers.

(1:6) Their names are legion, but we will not go beyond the names the course itself employs.

The biblical reference in the first phrase pertains to the devil, the "unclean spirit" mentioned in Mark 5:9. Here Jesus takes the same word and turns its meaning upside down. The names of these helpers of God are "legion," meaning they are countless. *A Course in Miracles* uses two names—Jesus and the Holy Spirit—but there are many, many others. None matters as such, however, as long as it symbolizes a non-ego presence of love beyond our self.

(1:7-9) God does not help because He knows no need. But He creates all Helpers of His Son while he believes his fantasies are true. Thank God for them for they will lead you home.

God is not the form of the help, although we may cherish such a concept. Recall that there is nothing in need of help because nothing happened. Nonetheless, within the dream we need help because we believe something did happen—*us*.

Helpers is capitalized, which means these are not the forms; for example, God did not create Jesus as a body. The Helper God created is love, which does not help; nor does it teach, since it does not know need of learning (W-pI.193.1-2). Indeed, God does not do anything. He simply is. However, since we made helpers into special idols, we need the right-minded corrections that translate the abstract Thought of God and His Atonement into forms we can accept and relate to. Jesus is one of these.

(2:1-3) The name of *Jesus* is the name of one who was a man but saw the face of Christ in all his brothers and remembered God. So he became identified with *Christ*, a man no longer, but at one with God. The man was an illusion, for he seemed to be a separate being, walking by himself, within a body that appeared to hold his self from Self, as all illusions do.

This tells us that the form—the person the world has called Jesus—is an illusion. He must be because he has been regarded as a separate body with a personality. The reality of Jesus, however, is not part of homo sapiens. Indeed, this reality is not even called Jesus, which is a name used to identify a presence within the dream that expresses the egoless Love of God, a resplendence of Love's light that is beyond the artificial light of the ego's world of specialness. Yet despite the illusion, we need a figure—a person—who represents the antithesis of what we regard ourselves to be: "the home of evil, darkness and sin" (W-pI.93.1:1); a correction in a form we can accept and recognize: a form who represents the home of light, joy, and peace (W-pI.93).

(2:4) Yet who can save unless he sees illusions and then identifies them as what they are?

The non-specific Thought of God is of no help if we do not experience it as applicable to our lives. Since we think of ourselves as a body, the Thought of God must be experienced as a body that shares our language. That is why It appeared as Jesus, among so many others.

(2:5-6) Jesus remains a Savior because he saw the false without accepting it as true. And Christ needed his form that He might appear to men and save them from their own illusions.

---

* *The Gifts of God*, pp. 82-83.

Repeating the central concept, the form of Jesus is nothing. What matters is the thought behind the form, the source behind the symbol. Paragraph 5 below refers to Jesus' "little life on earth." The figure of Jesus the world worships and whom we think of as author of this course is an illusion, a symbol of the Thought of Love that is the true Source, not only of Jesus but all of us. The only difference between us is that we still identify with the ego as source—a thought of separation, guilt, and hate.

This concept is difficult to relate to because if Jesus is an illusion, so are we. Faced with this threat, it becomes mandatory to make him real. Perhaps we would like a nicer Jesus than the one we grew up with, but under no circumstances do we want him taken from us. Students like the Jesus of *A Course in Miracles* because he is kind—he does not rant and rave, accuse and blame; he does not believe in suffering and sacrifice, nor demand things of us. Yet this kind Jesus is also illusory. That does not mean he is not helpful, and it certainly does not mean we should not go to him for help. However, we must eventually realize that the need to see him as real is our need to see ourselves that way. This is important to understand, for the need keeps us rooted in the idea that there is an actual Jesus. Again, he tells us in this passage that he is not real. This is implied in the Course itself, but could not be more explicitly stated than it is here.

(3:1) In his complete identification with the Christ—the perfect Son of God, His one creation and His happiness, forever like Himself and one with Him—Jesus became what all of you must be.

Jesus is the name we give to one of the seemingly separated fragments of the Sonship that remembered completely—the one who said the ego lies and the Holy Spirit speaks truth. It does not matter *when* he did it, because linear time is an illusion. What does matter is that we speak of Jesus as a symbol for what all of us want to become. Just as in Helen's lovely poem "A Jesus Prayer,"* we want to become like him. This means we want to make the same choice he did—not to live like him in *form*, but in the *content* of the mind's capacity to choose again, and correctly. We thus ultimately want to be like the non-specific thought of love that manifested as Jesus.

(3:2-5) He led the way for you to follow him. He leads you back to God because he saw the road before him, and he followed it. He made a clear distinction, still obscure to you, between the false and true. He offered you a final demonstration that it is impossible to kill God's Son; nor can his life in any way be changed by sin and evil, malice, fear or death.

This is a reference to the biblical story that, regardless of its historical inaccuracy in many respects, has been revered as true. The crucifixion of Jesus is the great Western myth, whose right-minded content offers a demonstration that you cannot destroy the Love of God. Remove the symbolism and mythological imagery, and the core of the story clearly emerges: you cannot kill God's Son. This, too, is the Course's message: "Not one note in Heaven's song was missed" (T-26.V.5:4). Nothing happened; nothing was changed. Jesus, as symbol, thus illuminates the powerlessness of the ego to offset truth. The ego's only power is what the decision-making part of the mind gives it. When belief in it is withdrawn, the ego is without power. Thus sin, evil, fear, and death are nothing; they, along with the ego, disappear back into the nothingness from which they came. Jesus, then, symbolizes the power of Christ—Who we are—while the powerlessness of the ego is who we thought we were. The teacher's manual makes the same point: since Jesus completed the journey, why would we not follow him? (M-23.5)

(4:1) And therefore all your sins have been forgiven because they carried no effects at all.

By saying the ego has no power, we are saying there is no sin. The ego can bluster and bellow, but it is nothing, doing nothing. The figure of Jesus highlights this nothingness, and we need to relate, not to him *per se*, but to the thought system he represents: nothing of the ego can affect God's Love or remove from us the remembrance of Who we are as Christ. We thus want to identify with the Atonement that was not his alone, but all of ours as God's one Son.

We have within us two thought systems: the falsity of the ego and the truth of the Holy Spirit. Jesus is telling us here that he made the choice that is open to all of us in our everyday world of special relationships. It is not important what Jesus supposedly did or did not do. Instead, we should think only of the thought system he represents—choosing against the ego. We need to practice diligently, that we may come to realize our sins had no effect: we have not separated from anyone; no one has separated from us. Looking at the world through Jesus' eyes of shared interests brings this happy realization home to us.

(4:2-4) And so they were but dreams. Arise with him who showed you this because you owe him this who shared your dreams that they might be dispelled. And shares them still, to be at one with you.

As we have seen, resurrection in *A Course in Miracles* has nothing to do with a physical body, or with a post-crucifixion event (M-28). It is awakening from the dream of death, the choice against the ego and for the Atonement that places us in the real world. And so Jesus tells us: "Arise with me and awaken." He shares our dreams by standing outside them, helping us realize the unreality of our lives. He is within the split mind that sleeps, yet knows it but dreams. The world, however, brought Jesus into its dream as if he could share it. Yet, our reality forever lies beyond it, and therefore Jesus did not share his life in a world that but dreams of life. He remains in our minds, that when we choose to go to him we may see all this for what it is. Thus our dreams do not have to be forgiven; merely looked at and gone beyond. We do nothing with sin but see its true nature—a fragile veil with no power to hold back Christ's light.

(5:1-2) Is he the Christ? O yes, along with you.

Jesus is identified with Christ, but so are we. He is an important symbol for us who remain asleep, but outside the dream he has no name but one—Christ—the same as ours.

(5:3-4) His little life on earth was not enough to teach the mighty lesson that he learned for all of you. [Not some or many—*all*.] He will remain with you to lead you from the hell you made to God.

What remains with us is not the historical Jesus, but the thought of love which Jesus reflects. We call that thought by a specific name because we call ourselves by specific names. Yet we are reminded not to confuse symbol with source, form with content. Jesus is not a man running around in the mind speaking to us, any more than he was running around in Helen's mind. What is in the mind—what is in *everyone's* mind—is the non-specific, abstract Thought of Love, the memory of Who we are as God's one Son. To the extent to which we identify ourselves with a specific self, we will, again, identify that thought as a specific self named Jesus, or any other name we choose. This is natural, as long as we think we are specific. Yet we need to remember that we want to grow and become like him, as in these words from Helen's aforementioned poem: "A child, a man and then a spirit."* We do not want to remain little children, continually asking our big brother for help, for we will never grow to remember our identity as spirit if the relationship remains on this level. We need to keep in mind that our ultimate goal is to truly become like Jesus, sharing with him the nameless Thought of Love.

(5:5) And when you join your will with his, your sight will be his vision, for the eyes of Christ are shared.

As I release my guilt and false perceptions, I automatically join with Jesus' perceptions. When I let go of one, I automatically choose the other, for *one or the other* is the principle of the split mind. If I look at you through the eyes of specialness, I have made the ego real—the thought system I am reinforcing. When I realize the pain this causes me and choose to let the ego's perception go, I automatically see through Jesus' eyes—no longer seeing others as separate, but sharing the same ego and Thought of Atonement.

(5:6) Walking with him is just as natural as walking with a brother whom you knew since you were born, for such indeed he is.

In other words, our relationship with Jesus is not in the body, but in the mind that is outside time and space. His Thought of Love is always with us. To repeat, when we identify with a specific self we attach that Thought to a specific self. As the text says:

> You cannot even think of God without a body, or in some form you think you recognize (T-18.VIII.1:7).

---

* "A Jesus Prayer," *The Gifts of God*, p. 82.

Since we see ourselves as bodies, we see God and His representatives as bodies, too. That is when we give the Thought a name—e.g., Jesus. In the end, however, we want to transcend our personal identity, which means transcending his personal identity. We are both the same Thought; we only think we are different from him.

(5:7) Some bitter idols have been made of him who would be only brother to the world.

You need not know much history to understand Jesus' words here. These are not merely bitter idols of hatred, judgment, persecution, and exclusion, but of special love as well. People have always made Jesus special and different. After all, he is said to be the only Son of God, which is why he goes to great lengths in the early pages of the text to shatter this specialness, stating he is different from us in time, but not in reality (T-1.II.3:10–4:1).

(5:8-9) Forgive him your illusions, and behold how dear a brother he would be to you. For he will set your mind at rest at last and carry it with you unto your God.

In the text, too, Jesus asks us to forgive the illusions we projected onto him (see, for example, T-19.IV-B.6,8; T-20.II.4). Whether illusions of special hate or special love, they cloud over who he really is to us: a mirror of our Self. To paraphrase lines from the workbook, he the end we seek, and he the means by which we come to him (W-pII.302.2:3). The end we seek is the Love of God, which translates into Jesus' form to become the means by which we come to him, the abstract Thought of Love in our minds.

Jesus therefore asks us to let go of our illusions and misconceptions—based on the past—so that we may see him as he is: neither Christian nor Jew; not as anything but a symbol of love representing the Thought of Love we are. Yet he cannot lead us to this Thought unless we free him from the prison of illusions we projected onto him, and so we need to set aside two thousand years of blood-drenched specialness and not place it on the figure of Jesus we find in the Course. If we do, we lose sight of Who he is in truth—our Self. Moreover, it takes vigilance to stay on the right path, for it is tempting to fall back onto old concepts. Thus the ego does not want to lose the biblical Jesus because that image enables us to hold onto our separated self.

(6:1-3) Is he God's only Helper? No, indeed. For Christ takes many forms with different names until their oneness can be recognized.

It is important to remember that Jesus is not the only form. He is *one* form, and in the end the forms disappear into the One. We need separate forms only to awaken us from the dream and lead us home, but until we recognize their oneness we need different helpers, in different forms, with different names.

(6:4-5) But Jesus is for you the bearer of Christ's single message of the Love of God. You need no other.

In this paragraph we see Jesus alternating between two thoughts: "I am not the only one and you can do this without me. Yet I can help you if you let me." In the manual for teachers, Jesus discusses this same idea—mine are the words you can accept, love, and understand (M-23.7:1). He is assuming that most people who read this book have grown up in a Christian world—whether believing Christians or not. For them, then, Jesus is the great symbol of God's Love in the true sense, as he is also the great symbol of His Love in the special sense, the source of bitter idols.

Asking Jesus' help, however, does not mean that we must ask him, and that we are errant children who will not reach Heaven if we do not. He is hardly threatening us. The right-minded way of approaching this issue is to examine the role Jesus has played in our lives. We need to examine our past experiences of him, and if they have reflected specialness—as they have for most people—we have unforgiveness we need to undo. This is accomplished when we let illusions of him go—as he said to us in the previous paragraph—so that his true nature as Helper can emerge.

But now Jesus says:

(6:6) It is possible to read his words and benefit from them without accepting him into our life.

In the end, it is Jesus' message alone that is important. The message and practice of *A Course in Miracles* stand apart from him, but do not stand apart from going within to ask help of our inner teacher—a mandatory part of the curriculum—but this need not be in a Christian context. Yet the Course does come in such a context, and Jesus is the first person speaking throughout. However, again, we do not want to fall into the trap of the churches—that if we do not confess Jesus as our Lord we will not get to Heaven. That is certainly not the point.

Now Jesus returns to the other side:

(6:7) Yet he would help you yet a little more if you will share your pains and joys with Him, and leave them both to find the peace of God.

Jesus would help all the more if we went to him for help, bringing our joys and pains, loves and hates—to him there is no difference. Seeing the world as the source of joy and happiness is no different from seeing it as the source of pain. We thus bring both to the altar, so we can be taught to find and then know the peace of God.

And one more time:

(6:8) Yet still it is his lesson most of all that he would have you learn, and it is this:

The bottom line is not the person of Jesus, but his message of Atonement:

(6:9) *There is no death because the Son of God is like his Father.*

Death came into existence when we believed we were different from God. From that perception of differences—the belief in separation—came the first judgment, the origin of our specialness: the belief in sin, the experience of guilt, the feared punishment of which death is the ultimate expression. Since we believe we seized life from God, we inevitably believe He will seize it back—thus is death made real.

(6:10) *Nothing you can do can change Eternal Love.*

A lovely statement of the Atonement principle—nothing we can think, feel, or believe can change reality.

(6:11) *Forget your dreams of sin and guilt, and come with me instead to share the resurrection of God's Son.*

In our dreams we believe we have changed Eternal Love and made it into special love. Yet these are only dreams, and *resurrection* is awakening from the dream of death. We enter the real world by saying without reservation: "I no longer want the ego's crucifixion." And so we turn our backs on what is false and accept the truth of resurrection. Jesus thus says to us: "I want you to become like me because you *are* like me." The *you* that is like him, and the *he* that you are like, is one unseparated Self. That is why this final line is so important, and goes to the heart of the daily practice of the Course:

(6:12) *And bring with you all those whom He has sent to you to care for as I care for you.*

Bring everyone, for God has "sent" us all people—everyone we think of, meet, have ever known, or anticipate knowing in the future. *Everyone*. If we want to share the resurrection's thought system of love and awaken with Jesus from the dream of separation, we cannot exclude a single person. In effect, Jesus says: "The same caring love and gentle kindness you feel from me, I ask you to extend to everyone, without exception. If you do not, it is because you have not accepted it from me, for love, kindness, and gentleness are one, embracing all God's Sons." Thus the core message of *A Course in Miracles* is the all-inclusive nature of forgiveness, which undoes our belief in separate and special interests. And as we forgive, we joyously waken to share the resurrection of God's one Son.

6. THE HOLY SPIRIT

We will see here that Jesus says about the Holy Spirit what he just said about himself.

(1:1) Jesus is the manifestation of the *Holy Spirit*, Whom he called down upon the earth after he ascended into Heaven, or became completely identified with the Christ, the Son of God as He created Him.

The first sentence is borrowed from the opening of the Acts of the Apostles, where Jesus is described as having ascended to Heaven and called forth the Holy Spirit upon his disciples (Acts 1:1-11). This ascension, however, has nothing to do with the Church mythology of bodily ascension. It is lovely imagery, as long as you see it as theological and not historical. Jesus teaches here that ascending to Heaven symbolizes our complete identification with Christ—letting the ego go and entering the real world. Jesus' acceptance of the Atonement makes him the manifestation of the Holy Spirit, and, as we have seen, his is the name we give to a form that represents God's perfect Love. The memory of that Love, which we took with us when we began the dream of separation, is the Holy Spirit, Who reminds us of our Identity as God's one Son. We personify the thought of oneness as Jesus because we, as bodies, personify separation. We name the form, mistakenly believing it is reality, and so Jesus corrects our distorted thinking.

The Holy Spirit thus symbolizes the abstract, non-specific Thought of God's Love in our sleeping minds. Within the world's dream, Jesus is a symbol of that symbol. If we remember that words are "symbols of symbols" and therefore "twice removed from reality" (M-21.1:9-10), Jesus can be thought of as a symbol for the Holy Spirit's symbol of reality, and thus is twice removed from the truth. That is why we need to be vigilant against worshipping the form, even though we need it to reverse the ego's insane journey and return home—undoing all thoughts of separation and specialness. At the end of this section we will be asked to become Jesus' manifestation, and therefore to become a symbol of a symbol of a symbol.

(1:2-3) The Holy Spirit, being a creation of the one Creator, creating with Him and in His likeness or spirit, is eternal and has never changed. He was "called down upon the earth" in the sense that it was now possible to accept Him and to hear His Voice.

Jesus reinterprets what it means to "call down" the Holy Spirit, meaning that he teaches us about this Symbol of the split mind's Thought of love, making Him more accessible to us. It is possible to accept Him and hear His Voice because we now have Its concrete manifestation in the dream. This Voice is an illusion, yet it remains the only way we can relate to the Thought that is not of this world. Remember, God and His Love know nothing about the world, and so we need symbols to represent that Love—the Holy Spirit being the Thought, and Jesus Its manifestation. Yet these symbols should never be confused with their source.

(1:4-5) His is the Voice for God, and has therefore taken form. This form is not His reality, which God alone knows along with Christ, His real Son, Who is part of Him.

The content—the Holy Spirit's reality—is love. It does not have a name, a voice, or even a function, and so the form we call the Holy Spirit—used in the Course to describe the loving Presence in our split minds—is an illusion. Therefore, as we mentioned in the last section about Jesus, God and Christ alone know Who the Holy Spirit is. This means we do not know, for we know only illusions. Yet because we are symbols of separation we need a symbol of oneness; however, Jesus alerts us to the trap of worshipping the symbol. We refer to the Holy Spirit as a Person, Teacher, Mediator, Corrector, Helper, Voice, but these are not Who He is. Similarly, *Jesus* is only the name we give to a concrete manifestation of that Presence. Once again, we need these symbols because we need a correction for the symbol we made ourselves to be. However, the correction is vitiated if we do not move beyond the symbols to the truth.

(2:1) The Holy Spirit is described throughout the course as giving us the answer to the separation and bringing the plan of the Atonement to us, establishing our particular part in it and showing us exactly what it is.

6. The Holy Spirit

In a lovely passage, Jesus explains that our particular part is forgiving our special relationships:

> To each who walks this earth in seeming solitude is a savior given... (T-20.IV.5:3).

The savior is you—whoever the *you* is in my life, beginning with my family, and encompassing everyone I meet or even think about. My special function—my part in the plan of the Atonement—is to forgive those special ones I have written into my script as foils in my ego's strategy of projection. This is not planned by the Holy Spirit, for He is merely the right-mind's loving and light-filled Presence to Whom we bring the darkness of our special relationships. In an earlier section, Jesus spoke of guilt and forgiveness lying side by side on the altar (C-4.6:7-8). In that context, the Holy Spirit can be seen as the Name given to the love that guides us to the altar, teaching us to bring the special relationship to the light of forgiveness.

(2:2) He has established Jesus as the leader in carrying out His plan since he was the first to complete his own part perfectly.

This makes it sound as if the Holy Spirit is God's General, Who establishes Jesus as His first lieutenant. These are helpful symbols to be sure, but we need be careful not to take them as literally true. Jesus says "he was the first to complete his own part perfectly"—this is to be taken symbolically as well. Think of the spiritual specialness that would erupt from taking this literally, that two thousand years ago the man Jesus was the first to have accepted the Atonement. What about Buddha and other holy people who lived before? This specialness trap is easily avoided, however, if we do not put Jesus' words in a linear framework, especially in view of his reminders throughout the Course that linear time is illusory.

We cannot comprehend the meaning of these statements because Jesus is not speaking of the world. Accepting the Atonement does not occur in time and space, but in the time-less mind that is the locus of decision. We think it occurs in the body because we think of ourselves as temporal/spatial creatures. And so, *Jesus* is the name we give to a *thought* that first accepted the Atonement. *When* in time that happened is anyone's guess, but be aware that the ego is primed to seize on this and make "Jesus" someone special—Christianity's tragic error that resulted in people proclaiming, in effect: "My savior is better than your savior."

(2:3) All power in Heaven and earth is therefore given him and he will share it with you when you have completed yours.

This is the same statement that is repeated several times in the text.* It is based on Matthew's gospel where the resurrected Jesus says that all power in Heaven and earth has been given unto him (Matthew 28:18). Jesus reverses this in the text, saying all power in Heaven and earth is given unto *us*—because we are of one mind. Thus he teaches us to insist not on his being different from us, but on our inherent sameness as decision-making minds that can choose between God and the ego.

(2:4) The Atonement principle was given to the Holy Spirit long before Jesus set it in motion.

The Atonement principle occurred in the same instant the separation came into existence. When the *tiny, mad idea* of separation from God seemed to happen, the split mind fragmented into three parts: the wrong mind that hears the ego, the right mind that hears the Holy Spirit, and the decision maker that chooses between them. The "plan" was thus set at the beginning, but it is not really the Holy Spirit's doing, as He, again, is only the *non-specific* Presence of truth in the mind to which we go for help. Yet even when we do not avail ourselves of this help, it is there.

The plan was "set in motion" when the figure of Jesus appeared, in the sense that there was now a tangible symbol to which the world could relate. Since linear time is an illusion, it is essential, as already discussed, not to be bound by the limited perspective of what we think of as history, and to keep in mind that *A Course in Miracles* was "given" to a Western—i.e., Christian—world. All we need know is that the abstract principle of Atonement is in our minds, and that Jesus is for us its greatest symbol. That is why he tells us in the text that he is the Atonement (T-1.III.4:1)—the manifestation of the Atonement principle that says the separation from God's Love never happened.

---

* See T-5.II.9:2; T-7.III.1:3; T-14.XI.2:4; T-26.VI.2:3.

(3:1) The Holy Spirit is described as the remaining Communication Link between God and His separated Sons.

The text teaches that the Holy Spirit is the link to truth in our minds (T-25.I), or, as the text says later, He is the "present memory" that undoes the past and future, returning us to the eternal present (T-28.I). Thus He is the Link between the ego thought system and Heaven. At the beginning, therefore, His Love basically said to us: "If you choose Me instead of the ego, I will take you home—the home you never left—because I am the Link."

(3:2-3) In order to fulfill this special function the Holy Spirit has assumed a dual function. He knows because He is part of God; He perceives because He was sent to save humanity.

In other words, He is a switch-hitter Who hits from both sides of the mind's plate! Once again, these are symbols that speak to us; but we should not regard them as anything more than that.

(3:4-5) He is the great correction principle; the bringer of true perception, the inherent power of the vision of Christ. He is the light in which the forgiven world is perceived; in which the face of Christ alone is seen.

The ego has a plan to keep us mindless, thereby keeping its own thought system intact. This needs correction—the plan of the Atonement—and the Holy Spirit is the symbol of this plan to undo the ego. To repeat our earlier discussion, we say *He* because we think of ourselves as persons. However, the mind is not part of homo sapiens. We are simply thoughts that antedate form. Since we think of ourselves as persons, we think of God, Jesus, and the Holy Spirit as Persons, too. Moreover, the ego has a myth that says we sinned against God, Who will punish us by dispatching His vengeful and wrathful General—the Holy Spirit—loaded with weapons poised to destroy us because we are bad. Thus Jesus kindly gives us a myth that says we have not sinned and God is not angry. We simply made a mistake, and our Father loves us so much He created the Holy Spirit and sent Him into our minds to bring us home—gently and lovingly. It is a comforting tale, what a caring parent would tell a child before it goes to bed. Yet it remains a story, a correction for the terrifying myth that uses the ego's symbols to communicate a message of forgiveness.

(3:6-9) He never forgets the Creator or His creation. He never forgets the Son of God. He never forgets you. And He brings the Love of your Father to you in an eternal shining that will never be obliterated because God has put it there.

Just as Heaven's light can never be extinguished, the memory of this light—its reflection in our minds—cannot be eradicated. While the above words are lovely and their imagery inspiring, it is only their content that is important. This can be applied on a practical level when, having a bad day—being angry, depressed, or riddled with guilt—we remind ourselves that our discomfort comes from our fear of love, which is not a sin but a mistake:

> Son of God, you have not sinned, but you have been much mistaken (T-10.V.6:1).

The Holy Spirit manifests this loving Presence, the memory of God's Love that says our mistake has had no effect on reality, though guilt mistakenly tells us it has.

(4:1-2) The Holy Spirit abides in the part of your mind that is part of the Christ Mind. He represents your Self and your Creator, Who are One.

There is no division in Heaven. The workbook teaches that "nowhere does the Father end, the Son begin as something separate from Him" (W-pI.132.12:4). That unity—a "Oneness joined as One" (T-25.I.7:1)—is beyond our comprehension. Yet we can understand the symbolic reflection of that Oneness, which is that you and I are one in purpose, for we share the same insanity *and* sanity. This recognition will lead us home. Again, the Holy Spirit represents Who we are in truth, for He is the Presence in our right minds that links us to the Mind of Christ.

(4:3-7) He speaks for God and also for you, being joined with Both. And therefore it is He Who proves Them One. He seems to be a Voice, for in that form He speaks God's Word to you. He seems to be a Guide through a far country, for you need that form of help. He seems to be whatever meets the needs you think you have.

6. The Holy Spirit

We have just read that the Holy Spirit is a link. Consider that when we think of a loved one who has died, we are filled with emotion—love, hate, mourning, joy. The memory links us to the person who is no longer physically present. Thus it is with the Holy Spirit. We believe we threw God away, but we retain the memory of His Presence in our minds—God's Voice—which unites us with our Source.

Note the repetition of the word *seems* in the above sentences. The Holy Spirit seems to be the One to meet our needs, but that is not Who He is. Remember that the overriding theme in this clarification of terms is symbol and source, form and content. Once more, it is imperative that we use symbols of love as long as we think of ourselves as symbols of separation—i.e., bodies. Thus we see the Holy Spirit as a specific Person and Jesus as older brother and teacher. Yet, we must eventually move beyond the symbols to what they represent, realizing that Jesus is only thought—no more a person than we are—and the Holy Spirit is not a Voice or Guide, but the Thought that represents the Oneness of God and His Son.

If we do not understand symbolism, we run the risk of making symbols into reality. It is therefore of vital importance that we identify with the thought behind the symbol. Otherwise, our progress in this course will be limited. We are a *thought* in the Mind of God, not a *body*. We are a *thought* of love, and Jesus is a *symbol* of that thought. Whatever needs we think we have, we will experience the Holy Spirit as meeting them; but in the end, He only symbolizes the light that guides our journey through the ego's far country, leading God's prodigal Son safely home at last.

(4:8-10) But He is not deceived when you perceive your self entrapped in needs you do not have. It is from these He would deliver you. It is from these that He would make you safe.

It is from our specialness needs—to be treated fairly and noticed as special—that the Holy Spirit will free us, when we bring them to Him. These needs lead to danger because they come from guilt that demands punishment. We thus believe the world will hurt us and, moreover, we want the world to hurt us because that proves guilt real—the ego requires that we deny our guilt and see it only in others: when you hurt me, you are the obvious sinner, not me. However, Jesus teaches us that specialness hurts only us, and is therefore not what we truly want.

(5:1-3) You are His manifestation in this world. Your brother calls to you to be His Voice along with him. Alone he cannot be the Helper of God's Son for he alone is functionless.

Having no ego voice in his mind, Jesus is the symbol of God's Love. When healed, we become symbols of that Love, too. Thus the functions of Jesus and the Holy Spirit are interchangeable, being but different forms of the one inner Teacher—the Presence of truth in the mind to which we bring our illusions. Jesus is no longer in a body and, as the manifestation of the Holy Spirit, he asks us to become his bodily manifestation in the world. As he says in the text and the workbook:

> Teach not that I died in vain. Teach rather that I did not die by demonstrating that I live in you (T-11.VI.7:3-4).

> You are my voice, my eyes, my feet, my hands through which I save the world (W-pI.rV.9:3).

It is clearly not the external world that is saved, but the inner world of the Son's mind. Simply stated, Jesus wants us to learn the lesson that the ego is wrong and the Holy Spirit right, so we may teach it.

(5:4) But joined with you he is the shining Savior of the world...

When we join with Jesus we become that "shining Savior"—the symbol of Christ in this world—living in an egoless state of mind. This is reflected here by a life that is gentle, kind, and helpful, in which we see no one as different—better or worse—than anyone else. Again:

(5:4-7) But joined with you he is the shining Savior of the world, Whose part in its redemption you have made complete. He offers thanks to you as well as him for you arose with him when he began to save the world. And you will be with him when time is over and no trace remains of dreams of spite in which you dance to death's thin melody. For in its place the hymn to God is heard a little while.

When Jesus awakened from the dream of death and accepted the Atonement, we were with him because minds are joined—"When I am healed I am not healed alone" (W-pI.137). Recall that we should not look at this from an historical or linear point of view, or we will become trapped in spiritual specialness. The Atonement's acceptance in the mind of God's Son occurs out of time. Indeed, it has already occurred and is fully present in us. Thus we have already awakened from the dream of death, ushering God's Sons into the real world where the forgotten song is remembered. When any part of the Sonship awakened, it was accepted for all because minds are one. However, we still retain the choice within our fragmented dreams to believe we can keep that acceptance apart from us by remaining asleep.

(5:8) And then the Voice is gone, no longer to take form but to return to the eternal formlessness of God.

The eternal formlessness of God is undivided and undifferentiated oneness. This means there is no trinity in Heaven—God, Christ, and Holy Spirit are symbols—but only the Godhead, to use Meister Eckhart's term that takes us beyond the idea of a personal God. At the journey's end, the Voice is gone as the Holy Spirit disappears, "no longer to take form but to return to the eternal formlessness of God." This is the same process Jesus speaks of early in the text when he discusses our final awakening: "... it is [the Holy Spirit's] special function to return you to eternity and remain to bless your creations there" (T-5.VI.12:6)—a lovely image that expresses the ineffable truth of perfect Oneness. As we read in the text:

> Heaven is not a place nor a condition. It is merely an awareness of perfect Oneness, and the knowledge that there is nothing else; nothing outside this Oneness, and nothing else within (T-18.VI.1:5-6).

EPILOGUE

We come now to the lovely Epilogue, written in blank verse. It seems as if Jesus saves his most poetic words for the end, with each of the Course books concluding beautifully and inspirationally—form and content—and it is an injustice to passages like these to explain them, because the imagery is so much richer in meaning than any commentary. Nonetheless, I will discuss it line-by-line, before presenting it without interruption. Although this concludes the clarification of terms, in a sense it can be seen as the conclusion to *A Course in Miracles* itself—perhaps not on the same level as the text's final vision, but still a beautiful expression of the journey's end. The Epilogue was written in the Christmas season of 1975, and contains five biblical references—more than is found elsewhere, except in the early pages of the text. The last reference, to Jesus as "the morning star"—the shining symbol taken from Revelation—is a fitting conclusion to our journey from darkness to the light that awaits us at Heaven's gate.

(1:1) Forget not once this journey is begun the end is certain.

Jesus tells us in the text that "The outcome is as certain as God" (T-2.III.3:10; T-4.II.5:8) because there is no journey. We need not worry about a final outcome since nothing happened and nothing changed. We remain "at home in God, dreaming of exile" (T-10.I.2:1), and dreams have no effect upon reality.

(1:2-3) Doubts along the way will come and go and go to come again. Yet is the ending sure.

Despite our vacillations between the ego and the Holy Spirit, we will surely awaken because we are already awake. Jesus told us in the text that this is a "journey without distance" (T-8.VI.9:7), and so the beginning and ending are one, for the journey ends where it began. We can invoke the words of Revelation here, where Jesus says: "I am Alpha and Omega…the beginning and the end" (Revelation 21:6). Jesus would tell us in *A Course in Miracles* that there is no space between the two, because nothing ever came between God and His Son.

(1:4-5) No one can fail to do what God appointed him to do. When you forget, remember that you walk with Him and with His Word upon your heart.

The *Word of God* means Atonement, which is the Holy Spirit's correction for the ego. It also can be seen as the memory of truth—the perfect Oneness of God and Christ—that we took with us into the dream. This Thought of Atonement, God's Word, is always within our right minds where it is personified by the Holy Spirit.

(1:6) Who could despair when hope like this is his?

We despair when we separate ourselves from hope. Yet Jesus' reassurance in the text comforts us: "This need not be" (T-4.IV). Whenever we are depressed, anxious, fearful, or guilty, we need but remember: "This need not be." We choose our ego feelings because the dream sustains our individual identity, and thus we do not take the hand of our Helper. However, we can and will choose otherwise.

(1:7) Illusions of despair may seem to come, but learn how not to be deceived by them.

As we saw in the manual, Jesus asks us not to despair because of limitations: "It is your function to escape from them, but not to be without them" (M-26.4:2). Reflecting this same gentleness, he asks us in the text not to be upset by the shadows surrounding our willingness (T-18.IV.2:4-5), saying, in effect: "Do not be upset when you have illusions of despair or terror. You will learn how to let them go for I will teach you to watch them without judgment or guilt, enabling them gently to pass away." Illusions become real only when we are afraid and want to do something about them. Then hope vanishes. Jesus helps us look at the ego's dream in all its forms—positive and negative—and see them as the same. A dream, after all, remains a dream, and therein lies our hope.

(1:8-9) Behind each one [illusion of despair] there is reality and there is God. Why would you wait for this and trade it for illusions, when His Love is but an instant farther on the road where all illusions end?

Jesus asks us why we make such monstrosities of our ego thoughts, when we can so easily move past them to the Love of God: "Would you trade this experience of Love for these silly things in yourself or others?"

(1:10-11) The end *is* sure and guaranteed by God. Who stands before a lifeless image when a step away the Holy of the Holies opens up an ancient door that leads beyond the world?

"The Holy of Holies" is the biblical term (Exodus 26:33) for the most sacred place in Judaism—the locus of the Ark of the Covenant that contained the two tablets Moses was said to have brought down from Mount Sinai. They were kept in the sanctuary of the temple where only the priestly caste was allowed to go. Jesus uses this as a symbol for the gate through which we pass, and which opens the ancient door leading to Heaven.

(2:1-3) You *are* a stranger here. But you belong to Him Who loves you as He loves Himself. Ask but my help to roll the stone away, and it is done according to His Will.

Throughout *A Course in Miracles*, Jesus tells us we are strangers in this world (see, for example, W-pI.160; W-pII.262) because we belong to God Who loves us the way He loves Himself. Jesus is also referring to the resurrection story in the gospels when the stone was rolled away from his tomb. Here, of course, it is used symbolically—that we ask his help to roll away the stone of the ego's thought system of crucifixion and death. When we take his hand we move beyond the ego, in accordance with God's Will that His Son is one—not separated, crucified, or a child of death.

(2:4-6) We *have* begun the journey. Long ago the end was written in the stars and set into the Heavens with a shining Ray that held it safe within eternity and through all time as well. And holds it still unchanged, unchanging and unchangeable.

This is similar to the imagery of the lovely passage near the end of the text:

> The Thought God holds of you is like a star, unchangeable in an eternal sky. So high in Heaven is it set that those outside of Heaven know not it is there (T-30.III.8:4-5).

Even when the separation seemed to occur and things appeared to fall apart, the truth remained aloft as a shining star, for God held us lovingly in His Heaven, ensuring our return to the Heart we never left.

(3:1) Be not afraid.

These were the words the biblical Jesus said to his disciples when he appeared after his crucifixion. It is what he tells us in *A Course in Miracles*: "Do not be afraid of the ego—yours or anyone else's—for it is nothing, lacking all power to put you to sleep, or prevent your awakening from the dream. How can you be afraid of nothing?"

(3:2-4) We only start again an ancient journey long ago begun that but seems new. We have begun again upon a road we travelled on before and lost our way a little while. And now we try again.

This is another of Jesus' comforting reassurances. "The very fact you study my course," he tells us, "is proof you take this journey with me. Let me help you, and do not despair or give in to the ego's temptations to have you believe it is more powerful than God. It is not. Do not be afraid, therefore, for you are safe in my love."

(3:5-7) Our new beginning has the certainty the journey lacked till now. Look up and see His Word among the stars, where He has set your Name along with His. Look up and find your certain destiny the world would hide but God would have you see.

The world would not want us to look up to Heaven's sky and see the shining star bearing our Name. It would have us see only our little name here, and all others that betray, abandon, and reject us. Thus the ego sees littleness instead of our magnitude as Christ.

(4:1) Let us wait here in silence, and kneel down an instant in our gratitude to him Who called to us and helped us hear His Call.

To "wait in silence" does not mean to do nothing. Jesus speaks only of silencing the ego's voice—its raucous shrieks and shrill cries of specialness: I need, I want, I demand. When we silence its voice, we will hear the Voice for God gently tell us Who we are. This course, therefore, is about silencing the ego, poetically expressed in these passages. Yet we cannot silence something until we first hear it, so Jesus teaches us to recognize the ego's voice, telling us that what we hear in others is a projection of the voice we made real inside—of separation, pain, judgment, and death. Learning to hear these words and thoughts at last, we gratefully choose against them. And then in silence we hear the Call that leads us home.

(4:2-4) And then let us arise and go in faith along the way to Him. Now we are sure we do not walk alone. For God is here, and with Him all our brothers.

In the beautiful Epilogue that ends the workbook, Jesus assures us that the Holy Spirit walks with us:

> Your Friend goes with you. You are not alone (W-ep.1:2-3).

He tells us we have learned the lessons, and are now to spend our lives putting them into practice with One Who will always be there to help us. At the workbook's very end, he says:

> …and of this be sure; that I will never leave you comfortless (W-ep.6:8).

Note again the word *all*—not just some, but *all* our brothers walk with us; otherwise, we walk the ego's path of specialness and death.

(4:5-6) Now we know that we will never lose the way again. The song begins again which had been stopped only an instant, though it seems to be unsung forever.

This refers to the brief instant when we believed we left God. Yet "not one note in Heaven's song was missed" (T-26.V.5:4): nothing happened, nothing changed—the song of God never lost its single melody.

(4:7) What is here begun will grow in life and strength and hope, until the world is still an instant and forgets all that the dream of sin had made of it.

It is not only that the mind is still, but so is the perceived world that reflects its stillness. We forget the world in the sense that it ceases to exist in our minds. The thought that held it in place, fulfilling the purpose of proving that sin is real, is gone, as are our thoughts and memories—there is nothing left to remember.

(5:1) Let us go out and meet the newborn world, knowing that Christ has been reborn in it, and that the holiness of this rebirth will last forever.

This is the real world, wherein Christ has been reborn. This has nothing to do with the external—the world is newborn because *I* am reborn. In the lesson "I will be still an instant and go home" (W-pI.182), Jesus speaks of the Child in us that yearns to go home. At some point on the journey we realize we are that reborn Child, and so our world is born anew from the ashes of pain, suffering, and death to become the pathway that returns us to eternity.

(5:2-3) We had lost our way but He has found it for us. Let us go and bid Him welcome Who returns to us to celebrate salvation and the end of all we thought we made.

We thought we made the world, but in reality nothing happened. Thus it is truly "a journey without distance" (T-8.VI.9:7).

(5:4) The morning star of this new day looks on a different world where God is welcomed and His Son with Him.

This is the real world, where there is no division or suffering. We are led to its welcoming gates by the light of our morning star Jesus, gentle companion and faithful guide on the journey.

(5:5-6) We who complete Him offer thanks to Him as He gives thanks to us. The Son is still, and in the quiet God has given him enters his home and is at peace at last.

Thus does the journey end. It began in conflict, and continued on a battleground drenched in blood. And now it is done. "The bloodied earth is cleansed" (T-26.IX.4:6) as our minds are gently healed. For an instant the blessing of forgiveness remains, until it disappears as well. We are still, as God takes the final step and lifts us home, where He would have us be (T-31.VIII.12:8).

Epilogue

Here now is the beautiful Epilogue in its entirety:

Forget not once this journey is begun the end is certain. Doubt along the way will come and go and go to come again. Yet is the ending sure. No one can fail to do what God appointed him to do. When you forget, remember that you walk with Him and with His Word upon your heart. Who could despair when hope like this is his? Illusions of despair may seem to come, but learn how not to be deceived by them. Behind each one there is reality and there is God. Why would you wait for this and trade it for illusions, when His Love is but an instant farther on the road where all illusions end? The end *is* sure and guaranteed by God. Who stands before a lifeless image when a step away the Holy of the Holies opens up an ancient door that leads beyond the world?

You *are* a stranger here. But you belong to Him Who loves you as He loves Himself. Ask but my help to roll the stone away, and it is done according to His Will. We *have* begun the journey. Long ago the end was written in the stars and set into the Heavens with a shining Ray that held it safe within eternity and through all time as well. And holds it still; unchanged, unchanging and unchangeable.

Be not afraid. We only start again an ancient journey long ago begun that but seems new. We have begun again upon a road we travelled on before and lost our way a little while. And now we try again. Our new beginning has the certainty the journey lacked till now. Look up and see His Word among the stars, where He has set your Name along with His. Look up and find your certain destiny the world would hide but God would have you see.

Let us wait here in silence, and kneel down an instant in our gratitude to Him Who called to us and helped us hear His Call. And then let us arise and go in faith along the way to Him. Now we are sure we do not walk alone. For God is here, and with Him all our brothers. Now we know that we will never lose the way again. The song begins again which had been stopped only an instant, though it seems to be unsung forever. What is here begun will grow in life and strength and hope, until the world is still an instant and forgets all that the dream of sin had made of it.

Let us go out and meet the newborn world, knowing that Christ has been reborn in it, and that the holiness of this rebirth will last forever. We had lost our way but He has found it for us. Let us go and bid Him welcome Who returns to us to celebrate salvation and the end of all we thought we made. The morning star of this new day looks on a different world where God is welcomed and His Son with Him. We who complete Him offer thanks to Him, as He gives thanks to us. The Son is still, and in the quiet God has given him enters his home and is at peace at last.

Index of References to *A Course in Miracles*®

TEXT

T-in.1:1-5	21
T-in.1:6-7	50
T-in.2:2-4	140
T-1.I.1	23
T-1.I.1:1	48, 101, 114
T-1.I.1:4	23, 24, 67, 68, 175
T-1.I.2:1–3:2	127
T-1.II.1:5	175
T-1.II.3:10-13; 4:1	31
T-1.II.3:10–4:1	230
T-1.II.6	12, 16
T-1.III.4:1	234
T-1.V.3:6	134
T-1.VII.1:4	179
T-2.III.3:10	21, 107, 147, 239
T-2.IV.1:2-5	149
T-2.IV.4	57
T-2.IV.4-5	57
T-2.IV.5	30
T-2.V.2	57
T-2.V.5:1	150
T-2.VI.5-6	35
T-2.VII.5:14	83
T-2.VII.7	155
T-2.VIII.2-5	105
T-3.I.4:1	36
T-3.I.8:2	80, 201
T-3.III.4:6	222
T-3.IV.2:1	201
T-3.IV.7:12	11
T-3.V.6:3	134, 177
T-3.VI.3:1	81, 132
T-4.II.5:2	37
T-4.II.5:8	21, 107, 239
T-4.II.11:8	193
T-4.III.4:6	131
T-4.III.7:10	186
T-4.IV	239
T-4.V.6:8-11	161
T-5.I.1-2	46
T-5.II.7:1-4	59
T-5.II.9:2	234
T-5.V.5:4-8	55
T-5.VI.3:5; 4:2	15, 204
T-5.VI.11:6-7	36
T-5.VI.12:6	237
T-6.V-C	112
T-7.I.6-7	29
T-7.III.1:3	234
T-7.VIII.3:11	126, 224
T-7.X	95
T-8.I.1:1-2	203
T-8.II	95
T-8.III.4:1	21, 109
T-8.V	37
T-8.V.5:4-6	169
T-8.VI.1-3	212
T-8.VI.9:4	171
T-8.VI.9:7	151, 219, 239, 241
T-8.VII.7:2	161, 222
T-9.III	125
T-9.VII.4	169
T-9.VIII	128, 176
T-10.I.2:1	173, 239
T-10.V.6:1	235
T-11.V	193
T-11.VI.7:3-4	4, 27, 236
T-11.VII.1	212
T-11.VIII.15	29
T-12.I	80, 194, 118
T-12.III.4	126
T-12.VII.1:1-4	48
T-13.in.2:2	16, 99
T-13.in.2:2–3:1	212
T-13.in.3:1	179
T-13.I.3	16
T-13.III	105
T-13.III.1:10-11	58, 134
T-13.III.2:6; 4:3	58
T-13.III.10:1-4	169
T-14.IV.1:7-8	24
T-14.XI.2:4	234
T-15.III	176
T-15.V.5	33
T-15.IX.7:3	133
T-16.I	68
T-16.I.6:5	126
T-16.II.1	91, 192
T-16.IV.6:1	89, 138
T-16.V.10:1	97
T-16.V.12:2	203
T-16.VI.11:4	36, 167
T-17.II	132, 224
T-17.III	165
T-17.IV.2:3	33
T-17.IV.7	46
T-17.IV.7:1	114, 119, 121
T-18.I.4:3	88

TEXT (continued)

T-18.II.6	33
T-18.IV.2:1-5	175
T-18.IV.2:1-6	9
T-18.IV.2:4-5	239
T-18.IV.7:5	17, 81
T-18.VI.1:5-6	237
T-18.VI.3:1	61
T-18.VII	127
T-18.VII.3:1	114
T-18.VIII.1:7	144, 230
T-18.IX.4-5	224
T-18.IX.5:4; 6:1,4	223
T-19.I.16:1	35
T-19.II.3:6	133
T-19.IV-A.i	106, 128
T-19.IV-A.12	72
T-19.IV-B.6,8	230
T-19.IV-C	179, 181
T-19.IV-C.2:15	212
T-19.IV-C.10:8	100
T-19.IV-C.11:2	212
T-19.IV-D.6:1-3	195
T-19.IV-D.12:8	129
T-19.IV-D.19:1	220
T-20.II.4	230
T-20.III.7-8	46
T-20.IV.5:3	234
T-20.IV.6:5	129
T-20.IV.8:12	64
T-20.V.4:7	31
T-21.in.1:1	70
T-21.in.1:1-3	183
T-21.in.1:1-5	138
T-21.in.1:5	7, 34, 84, 225
T-21.in.1:7	88, 220
T-21.II.2:6–3:2	56-57
T-21.VII.7:8	5, 36, 75, 203
T-21.VII.12	138
T-22.III.5-6	72
T-22.III.5:6	223
T-22.III.6:7	4
T-22.V.3:5	171
T-22.VI.9	192
T-23.I.2:7	77, 128
T-23.II	15
T-23.II.2	79
T-23.II.2-3	24
T-23.II.2:3	74, 119
T-23.II.4-8	121
T-23.II.9-11	222
T-23.II.9-13	68
T-23.II.19:1	90, 140, 181
T-23.IV	55
T-23.IV.1:10	69
T-23.IV.9:1-4,7-8	43
T-23.IV.9:8	107, 216
T-24.in.1:1	187
T-24.in.1:1-2	175
T-24.in.2	60
T-24.I	116
T-24.II.4:3	146
T-24.II.4:3-6	43
T-24.II.4:3–5:1	89
T-24.VII.1:11	71
T-24.VII.1:11; 10:9	12, 211
T-24.VII.10:9	93
T-25.I	235
T-25.I.7:1	3, 4, 15, 62, 87, 88, 235
T-25.I.7:2-5	16
T-25.VII,VIII	5
T-26.I	95
T-26.IV	132
T-26.V.3:5-7	20
T-26.V.5:4	36, 67, 80, 85, 126, 194, 229, 241
T-26.V.13:1	94
T-26.VI.2:3	234
T-26.VII.7	83
T-26.VIII	152
T-26.VIII.1:3	24
T-26.IX.4:1-3	64
T-26.IX.4:6	241
T-26.IX.8:8-9	135
T-27.I.4:6	145, 185
T-27.III	144, 204
T-27.IV	204
T-27.V.10:4	25
T-27.VII.10:2	140
T-27.VII.12:1	180
T-27.VII.14	99
T-27.VIII	93, 164
T-27.VIII.6:2	69
T-28.I	156, 224, 235
T-28.I.1:6-7	155
T-28.VI.2	72
T-28.VI.6:1-5	107
T-29.V	126
T-29.VI	221
T-29.VI.6	14
T-29.VII.1:9	41, 77
T-30.I	76, 110
T-30.III.8:4-5	240
T-30.V.9:10	44

TEXT (continued)

T-30.VIII	126
T-31.IV.4:3,5-6; 9:3-5	13
T-31.IV.8:4-5	5
T-31.V	69
T-31.V.2-4	139
T-31.V.17:9	204
T-31.VII.9	139
T-31.VIII	14
T-31.VIII.2:3	195
T-31.VIII.2:3-7	32
T-31.VIII.8:5	47
T-31.VIII.8:5-7	107
T-31.VIII.9:2	8, 121
T-31.VIII.10:1	195
T-31.VIII.10:8	208
T-31.VIII.12:5	100, 173, 187
T-31.VIII.12:8	241

WORKBOOK FOR STUDENTS

W-pI.21.2:5	119
W-pI.23.5	225
W-pI.24	80
W-pI.46.1:1	131, 217
W-pI.49	147
W-pI.72.2:1-3	224
W-pI.91.6:7	38
W-pI.93	228
W-pI.93.1:1	49, 228
W-pI.95.7-10	111
W-pI.95.11:2	39
W-pI.108	154
W-pI.126	65
W-pI.131	138
W-pI.132.6:2	9
W-pI.132.6:2-3	34, 129, 155
W-pI.132.11:1-5	59
W-pI.132.12:3-4	4
W-pI.132.12:4	235
W-pI.133	34
W-pI.134.9:3	117
W-pI.136	53, 152
W-pI.136.1-6	91
W-pI.136.3-4	139
W-pI.136.5:2	180
W-pI.137	13, 62, 129, 156, 236
W-pI.153.2-9	223
W-pI.153.3	119
W-pI.154	11
W-pI.155	146
W-pI.155.1	90, 176
W-pI.158.3-4	20
W-pI.158.4:5	19
W-pI.160	240
W-pI.163	179, 187
W-pI.167	179
W-pI.169.10	16
W-pI.169.11:1-2	17
W-pI.170.8:7	133
W-pI.rV.9:3	236
W-pI.182	241
W-pI.182.10:1	83, 100
W-pI.183	156
W-pI.183.7:3-5	143
W-pI.184	156
W-pI.188	138
W-pI.190.3:3-4	181
W-pI.190.3:4	45
W-pI.190.9	139
W-pI.193.1-2	228
W-pI.193.13:7	132
W-pI.195	157
W-pI.195.4:2	168
W-pII.234.1:2-4	36
W-pII.3.2:1	119
W-pII.3.2:1,4	212
W-pII.3.2:1	83
W-pII.3.2:4	83
W-pII.4.5:2	94
W-pII.5.5	113
W-pII.262	240
W-pII.294	165
W-pII.301	82
W-pII.302.2:3	155, 230
W-pII.10.3-5	105
W-pII.10.5:1	133
W-pII.13.5:1	20, 86, 94
W-pII.13.5:4	212
W-pII.14	204
W-pII.14.1	194
W-pII.14.2:1	146
W-pII.358:1:7	35
W-ep.1:1	110, 203
W-ep.1:2-3	241
W-ep.4:1	111
W-ep.6:8	241

MANUAL FOR TEACHERS

Reference	Page
M-in.2:1	42
M-1.1:2	3
M-1.3:5	80, 183
M-1.4	203
M-1.4:1-1	159
M-1.4:1-2;1.3:5	88
M-1.4:4-5	225
M-2.2	83
M-4.1:4-7	15
M-4.IX.1:10	155
M-4.X.3:7	217
M-5.III	102, 154
M-9	87-88, 150
M-10	192
M-12.3:3	43
M-13.1:2	85, 223
M-13.7	149
M-14	127
M-16	143
M-16.8-9	57
M-18.4:6	147
M-21	194
M-21.1:7	146, 164, 175
M-21.1:9-10	15, 203, 233
M-23	227
M-23.5	229
M-23.6:9-10	105
M-23.7:1	231
M-26	155
M-26.2:2	9, 29
M-26.4:2	239
M-27.7:1	183, 187
M-28	156, 229
M-28.2:5	188
M-29.2:6	75, 110

CLARIFICATION OF TERMS

Reference	Page
C-in.3:1	15, 144, 175
C-3.2:1	187, 209
C-4.6:7-8	227, 234
C-5.1:3-5	88
C-5.2:3	159
C-5.3:1-2	60
C-6.5	158
C-6.5:5	60, 105

PSYCHOTHERAPY: PURPOSE, PROCESS AND PRACTICE

Reference	Page
P-2.II.4:4	164
P-2.VI.6:3	129
P-2.VI.6:3-4	63
P-3.II.6:1	63, 154

THE SONG OF PRAYER

Reference	Page
S-1.I,II	193
S-1.I.2-4	167
S-1.I.3	159
S-1.V.3:12	39
S-3.II.1:8–2:1	90
S-3.III	61, 68, 143

THE GIFTS OF GOD

Reference	Page
"Gifts of God, The" (prose poem): *The Two Gifts* (p. 118)	44
"Gifts of God, The" (prose poem): *The Two Gifts* (p. 119)	188
"Gifts of God, The" (prose poem): *The Two Gifts* (pp. 118-19)	95
"Jesus Prayer, A" (p. 82)	230
"Jesus Prayer, A" (pp. 82-83)	228
"Transformation" (p. 64)	22

Foundation for A Course in Miracles®

Kenneth Wapnick received his Ph.D. in Clinical Psychology in 1968 from Adelphi University. He was a close friend and associate of Helen Schucman and William Thetford, the two people whose joining together was the immediate stimulus for the scribing of A Course in Miracles. Kenneth had been involved with A Course in Miracles since 1973, writing, teaching, and integrating its principles with his practice of psychotherapy. He was on the Executive Board of the Foundation for Inner Peace, original publishers of A Course in Miracles.

Gloria Wapnick has a Master's degree in History from Hunter College (1970), and taught social studies in a New York City high school, where she was also Dean of Students. Gloria has been working with A Course in Miracles since 1977, and conducted her own group for several years.

In 1983 Kenneth and Gloria began the Foundation for A Course in Miracles, and in 1984 this evolved into a Teaching and Healing Center in Crompond, New York, which was quickly outgrown. In 1988 they opened the Academy and Retreat Center in upstate New York. In 1995 they began the Institute for Teaching Inner Peace through A Course in Miracles, an educational corporation chartered by the New York State Board of Regents. In 2001 the Foundation moved to Temecula, California and shifted its emphasis to electronic teaching. After Dr. Wapnick's death in 2013, it was decided to move to a smaller facility, which happened in October 2018 when the Foundation moved to Henderson, Nevada.

The following is Kenneth's and Gloria's vision of the Foundation:

In our early years of studying *A Course in Miracles,* as well as teaching and applying its principles in our respective professions of psychotherapy, and teaching and school administration, it seemed evident that this was not the simplest of thought systems to understand. This was so not only in the intellectual grasp of its teachings, but perhaps more importantly in the application of these teachings to our personal lives. Thus, it appeared to us from the beginning that the Course lent itself to teaching, parallel to the ongoing teachings of the Holy Spirit in the daily opportunities within our relationships which are discussed in the early pages of the manual for teachers.

One day several years ago while Helen Schucman and I (Kenneth) were discussing these ideas, she shared a vision that she had had of a teaching center as a white temple with a gold cross atop it. Although it was clear that this image was symbolic, we understood it to be representative of what the teaching center was to be: a place where the person of Jesus and his message in *A Course in Miracles* would be manifest. We have sometimes seen an image of a lighthouse shining its light into the sea, calling to it those passers-by who sought it. For us, this light is the Course's teaching of forgiveness, which we would hope to share with those who are drawn to the Foundation's form of teaching and its vision of *A Course in Miracles*.

This vision entails the belief that Jesus gave the Course at this particular time in this particular form for several reasons. These include:

1) the necessity of healing the mind of its belief that attack is salvation; this is accomplished through forgiveness, the undoing of our belief in the reality of separation and guilt.

2) emphasizing the importance of Jesus and/or the Holy Spirit as our loving and gentle Teacher, and developing a personal relationship with this Teacher.

3) correcting the errors of Christianity, particularly where it has emphasized suffering, sacrifice, separation, and sacrament as being inherent in God's plan for salvation.

Our thinking has always been inspired by Plato (and his mentor Socrates), both the man and his teachings. Plato's Academy was a place where serious and thoughtful people came to study his philosophy in an atmosphere conducive to their learning, and then returned to their professions to implement what they were taught by the great philosopher. Thus, by integrating abstract philosophical ideals with experience, Plato's school seemed to be the perfect model for the teaching center that we directed for so many years.

We therefore see the Foundation's principal purpose as being to help students of *A Course in Miracles* deepen their understanding of its thought system, conceptually and experientially, so that they may be more effective instruments of Jesus' teaching in their own lives. Since teaching forgiveness without experiencing it is empty, one of the Foundation's specific goals is to help facilitate the process whereby people may be better able to know that their own sins are forgiven and that they are truly loved by God. Thus is the Holy Spirit able to extend His Love through them to others.

Made in the USA
Las Vegas, NV
11 November 2024